SAGE

by Colonel Jerry Sage

SAGE

by Colonel Jerry Sage

Miles Standish Press

Published by
Miles Standish Press, Inc.
353 West Lancaster Avenue
Wayne, Pennsylvania 19087

ISBN: 0-440-07580-7

First printing—January 1985

10 9 8 7 6 5 4 3 2 1

Printed in the United States of America

In Memory Of

My son, Terry, Captain Terence F. Sage, West Point 1963. Killed in action in the counterattack to the Communist Tet Offensive, 31 January 1968, on Tan Son Nhut Airbase, Vietnam. Posthumous awards included the Silver Star for Gallantry, the Bronze Star, the Purple Heart, the National Order of Vietnam, and the Gallantry Cross with Palm from the President of the Republic of Vietnam.

In loving memory also of my daughter, Barbara Ellen Bussard, my brother Eugene H. Sage, and with most grateful remembrance of my parents, Ruth and Howard Sage.

Dedication

Dedicated to my wife, Mary Jon, who gave me loyal and generous support during the long hours of writing and re-writing.

Also to my sister Wanita and her husband, George Thompson, and to my other children, Mike and Regina Sage, Patti and Buck Kistler, Stephanie and Dave Long, Mary Jon and Al Sneckenberger, and Walt and Susie Harris, and to my grandchildren—and to all youngsters I've worked and played with who like to call me grandpa, or uncle, or friend.

Jerry Sage
Colonel, U.S. Army Ret.

Acknowledgments

Many of my old colleagues have given me fine support and encouragement in producing this account of our adventures. I particularly want to thank the following for their contributions of photographs, sketches, and reminders or verifications of anecdotes and happenings of over forty years ago:

From Stalag Luft III
John M. Bennett, Col., USAF Ret.
Robert M. Brown
Henry Burman
A.P. Clark, Lt. Gen., USAF Ret.
C. Wally Floody, ex-Royal Canadian Air Force
Charles G. Goodrich, Col., USAF Ret.
and our beloved senior American officer
Willard Heckman
Robert B. Hermann
Charles C. Huppert
David Mudgett Jones, Maj. Gen., USAF Ret.
Richard "Wings" Kimball
Richard P. Klocko, Lt. Gen., USAF Ret.
Robert "Maxie" Menning
William Nance
David Pollak
Dick Schrupp
Donald A. Stine, Col., USAF Ret.
Alvin W. "Sammy" Vogtle, Jr.

From Oflag 64
Charles Kouns, Col., U.S. Army Ret.
Herb Johnson
John Slack
John Knight Waters, General, U.S. Army Ret.

From the OSS
Stephen Byzek
Lucius ''Jump'' Rucker
and others

From Sweden
Neutral Power Representative Henry Soderberg

And much earlier from
''Wings'' Day and many other RAF cohorts

And grateful thanks to my publisher, Peter W. Tobey, and to my skilled and patient editor, Edward B. Claflin.

INTRODUCTION

In the spring of 1943, Jerry Sage, then a paratrooper major, arrived at POW camp Stalag Luft III, in Sagan, Germany.

Run by German Luftwaffe officers, Stalag Luft III was exclusively for Allied airmen who had been shot down and captured in Europe and North Africa. Since Sage came in with a group of airmen, no one suspected that he had actually worked for Wild Bill Donovan's undercover OSS behind Rommel's lines in North Africa. If the Germans had known, they'd have shot him, but when he was captured, Sage was able to jettison his OSS hardware and he soon escaped from a boxcar with two bona fide shot-down airmen. On recapture they convinced the Germans that Sage was also a shot-down flier trying to return to friendly lines. The Germans bought the story and sent him to our camp. By the end of the war, I am sure, many a German regretted having captured him in the first place, for he was a tough and skilled guerrilla fighter, a born leader and a persistent escaper.

We soon came to know him well—this big, rowdy, football-playing Phi Beta Kappa from Washington State. Other men instinctively deferred to Sage, not because he displayed outstanding authority or dignity, but because he had great *presence*. His physical stature was imposing: He was tall, blond, fine-looking, in exceptionally fit condition. And his positive attitude communicated itself in everything he said and did. All the men responded to the spirit of his deep, jolly voice, to his inexhaustible enthusiasm and his irrepressible gung-ho attitude. He was a blithe spirit, always affable, always ready for anything, and his merriment was an important morale booster in the camp.

The younger men related to Jerry Sage because he was always looking for ways to escape, no matter how improbable or impossible escape seemed. To the restless officers in our camp he quickly became a hero, a kind of Pied Piper whom they would follow anywhere. Having taught them many of the grim techniques of "silent death," he led them in many escape activities and in harassment of our German captors, as well as in lusty tomfoolery and fun.

One episode in particular will be remembered by every POW who witnessed the event. On July 4, 1943, after many days of careful planning, Jerry, as Uncle Sam, led nearly six hundred Americans in one of the greatest Fourth of July celebrations of all time. At the early morning "unlock"—when the Germans opened the barracks—a motley column of American Colonial Revolutionaries burst forth from the huts, led by a traditional color guard complete with fife and drum. Jerry paraded this full-dress Revolutionary Army across the grounds and roared into the British huts, taking the English airmen completely by surprise.

It was the beginning of a full day of fun and games spiked with liberal quantities of kriegie home-brewed "wine"—a day none of us will ever forget. Jerry was in his element. He was everywhere, involved in every conceivable sport and escapade, from the baseball game between senior and junior officers (with a drunken British officer running bases) to a dunking that ended up with all the senior officers being thrown into the fire pool.

Our German guards didn't always know what to think of Major Sage. I believe they grudgingly admired his prowess and even laughed at some of his light-hearted antics. But they were also wary of him—his escape attempts were no laughing matter, and he made no bones about still being at war with the Germans. I do not know just how many times Jerry Sage attempted to escape, but they were numerous.

The normal punishment for an escape try was a stretch of solitary confinement in the "cooler" cell. Sage spent many stretches in the cooler for his escape activities, plus two or three stretches for resisting the bullying tactics of his captors.

Tension grew in Stalag Luft III in the spring of 1944. The Nazis executed fifty officers recaptured after the "Great Escape" tunnel break from North Camp. Guards shot into the American South Camp, killing one

POW and wounding another. When rumors spread of Nazi plans to liquidate POWs, our senior officer, Colonel Goodrich, asked Sage to train a hand-picked group of men to take over the camp, to at least avoid being killed like rats in a trap.

Despite our security precautions, perhaps the Germans saw Sage teaching his "silent death" techniques. They certainly knew his past cooler record. At any rate, Colonel von Lindeiner, the old German commandant, ordered Sage purged from the camp as a troublemaker. The escort guards could not or would not tell Colonel Goodrich where Major Sage was going. Many feared he would be shot.

I clearly remember the day over forty years ago when Jerry Sage was marched out of Stalag Luft III. As he started for the gate, all the POWs rushed out to bid him farewell. He was cheered all the way to the gate by the two thousand young American flying officers in the camp, and we all hated to see him depart.

That was the last time I was to see Jerry during the war. I learned later that after some weird adventures in southern Germany he was eventually taken to Oflag 64 in Schubin, which was evacuated ahead of the Russian advance. You will enjoy reading the story of how Jerry found the chance he had been waiting for, and of his incredible adventures on his final escape from the Germans—going east across Poland and the Ukraine to Odessa, then back to the OSS in Egypt and home in March of 1945.

We never lost touch with Jerry after the war, and he has brightened many a Stalag Luft III reunion with his presence.

Many of us personally observed this remarkable soldier's experiences. We know what it meant to spend long, grim days in the camps behind enemy lines—and what a difference one person could make in the lives of us all. Those of us who spent time with Jerry Sage behind the wire in Germany will always cherish fondness and respect for this big, flamboyant and warm-hearted guy who made our days more bearable.

Lieutenant General A.P. Clark
USAF Ret.

Chapter 1

Early in the fall of 1941, I was driving my little Procter & Gamble Chevrolet down Montgomery Avenue in San Francisco, listening to a radio commentator discussing the war in Europe. He reviewed Hitler's stealing Poland and dividing it with the Soviet Union in late 1939, then overrunning France and the smaller coastal countries in 1940, and trying to bomb Britain to its knees. During this "blitz" of London, which lasted till the summer of 1941, we had all heard Edward R. Murrow of BS say, "This is London," and tell of the heroism of the British, standing practically alone against Nazi tyranny. The United States was maintaining its neutrality, though President Roosevelt was obviously in favor of supporting England.

Now the commentator was telling how Hitler's forces had taken Yugoslavia, Greece and Crete and were crashing their way into the Soviet Union. Hitler had sent his best general, Rommel, to North Africa to strengthen the Axis there against the extended British forces. The announcer also talked of the Nazi atrocities against their captives and ones they considered "lesser people."

The twenty-four-year-old Procter & Gamble salesman, Jerry Sage, had felt a slow burn of revulsion against Hitler for two years. This broadcast crystallized my growing conviction that the United States of America would have to fight the Nazis. Without a second thought, I turned around in the middle of the road and headed for the nearest Army recruiting office. I knew just what I wanted to do.

Approaching the recruiting officer, I said, "My name is Jerry Sage. I'm a first lieutenant in the reserve, reserve commission from Washington State. I'd like to go on active duty. I think we've got to stop this Hitler clown."

The officer looked up and nodded. "Welcome aboard," he said, and he started right in on the paperwork.

It did not take me long to tell him about my past. I was a graduate of Washington State University, where I had played football and earned a Phi Beta Kappa key. During college, I paid my way by scrubbing the athletic shower room floors and by selling wholesale candy and tobacco to the student commissaries in each fraternity, sorority and dormitory. Having taken advanced ROTC in college, I graduated with an Infantry commission in the United States Army Reserve.

Immediately after graduation, I had gone to work for the Procter & Gamble Distributing Company, handling the Crisco-type products called Primex and Sweetex, which were sold mainly to bakeries and restaurants, often through large distributors. I was three and a half years with Procter & Gamble, first as a junior salesman and later as a representative for the territory of Washington and Alaska. Before signing up for the Army, I had been promoted to senior salesman for the area covering San Francisco, northern California and the Hawaiian Islands.

* * *

I was ordered to appear for duty on the ninth of December 1941, but I showed up before Thanksgiving. I reported to the Presidio of San Francisco, and the Army detailed me to the Quartermaster Corps, placing me in command of the field bakery platoon at the Presidio, evidently because I had sold shortening to bakers! For a time, I had to give up my crossed-rifles Infantry insignia.

Then came Pearl Harbor. Ships that were headed for the Hawaiian Islands and Philippines had to turn back and their troops camped in Golden Gate Park. In order to serve these troops, I set up my field oven in the park and began baking bread. It was good bread, too—great big loaves of it.

After three or four weeks of this, the outfit was suddenly moved to Fort Lewis, Washington, in early January 1942. We were preparing to ship out to some Pacific island—I didn't know where. But I sensed that we should start to get ready, and I put the men on a rigorous training program to prepare for combat. We were probably the only bakery outfit in the United States Army that went up and down cargo nets wearing our full packs, each of us with a loaded rifle over one shoulder. Clutching the nets one-handed, we dragged aboard big, heavy sections of field ovens for baking bread. I insisted that my men were combat bakers, not rear echelon troops. When the time came to see action, I wanted my men to be ready to board the ships and go.

I had been training the men for three weeks or so when I was called out to be an instructor at an Officers Training School at Fort Lewis. My new job was to train people who had been off duty and to help them get into shape for their units.

That job did not last long either. Within a few days

I received a telegram that said First Lieutenant Jerry M. Sage, Inf, 0326876, was to report by the earliest available aircraft to Washington, D.C. My assignment was to the Q Building at the Office Coordinator of Inf.

The message was cryptic. I did not even know what the Office Coordinator of Inf was, though I assumed Inf meant infantry. (It was a wrong assumption, as it turned out, but I would not know that until I got there.) I packed up, threw my gear over my shoulder, climbed aboard a plane, landed in Washington, D.C., and got a cab.

I asked the driver, "Would you take me to the Q Building?"

He asked, "Where's the Q Building?"

We drove around awhile and asked some other cabbies. Finally, one of them said something about a brewery and an old health center. My driver seemed to understand, and we sped off toward the Potomac. He took the time to drive me around the Lincoln Memorial a few times—I had never seen it before—and then we followed the Potomac toward an old brewery.

We came to a heavily guarded building cordoned off with barbed wire. The guards at the gate blocked the cab. I paid the driver, got out and walked in alone. One building had a sign that read "Entrance, Adjutant." I went in. A first lieutenant was sitting at the desk and he introduced himself as Lieutenant Dick Oliver.

"Who are you?" he asked.

"I'm Lieutenant Jerry Sage." I handed him the telegram.

"Oh, yes," he said. "Colonel Donovan will see you."

I still didn't understand. "What the hell is the Coordinator of Inf?" I asked.

"It's the Office of the Coordinator of Information. The man you're gonna see is Colonel Donovan."

A little light bulb went off in my head.

"Holy smoke, it couldn't be!" I said. "Not Wild Bill!"

"The same," he replied.

William J. Donovan, known to everyone as "Wild Bill," was one of the two greatest heroes of my childhood. (The other was Sergeant Alvin York of Tennessee.) I had first read about Donovan in a book about World War I. To me, he was a larger-than-life character. During the First World War, he had won the Congressional Medal of Honor, the Distinguished Service Cross, the Distinguished Service Medal, and the Purple Heart in the Fighting 69th. Afterward he had become a lawyer and held many public service jobs. He once ran for the governor of New York. He also had been an outstanding fullback at Columbia University.

Now Donovan was back in Washington. I had heard news of his meetings with FDR and his conferences with Churchill. Beyond that, no one knew of his precise role in the war effort.

I was ushered into his office. I popped to with a salute and held it.

Seated behind the desk was an imposing, somewhat heavyset man—not as tall as I, but with good shoulders. He had piercing Delft-blue eyes. His gaze did not waver for an instant. I held the salute.

"Oh, sit down." He waved to an easy chair. "Do you have any idea why you're here?" he asked.

"Not in the slightest, sir."

The truth was, I was not entirely pleased to be in Washington, D.C., at all. I was ready to go out and fight the Japanese. The move to Washington meant I was now in real danger of being stuck in an office job.

"Well, the reason you're here is that you've been hand-picked," he said. "We have information from my friends at Fort Lewis, and the FBI also mentioned you. Apparently you're not afraid to mix it up. You're not afraid to use your fists, you're a good athlete, a football letterman, and you learn fast. My guess is you can learn rapidly enough to keep up with the people who do what we do."

I was about to ask what they *did* do, but he quickly continued. "This is a completely volunteer outfit. I want to tell you what it's like. If you join us here, you will be working on the most dangerous assignments in the military. We'll be seeking a payoff from your work. You'll be an agent, a saboteur, maybe an assassin, certainly a guerrilla fighter. . . ." (With each word, my grin got a little bit bigger.) "Your folks will never know where you are. They'll communicate with you only through a post office box in Washington, D.C. You won't ever earn any medals. Nobody will know anything about what you do. But it will be a great service for your country. We can really hit 'em where it hurts most, behind their lines, and we can bring out the intelligence that we *must* have to win this war."

He paused a moment and then asked, "Do you want to come aboard?"

"I like it," I replied immediately. "I'm aboard. Yes, sir."

"Well, fine," he said, and then he talked some more about what was involved. Finally, he asked, "Have you ever been in Washington before?"

"No, sir," I said, "I've never been east of the Rocky Mountains before."

"Would you like to see some of the nation's capital?"

"What's the alternative?" I asked.

He must have been expecting me to say that, because he immediately offered, "Well, we have our camp up in the Catoctin Mountains, near Frederick and Thurmont, Maryland. We call it Area B2. It's one of our first training camps. You'll meet some interesting people and you'll help train others, if you'd like to do that."

"I certainly would," I said.

I was loaded aboard a little three-quarter-ton truck. I guess no one was supposed to see my face now that I was a member of this special outfit. They pulled the curtains and fastened the flaps on the back of the truck. At the gate, the driver showed proper identification, and then we bounced away down the road.

After we were well away from the headquarters area, the driver brought me up to the front of the truck. We headed up Wisconsin Boulevard, got on the highway and turned toward Frederick, Maryland. After passing through Frederick we continued to the village of Thurmont, then followed a little road up through the hills. There were guards and barbed wire, and we were stopped several times along the way.

Area B2 had some log cabins, a big mess hall and kitchen and a headquarters building surrounded by trees. There was a swimming pool and a large green field, possibly for football or soccer. Men were strolling around. A loudspeaker seemed to be going all the time, blaring out music and messages. The music ranged from selections of the Andrews Sisters such as "The Boogie Woogie Bugle Boy from Company B" to "American Patrol" by John Philip Sousa. I loved all of it.

* * *

One of the first men I met was an Armenian whose name I do not recall. He had reportedly been with Lawrence of Arabia, which added a touch of adventure for me—I had read Lawrence's fantastic story of desert fighting.

The Armenian's favorite song was "American Patrol." The man who ran the sound system would put on the record and wait for the Armenian to start singing. I can still hear that enormous voice, with its pronounced accent, as the Armenian bellowed, "Ve must be wigilant, Ve must be wigilant, American Peetrol, mit arms for the army, sheeps for the navy," and so forth. His droll rendition was habit-forming. Soon we all sang it that way with him. Even today when I start to sing that song, the first line comes out, "Ve must be wigilant. . . ."

Like most of the men in that B2 camp gang, the Armenian was ready for anything. It was an inspiration to be with those men. Even when I didn't like what I was doing, I liked the people I worked with. They had a lot of guts and a lot of drive. They had imagination.

One of the men at B2 was Ilya Tolstoy, a descendant of Count Leo Tolstoy, the author of the epic *War and Peace*. Ilya trained hard at B2. Later on, he went to Tibet with Lieutenant Brooke Dolan, where he served as an envoy to reassure Tibet of American friendship.

At B2 I also met Major William E. Fairbairn. Strong-jawed, grizzle-haired Bill Fairbairn had been on the Shanghai police force for thirty years. For much of that time he was the head of the Shanghai riot squad, which broke up fights and gang wars (tong wars) in the Shanghai area.

Fairbairn was an expert at judo and jujitsu long before martial arts were much known in this country. Fairbairn knew all the techniques of hand-to-hand combat, instinctive or hip-shooting, and knife-fighting—what he called "silent killing." He taught us well. I picked Fairbairn's brain and absorbed the lessons.

As I came to know Bill Fairbairn better, I began to call him "Delicate Dan." He was polite, adroit and nimble. He was always courteous. He would say, "Excuse me, please," as he demonstrated how to break an opponent's arm, neck or back. He could flick a knife and twist it different ways with great dexterity. We always said that he could cut the pit from a cherry without bruising the fruit.

Fairbairn used a Sikes-Fairbairn fighting knife, which had been invented by him and a colleague named Sikes. In cross section the blade was diamond-shaped for strength and as long and sharp as a stiletto. The Síkes-Fairbairn had a knurled handle and very good balance. This was one weapon we used a lot later on, when we were behind enemy lines.

Fairbairn had been commissioned a major, training Commandos in the British Army, when Donovan brought him over to help us get started in our close combat course.

Delicate Dan Fairbairn was about twice my age. He stood five feet ten inches and weighed one hundred seventy pounds. Fairbairn was in great shape. In martial arts training he always picked a bigger man to attack him just to prove that the smaller man could win if he learned Fairbairn's techniques. Because I was six feet two and weighed two hundred lean pounds, I was picked to be his assistant and stooge.

His system looked very good when he demonstrated how he could throw me around easily. We performed several demonstrations for other branches of the service. Once we did a guest appearance for the Navy at the Waldorf-Astoria Hotel in New York. Included among the Navy men were heavyweight champs Gene Tunney and Jack Dempsey. Pro wrestlers and footballers in the conditioning program of the Navy were also there. Fairbairn gave them a good taste of his course, then sold some copies of his newly published book, *Get Tough*. In each of the demonstrations, I would attack Fairbairn and he would flip me around the room, winding up with lethal blows or kicks.

After that demonstration at the Waldorf, one of the wrestling pros came up to me and said quietly, "Say, Captain, just tell me, aren't you sort of going along with the old man? Aren't you putting on a little show to make him look good?"

"Well, what would you do if the old man had you by the hand like this"—I seized his hand—"and did this?" I flipped him underneath the table.

What I demonstrated was just a good judo wrist throw, but it was new to him. As he got up he said, "Shees, that's good!"

As the demonstration continued during the next few days, the Navy men began to pay a bit more attention. They were awed by the story of how Delicate Dan could cut a man in half with a tommy gun as he had done in Shanghai. We also impressed them with tales of Dan and his amazing Commando fighting knife. We didn't use the illustration of his pitting a cherry in one sweep. Instead, we told what Dan did to mosquitoes. Back in camp, when a mosquito buzzed across above his head, Dan just whipped out his knife and made a quick slash upward. Away screamed the mosquito, buzzing about two octaves higher!

Chapter 2

In those early days at Area B2 and during trips to Washington and New York, I learned more about Wild Bill Donovan. From my earlier reading, I knew he had won the Congressional Medal of Honor and the other top military awards in the Fighting 69th during World War I.

Many of the people he brought with him to form the new super-spy unit had served with him during World War I. Among them was Edwin ''Ned'' Buxton, who had been the commanding officer for sharpshooting Sergeant Alvin York of Tennessee. Buxton's courage and far-ranging mind were much admired by Donovan, and he became a right-hand man in the new spy and sabotage agency.

Between the wars, Donovan had worked for a New York law firm and had served as an antitrust prosecutor for the Department of Justice. From his extensive contacts as a practicing lawyer Donovan brought in financiers, explorers, war correspondents, college presidents and professors, law men, narcotics agents and publishers. Occasionally he also brought in an ex-convict with a particular skill such as forging or safecracking to help us on the operational side.

Among those I met on visits to Washington from training area B2 were financier Charles Cheston and diplomat David Bruce. The latter I respected especially as a very fine officer and organizer. From Donovan's law firm came Oley Doering. Then there were Ellery Huntington, a former Colgate football player, and Preston Goodfellow, a New York publisher. I also met barrel-chested Carl Eiffler and West Pointer Ray Peers, who later became leaders of Detachment 101, the first operational OSS outfit in Asia.

Though Donovan was a Republican, he was greatly respected by presidents of both parties. In the late thirties and early forties, Donovan was sent by FDR to conferences with Churchill. He reported on England's defense and intelligence activities.

Even before Pearl Harbor, Roosevelt was acutely aware that the United States did not have a sufficient intelligence network to become a skillful participant in the war. Americans looked down their noses at spying. During that era, we had people in the State Department who thought that spying wasn't quite cricket. They wouldn't read the Japanese mail even if it was left open for us!

Donovan had the talent of being able to pick up knowledge in a hurry. He traveled to the Balkan countries, Yugoslavia and Greece, as well as other areas of Europe and Asia, collecting information about Hitler's blitzkrieg. He tried to assess the ability of those countries' armed forces and to evaluate their will to resist.

Before the war Mussolini, *il Duce*, was reported to be amassing Italian troops in Africa, but no one was allowed to see them. Donovan visited Mussolini in Rome and asked if he could visit the troops. When il Duce refused, Donovan goaded Mussolini with a shrug and an offhanded, "Oh, it doesn't matter. We know the Italians don't have much of an army anyway!" Furious, Mussolini gave orders that this American unbeliever, Donovan, could go everywhere and see everything. That was how Donovan gathered his information about the Italian Army.

When Roosevelt asked Donovan to set up a new intelligence agency, they called it, for cover, the Office of the Coordinator of Information. That was the office that I joined in March of 1942. By summer, the name was changed officially to the Office of Strategic Services (OSS).

In starting the OSS, one of Donovan's first goals was to win the confidence of British Intelligence. British leaders were well aware that if we got into the war, it would prove to their benefit. They furnished advisors, equipment and valuable information to help the U.S. intelligence agency grow from its infancy.

One of the missions of the OSS was the obvious one, "to collect and analyze strategic information." A second goal was "to plan and operate special services." The latter mission included sabotage, psychological warfare and similar clandestine operations that did not fall within the jurisdiction of the regular armed forces.

Donovan was the perfect man to lead these operations. He was curious, imaginative and full of new ideas. Always willing to try something new, he was the first to say "Yes" to an unprecedented way of doing things. He was a determined man, a risk-taker and a winner.

Donovan had drawn together a large group of people who were the backbone of the OSS efforts to catch up on worldwide intelligence. The research organization comprised academic specialists in such fields as anthropology, science, business, economics, and social science. There were also linguists who could translate foreign materials. Much information was already available, but it had not been fully assembled. Donovan's people had to draw this material together, boil it down, then analyze and distribute it for use.

Other researchers were developing weapons, explosive devices, documentation and clothing for use in operations. The clothing looked authentically European, but there were concealed flaps and pockets for hiding various undercover devices.

I had only limited contact with Donovan's researchers, since I was in training for operations. At OSS Camp B2 I quickly discovered that training was rigorous. Delicate Dan Fairbairn taught us how to fall, roll and come up on the offense. We became skilled at very gentle come-along grips, which were done by twisting the finger, wrist or elbow joint of the enemy. Fairbairn taught vicious blows that could dislocate a man's shoulder or break an arm or a leg.

The most lethal silent kill was the Japanese strangle or sentry kill. The goal was to take a sentry by surprise. The attacker would approach from the rear, drive his right fist into the enemy's kidney and snap a left forearm like a bar across his throat, with fingers stiff and tucked inside his right elbow. Using his right elbow as a pivot, the attacker then vised down with the right hand on the back of the enemy's head. The sentry had no chance to scream. He would die by strangulation or of a broken neck.

In time, Fairbairn taught us all the martial arts—judo and karate, the most useful blows of Chinese boxing, the high kicks of the French savate, and many other tricks of gutter fighting picked up in the alleys of the Shanghai waterfront. Among the weapons he taught us to use were his own stiletto-type Sikes-Fairbairn knife, a jungle machete and another weapon he called a smatchet. The smatchet was a hybrid between a machete and an axe, with a very heavy slashing blade. We also learned how to fight with meat hooks, bailing hooks, hatchets and other types of cutting and striking instruments. Fairbairn taught us how to get rid of an opponent using normal everyday items such as a rolled-up magazine or newspaper, a matchbox, a pen or a pencil. He showed us the pressure points on crucial arteries and demonstrated the sensitive nerve areas where a single blow could immobilize an enemy. With every tactic we also learned the counter-measures to protect ourselves from a similar attack.

Fairbairn also taught us what he called instinctive shooting. This was shooting from the hip with a revolver, submachine gun, rifle or shotgun. The ultimate test of our instinctive shooting ability was Fairbairn's specially designed house of horrors, which we faced at the end of the course. In the house, pop-up targets that looked like Nazis would appear suddenly in darkened rooms, their appearances accompanied by simulated shots and flashes of light. When the OSS student heard the sounds of shots, his objective was to swing his weapon in a rapid arc up the target's midriff, getting off two shots in rapid succession between the enemy's crotch and head.

As Bill Fairbairn's assistant instructor, my duties were to indoctrinate the new recruits—who were everything from jailbirds to college professors—and teach them the fundamentals of soldiering and physical conditioning. Since all the countries had men in uniform, the simplest cover for an OSS officer was that of a soldier. The first few officers who were recruited and sent to Camp B2 all had a hand in making the trainees, mostly civilians, look and act as much like soldiers as possible. We taught them how to march and react like military men. Then we turned our emphasis on the tough training—physical conditioning, explosives work, hand-to-hand combat and knife fighting. Ultimately, every man learned how to survive as an agent behind enemy lines, how to collect intelligence on the enemy and get it through to our side, and how to sabotage the enemy's efforts against us.

Some of my colleagues at B2 were old friends from Washington State University. Of the first ten military officers who were trained as instructors and behind-the-lines operators, at least half were from Washington State. One was my best friend Chris Rumburg, who had played center on our football team when I was playing end.

Chris and I were about the same size, but he was just a little bit heavier and stronger. Though Chris weighed a bit over two hundred pounds, he was a skillful rope climber. He would start from a sitting position, legs straight out, with the rope between his legs. Reaching hand over hand, he would pull himself up to the cross-beam thirty feet above. He never changed from the sitting position and never used his feet at all. I worked at the rope climb until I could go up the same way.

A man who was more agile by far than either of us was little Joe Collart from Washington State. At State he had been a tumbler, a gymnast and a diver. He was strong and very well coordinated. With the help of some of the others, Joe and Chris built from logs a great trainasium, as they called it. Tall logs were planted in the ground like pilings, with cross-logs arranged at various levels. In walking the logs at great heights the men were forced to overcome fears and dizziness, and the training helped them to gain confidence in their own agility and sense of balance. This training was to prove invaluable to me later on during operations and escapes from enemy camps.

Among the recruits from Washington State were Arden Dow, a close college mate, and Elmer "Pinkie" Harris, a red-haired officer commissioned in the Marines. Others included Rex Applegate from Oregon, Jim Johnson from the Midwest, and Ainsworth Blogg from Seattle, Washington.

Our head instructors in the use of demolitions were young engineers from Penn State. Two of these men were Charlie Parkins and Frank Gleason, who were commissioned in the engineer reserve. Frank, the youngest officer at B2, was the only second lieutenant in the outfit. He loved to blow up simulated enemy targets. With a wide grin, he would discuss our upcoming demolition blasts, calling them big booms. The devices he worked with came from regular Army stock and from the OSS research department.

Among the devices we used was an initiator called a time-pencil, which looked like a thin fountain pen. It had a striker held back by a spring. The spring, in turn, was retained by a fine wire. In the center cavity with the wire was a small capsule of sulfuric acid. To start the action we merely squeezed until we broke the capsule. As the acid ate through the wire, it released the striker, which hit a percussion cap.

The length of time-delay depended on the thickness of the wire. A thin wire would give us ten minutes to get away from the explosion site. A thicker one gave us thirty minutes.

We also had booby traps. There were push-pull devices, pressure-sensitive detonators and release mechanisms that would go off from hand or foot pressure. We used numerous explosives. Dynamite was common, though we preferred TNT for destroying concrete structures. When we knew we were going to blow a bridge, we carried TNT. Our standby, however, was a plastic explosive made by DuPont and called Composition C. For its weight and volume, it was the most economical to carry and it was by far the most powerful.

Composition C was a malleable plastic that was very fast-burning and could cut through steel. We would carry it in various forms, as a ball or in lengths, along with an explosive detonating cord called primacord.

At night we used to lie around the campfire and dream up things to do with Composition C. We imagined presenting the Nazi leaders with a gift of chocolate-covered cherries. The cherries would be hand-molded plastic embedded with pressure-cap detonators and dipped into Hitler's, Goebbels' or Göring's favorite chocolates. Just let them take a bite!

We studied in considerable depth what type of charges should be used to achieve certain effects. We could rig a charge so that it would simply cut a rail line or we could set it up so the detonation would go off just before a locomotive arrived. If we could derail the locomotive in a tunnel, all the better—that would tie up traffic longer.

We learned how to pick the key bottlenecks. To cut the engine's electric power, we would aim to knock out the biggest turbine in a power plant. We could make a bridge fall as we wanted it to, using the least amount of explosive.

We had a prestigious neighbor in the Catoctin Mountains. Up the road from our camp, some new construction was under way for a structure that looked like a big Western hunting lodge. We soon discovered that the lodge was for President Roosevelt. This lodge Roosevelt named Shangri-la, after the mythical paradise on Earth that had been popularized in the novel and movie version of *Lost Horizon.* President Eisenhower later renamed it Camp David after his grandson David.

Since the grounds of our OSS camp and the President's lodge were in the same national park in the Catoctin range, a single national park ranger had clearance to enter both our camp and the land designated for the President's retreat. One day, the ranger came down in his pickup truck and Charlie Parkins and I went to the gate to talk with him.

"I need a bit of help," he said. "I understand you're using a lot of explosives here. We're digging a sewer line for the President's lodge and we've run into some of this Maryland schist. It's the toughest rock I've ever seen. We've got to cut down to get the line to run into the house through the basement. I thought maybe you could help us blow some of this rock."

Charlie said, "Fine, let's go."

We picked up Frank Gleason. He, Charlie and I took a load of dynamite and Composition C, along with our detonators and fuses, jumped into a jeep and headed for the President's house. That day we created numerous big booms. One of those booms, which I confess I set myself, blew a big hunk of rock through the newly installed huge bay window in the President's lodge. Here I was, trying to win the war against the Nazis, and I'd only succeeded in breaking the President's window!

On President Roosevelt's first visit to his new retreat, some of us from the OSS were to augment the security forces of the Secret Service. Of course, we were happy to oblige. During the pre-visit briefings we were warned repeatedly that it was to be kept a complete secret that Roosevelt was coming. We played the hush-hush game to the hilt, but everyone found out soon enough.

On the great day, one of our colleagues happened to be buying some odds and ends of hardware in the sleepy little town of Thurmont, Maryland, at the foot of the road leading to the camp. The newest car in Thurmont was usually a 1928 Ford, but suddenly the town was alerted by the appearance of three shiny, armored limousines. Two Packards and a Cadillac roared through the village, men in slouch hats perched on the running boards, en route to the "secret" rendezvous. According to our colleague, the whole town turned out to watch. Some security!

I was in the guard detail at the lodge. I recognized only two of the visitors who accompanied the President, his secretary Missy LeHand and his advisor Harry Hopkins. Roosevelt looked very tired. However, he came out on the verandah and exchanged a few words with the other guard and me. We were standing immediately below his replaced bay window. I had a little guilty conscience, but not much.

Games with explosives were fairly common. At the camp, we booby-trapped almost everything, and everyone had to be wary all the time. It was good training for agents, as we learned the value of closely scrutinizing every object we approached. OSS men would not lift, push or pull anything without carefully checking first. Something as simple as opening a door could set off a push or pull device, or a pressure-release switch that would set off various detonators and charges. Sometimes, you would see an OSS man open the dining-room screen door with a long stick. His precautions were well-founded. As soon as the door opened, you would hear a detonator or a mild charge go off.

Once Charlie Parkins booby-trapped the flush toilet at the end of the hut. Always on guard, I took the precaution of trying the flush handle before I sat down. Fortunately, I received nothing worse than an unexpected shower. If I hadn't tried out the flush handle, I might have become a eunuch.

I waited a few days before I took my revenge on Charlie. Parkins was a late and heavy sleeper who rarely got up in time for breakfast. Like the rest of us, he slept in a cubicle in the Catoctin camp hut. The cubicle had high partitions that came within eighteen inches of the ceiling, leaving a small ventilation gap between the top of the partition and the ceiling of the hut.

One morning, I came to Charlie's room with a CN-DM (chloracetophenone and adamsite) grenade.

"Charlie," I called, "wake up! Beddie-bye is over!"

"Go away!" he grunted.

I pulled the pin on the grenade. "You'll be sorry, Charlie!" I warned, as I rolled the grenade under his cot.

I strolled out, locked the door to Charlie's room and waited outside the door at the end of the hut.

Now, CN-DM is a combination of tear gas and nausea-inducer. Moments after I left Charlie's cubicle, I began to hear sputters, coughs and door-bangs, plus some terrible words. A moment later Charlie took a giant vault over the partition, landing spread-eagled on the floor with wild, streaming eyes. After staggering to his feet, he dashed for the shower room, one hand over his mouth and the other clutching his stomach.

After that episode Charlie started rising more promptly in the morning, and for a time we stopped booby-trapping each other.

Later at B2, Parkins and Gleason devised an outdoor obstacle course that corresponded to Delicate Dan Fairbairn's indoor horror house. The obstacle course had a similar array of pop-up targets that each man had to shoot down. Moving as rapidly as possible in an attack pattern through this course, we had to hit each enemy target and keep running, trying to beat the best time. Though Fairbairn had contributed a few ideas on the targeting, Frank and Charlie had built the course and set the explosives.

After the course was set up, I was chosen to run it the first time. I made one mistake at the start: I put on a big, loose sweat suit.

Frank and Charlie said, "Okay, Jerry, you're gonna be first. We expect you to set the record for everyone else to beat."

They handed me a tommy gun with a loaded clip and yelled, "Go!"

I sprinted off. A target swung out of a bush on the left and I gave it a quick burst in the middle. Another popped up from behind a rock on my right. I leveled it, running at full speed. This continued for about half a mile, with the enemy attacking from all sorts of hiding places.

Finally the trail came to a stream. I could hear Charlie yelling, "Keep moving! Keep moving!" Without breaking stride I raced to the bank of the stream and took an enormous leap.

I was in midair, halfway across the stream, when suddenly there was a great boom. A charge had gone off under my feet. It knocked me rear-over-teakettle and I landed in the rocks and gravel of the streambed.

I was still holding on to my tommy gun, but my sweat suit was soaked. As I dragged myself out of the water, Gleason grabbed the wet tommy gun, shoved a fresh one into my hand and yelled, "Keep moving!"

With every step, water squished through the sweat suit and added about fifty pounds to my weight.

After I had blasted a few more ground targets, Gleason yelled, "Drop the tommy gun!" I threw it down and he tossed me a pistol. All the time I was moving at a dead run.

For the final part of the course I had to negotiate the parallel wires. There was a tightwire to walk on and a second wire overhead for a handhold. Holding on to the overhead wire, I had to negotiate my way through the air, shooting at targets that jumped up on either side.

At the end of the course I chewed out Frank and Charlie about that midstream explosion. When I realized I wouldn't get much sympathy, we all shared a laugh. They had thoroughly enjoyed blowing me into the stream. As it happened, my time on the trial wasn't beaten for quite a while, even though I'd finished the course in a weighted-down sweat suit.

Shortly after the war, I met Frankie Gleason again. We had been apart for a long time, and I felt obliged to ask whether he'd had enough of his beloved big booms during his time in the service. Frankie threw back his head and gave a big Irish laugh. Then he told me about the biggest boom of his career.

It happened during the last year of the war, when the Japanese troops began an offensive that threatened General Chennault's air bases in China. Frankie was serving with OSS Detachment 101. He and an OSS demolition team found several huge ammunition dumps that held tons of arms, ammunitions and supplies belonging to the Chinese. The Japanese were only a few miles away and Frankie was certain they would soon overrun the Chinese base and seize the supplies. To ensure that the Japanese didn't benefit from this windfall, he and his lads used a wealth of the explosives on hand. The big booms, Frankie said, could be heard all the way to Japan.

Chapter 3

At Area B2 we had good instruction in radio communication procedures, but this wasn't my strong point. Though I was adept at handling weapons and all kinds of explosive devices, I never felt completely competent in radio work. By the end of that phase of training, I had come to the resolution that I would always take good care of my radioman. And I always did.

We learned how to be undercover agents in a foreign country. One of our instructors was Garland Williams of the New York Narcotics Commission, an experienced man in undercover work. He taught us how to change our appearance and how to find out whether our rooms or our luggage had been searched.

In a target country it was essential to have the right food or ration coupons and the proper papers. We wanted to look like typical citizens. We had to be very careful to carry no American or British cigarettes, pens or labels. Our possessions had to match those of the citizens. The wrong cigarette lighter, conspicuous foreign labels on the clothing or the wrong cut of clothes could give us away.

Training was not entirely physical work. General Donovan was very well read in the field of espionage and guerrilla warfare, and he maintained a good library in our training area. The book I recall best had nothing to do with espionage, however. It was a volume about Chief Joseph of the Nez Perce Indians.

"Here's one you'll like," said Donovan when he handed it to me. "It's from your part of the country, the Northwest."

Donovan was right: I did appreciate that book. Chief Joseph had been a fine guerrilla warrior who had kept United States troopers chasing him and fighting him for a long time before he finally decided that he would make war no longer.

I was further interested in the book because I had a distant connection to Chief Joseph. At Washington State I had become the blood brother of the great grandson of Chief Joseph, a man with the improbable name of Levi McCormick. McCormick, who later became chief of the Nez Perce, had played football with Chris Rumburg and me, and subsequently he became a professional baseball player.

One night in college after football season was over, McCormick and I were sharing a few beers when he told me about the blood-brother ritual among the Nez Perce. Accordingly, we scratched our wrists and mingled our blood in ceremonial style. I sometimes wondered whether the Indian blood helped me in my night fighting later on.

As training continued, each of the OSS men developed specialties. Instructors who had already been through the entire training were assigned to become instructors in other OSS areas. Those who had special areas of knowledge were trained for individual missions.

Each student went by a code name. Some code names were simply first names, but others were made up. In one class there were two men with very similar code names, one called Ski and another—a tall, regal-looking fellow—called Sky. Both gentlemen caught my interest. I suspected they were either Russians or Poles, and I wanted to know more about them. Later I got to know both of them well.

Sky, the tall gentleman, was then about fifty-four years old. His real name was Serge Obolensky, and he was a Russian prince who had fought against the Bolsheviks as a young cavalry officer in 1917 and 1918. Forced to flee Russia because of his noble background and czarist support, he came to the United States with other White Russian immigrants.

Sky was a hard-working, intelligent man who spoke very fine English with an Oxford accent. A hotelier and highly respected public relations man, he was very well known in New York society. But he was no playboy. He was a real man—tough, resilient, and good-humored. He trained hard, and despite his greater age, he kept up with all the younger fellows and did everything we did.

I will never forget his performance during parachute training, which the OSS carried out in an accelerated program. At the Army bases of Fort Bragg and Fort Benning there were many stages of ground indoctrination before the men started their qualifying jumps. But at the OSS we made it a point of honor to go through the indoctrination and all five qualifying jumps in one day.

Although Serge was much older than the average trainee, he wanted to take parachute training with the rest of us. After the first two jumps his legs began to bother him. He asked the medics to tape him up tightly. On the next jump the tape burst when he hit the ground. It did again on the fourth jump.

The jumpmaster said, "Okay, Sky, that's enough."

Sky gritted his teeth and told the medics to wrap the tape more tightly. Then he went up again. When the jumpmaster tried to stop him, Obolensky said, "Throw me out of the plane, damnit!" They threw him out and he qualified.

That was a proud and courageous man.

After the war, I learned how his jumping practice paid off. In 1950 Serge invited me to dinner with Ed Sullivan, then a columnist and later of TV fame, and Connie Woodworth of *Harper's Magazine*. During dinner Prince Obolensky related some of his escapades.

On his first OSS mission he parachuted into Sardinia with a suitcase and a radio. Gathering partisans, he organized resistance against the Germans and cut communications lines. Later he worked with the Maquis in France and took part in underground resistance activities throughout the greater part of the war.

The man with the code name Ski had a completely different background from Sky. Ski was a companion of two other men known as Milt and Irv. All three had fought with the communist-leaning Abraham Lincoln Brigade in the Spanish Civil War. At that time a few other communist sympathizers were training in the OSS, as they fully supported our drive to defeat Hitler. (And after Pearl Harbor, Russia was our ally!) Political leanings did not matter as long as we were all against the Nazis.

Another man I came to know well at Camp B2 was Captain John Ford of the U.S. Navy Reserve, the movie director who made John Wayne famous. Ford had done some pictorial work for the Navy and he was asked by Donovan to do a training film of the OSS. He came to B2 with a very fine cameraman named Joey, who was famous for taking the remarkable shots of Gunga Din climbing a great polished minaret in the movie *Gunga*

Din. The writer on the training-film project was Jack McClain.

Acting for John Ford was terrific fun. He filmed us swinging from the trees, throttling a sentry and blowing up huts and enemy materiel. All of the trainees wore masks to disguise their identities. We were all dressed in shorts.

Those shorts earned me my first nickname. Ford had told us it didn't matter what we wore as long as we performed, so I donned a pair of bright red shorts that I always favored in the heat of the Catoctin summer. As I came swinging out of a tree to attack a German, wearing nothing but those bright red shorts, somebody yelled, "Here comes Flash Gordon!"

Flash Gordon I remained for the duration of B2.

One of the first groups I trained included a number of men from Thailand, then called Siam. The leader of the group was Colonel Karb Kunjara. Kunjara was taller than the other Thais, and he was very intelligent and enthusiastic—a great companion for weekend festivities.

Kunjara had been assigned to the United States as the military attaché to Seni Pramoj, who was at that time the minister from Siam. Together Kunjara and Pramoj had started the Free Thai movement by gathering together Siamese students then in the United States for training at Area B2. The students were commissioned in the so-called Free Thai Army.

The Thais received the usual training in silent killing, use of weapons, infiltration and guerrilla warfare. We taught them how to use radios and other communications equipment, and schooled them in sabotage and undercover agent techniques. In return, the Thais taught us a few words of Siamese and a novel team sport that was similar to soccer but played with a smaller ball. They also taught us Siamese boxing, in which the opponents deliver blows with the feet as well as with gloved fists.

I left Camp B2 before the Thais were sent overseas, but I later learned of their fate from Nicol Smith, the explorer and author of the bestseller *Burma Road*. Having been put in charge of the group of twenty Thais from B2, Smith had engineered their infiltration into Thailand. From an airfield prepared by General Claire Chennault in South Yunnan province the Thais launched their mission through Burma to Siam. Some were lost in the long, hard trek through Burma, but others got through. Along with a few Americans from the OSS, they succeeded in establishing contact with the Regent of Thailand, Luang Pradit, and they set up radio communication with the other OSS stations.

Nick Smith's Siamese, as this unit came to be called, eventually built a strong intelligence network throughout Thailand. The network was partially protected by a dozen OSS-established guerrilla camps, and from these camps they tried to organize a general uprising. The war was over before the uprising ever got under way, but during the war the Thai group was a considerable impediment to the Japanese.

Norway also had its representative. His name was Ed Stromholt, and he was a Norwegian fenrik (lieutenant) who had come out of Norway in the British raid on the Lofoten Islands in 1941 or so. Lean and hard, Stromholt was an excellent skier, and he could outwalk anybody in our mountain camp. He was our instructor in map and compass work—orienteering, as it was called by the Scandinavians.

Often students had techniques they could teach to

their instructors. In particular, I remember a student in one of my silent killing classes, in which Charlie Parkins was an assistant instructor. The student, called Vic, was a solid, heavyset man with some fat on him. After a few classes he began giving Charlie a hard time.

Before each course we carefully explained the safety rules to all our students. The instructor would demonstrate a hold on a student and apply enough pressure to show its effectiveness. When the student had had enough, he tapped the instructor, who immediately eased his hold. The same rule operated when a student tried out a hold or throw on an instructor or classmate.

One day Charlie was demonstrating a wrist throw with Vic. Instead of giving the tap for release, Vic jerked free and sprained Charlie's wrist.

I stepped in, got a good grip on Vic and said, "Let's be gentle with one another, shall we? You don't hurt instructors, you follow the rules!" Then I repeated the instructions about tapping for a release.

Vic growled a bit, but he finally said, "Okay."

After class was over, he came up to me and said, "Captain, could I talk with you a minute?"

"Sure," I said.

"Let's go over to the mat."

We went across to the long wrestling mat that was laid out on the grass.

"Show me how you would attack," he said.

I came in slowly toward him, intending to be gentle about the whole thing. Suddenly Vic made a sharp movement upward. It was a good feint. I looked up for just a second.

The next thing I knew, I was eating field grass, dirt and gravel with Vic on top of me.

The maneuver was remarkable for a man of his

size. Vic had distracted my attention, then leapt forward legs first. With a flying scissors he caught me around the legs as he rolled over. I rolled with him, landing face down on the ground.

I turned over, spat out the gritty grass and said, "Vic, that's darn good! Where'd you learn that? I've never seen such speed."

"That's my specialty in the ring," he replied. "It's called the flying scissors."

As it turned out, he was a professional wrestler, and that maneuver taught me a lesson that I passed on to all my students. Never fall for a feint, nor underestimate an opponent.

As a rule, we didn't try to change the habits of a man who was already a good boxer or wrestler. If he could knock someone out with a punch or a throw, we didn't try to convert him to karate chops, judo blows or French savate kicks. We taught everyone that the best way to dispatch an opponent was the quickest and easiest way for the student himself.

However, we did try to break the habits of fistwork by men who were not excellent boxers. If a man hit an opponent with his fist, he stood a good chance of breaking his own knuckles. We taught the edge-of-the-hand chop and the vicious uppercut to the chin with the heel of the hand, using the fingers in the enemy's eyes. The men who banged up their fists or were too squeamish or hesitant had to unlearn their bad habits before they were ready for effective agent work.

Among the other students in our classes were Greeks and Yugoslavians. The Greeks were primarily first-generation Greek-Americans and I remember only their code names, since no one bothered to pronounce their real names; Nikipopoulos, for instance, was conveniently shortened to Nick or Pop. When they left B2 they fought the Nazis in Greece, and some stayed on after the war to fight the communists.

The Yugoslavs were primarily Serbs, though there were also some Dalmatians and Montenegrins, including many great mountain men and knife-fighters. These men loved to use explosives, and they relished any kind of rough going. I enjoyed working with them. Though a little impatient with espionage training, they took to guerrilla fighting like ducks to water.

The Serbs were great singers. From them I learned a great old Serbian patriotic song, originally called "Marching, Marching, King Peter's Guard"—a title that was later changed to "Mihailovic's Guards," after Colonel Draza Mihailovic, the leader of the Chetnik guerrilla fighters, a man loyal to King Peter of Yugoslavia. When the king was deposed, the name of the song was changed to honor Mihailovic, who put up the only resistance to the Germans when they first invaded Yugoslavia.

Sung in Serbian, the song is powerful and beautiful— "battles fighting, fighting, flags waving, waving . . . new heroes being born." The last phrase is "Za slobodu sviyu nas," which means, "For liberty for all." I learned the entire song in Serbian and I believed every word of it. On later occasions I shouted out, "Za slobodu sviyu nas!" The Poles and Czechs also loved it.

In Ford's training film there is one segment where the Serbs loudly sing "Mihailovic's Guards." One summer evening Ford grouped the Serbs around our little swimming pool in Area B2, with me up front leading the singing, waving my Sikes-Fairbairn stiletto. I could see the muscles stand out in their proud necks as the

Serbs roared out their song with the cameras rolling. When we finished there was a deep silence.

Afterward Ford told me, "That is one of the most stirring scenes I have ever done. Those men know what they are fighting for."

He was right. They knew what they were fighting for, and they went over to the hills of Yugoslavia and did a very great job. The tragedy came later, when Tito and the communists, with the support of the Russians, came into power at the end of the war. The hero of that song, Mihailovic, was executed on Tito's orders.

In July of 1942 a few men from B2 were sent to England for special classes at the British Special Operations Executive (SOE) School of Industrial Sabotage. I was there for six weeks, four of which were spent in Hertfordshire at SOE Station 17 and the rest in London.

Station 17 was one of many top-secret installations under the SOE, which had been organized by William Stephenson, the man called "Intrepid" by Winston Churchill. He was also the head of Britain's Secret Intelligence Service (SIS) and the Counterintelligence Agency. The SOE's mission included undercover actions, sabotage, subversion, and underground propaganda. I was in the counterpart element of the OSS.

In addition to SOE and OSS clandestine trainees, British servicemen were brought in from the Special Air Service (SAS), which had been started by David Stirling in Egypt, and there were resistance fighters from all the Nazi-occupied countries of Europe. Our goal was to learn the methods of industrial sabotage that the British had been developing for some time. We also wanted to find out what were the key bottlenecks in the enemy's industry so we could destroy the equipment and supplies that were most difficult to replace. In addition, some of us planned to accompany the British and observe their methods of infiltrating the Low Countries, Belgium and the Netherlands, by crossing the English Channel.

Among the agents in our classes were a number of men who were destined to return to occupied Europe. In particular I remember a man named Van der Hook who returned to Holland to conduct sabotage. (The word sabotage, incidentally, is derived from a Belgian word, *sabot*. In previous wars the workers threw their wooden shoes, sabots, into the machinery in order to sabotage the war effort.) Van der Hook went into the Dutch resistance, where he later aided American troops in river crossings and helped destroy a number of enemy-held bridges. His intelligence reports after D-day were invaluable.

Station 17 also included a Norwegian, Peter (Per in Norwegian), who was an excellent pianist. After dinner he would play for hours, entertaining us with the works of Grieg and other composers. Most of the men would listen to his impromptu concerts, and then afterward we would play Ping-Pong or retire to a local pub. Much later I discovered that Per went back to Norway and helped sabotage the German efforts to develop "heavy water," a critical element in early experiments with the atomic bomb.

In working with the British, we swapped a lot of information about explosives and undercover techniques. At that time the British were still using an explosive called gelignite, which had an almost overpowering sickly sweet smell. They also had dynamite and TNT, but our Composition C plastic explosive was something new to them.

As time went on, we exchanged information about the various kinds of time-pencils and other devices we used to delay explosions. Then we concentrated on how to destroy specific targets in order to cause maximum damage to the Germans.

Among our practice exercises was the infiltration of London dock areas, where we tried to lay charges without being spotted. Our targets in these training sessions were the huge cranes used to load and unload the ships in port. We knew that if we could enter the harbors of occupied countries and sabotage enemy operations, the Germans would not be able to get their ships in or out, or to load or unload them once they were docked. In the London shipyards we laid all our lines just as though they were fuses and set mock charges underneath each of the cranes. Small blocks simulated the explosives.

Other trial targets included locomotives, generator turbines and factories that made specific war-related materials like ball bearings. Locomotives were hard to replace and very expensive to build. The destruction of one locomotive cost the enemy a fortune in labor and steel. Power plants were also critical. If we wanted to put a big electrical power plant out of commission, we would plan to hit one of the turbines. Each turbine was a huge screwlike piece of steel produced from a single casting, enormously costly to produce. So we practiced blowing up turbines.

From the British we learned that the German forces were short of ball bearings. The RAF and the USAF had already made the German ball bearing plants, such as Wurzburg, primary targets in their bombing raids. But air raids were costly and inefficient, and we needed men on the ground who could do the sabotage work. Fifty or a hundred airplanes might or might not hit the critical parts of the factory, but one man, properly placed, could infiltrate a critical part of the factory and destroy the vital key to the plant's production.

One of my special friends from the British SOE was Captain Watts of the British Army, a great raconteur and an enthusiastic adventurer. Some of his jokes were fairly rough, but he had a dry sense of humor and a lot of good common sense. He led many of the expeditions to the London dock areas where we practiced destroying the cranes with mock charges.

Watts also taught us how to set limpets, magnetic charges that were used against enemy shipping. To set a limpet you had to dive underwater, approach the enemy ship without being seen, attach the limpet just below the water line and then swim away before the electrical timing device set off the charge.

One night as we were returning late from the dockyards, we passed through a small village that Captain Watts seemed to know.

"Let's stop here," he said suddenly.

We pulled over and went into an old pub. Captain Watts called over the publican and whispered something in his ear. At first the owner of the tavern just shook his head. Captain Watts brought out a little wad of bills and pointed at me. Obviously he was telling the publican that I was an American and he wanted to show me something special.

The man finally nodded. Having descended the stairs to his cellar, he returned with two bottles, cellar-cold.

Watts presented these to me with the words, "And here, my friend, is Benskin's Colne Springs Ale."

"That's just beer," I said, glancing at the bottles. "And I don't even drink beer."

Watts smiled. "You have never tasted such nectar as this. Just try it."

I noticed the loving way the publican handled the tall bottle of ale as he gently poured it into a slim glass.

"Cheers!" he said.

"Cheers!" we replied, and I took my first sip of ale. It didn't taste bad. In fact, to me it tasted just like any other beer. Since we were thirsty, I quickly finished the first glass and then downed another.

After the second glass, I said, "Well, that's pretty tasty, but I don't know what's so special about it."

Then I realized I was speaking very carefully. I had to space my words judiciously to keep them from slurring together.

"Pardon me," said Watts. "Would you please hand me my hat from the hat rack?"

I stood up to oblige, and that's when I realized Benskin's Colne Springs Ale was something special. The room started spinning or maybe it was my head. I still don't know what was in that ale, but it was the strongest beerlike substance that I've ever had in my life. No wonder the bartender treated it like liquid gold!

Captain Watts also goaded me into one of my most dangerous adventures on English soil. It occurred in a roundhouse in a railroad siding in Hertfordshire.

A roundhouse is a mammoth repair shop where locomotives come in to be serviced. The floor of the structure turns like a revolving stage. Lengths of track set into the floor point out from the center of the roundhouse like the spokes of a wheel. When a locomotive comes in to be serviced, it runs frontward or backward onto the piece of track. The floor can then be turned so that the locomotive is over a service pit, where mechanics can work on the undercarriage. Or the floor can be revolved one hundred eighty degrees so the engine is turned around for its exit.

In describing a roundhouse to me Watts mentioned that there was one nearby in Hertfordshire. An idea occurred to him as he spoke.

"Jerry," he said, "I think you might be the first man to steal a locomotive out of that place. Do you think you can do it? Are you game?"

"Let's go," I replied.

I had never been in a roundhouse before, but I had already learned how to drive a steam locomotive just in case I had to make a getaway in one.

One evening just as it was getting dark, we approached the roundhouse during a change in shifts. A locomotive was all set up on its track, smoke and steam puffing from its stack, ready to leave the roundhouse.

As my friends arranged a distraction, I climbed aboard. The pressure gauge told me there were already live coals in the firebed and a head of steam.

I quickly threw on more coal and shoved the throttle forward. The engine roared out of the house along a switch track leading to the main line. I didn't know where the line went, but I recalled Watts' warning: "Don't stay out there any longer than four minutes."

It wasn't long before I realized why he had given me that warning. As I roared down the track, I saw the semaphore signals begin to change from green to red. Three signals had already changed to red before I heard a big whistle overriding the noise of the steam engine. Up ahead, around the bend, came the London Mail.

I jerked the brakes on full, slammed the shift into reverse and roared back toward the roundhouse faster than I had come out. By now many workers were staring at the locomotive, but they all seemed to be shocked into paralysis. Some men who were leaving through a nearby gate stared at me as I screeched to a halt, threw the engine into idle, and jumped down from the locomotive. In a moment I had slipped past the workers and was gone.

In my entire wartime experience that was the first and only time I ever borrowed a locomotive.

In some respects, Station 17 was run like an old boarding school. The major who ruled over the station was a sourpuss whom we called "the headmaster." Like a true headmaster, he believed in repeating instructions until we had absorbed them completely. The repetition was tiresome, but he firmly believed that practice makes perfect.

At night we were often looking for something else besides Norwegian Peter playing Grieg or a game of Ping-Pong in the barracks, so we would head for the nearest pub even though the headmaster had decreed that the doors were to be locked at ten o'clock. Not having been treated as schoolboys for some time, we were inclined to ignore the curfew, and each of us found his own way to get in later.

We discovered that the doorkeeper would unlock the gate after ten, but he conscientiously reported latecomers to the headmaster. If you came in through the gate, you had to go on report and contend with the major the next morning. The preferred method of return was to climb up the trellis of the old school building and go in through a window.

Despite our high jinks, there were also moments of sober reality when the war was brought home to us. I remember accompanying Captain Watts and a group of SOE officers one evening to watch the departure of a pair of Belgian operators who were on their way home to join the Belgian underground.

We drove the men down to the waterfront and

watched them board a fishing boat that would take them across the Channel. It was a risky mission, but the crew comprised experienced men who knew the coast very well and had good lookouts. There was a small radar aboard to help them look for mines. Nonetheless, I seriously wondered whether that boat would make it through and I wondered how long those two operatives would survive in their own country.

Chapter 4

Although our time at Station 17 was well spent and we gained invaluable experience and knowledge from our contact with the SOE, we were all anxious to get to London as soon as the session was over.

Back home we had all listened to the beautiful, mellifluous voice of Edward R. Murrow as he began his nightly broadcasts with his famous phrase, ''This . . . is London.'' Finally I was there, and I wanted to see everything I could of that city.

During the day, wartime London seemed to be quite normal, though the occasional air raid sent people running for shelters. London at night was a different story. Then I knew we were in a war zone. The streets were blacked out. Trafalgar Square, Piccadilly Circus, Nelson's statue and Hyde Park, where orators on soap boxes gave their speeches—all were silent at night. The city was cloaked in black. You might walk along the dark streets and hear the disembodied female voice of a streetwalker calling from the doorway, ''You want some company? Are you lonely?'' Or you might bump into someone in the street, hear a polite, ''Excuse me,'' and pass without ever seeing the face of the person you had bumped into. It was impossible to find your way around those darkened streets without asking directions again and again.

One night a couple of us went to the Haymarket Theatre to see Vivien Leigh, of *Gone with the Wind* fame, in George Bernard Shaw's *A Doctor's Dilemma.* Another evening we enjoyed a musical about springtime. I can't remember the title, only the lead song, "When You Have a Little Springtime in Your Heart." People went to dinner and attended the theater as usual, but at any moment an air raid siren could send us all scurrying for the underground bomb shelters, many of them in London's subway system.

Food was scarce throughout England. The oranges that we Americans brought in were great treats to the British. Fresh eggs were available in the country, but in town they were expensive and hard to obtain. Elite restaurants still carried delicacies, but everything was enormously costly.

Fortunately I was rarely tempted to dine at the more expensive restaurants, mostly because of the strong-flavored game meat they served. In Washington State where I grew up, my father was a great hunter, and I was accustomed to eating deer, bear, and game birds such as pheasants. However, the British liked to let their pheasants and other game "hang" for several days in order to improve the flavor. The high-priced restaurants served well-hung pheasants that the British thought were magnificently cured. To me the meat was completely unappetizing. The birds smelled as if they had died a noxious death from some dread disease.

On the other hand, I came to admire what the British cooks could do with a few leftovers during those days of scarcity. At Station 17 and in many homes, the cooks made little sweets for dessert by adding some custard to a bit of canned pear or peach, sometimes topping off this dessert with a little cookie. I also became accustomed to the English breakfast of oatmeal or porridge, often accompanied by some kippers (salt fish).

The blackout brought people together, sometimes in unusual circumstances. One night as I was making my way around London, I bumped into three men who had accents I didn't recognize. It turned out they were Australians. I learned they were Navy men who had helped transport the troops to Dieppe, France, in a huge raid to test the German defenses, mislead them as to D-day landing plans, cover the infiltration of highly specialized agents, and blunt Soviet insistence on a British invasion of the continent. Most of the aims were achieved, but at great cost. Three fourths of the five thousand men, the bulk of the landing force, were killed or captured.

Having joined forces with the Aussies, I soon helped them attack several bottles of ship's rum. Eventually they and their rum wound up in my hotel room, where they proceeded to teach me a number of Australian songs. I was an apt pupil, and I swapped a few American lyrics for their Australian ones. When I had finished my rendition of "Ragtime Cowboy Joe," they responded with "Waltzing Matilda," which was more or less their national anthem.

I immediately liked "Waltzing Matilda," so they taught me all the verses. Sprawled out on the bed with a scrap of paper on the floor and a pencil in hand, I attempted to write it down for posterity while two Aussies sat on my back shouting verses at me. With a jug or two of rum for fortification and the aid of their patient assistance, I finally managed to learn all four verses, plus the chorus. I still have in my possession the almost totally illegible script of that song, and I can still sing all four verses from memory.

While we were in London, I also went to a party hosted by John Ford at Claridge's, a grand old hotel. Ford was a gracious host, and we spent some time at the party reminiscing about our time together in Area B2 when I had acted in the training film he directed. At the party I had the opportunity to meet Sir Alexander Korda and Douglas Fairbanks, Jr. I had admired Fairbanks' father in the silent pictures, and I was gratified to see that the son looked exactly as he had in *Gunga Din*.

Garson Kanin had come along with Korda, and there were many other luminaries as well, including government officials and agents who were active in the British Special Operations Executive. It was an evening of good hospitality, lively conversation and many shared experiences.

In a short time I would have to return to the United States, but I was anxious to see Oxford before I went. In 1938, when I graduated from Washington State University, I'd had a good chance of winning a Rhodes Scholarship, but a fine halfback from Colorado named Whizzer White was chosen. His real name was Byron White. He did go on to Oxford and later became a Supreme Court Justice. When I was in the running for the Rhodes, I saw pictures of the beautiful colleges of Oxford University, such as Magdalene (pronounced "Maudlin"), and now I figured this was my chance to see it. One morning, I took a train to Oxford.

Oxford in those days was a beautiful, quiet town that seemed totally cut off from the war. As soon as I got off the train, I went to a little tea room—the epitome of the small village restaurant—where I had a crumpet or scone with a dab of orange marmalade. Then I walked around the grounds of the university, thinking of all the great men of England who had gone there. The quiet greenery and the seclusion of the place were in marked contrast to all my work with explosives and a contrast, as well, to the hubbub of London.

On my return to Washington I reported to OSS headquarters in the Q Building. There I was given new orders transferring me from Area B2 to another OSS camp on the Potomac River at Indian Head, Maryland.

The commanding officer at Indian Head was Albert Seitz. As his executive officer, I was supposed to help him develop light plane and marine movement so we could infiltrate by submarine and small boat.

One of my first assignments under Al Seitz was to build a landing strip for light planes, where we would experiment with short takeoffs and landings. To build a landing strip we needed a bulldozer, but the nearest one was in Fort Meade, Maryland, where the Army had extra equipment in its engineer motor pool.

I recruited an experienced farm boy from among our OSS enlisted men, and together with another OSS operator, we hopped into a jeep and headed for Fort Meade. We anticipated a lot of red tape, and it was critical that we obtain that bulldozer as soon as possible in order to save ourselves a lot of unnecessary work scraping ground and pulling up tree stumps. In order to avoid the delay of lengthy explanations, we OSS agents practiced some of our appropriation techniques. Soon our farm boy was out on the road with the bulldozer, my fellow agent and I bringing up the rear in our jeep.

As it turned out, we didn't have to return that bulldozer for some time, because no one missed it from Fort Meade. We saved hundreds of man-hours using it to tear up the trees and stumps for our little landing strip.

Unfortunately, the strip wasn't quite long enough for the particular type of plane that first flew into the Indian Head camp. The first test-landing was made by Lieutenant Colonel Adams, an excellent pilot who certainly deserved a better field than the one we had built. Adams executed a perfect landing, but when he tried to take off, he encountered an unforeseen obstacle just off the end of the runway. As the plane lifted off the landing strip runway, our camp flagpole loomed straight ahead. Adams banked sharply to avoid the flagpole, slipped vertically in the bank and crashed on one wing.

No one was seriously hurt, but the airplane was a mess.

At Indian Head we learned amphibious training, including submarine and small-boat work. One of our instructors was the Navy's Lieutenant Shaheen, who later operated an OSS small-boat navy in the Mediterranean off the coast of Italy.

While I enjoyed the small-craft work, I always felt crowded in a submarine. Because of my size I felt there was no escape from a submarine except out the torpedo tube, and I was a bit too big! I endured as much as I had to and then requested jump training, which came through in fairly short order.

Meanwhile, we continued to develop our explosives work for sabotage training. We experimented with new types of time-delay pencils and we practiced blowing up critical structures.

During one of the training sessions I came very close to ending my career with the OSS. We were using blocks of TNT to knock down concrete bridges and small buildings. One day I set the charge and then started to move away. Fortunately my head was lowered, and I was still in a crouched position, backing away from the charge. For some reason the timing device went off too early and a pound of TNT exploded only a few feet in front of me.

On that particular day the Lord must have been watching over me, because I had my helmet on for a change, and it took the brunt of the blast. The explosion blew me rear-over-teakettle and my ears rang for weeks.

Infection from shrapnel wounds was also an occupational danger. Once while I was working with explosives, a piece of fragment caught my forehead near the left temple. The wound became infected. I didn't pay much attention to it, but the infection kept getting worse. Finally the camp doctor said, "You'd better get to Walter Reed and have the doctors take a look at that."

At Walter Reed, the doctors immediately put me to bed. They applied a black goo to the wound—a medicine that the nurses called anti-phlogistine, intended to suck out the infection. In addition, the nurses applied heat pads and wet compresses.

Eventually the wound healed. The doctors and nurses seemed mightily relieved. The temple is a very poor place to have blood poisoning, and the doctors feared a serious infection would destroy whatever brain I had left.

The night I was released, I had a celebration at a Chinese restaurant with three of my best buddies—Chris Rumburg, Ernie Krom and Lou Rucker. Rucker was a paratroop captain pulled into the OSS from Army parachute school. He obtained official permission relieving me from submarine duty to start parachute training.

I was grateful. Parachuting seemed like the fastest way to infiltrate behind enemy lines and far more efficient than submarine or small-craft invasion. And of course I preferred it because I like to have a lot of space around me. I was glad I didn't have to look forward to any more submarine missions.

Rucker's first name was Lucius, but we called him Lou, Ruck or Jump. Lou hailed from Jackson, Mississippi. He was a great soldier and avid paratrooper, and we always said he could jump out of an airplane faster than he could talk. His southern pace of conversation was notoriously languid, and when anyone around him talked too fast or was in too great a hurry, he would drawl, "Take it easy, greasy!"

It was Rucker who made all the arrangements to get me jump-qualified, but the only day we could make the jumps was Thanksgiving Day, 1942. True to OSS tradition, I had to qualify all in one day rather than go through all the steps of the regular Army parachute course, which lasted several weeks.

On the day of my qualifying jumps Rucker met me at Bolling Field in Virginia, just across the Potomac from Washington's National Airport. With him was Sergeant John Swetish, the man who once set a record for the most jumps in twenty-four hours.

Breakfast was at the Bolling Field Club. After Rucker, Swetish and I had eaten, we walked out on the club grounds. Some park benches were scattered about the lawn.

"Jerry," said Rucker, "you have never done any ground training, have you?"

I shook my head.

"Ever done a PLF?"

"I don't even know what a PLF is," I replied.

"That's a parachute landing fall," he explained.

"Well, let's do it."

"Okay," said Rucker. He turned to Sergeant Swetish and told him, "Sit on one end of that bench over there."

When Swetish had taken a seat, Rucker placed himself on the other end of the bench and ordered, "Now, Jerry, get up on the back of the bench. See if you can balance there."

I climbed up on the back of the bench and put one hand on each man's head.

"Okay," said Rucker. "Now stand up straight and then fall forward and roll. Do a somersault."

I had played a lot of football and I'd had extensive Commando training. With the rigorous physical exercise I had seen at Area B2 and with the British SAS exercises, I was in good shape. I did my forward roll without any mishap.

"All right," said Rucker, "now get up and face toward the front of the bench. Fall off backward and roll."

When I had done that, he beamed. "You have just qualified in your ground school. Let's fly!"

The airplane was either a B-10 or B-18. Taking off from Bolling Field we headed for Lakehurst, New Jersey, where we were to join in a jump with the Marines at the Navy Marine Parachute and Dirigible Base.

At Lakehurst there was plenty of activity on the base, but a big clear field in the middle of the post was empty. We circled once and headed for the field.

"Get in the door," Swetish ordered, "and when I say go, you go!"

I squatted in the doorway of the plane and waited for the word. But when he said "Go!" I evidently didn't move fast enough. I felt his big foot in the middle of my back, and suddenly, I was out.

I had hooked up to a static line inside the airplane,

and it automatically pulled my chute loose. It was a great feeling when the chute opened and I sailed down over the field. I pulled myself up on the risers lines of the parachute and managed to do a reasonable PLF. The risers are webbing straps that connect the harness to the nylon parachute lines. Then I rolled up my chute and brought it in.

On the next run Rucker and Swetish were both wearing parachutes themselves.

"What's going on?" I asked.

"We're doing a free jump," Rucker replied.

I knew that was a jump without a static line: You had to pull your own ripcord to open the chute.

"Well, gosh, I want to do that too," I said.

Rucker shook his head. "You've had only one jump. I'm sort of sweating this out myself, and I've had well over thirty jumps."

But I wouldn't give up. "I want to go," I insisted.

"Okay," he shrugged. "Just remember this: It don't mean a thing if you don't pull that string."

Rucker requested that the Marines issue me a free-fall chute. This time we would be flying in a blimp instead of the airplane. We lined up to get aboard the blimp, and after it took off, the officers lined up our stick (group) of jumpers.

A captain of the Marines led off, followed by Captain Rucker. Another Marine captain came third, the greenhorn Captain Sage came fourth, and I was followed by another couple of Marine officers. Among the Marine noncommissioned officers was Sergeant Swetish.

The jumpmaster gave us careful instructions. Each man was to come forward to the front of the blimp until he stood opposite the door on his left. Then we were to make a left turn, march to the door, click our feet, come to attention and—still at attention—fall out the door.

"Stay at attention until your head is below the level of your feet," the jumpmaster told us.

He also instructed us to hold onto our ripcord handles, since the cord would be used again when the chutes were repacked. The rule was that anyone who let go of his ripcord had to buy drinks for all.

The first three men got away. Then it was my turn at the door.

As I popped to attention and started to fall forward, I thought to myself, "Shucks, I'm gonna delay pulling my ripcord and try to catch up with Rucker."

And I did. I stayed at attention until my head fell below my feet. Then I just kept falling, almost like a diver. When I was level with Rucker, I looked at him with a grin and pulled the ripcord.

I was having so much fun that I forgot about the penalty for losing the cord. As I gave that cord a yank, I let go of the handle and threw it from New Jersey halfway across New York.

Rucker and I landed safely near each other and swapped happy congratulations.

That day, they finished qualifying me and then we joined the Marines at their club. I bought the Marines a round of drinks—my penalty for throwing away the ripcord—and then they bought me a couple of drinks as reward for qualifying all in one day and for celebrating Thanksgiving with them.

Rucker, Swetish and I loaded up the B-10 (or B-18) and flew back to Bolling Field. There I got in the car and went home for Thanksgiving dinner at Indian Head, Maryland. I was now an officially prepared parachutist, ready to drop anywhere at a moment's notice.

Chapter 5

After that Thanksgiving weekend, I went on to Washington headquarters. By that time I'd had my fill of training and was anxious to "get operational." I told the people at headquarters that I wanted to get out in the field and do some of the things I had been trained to do.

In December of 1942 I had several briefings in Washington headquarters in preparation for being shipped overseas. At that time two "deep" missions were being considered, both of which would be staged out of North Africa, which Allied forces had invaded in November. The first deep contingency was to go into Spain if the Fascist leader Franco, already sympathetic to the Nazis, actually committed Spain and its resources to the Axis. That could make Spain another jumping-off point for German troops to attack us in North Africa. We wanted to have OSS-trained Spanish speakers available to disrupt such proceedings. My other contingency assignment was to Yugoslavia, where I might be parachuted in to work with my Serb friends from B2 under Draza Mihailovic.

Both of these were mountainous areas, so we were issued appropriate wearing apparel consisting of brand-new jackets, leather lined with alpaca fleece, from New

York's Abercrombie & Fitch. They had ample pockets for weapons, explosives and detonators, and they were extremely warm. As always, the OSS went first class.

In my outfit were three men who strongly wanted to go to Spain—Vince Lassowski, Irving Goff and Milton Felsen. All three were experienced guerrilla fighters who had fought with the Partisans against Franco's forces in the Spanish Civil War from 1936 to 1939. Since they had served in the Abraham Lincoln Brigade, I assume they were communists, though their political affiliations made little difference to us at that time as long as they would fight Hitler and the Nazis. We would have to wait and watch Franco for any decision to go into Spain. In the meantime we prepared for our trip to North Africa. Our alpaca jackets came in handy earlier than expected. We needed them when a severe blizzard hit North Africa in January.

My orders were to report to Marine Colonel William Eddy in Algiers. Along with my orders I was given carte blanche to requisition transportation and supplies for the mission. My orders said that I could use any available civil or military aircraft, any surface craft, water craft or submersible, or any type of train, conveyance or automobile that would aid me in my secret mission. In other words, I could go anywhere in the world and use any method to get there. I was also allowed a per diem to cover expenses during my time overseas. No one knew at that time that I would be gone for two full years, and I never did collect my per diem.

After we received our orders, Donovan gave me a money belt containing about $35,000 in various currencies, including gold, silver and sterling coins. Donovan's orders left a lot up to the agent. He simply described the mission: Get behind the German lines and hurt the enemy. He did not specify methods or how we should spend the money we were given. (It so happened that when I was captured the money belt was safely in the hands of my adjutant in the OSS detachment.)

I did ask Donovan about Colonel Eddy and another man I was supposed to meet, Robert Murphy. Colonel William Eddy was a former professor and college president who had won the Distinguished Service Medal and the Distinguished Service Cross in World War I. A man who spoke fluent Arabic, he was instrumental in making preparations for the Allied invasion of North Africa called Operation TORCH, and he later became a United States representative to Saudi Arabia.

Robert Murphy was a U.S. career Foreign Service officer in France at the time of the Nazi occupation and continued on at the U.S. embassy at Vichy. He maintained his diplomatic position even after Vichy became a collaborationist government that cooperated with the Germans, and still later represented our State Department in Algiers. He had worked out trade agreements with General Weygand, Vichy's commander in North Africa, and he attempted to win the support of French forces for our cause in the event that we decided to invade that continent.

In his role as consul, Murphy hired and brought to North Africa a dozen people whom he called vice consuls. Their mission was ostensibly to see that American goods coming into the French army were not transshipped to Germany from North Africa by the Vichy people. But the real purpose of Murphy's vice consuls, beginning in the summer of 1941, was to collect intelligence. The vice consuls made charts and maps of the fields and coastline, and they kept attuned to the morale of the local population. Any information they acquired eventually reached the OSS.

When Bill Eddy was sent by Donovan into North Africa, he met with Murphy and together they worked out a coordinated OSS/State Department intelligence group under their combined control. They set up radio stations in the coastal cities—Tangier, Casablanca, Oran, Algiers, Tunis and other coast-watcher stations along the Mediterranean—from which they plotted the movements of Nazi shipping. As it developed, Eddy, Murphy and the group of vice consuls were of great assistance in planning and executing the U.S. landings in North Africa. In addition, they fed false information to double agents concerning landing points of Allied forces.

During all of December 1942 I was busy making sure that all the personnel who were to accompany me were properly processed, fully equipped and prepared to go to North Africa. There were nearly twenty men under my command; some were to remain with me, while others had missions elsewhere in North Africa. Among those who accompanied me to the port of embarkation in New York were Richard Crosby, a Bostonian and my adjutant; Captain Harold Rossmiller, a doctor; the three Abraham Lincoln Brigade sergeants: Goff, Felsen and Lassowski; and a man who was to become invaluable to me, Sergeant Steve Byzek, recruited a few months earlier from the parachute school at Fort Benning.

Our alpaca-lined Abercrombie & Fitch leather jackets were issued to all, but the choice of weapons was left up to each individual. Each man selected the weapons that he thought would be most effective behind enemy lines as well as the ones he used with the most skill. I carried two Sikes-Fairbairn knives, a switchblade, a special demolition pocketknife and a spring cosh.

The cosh was a lethal type of metal blackjack. It was an innocent-looking black cylinder about five inches long, with a leather loop at one end that went around the wrist. Inside the cylinder was a spring-loaded ball of lead. When an attacker swung the cylinder, the chunk of lead popped out the end of the tube, given added impetus from the spring inside. One blow from the cosh could split a man's head open or break his arm. Carrying the loaded cosh up my sleeve, I could go into action with one sweep of the arm.

In addition to hand weapons we had our choice of pistols or tommy guns. I had a regulation Army .45 automatic, and I also carried a snub-nosed .38 revolver with a sawed-off trigger guard in a small holster behind my belt buckle. I could slap the revolver out of the holster and fire instantly at close range.

The .45 and the .38 "belly gun" were only for close work. In addition, we carried British Sten pipestem automatic submachine guns for guerrilla combat. The Sten guns were cheap, light, easy to break down and carry, and quite effective.

By Christmas we were fully equipped and all our personal matters were straightened away—allotments to the wives and final farewells. On our way to the port of embarkation we stopped for a moment for some parting toasts at the Waldorf-Astoria. Having bade our goodbyes to the United States, we embarked on the *SS Evangeline*, which brought to mind the Longfellow poem beginning, "This is the forest primeval." The *Evangeline*, judging from her age, might have been built from that very forest.

We joined a convoy bound for North Africa, and soon we were being tossed about on the high seas. During the crossing we spent many hours playing cards. I also spent some hours learning French from one of the

OSS language specialists. I started my lessons with the children's song "Frère Jacques," later "La Madelon," then "Auprès de Ma Blonde" and "Les Chevaliers de la Table Ronde." By the end of the voyage, I had learned about four verses of "The Knights of the Round Table."

I discovered that anything I could learn about languages would stand me in good stead. When I later met people from the Lafayette Esquadrille, I was able to establish rapport with them just by knowing French songs. Everywhere I went, I found that being able to sing songs and to say thank you readily in a foreign language was like Ali Baba saying "Open sesame!" People appreciated my efforts, and they warmed up more readily if I could speak the words they knew. In the end I wound up learning songs and "thanks" in at least twenty languages.

We were very security conscious aboard ship, and we never breathed a word about the OSS. Many people asked, "What outfit are you with?" We just told them we were replacements or the usual cannon fodder. The GIs soon learned that they wouldn't get much out of us and soon enough stopped asking questions. Only one person, a subordinate directly under the skipper of the ship, knew our true role.

We received an unpleasant surprise when we arrived in Oran, our destination in North Africa. At the docks were signs and arrows pointing to the different areas where the units were supposed to assemble. As I walked down the gangplank followed by my band of twenty men, all carrying their gear for the mission, I was appalled to see a sign saying, "OSS DETACHMENT ASSEMBLE HERE."

Turning to my outfit, I hissed in an undertone, "Eyes forward! Keep moving!"

Without glancing to left or right, the men followed close on my heels. I led them past the signs, through town and up a hill overlooking Oran. We camped there that night.

I have no idea who put up the sign, but I didn't like it. There were many Nazi spies among the Arabs and many foreign sympathizers who might well have betrayed us. Wars are strange things: They create spies everywhere.

Glad to be off the boat at last, we spread out our sleeping bags and bedrolls on the sandy hill and slept soundly. But in the morning when I awoke, North Africa presented me with my second unpleasant surprise (the first had been that sign). Perched on the lip of the sleeping bag with its tail curled over its back was a creature I recognized instantly as a scorpion. It was gazing down at my face, but I knew it didn't love me. The tail was not far from my eyeballs, which at that moment must have looked enormous to him.

I lay as quietly as I could. I was afraid if I moved my arms, I would startle the creature into attacking my face. Gradually I inhaled deeply, at the same time tensing my stomach muscles. When my lungs were full of air, I blew as hard as I could in the scorpion's face. In the same instant, I rolled up fast from the waist, performing the quickest sit-up of my career.

The little beast scuttled away across the desert and I breathed quietly, "Thank you, Lord!"

In Oran I located one of Murphy's vice consuls, who helped me get in touch with Colonel Eddy and arranged for my outfit to take a train to Algiers. In Algiers we were met by someone from the OSS and taken to a house near the Armed Forces headquarters.

The OSS had a couple of villas near a big hotel on a hill overlooking Algiers, and Colonel Eddy had his own residence and office in one of them, the Villa Rose. My detachment stayed in the Villa Sinetti.

The first night in the Villa Sinetti we were welcomed with a German air raid. Showing more curiosity than brains, we went up to the roof to watch the Nazis bomb Algiers. The only casualties we suffered, which were minor, occurred when our own antiaircraft flak fell on the roof of the villa.

In those days the OSS was not too well organized logistically. Somehow no one had thought about transportation for all of us, and it was up to me to arrange for a couple of jeeps and trucks. OSS supply gave me a beautiful French Peugeot limousine, perfectly suitable around Algiers, but useless when we began operations behind the lines.

By early January, there had been some changes in our outfit. Dr. Rossmiller joined the OSS medical staff stationed in Algiers, and some of the French-speaking language specialists were assigned to other jobs.

During the first few days in January a few Spaniards were added to my outfit. These were sailors who had rebelled against their Franco officers, hijacked their ships and sailed to North Africa. Upon arrival the Spaniards were interned by the Vichy French, but Murphy, Eddy and a man named Downes brought them out of internment camp and added them to my outfit. The new men had some military training, and as internees they also came to know the terrain around North Africa. At that time the mission to Franco's Spain was still only a contingency plan, but we knew the Spaniards would be useful even if the Spanish mission didn't materialize.

My outfit was given a long but innocuous code name, Experimental Detachment, G-3, AFHQ (Allied Forces Headquarters), a meaningless designation that covered our true mission. In Algiers we had an assortment of tasks. One of the most memorable assignments for me was playing bodyguard to an OSS agent who was meeting a double agent in the Casbah.

At that time Algiers was filled with informers, and I soon got a feel for that kind of work. Everyone, it seemed, was doing some kind of double-agent work and there were so many people lying to each other that the whole situation seemed ridiculous. I began to take everyone in North Africa with a grain of salt and to look at each new acquaintance with a jaundiced eye.

The Casbah was the prime meeting place for undercover agents and informers. This famous old Arab quarter of the city, a labyrinth of winding streets and twisting, narrow alleys, was no place to go at night. But I already had a romantic image of the Casbah from the movie *Algiers*, starring Hedy Lamarr and Charles Boyer. As I climbed those narrow streets, I had the fleeting hope that Hedy Lamarr would somehow appear around the corner.

In reality my mission was simple, to accompany another OSS man to his meeting with an informer and then see that he got back safely. To assure his protection I carried a large snap knife in my hand. This weapon gave me two options. If I pressed a button, the blade would shoot out. But if I just held it in my hand and didn't use the blade, the bulk of the weapon made a solid fist. Hitting someone with that knife was like clobbering him with a billiard ball.

The streets were growing dark as we started into

the Casbah, and we had to feel our way up the steep steps and inclines. It was growing darker all the time, and soon the hubbub of the city below faded away to nothing. The only noise came from the Casbah shops and bistros, but it seemed as if these night places also became eerily quiet as we drew near. I could sense the presence of dark shapes passing us in the night, even though I could see little or nothing of these shadowy figures.

It was my duty to protect the OSS agent from anybody, German or Arab. At one point I felt a hand slithering along my side. In all probability the man was just trying to rob me, but I reacted instinctively to his touch. Whirling around, I snapped my blade open. I stuck it about a quarter of an inch into him, not very far, and wiggled it a bit. With a great wail the man roared off into the darkness, followed by his companions.

We were left alone after that, and our agent accomplished his mission.

In preparation for OSS work behind enemy lines, I enlisted the help of Dr. Carleton S. Coon, a former professor of anthropology from Harvard and one of the vice consuls who worked with Robert Murphy and Bill Eddy's intelligence team. Coon spoke fluent Arabic and he was very familiar with the North African geography and peoples. Together Dr. Coon and I developed a zany but effective weapon to use against Rommel's Afrika Korps and the Italians.

The weapon, a manure bomb, was the perfect solution to a geographical handicap. The area around Algiers consisted of arid or semi-arid desert with only a few cacti growing in the sand, so there were few places to conceal explosives. Since people traveled primarily by camel, donkey and horse, however, piles of dung were the most common sight along the roads. We created explosives by molding Composition C into the same shape as camel or donkey dung, then implanting a pressure cap in the middle. These were the first explosives we put to use when we were turned loose behind enemy lines.

Rommel was doing well against our inexperienced troops and had pushed far into North Africa. When I asked Colonel Eddy what we could do to help, his reply was much like that of General Donovan: ''Get behind them and hurt them as much as you can.''

It was late in January 1943 when we started out for the front. Our first adventure proved beyond a shadow of a doubt, if any proof was needed, that we required better transportation. Four of us loaded into our French limousine and worked our way behind Rommel's front lines. Taking back roads on the edge of the desert, we finally came around to our target near the coast—a small railroad bridge. All the supplies for Rommel's troops had to pass over this single bridge.

From behind a small cactus-covered hill we planned where we would place our explosives and prepared for rapid emplacement. When no one was in sight, we attached our charges to key supports, lit the fuses and took shelter behind our little hill. The limousine was idling, ready to head out.

The charges went off with a roar and we saw the bridge settle into the wadi, the dry stream bed. Feeling victorious, we climbed aboard our Peugeot and set out across the desert, proceeding slowly around the cacti and ditches. When we reached a desert road, we sped up. As we rounded a curve, we hit an unexpected chuckhole, and the limousine slammed to a halt. We climbed out to inspect the damage—a broken axle.

* * *

After a tiresome hike back to the bivouac I was in no mood to brook further delays while the Army tried to requisition jeeps and trucks. I wanted wheels, pronto.

At this point Steve Byzek gave proof of his invaluable ability to acquire things. Using the same methods that had won us the bulldozer from Fort Meade, Steve managed to obtain a motorcycle. The motorcycle, in turn, provided transportation to a big U.S. motor pool that seemed to have everything we wanted. As we surveyed the motor pool, we realized that the Army units had all kinds of transportation, while we didn't have any. In order to even out the balance somewhat, we took unauthorized possession of a jeep and drove away.

What we needed most desperately were a couple of six-by-six trucks. We had in our possession one of the big tarpaulins that went over the back end of a six-by-six. All we needed was the truck to go under it. Steve and I decided to use that tarpaulin as a means to an end.

We loaded the tarpaulin into the back of our jeep, and drove to an Army motor pool, where we parked and went inside. Approaching the first sergeant of the motor pool, we explained, "Look, we've got this tarpaulin, but we lost the truck. We need a truck to put the tarpaulin on."

The motor sergeant grinned, shrugged and looked out the window. "Well," he said, "there's one truck sitting right over there," and he handed over the key.

We threw the tarpaulin into the back of the truck, Steve hopped inside, and he drove away in the truck while I took the jeep. One down, one to go.

The second six-by-six was delivered via a proper requisition from OSS headquarters and was properly assigned to our Experimental Detachment, G-3, AFHQ. At the heavy truck battalion where we picked it up, the commander made us sign some papers. Then the six-by-six appeared, driven by a big fellow named Corporal Drake.

I thanked the commander. "But we just need the truck," I added. "We don't need a driver. We can drive it ourselves."

"You can't get the truck without the driver," the commander replied. "When you're through with the truck and the driver, you send them back together."

That was fine with me. "Thank you very much," I said, and left.

At that time the Army was still segregated, and Corporal Drake's was an all-black transportation outfit. A Detroit man, he was a great driver and also eager to learn about our work. I soon taught Corporal Drake knife-fighting and explosives work and he eventually became the first black operational man in the OSS.

Every now and then someone would forward a query to me: "When are you going to send back Corporal Drake and that truck?"

I didn't pay any attention. Drake was a great soldier and we needed him on our missions. I wasn't going to give him up willingly.

One day when Colonel Eddy came to see me on other business, he brought up the subject of our driver. "By the way, some outfit keeps calling us, saying you've got a Corporal Drake up here and they want him back."

I turned to my adjutant. "Would you bring in Corporal Drake, please?"

Corporal Drake came in and saluted, and I introduced him to Colonel Eddy.

"Corporal Drake," I began, "what were your exact orders when I picked you up in Algiers?"

"I was to take you where you wanted to go," he

replied, "and when you got through with me, I was to take the truck back to Algiers."

"Have I ever told you that I was through with you?" I asked.

"No, sir," he said.

"Do you want to leave us?"

"No, sir."

"That's all," I said. "Thank you."

When Drake had left the room, Colonel Eddy—a wise, bold old Marine—just grinned at me.

So we wound up with two big trucks, a jeep, a motorcycle and a new man in our outfit. We were ready for action.

Chapter 6

My outfit was an ever-changing mixture of nationalities and personalities. By the time we acquired our jeep and two trucks the unit had an international flavor, with nearly twenty Spanish ex-sailors, two or three French part-time volunteers and a couple of loyal Arabs. OSS men included my adjutant, Dick Crosby; Professor Coon; the three Abraham Lincoln Brigade sergeants; occasionally a doctor; my informal supply sergeant, Steve Byzek; and informally, Corporal Drake. Some people from the British SOE whom I had met in Algiers would come and go. Among them was Major Quiney, who served with us briefly and was replaced by Captain McIntosh from Gibraltar.

The final addition to our outfit was a British captain who had been on Franco's side in the Spanish Civil War. His presence created immediate problems. Now we had people who had been on opposite sides during the civil war, and there were bitter feelings between the two factions. The Spaniards and the men from the Abe Lincoln Brigade called the captain a Nazi and a fascist, and he thought they were just communist rabble. Whenever we went out on an operation, I always placed myself between those two ex-antagonist groups because

I was afraid they might knock off each other before we came back.

We harassed Rommel by blowing up supplies and soldiers behind the lines. The manure bomb proved useful. We strewed the roadways behind the lines of the Afrika Korps with manure bombs, and Arab line-crossers or friendly patrols told us what happened. Wheels were blown off the German trucks. Nazi Tiger tanks lost their treads. Numerous German and Italian infantrymen were killed or wounded. The results were certainly grim, but we were doing our job, slowing up the famous Afrika Korps.

At that time, the Afrika Korps fighters were touted as being the most experienced, best-trained and best-led troops in the world. So there was a certain satisfaction in seeing them fall prey to manure bombs. We took great pleasure in knowing that the famous Afrika Korps soldiers had to act as street sweepers before they could go anywhere. The Germans never knew which dung in their path was the real thing and which was a camouflaged bomb.

Our main targets were the railroads, the locomotives and rolling stock particularly, although we also aimed for tanks and a few airplanes. Wherever we went, we left a trail of manure bombs on the way in and another line of bombs on the way out.

In these operations we had our first chance to test our OSS training in the field. When we had to dispatch guards with our knives or hands, we used the sentry kill that we had learned from Delicate Dan Fairbairn. All our training in the use of explosives now had to be put to use.

Many Arabs cooperated with us. Their donkeys could carry a hidden burden of lethal cargo. Explosives with detonating kits were sewn into their donkeys' saddles. Carleton Coon wrote out complete directions in Arabic for the line-crossers, telling them how to set the charges on a locomotive or a tank, or in a supply depot. We rarely learned the results of these missions, since the Arabs did not report back to us. But occasionally we received word that one of our designated targets had gone up in smoke—a railroad bridge, a locomotive or a large number of German vehicles. Our greatest under-cover victory was the destruction of a big German gasoline dump in the area between Feriana and Tunis. Each of these successes cost Rommel dearly, since he desperately needed fuel and transportation vehicles to maintain German mobility in North Africa.

There was some minor cost to our side as well. By this time Steve Byzek had acquired a third big truck for the outfit, and one day our convoy ran into some artil-lery fire. In pulling off the road our latest vehicle ran off the shoulder just as a couple of the Spaniards were trying to jump off. One suffered a broken arm and the other an injured leg. We were still lucky with no serious losses, but we were getting a little tired.

Throughout these missions we slept in the vehicles, under them or on the ground nearby, in all kinds of weather. Some men had colds and sore throats, and there was a general feeling of fatigue. I wanted to give them a bit of a change and some rest before we went on.

We were fortunate to find an abandoned mine, a long cave that had once produced potash or some such material. Among ourselves, we just called it the salt mine. It was a welcome discovery, since the mine gave us a warm, dry place to rest up, regroup and plan for future operations.

The night we moved into the cave, a Scotsman

from the British Special Operations—the counterpart of the American OSS—came to pay us a visit. His name was Colonel Young.

Colonel Young appeared wearing a kilt and carrying a bagpipe. Fortunately, he was also toting a couple cases of Scotch whiskey and some beer, which he said was for the other ranks—the British term for enlisted men.

"Shucks," I said, "we all deserve a break and a party. We'll all drink the Scotch as long as it lasts and then break out the beer."

Inside the salt cave, there were low ledges that had been cut in the wall by some long-ago visitors. We sat on them while we talked and drank. We put candles in niches high up on the walls. Their soft, flickering light illuminated the stalagmites and stalactites, and cast their sharply pointed shadows on the cave walls.

As we sat around talking, drinking and singing, a warm camaraderie developed. Each man who took a swig of Scotch was obliged to sing or say a few words in his own language. The Frenchmen of the Lafayette Esquadrille wished us "bonne santé et bonne chance" (good health and good luck), and I joined them as they broke into a verse of the stirring "Marseillaise."

The Arabs in our group—garbed in flowing robes and headdresses—temporarily disregarded Mohammed's taboo on alcohol and joined us in offering a toast in Arabic, which Carl Coon translated. Leaping to his feet, Colonel Young skirled a wild Scottish air on his bagpipe, while three or four of us presented our own rendition of a Scottish sword dance and the others clapped out the rhythm.

The Spanish ex-sailors led us in "Cielito Lindo," while we all joined in the chorus, "Aye, yi, yi, yi, cantai no llores.'' (Sing, do not cry). This was followed by ''La Cucaracha'' from the Spanish Civil War era.

Then, in truly heroic style, a soldier from the Barcelona region sang a flamenco song that told of our exploits. In a wailing chant that reminded me of a Caribbean calypso song, he told of some of our recent adventures—how fast we moved, what we blew up, and what great feats of daring we all performed. His audience clapped, nodded and yelled ''olé'' whenever we felt like it, which was frequently.

The evening ended with a French lyric that was our outfit's favorite victory song. It had burst from me one day after a particularly tense mission on which we had stealthily infiltrated the enemy lines, neutralized guards, placed our explosives and time-pencils, and worked our way back out. When at last we were safe in a home area, I stood up and sang, loud and clear, the first line:

''Eh, voilà, c'est-ce qu'est bon, est bon!''

By now, all the men knew the chorus:

''Eh, voilà la vie, la vie, la vie, la vie, chérie, ha ha!

''Eh, voilà la vie que touts les moines font!''

My first line, roughly translated, said, ''Ah, this is what is good, is good!'' and their reply was, ''Oh, this is the life, the life, the life, my dear, ha ha!'' And we all ended with the wry line, ''Oh, this is the life the monks lead!'' It was a lusty tune, filled with the gladness of being alive, and we began to sing it after every mission. That night in the salt mine, we repeated it many times.

In a polyglot of four or five languages I told the men that I was very proud of them. Colonel Young echoed these sentiments, adding that he loved to be with an outfit that showed such spirit.

Eventually we called it a night and slept the sleep

of slightly inebriated, happy warriors. But that night in the salt mine has stayed with me, a memory tinged with the romance of a foreign war—a night when high-spirited men of courage and good will celebrated together their fight for a worthy cause.

The day after our celebration in the salt mine, I went to the headquarters of General Orlando Ward, commander of the First Armored Division, and asked if there was anythng he wanted done. He said, "Well, go see General McQuillan in Combat Command A, up forward."

Accordingly, the next day I drove to Sidi Bou Sid, where Brigadier General McQuillan had his combat command post. When I offered our services, McQuillan replied immediately, "Yes, there is one thing I would like you to do. See if you can get behind the lines in back of Faid and spike those German 88s. They are outgunning us and doing a lot of damage."

Having returned to my outfit, I told the men to get ready for the new mission. Everyone knew those big guns would be well protected by the enemy as well as a target of our artillery and bombers. We had reason to be concerned.

One of the greatest dangers in working behind enemy lines was the threat of being bombed or shot at by our own planes or artillery. Behind the lines we had to be afraid of all the planes, not just the ones with swastikas.

Often, when planes started to buzz us, someone would yell, "They're ours!" The next thing we would hear was a boom or the rat-a-tat-tat of machine gun fire from U.S. or British planes. Eventually, the phrase, "They're ours! Boom!" became a stock gag of ours, but the danger from our own aircraft was no laughing matter.

One episode was all too vivid in our memories at that time. At one point, five or six of us were trying to reconnoiter routes through the mountains near Faid Pass. Suddenly artillery rounds began to explode quite near us. We dropped to the ground, trying to find holes and gullies to lie in. The explosions increased and came closer and closer. Somebody yelled, "Is that the krauts?" and another voice replied, "No, that's ours!"

Both men were right. We were caught in the middle of incoming rounds from our friends and enemies. But the good Lord was with us and no one was seriously hurt. Soon there was a break in the shelling, and we raced into a dry wadi and worked away from the line of fire in the shelter of its banks.

Working behind the lines, we also met Arabs of questionable loyalties. One encounter still fresh in all our minds had occurred on a hill near Kasserine Pass.

I had met an Arab going the other way, and as our paths crossed, I began to interrogate him. He seemed friendly enough, and we conversed in pidgin English and French. Since he was coming from the direction of the German position, I asked him about the placement of the big guns and other dispositions.

Without any warning, he whipped out his curved Bedouin knife and slashed it toward my throat. It was fortunate that Dan Fairbairn had taught me well. When the Arab snatched out his knife, I leaned backward and kicked instinctively, rapidly and without telegraphing my counterattack. The kick caught him full force between his legs, putting him completely out of action.

I walked away from the encounter with a big cut in my right leg from his knife. I made a tourniquet with my belt, but it took a while for the wound to heal.

Fortunately the wound did not slow me down too much, but a big scar still remains to remind me of my Arab attacker. That scar is a cheap price to pay for saving my throat.

My supply man, Steve Byzek, was the one who made me realize that the outfit fully understood the dangers of the mission that lay ahead. But he did so in an oblique way.

Back at Washington State, Chris Rumburg and I would occasionally buy a box of fancy cigars. At the end of football season we would stroll around campus puffing those cigars to celebrate our past victories. In honor of that tradition I had brought along to North Africa one box of good cigars. I had smoked only a few of these, and I asked Steve Byzek to take care of the rest because I knew there were none to be had anywhere in North Africa. Now and then after a difficult raid I would take out a single cigar and relish a long smoke.

The day before our new mission was to begin, Steve Byzek approached me and said with a perfectly straight face, "Major, if we're starting off to spike those 88s, don't you think you should smoke those cigars a little bit faster? You'd hate to have something happen and see all those cigars go to waste."

Laughing, I replied, "Well, I guess you'd better help me smoke them, Steve!"

So he took a pocketful of cigars with him when we set out the next day.

I had never before taken along the whole detachment on any one raid, but I knew that the four German 88s would have a lot of protection, and I would need all the manpower I could muster to carry out the mission. I took along all my men, vehicles, supplies and explosives.

I consolidated our forces in a field bivouac not too far from the town of Sbeitla in Tunisia.

During the night we heard the rumble of artillery, but we were used to that sound, so we rolled over and went back to sleep. In the morning we started out for Faid Pass.

Along the road to Faid, we met numerous Americans who were heading back. I asked one officer, "What's going on?"

"The Germans have attacked," he replied. "Don't go up this road. You're running into the spearhead of Tiger tanks."

Obviously, the situation had changed since I had spoken to General Ward. In light of the new offensive, I sent most of the outfit back to the cactus-patch bivouac and told the men to wait for me there. Accompanied by two or three sergeants, I went to find General Ward at the headquarters of the First Armored Division.

"I'm Major Sage," I introduced myself. "I was going to do the sabotage job up front for General McQuillan, but I think the mission may have changed in view of what's happened here."

"Yes, they've hit us hard," General Ward replied.

"What can I do to help?"

"Find General McQuillan for me. We have lost radio contact with his Combat Command A. His forces took the brunt of Rommel's attack, and McQuillan may need help. Try to locate him."

After I left Ward, I told my sergeants, "You don't need to go with me on this."

"We wouldn't miss it!" they yelled.

We took off in the jeep in the late afternoon with a sackful of hand grenades and some Sten pipe-stem submachine guns. As we rolled toward the front, we passed wrecked machines and crumpled bodies. I recalled

Sherman's saying, "War is hell!" and I revised that saying in my own mind: War is just a mass of confusion and destruction.

The best tanks that the United States had were in the field at that time, and all seemed to be out of action. One young man, a lieutenant, was standing beside his disabled tank, and I went up to him.

"Son," I said, "have you any idea where I'd find General McQuillan's headquarters?"

The youngster couldn't reply. He was in shock. He just stared at me with a blank look.

After a moment he managed to speak. "We can't stop 'em. I bounced a round off the turret, and it doesn't stop 'em."

Stunned with disbelief, he repeated those words over and over again. His tank was completely burned out, and he was lucky to be alive.

In that battle we had been outgunned by the German Tiger tanks. This was the first time Rommel had hit the U.S. forces with his experienced and well-armed Afrika Korps, and our men were reeling from it. It was a real setback for our less-seasoned troops.

As darkness began to fall, the sergeants and I continued to cruise back and forth across that confused front, asking for General McQuillan. The reaction of the tank gunner we had met earlier turned out to be typical. Several men were dazed and confused. No one knew where to find General McQuillan.

In the darkness we encountered small-arms fire, but we kept the jeep moving forward. There was no straight-line front to define the location of the American and German units. The forces were all mixed up. If someone yelled "Who's there?" from the dark, we would ask if he knew where we could find General McQuillan. Some soldiers would shout out directions, but they were just guessing. Others would say, "Damned if I know!" and we'd roar off across the desert. If the voice that called out from the darkness was in German, we would throw a live grenade to keep him warm and then move on.

In the middle of the night we finally found the general's headquarters in a salt cave much like the one we'd used for our bivouac. After we identified ourselves, the sentry waved us inside. General McQuillan was seated in a camp chair surrounded by maps pinned to the walls.

"Sage, I guess our plans are changed," he said, looking up.

"Yes, sir," I replied. "General Ward sent me to find you. He hasn't heard anything from you on the radio."

McQuillan nodded. "We're having radio trouble, but we should be okay soon."

He gave me the coordinates of his position for me to report to headquarters. As I left, he added, "We're sure getting the hell kicked out of us."

Back at General Ward's headquarters, I reported General McQuillan's location and asked for further orders. In reply General Ward just told me what I'd already heard twice before: "Get behind the lines and hurt them."

"Any particular area, sir?"

"Well," he said, "you might try the right flank. That's being held by the Derbyshire Yeomanry, a British outfit. Wherever you can get through, cut communications, mine the roads, blow up tanks—do anything you can to harass the Germans when we start shoving them back."

Ward told me the Americans would be getting

reinforcements and supplies. He thought Rommel had about used up his momentary little punch and that the American troops were hoping to move forward soon.

As I saluted preparatory to leaving, he added once again, "Just get behind them and slow them up a little."

Chapter 7

The next day, I reported to the brigadier who commanded the Derbyshire Yeomanry. When he asked for my code name, I told him that I was called the Dagger. This was the name I had been given by a British colonel in Algiers who was impressed by the look of my Sikes-Fairbairn knife, and it was the code name I used in all radio communications.

"Oh, Daggah," the brigadier replied with his accent, "that's good. We've heard good things of you. You have been quite mischievous behind the German lines. As I hear, you've given them a spot of trouble with your camel-dung bombs and such."

"Well, we've tried to, sir!" I replied. But I was almost laughing when I said it because of the droll face he made as he minced the words camel dung.

The brigadier described to me the situation on the right flank, where the Derbyshire Yeomanry were holding the line. Some of Rommel's Afrika Korps units now occupied the high ground on either side of a small pass in the mountains just forward of the town of Feriana, Tunisia. The British unit's forward observers had reported some Germans working at the entrance to the pass, and the brigadier was concerned. He suspected that the Germans were laying mines at the exact location where he planned to attack the next day.

"I understand you're quite effective at this infiltration stuff, Majah Daggah," he said. "Can you get up there and find out just what the Germans are doing?"

From where we were standing, I could see the mouth of the pass. Two deep wadis trisected a sandy plain that was bare except for scattered clumps of cacti.

"I think we can use the wadis for an approach, sir," I said. "But if I get up to the pass and the tanks come out, what kind of diversion can we count on? We'll need a way to get back."

"I have a couple of 75s on halftracks," the brigadier replied. "The Germans don't know we have them. If they make trouble, the 75s will open up."

He immediately gave orders to have the weapons moved forward, and I made preparations to depart. As always before such a mission, I handed the money belt from Donovan to my adjutant, Dick Crosby, for safekeeping. Then I gave orders to the men.

Sergeants Goff and Felsen were to accompany me up the nearest wadi that led directly to the pass. At the same time, Captain McIntosh and another sergeant would approach the suspected minefield by way of the left-hand wadi, which led to an area of high ground. As soon as everyone understood the plan of action, we took off.

My party advanced in its usual triangle formation, with me in lead, Goff and Felsen a short distance behind. When we were about halfway up the wadi, the stillness of the hot afternoon was suddenly broken by a mournful wail that sounded like a muezzin's call to prayer.

The eerie sound was picked up and repeated by other Arabs, the message traveling toward the German position. Certain that the Arab underground was signaling our approach to the Germans, I felt a chill run up my back. The Arab grapevine had hurt us before, and we had learned to be cautious.

We moved forward warily. After about half an hour, we came to a bend in the ravine where the wadi turned and ran parallel to the enemy lines. When we raised our heads over the top of the wadi, we could see the tracks of German tanks and other vehicles. The sand showed all the signs of a minefield.

It wasn't enough just to know that the minefield existed. We had to find a pathway through the field of destruction, and do it before we were spotted by the enemy. To explore farther we would have to leave the protection of the wadi.

As we walked gingerly onto the open plain, each of us scanned a sector, noting disturbances in the ground where the Germans had buried their mines. This kind of observation could only be done in broad daylight: At dawn or dusk the ground marks would have been imperceptible.

We walked carefully but worked fast. When we had made our observations, we met to piece together the plan of the minefield. We were in a lonely position, dangerously close to the enemy installations, and we were glad that all was quiet for a while.

Our peace didn't last long. Suddenly we heard a familiar whistle followed instantly by two booms. We all hit the ground at once. I looked toward Goff, laughed and said, "Well, here we go again!"

Quite a few times before we had been caught in the midst of artillery exchanges. We had learned that a whistling sound meant the shell would pass over us, so we weren't worried.

Then we heard the roar of tanks or armored cars,

winding down the pass directly toward us. We were in an exposed position several hundred yards from the wadi. Our only chance was to run.

We lit out for the wadi, racing along the mine-free path that we had traced out so carefully. I thought to myself, "Come on, British, open up with your 75s!" But we heard nothing from the Yeomanry.

The next time two shells exploded there was no warning whistle. They were right on top of us. Fragments filled the air. Felsen was about thirty feet closer to the wadi than I was. He staggered, grabbed his head and shrieked, "They got me!"

My first thought was, "I've got to keep him running. Lord, help me!"

Out of the corner of my eye I saw Goff start toward us. I grabbed Felsen's arm to help him keep going, but the next round came in and knocked us both down.

I landed on my head and shoulders. I didn't know whether I had been hit, or where, until I started moving. But when I got up to walk, I was limping. I realized then I'd been hit in the leg. Later on, a pain in my shoulder told me I'd been wounded there too.

Shells were exploding all around us. Felsen moaned. He was bleeding from the leg and head. Goff caught up with me and we pulled out our first-aid kits. Working rapidly, we wrapped Felsen's wounded leg and bandaged his head to stop the bleeding.

I was groggy from the impact of the shell. I kept thinking, "I've never lost a man, and I don't intend to now." I tried to crawl, dragging Felsen along the ground behind me. He told me to leave him and run.

Shells exploded all around us. I tugged at Felsen, but I couldn't drag him any farther.

"Listen," I said, crouching over him, "Goff and I are going ahead. We'll come back to you after dark."

I ordered Goff to run ahead, make his way down the wadi and take back the information. Then I started to crawl away from Felsen.

By then my leg was no longer working. I couldn't even stand. I could hear the tanks roaring behind me, but I couldn't get away. They seemed to be coming right up my back.

I crawled a short distance ahead of Felsen when I heard a British voice, Captain McIntosh's, yell out, "Lie still, Major, they won't see you."

I was in a slight depression in the sand. McIntosh must have been on higher ground, where I couldn't be seen by him. Since he couldn't see me, he assumed I was hidden from the Germans as well.

I had no choice but to take his advice. I squirmed down in the depression, covered my arms and face with sand, and lay still.

The roar of the tanks grew louder, then stopped. There was a strange silence. Then I heard German voices behind me. They had found Felsen.

I lay on the ground like a stone. For a while, everything was quiet. Then I heard feet padding across the sand behind me. A voice spoke in broken English, "Get up. Are you wounded?"

I pulled myself to my feet. Several Germans stood a few yards away, machine pistols trained on me.

"Where are your comrades?" one of them asked.

"There were only two of us," I told him curtly.

To divert his attention from Goff and McIntosh, I began limping toward Felsen.

Several tanks, two armored cars and several more Germans were gathered around Felsen. Evidently the Germans were as anxious as we were to get out of the area. As I came up, they quickly hoisted Felsen onto a tank, then ordered me to climb aboard.

The Germans' haste worked in my favor. Before I boarded the tank, I had a moment to unload my OSS equipment covertly. As I clambered up on the tank, I pulled the dagger from my belt and the spring cosh from my sleeve and dropped them under the treads.

When the tank reached the pass, the Germans ordered a halt and began to interrogate Felsen and me.

Felsen was still bleeding profusely. I began to raise hell, demanding that the Germans provide a doctor to look after him. When the doctor finally arrived, all the Germans turned their attention to me.

They were very excited when they saw my gold leaf and realized they had captured a major. They also seemed amused, informing me that I was a *dummkopf* to be caught in front of the lines. At that moment, I thoroughly agreed with them.

From the moment of our capture I was determined to escape. As soon as I was alone with Milt Felsen, I said, "Hurry up and get well, Milt. We're leaving. I want to get back to the outfit." He was in such bad shape that he couldn't answer.

When the doctor was finished with Felsen, he bandaged my leg and shoulder, which had bled profusely. Within twenty-four hours I was put aboard a truck bound for Gafsa, Tunisia. All the time I was looking for a way to escape.

However, there was no opportunity to leave the truck, even for a moment. Whenever I had to relieve myself in the bushes, three well-armed guards went with me. Furthermore, the bad leg was beginning to stiffen up, and that was an impediment.

By the time we reached Gafsa, my spirits had hit a

new low. Trying to cheer myself up, I reminded myself that Goff had at least escaped with all the information we had about the minefield. Yet I felt that our risk and capture had been close to pointless. And I was still disgruntled because the 75s that the brigadier had promised for a diversion never opened up. If they had, we might have escaped.

In addition, I was angry at the Germans. They had stolen at gunpoint my Abercrombie & Fitch leather jacket and the Girard-Perigot chronograph that had been a gift from a friend named Flynn.

We stayed only one night in Gafsa, and the Germans let me sleep in a bed. The next morning, after some rest, I felt better. My wounds were stiff, but as I moved about they loosened up. Again I began to think about escape.

That day I was taken to Gabes in a big truck, accompanied by seven or eight German guards. At noon we stopped for lunch and the Germans spread out their food on the tailgate of the truck. They had heavy loaves of brown bread, sausage and a soft cheese that they carried in tubes like toothpaste. For lunch they gave me a piece of bread and some of the cheese.

Carrying my lunch, I limped toward the cab of the truck. The guards shook their heads and yelled, "*Nein*, get away!"

I kept telling them I was tired and hurt. Pointing to my bandaged leg, I tried to look even weaker than I was. They soon tired of arguing with me and finally didn't pay any more attention. Feigning complete exhaustion, I slowly climbed up into the cab and closed the door. Immediately, I tried to figure out how to run it.

An H-shaped diagram showed how the gearshift worked. I spotted four forward-speed positions, numbered one through four, and an unnumbered position that I assumed was reverse. Shifting gears seemed to be no problem.

The key was in the ignition switch in a vertical position. I examined the markings on either side of the switch. The one on the right was marked "ein," the other "auf." I thought, "This is easy. Any red-blooded American boy can tell at once that *ein* means 'on' and *auf* is 'off.' " Or so I assumed.

Confidently, I turned the switch to *ein* and pressed the starter. There were several mechanical noises and loud clicks, but the engine didn't start. I was cursing and praying, but the only response was that mechanical clicking sound. The next thing I knew, a rifle butt slammed against my head and shoulder.

The Germans were furious because they had been taken in. I was equally furious, but for a different reason.

It wasn't until much later—when I was in prison camp—that I learned how to say "on the table"—"*auf dem Tisch*." But long before then I had realized the error of my ways. My assumptions had been wrong: *Auf* meant "on" and *ein* meant "off." My first great escape began with trying to turn a truck engine off!

Though the Germans watched me continuously for the next few days and nights, I didn't stop thinking about escape. I stole a German hat, thinking I could disguise myself as a German driver and flee in another vehicle. Later, in Gabes, I tried to escape by jumping out of a second-story window. The Germans caught me immediately, threw me into a solitary cell and started guarding me more closely. In that attempt, I succeeded only in aggravating the pain in my wounded leg.

A short time later all the British and American

prisoners were moved out of Gabes. Before we were loaded into boxcars, I joined the other prisoners in the compound. There I met the two men who were to become my companions in the next escape attempt. They were Lieutenant Dick Kimball, an American, and Lieutenant Charles Southard, a South African. Both were fighter pilots.

Along with Kimball and Southard, I was loaded aboard a boxcar with a number of captured soldiers, many of them wounded. The boxcar was solidly built. The only windows were near the top of the car, and there were iron bars across them. On the outside each window was covered by a large sheet of metal.

I wanted to know how the sheet was fastened on the outside, so I asked the guard if I could relieve myself. Outside the car I stood near a window and inspected it.

A vertical, sliding metal arm held the metal sheet. The bottom of the sliding arm was fastened to the boxcar's side by a metal hasp. In order to move the metal sheet, we would have to unfasten the hasp and slide the metal arm out of the way.

To judge the location of the hasp, I counted the number of boxcar boards from the bottom of the car. That gave me the vertical position. Lengthwise, I estimated, the hasp was about two yards back from the front end of the car.

I still had a spare demolition knife that I always carried concealed in my boot or strapped to my lower leg. When I returned to the boxcar, I took out the knife, located the hasp from the inside and began digging at the sturdy board.

The wood was hard and tough, and my knife dulled rapidly. One of the wounded soldiers, Sergeant Armie Hill of Phelps, Wisconsin, lent a hand. Being from an engineer outfit, he always carried a whetstone, which we used frequently to sharpen the knife.

Having a whetstone along with a knife was almost too good to be true. I remember saying quietly, "Thank you, Lord!" Many inside that boxcar offered prayers for our success. One soldier had a tiny Bible with him, and he wanted me to read a passage before we left. I opened the Bible at random and hit upon the text of the Prodigal Son. As I read about the son's return to his home, I silently prayed that I too would be one to return home.

As my hands started to blister from hacking at the wood, Kimball and Southard spelled me at carving. Guards with a machine gun were on a flatcar immediately behind our car, so we were concerned about the noise of our activities. Whenever the train came to a halt, we asked everyone to sing "I've Been Working on the Railroad" and other songs to drown out the noise of our work. As long as the train was moving, we knew we couldn't be heard above the rumbling of the cars.

After several hours we managed to make a hole big enough to reach through to the hasp. Then we went to work at the window, loosening the lower ends of two steel bars. When the train was rolling, we reached through the hole in the boxcar's side, removed the fastening hasp and slid down the metal plate. I grasped the lower ends of the two steel bars, asked the Lord for extra strength, and pulled them far enough apart to get through.

By this time darkness had fallen, the train was rolling along, and I was certain it was time to leave. Kimball and Southard wanted to go with me.

I turned to the other men and said, "These two are going with me now. If anyone else feels up to it and wants to use the window, you can follow us when you like. It's as good a time as any."

I knew that many of the men were wounded and wouldn't have a chance of getting away, but I wanted each of them to have the choice.

Being bigger than Southard or Kimball, I went first through the window. The other two helped me up and started pushing. Halfway through I got stuck, but with everyone shoving from behind, I managed to pull myself clear.

Twisting my body around, I grasped the outermost rim of the car. I planned to hang on until the other two got out. Inching along hand over hand, I made room for two more on the roof's edge.

Soon Kimball wiggled out, clutched the rim and hung on. He was followed by Southard. By the time Southard emerged, my fingers were in agony. Furthermore, we were in danger of being seen. From where I was hanging, I could see the Germans on the flatcar with their machine guns and antiaircraft battery. They were lounging around, smoking cigarettes and talking. I figured if I could see them that clearly, they could spot us at any moment.

The train began to slow up. Looking ahead, I saw the engine disappear around a curve. I jerked my head as a let-go signal, and the three of us dropped together. Fortunately, the outside of the curve was banked. As all paratroopers know, the easiest place to land is on an incline, where you can roll over quickly to minimize the shock of the fall.

Having rolled down the embankment, we scooted behind a cactus patch. We lay there for a moment, watching the train pull away into the distance. No one had seen us. The train rumbled out of sight. We had made it that far, at least.

* * *

Many years later, at a reunion of men from Stalag Luft III, I met a U.S. flier by the name of Allen Karstens who told me the rest of the story of the boxcar escape. Karstens, another American flier called Ralph Johnson, and a British sergeant all followed us out the window. Their experiences in the desert were much like ours, though our paths did not cross again for a long time.

After the train disappeared out of sight, I set a course due west, keeping the North Star on my right. I knew that our lines in Tunisia were to the west, and we would eventually get there if we could just keep walking. Though it was tough going, by morning we had covered quite a few miles and had left the more thickly settled area near the Mediterranean and were in the drier area inland.

There was quite a bit of Arab activity in the morning, so we hid in a cactus patch to wait for siesta time in the heat of the day. The morning seemed unbearably long. Our only food was a discarded orange peel, which we split three ways. We shared one partially filled canteen, but the water didn't last long. The combination of heat, hunger and thirst left us feeling weak and exhausted as the sun reached its peak.

Though it was hot, as soon as it was quiet we took off again. We made fairly good time that afternoon, and we were heartened by the knowledge that every step brought us nearer our lines. The sound of artillery in the distance ahead made us feel confident we were headed in the right direction. But we were mighty thirsty.

At one point, Kimball suddenly cried out, "Hey, Major, here's water, here's water!"

He pointed ahead, but I couldn't see anything.

"Come on, that's a mirage," I said. "We're not

seeing any water." Sure enough, as we continued walking, we passed through the area where he had seen water and discovered that it was all dry sand.

A short while later, however, Kimball again saw water. Again I refused to believe him, but there was a difference. This time I saw it too.

"No," I insisted, "it's another mirage."

But this time when we reached the site, we walked into water instead of dry sand. The water was up to my ankles before I believed it was real.

Gratefully we scooped up handfuls of water and poured it down our throats. A moment later all three of us were coughing, cursing and spitting. The water was alkaline, unfit for drinking.

So we plodded along, still thirsty, but it got a little cooler as the sun went down. Several hours later, as we were approaching a distant tree, I suddenly saw a white figure outlined in the darkness. For an instant I thought the moonlight was playing tricks on me.

Then I heard a long Arab wail, and I knew the figure ahead was no illusion. The wail was picked up in every direction. We heard barking dogs and braying donkeys, and lights began to flicker in huts up ahead. The desert grapevine was at work.

A moment before we could scarcely stagger. When Arabs started to appear from their huts, we ran like men possessed.

Even after we had left the village behind, we kept up a furious pace. We began to hear artillery fire again, and the sound raised our hopes. Soon, we thought, we would be crossing to our own lines—if exhaustion and thirst didn't bring us down.

Some time later, we threw ourselves down on the ground to rest. The artillery fire had stopped. For a while we listened, fully expecting to hear some Arabs repeat their warning cry. But there was nothing, only the silence of the night. I breathed a sigh of relief.

But my relief turned to anxiety when I looked up to find the North Star. To my dismay, I saw the sky was becoming overcast. Within fifteen minutes we could not see a single star. We had no idea in which direction we should be moving.

There was nothing to do but lie down in the sand and wait until the storm clouds passed. All of us were praying, I think. With a shock I realized I could hear my own voice in my ears. I was panting over and over again, "Please God, give us a cock-eyed star to see by."

No star appeared, but we did get rain. Holding our mouths open, we tried to catch a few drops to moisten our parched throats. We soaked up water in our handkerchiefs, then sucked the cloth dry.

After the storm passed, we decided to push ahead. Dawn was approaching, and we knew with the coming of daylight we would have to go into hiding again. We were now close to the lines, and the area would be thick with German vehicles and Arab sympathizers. Once again when daylight broke we would have to find cover and wait it out.

As we moved cautiously through an olive grove on the edge of an oasis, some Arabs spotted us. Several ran toward us while one took off in the opposite direction, shouting at the top of his voice.

We had no place to hide and no hope of catching the man who was running off. Our only alternative was to brazen it out.

The Arabs soon caught up with us. We told them we were Germans, which they didn't believe. Then Southard showed them his Arabic script, a standard certificate that the RAF gave to British pilots working out of Egypt. The certificate promised a large reward to any Arab who rescued an Allied aviator.

The Arab appeared to show great interest, but it turned out he was only toying with us. He gave some command in Arabic, and a few minutes later the whole village descended on us. Several hundred people, including men, women and children, all wearing white robes, ran toward us carrying guns, knives, scythes, sickles and clubs.

The menacing mob made gestures indicating that we were supposed to pull off our rings and watches, and hand these over to them. Prepared to fight them all, the three of us stood back to back, facing outward. I started waving my bared demolition knife quietly back and forth at stomach level. Of course we would not have lasted long if they had chosen to attack, but for some reason they did not do anything to us.

It was a stand-off until an armored car arrived, apparently summoned from a nearby camp that had been alerted by the uproar. The armored car contained Italian troops who seemed bent on taking us in. But before they could capture us, the Germans arrived.

Pushing the Italians aside, the Germans seemed to ask for the headman of the village, who stepped forward. One of the Nazi officers pulled out a small wad of German marks and handed a few to the headman.

Apparently, that was all we were worth—a few marks apiece!

Chapter 8

As we were driven away by the Germans, we joked about how little they had paid for us. One of the Germans overheard our conversation and in broken English tried to explain why the Arabs had relinquished us for such a small price. He said the Allied planes had just bombed Qairouan (Kairouan), one of the Moslem holy cities. The bombs were aimed at a German ammunition depot the Nazis had put next to a mosque expressly to deter our bombing it. To the Arabs it looked as if we were trying to bomb their mosque. And that's what the Germans wanted them to think.

Kimball and Southard, dressed in flying boots and winged jackets, were obviously fliers, and they told the Germans that I was their commanding officer. From that moment throughout my imprisonment in Germany, I was considered a shot-down flier.

This identity was convenient because I needed a cover. Hitler and Goebbels had frequently broadcast that if any of Donovan's OSS men were captured, they would be stripped of information—by any means—and buried twelve feet under. That was a condition I did not favor. At the moment of capture I had dropped the incriminating evidence under a tank, and the treads had ground my identity into the desert sand. Apart from those items, there was nothing to show that I was anything other than an American major.

When my fellow fliers and I learned that we were going to be transported to Italy in a JU-52 transport, we decided to make another escape attempt. While I knocked out the guards in the rear of the plane, Kimball and Southard would overcome the crew, take over the pilot's seat and fly the plane to our lines.

But the cards were against us. I was separated from them before the plane took off, perhaps because I was a field-grade officer and they were lieutenants. On the flight from Gabes to Italy I regretted the lost opportunity because I could see it would have been very easy to take over the plane. The guards slept most of the way, and they didn't pay much attention to me. But since I couldn't fly the plane myself, I was forced to let the opportunity pass.

We landed in Naples, where I was placed in solitary confinement. The treatment was rough and the food was poor. My condition was worsening. I had infection in my wounds and severe diarrhea.

From Naples I was sent to Rome, where the Germans placed me in an upstairs cell. My fever was high and my head was so hot that I thought my brains would boil out my ears. I pounded on the door, shouting, "*Heiss, heiss*!" which is German for "Hot, hot."

Finally a medic came by and stuck a thermometer in my mouth. My temperature was 104 or 105 degrees. The medic ordered me to a hospital bed.

From my first days as a POW I tried to learn German, primarily so I could understand my captors and figure out a way to escape them.

Initially my knowledge was less than rudimentary.

The first time they shouted "*nein*" at me, I thought they were counting. I knew "Bei mir bist du schön" and "Auf wiedersehen, my dear," from the Andrews Sisters, and by the time I arrived in Naples, I fortunately knew "*heiss*," for "hot." But that was the limit of my knowledge, and I wanted to learn more.

In the hospital I finally was able to speak to some German people other than the guards. Some patients taught me the words to an old song I had heard back in Spokane, "Du, Du, Liegst Mir im Hertzen." It was an old folk song that had been sung by the German people long before Hitler's Nazis took over. The words of the title mean, "You, you lie (stay) in my heart."

I also knew the classic Italian song "O Sole Mio," which indirectly served to obtain me better care in the hospital. During the first few days in the hospital, the German and Italian nurses treated the other patients before they came around to me. I knew I needed attention. I was getting weaker all the time, and my wounds weren't healing properly.

One of the Italian nurses was a big, fat mama-mia. One day, to get her attention, I started to sing "O Sole Mio" in Italian. At once she broke into a delighted laugh and began to sing with me. When we had finished the chorus together, she parted with a friendly smile. Within an hour she returned with some minestrone soup and solid food. Apart from some moldy rye and potato bread that the troops had given us, this was the first decent meal I'd had in weeks.

For the German nurse I sang a bit of "Du, Du, Liegst Mir im Hertzen." She chuckled at that and gave my infected shoulder a little bit better care.

But I wasn't allowed a long time to rest. As soon as a Nazi doctor said I could be moved, I was sent by rail to Frankfurt. I arrived in March 1943.

During the trip north from Rome I still had a high temperature. I don't remember anything about northern Italy, but as soon as we crossed the Brenner Pass to Austria, my health seemed to improve. I had a vivid memory of one little Austrian railroad station where we stopped for a while. There was snow on the ground. Healthy-looking, suntanned skiers passed by the windows, fresh off the slopes of the Tyrol, looking carefree and hearty. Carrying skis on their shoulders instead of rifles, they seemed oblivious to war.

As we continued on our way, I gazed out the window at the Austrian and Bavarian towns. The houses had wide overhanging eaves with rocks on the roofs to hold down the thatch in winter storms. Each house had flower boxes in the windows. Potted geraniums had been placed in the sun to catch the heat of the day.

In a little station that looked just like an illustration from a Grimms' fairy tale, I began thinking of Christmas and the snows of Spokane. As I looked out the train window, I thought, "This is the place for me. I think I'll come back and see this in peacetime."

Then I said to myself, "Why should I wait? I think I'll just leave now!"

I limped into the train's lavatory. By this time all the guards knew I had been sick, and they'd seen me dozing fitfully throughout the journey. No one paid any attention when I went to the bathroom.

The next thing they knew, I was out the window on the station platform. The train guards shouted out to German military people who were milling about on the platform. I tried to run, but several travelers grabbed me immediately.

One of the train guards came right through the passenger window after me, while the rest streamed out through the door. They surrounded me with drawn weapons. I stood still and grinned at them.

"Where do you think you're going, *dummkopf*?" demanded the head guard. This was the second time I'd been called that. "You aren't strong enough to get any place anyway."

To tell the truth, he was probably right on both counts. It was a stupid try, and I was certainly too weak to get very far.

I arrived in Frankfurt on March 12, 1943. I had been told three times to get behind the German lines and raise hell. Now I was more than fifteen hundred miles behind the lines, a lot farther than I had planned, but I was in no condition to raise hell. However, I figured I had already done some pretty good work blowing up German railroads and military supplies, and harassing them with manure bombs and other explosives.

My goal now was to get out of Germany as soon as possible and return to my outfit. I was determined to cost the Germans a lot of time, money and effort in the meantime.

At Oberursel, a small town near Frankfurt am Main, I was escorted into the Luftwaffe interrogation compound called Dulag Luft. For the next eighteen days or so, I was kept in solitary confinement, mainly in an interrogation cell, plus a few days in a hospital cell.

Though I had never been thoroughly interrogated, my captors had asked me many questions, especially after each of my escape attempts. To every German who asked for information, I would reply to all questions by giving my name, rank and serial number, just as I had been taught to do. As far as I knew, the Germans now considered me nothing more than an air corps major. Because of my train escape, they didn't connect me with the man who had been picked up under peculiar circumstances at Feriana.

At Dulag Luft I was subjected to harsh, methodical interrogation by well-trained experts. Because I was wearing jump boots, the interrogator assigned to me was a paratroop officer of the Luftwaffe. He spoke perfect Oxford English. Throughout the days of interrogation he practically lived with me, doing everything possible to trip me up.

He could never be sure whether I was a paratrooper or a flier. Fliers often dressed hastily for a mission, and they rushed to their planes wearing everything from boots to house slippers. So he wasn't sure that my paratroop boots meant anything at all.

During interrogation I never said a word about my work behind the lines or let anything slip concerning the OSS. On one occasion, it seemed as if he had come close to guessing—but it may have been a shot in the dark.

My interrogator asked me, "Major Sage, when did you last see Colonel Sterling?"

Fortunately I had schooled myself not to blink an eye. As he was the head of one of the British SOE outfits, Sterling's name was very familiar to me. It was his outfit that had raided Rommel's headquarters and killed some of the people, though they had unfortunately missed Rommel, who had been gone the day of the raid.

I told him I had never heard of Colonel Sterling, and my reply apparently satisfied him. He never asked me anything further about the SOE.

Another ploy practiced on prisoners in Dulag Luft solitary confinement was the "Red Cross" man. One day a man came into my cell who was very different from my normal interrogator. He was a nice, pleasant little fellow with glasses who spoke in a very gentle manner.

"I'm from *das Rotes Kreuz*, the Red Cross," he said. Placing a sheet of paper before me, he said, "I am sure that your loved ones must be missing you and wondering how you are. If you would just put down your name and address and their names, we'll let them know where you are. I'll be very happy to see that we get a letter to your family through Red Cross channels. We'll tell them where you are and inform them that you are well, and we'll give them your greetings. Just fill in this form."

I looked it over. The questions at the top of the paper were innocuous enough, but we had been trained to give only name, rank and serial number, so I wouldn't list my family members or their addresses.

As I read the rest of the form, I realized that the man before me was no Red Cross official. The form was carefully designed to draw out information. It asked for our commanding officers, "so we can let them know you're okay," our units, the number of men in each unit, where they were positioned last, where they were going and their activities.

It would have been taboo to answer any of the questions on that form. I later heard that a number of young soldiers fully believed the "Red Cross" fellow and filled out some of the information. The Germans would collect this information and then spring it on others so they could start new men talking more easily. The "Red Cross" questionnaire was gentle, but it gleaned a great deal of intelligence for the enemy.

Many sterner methods were used to break down prisoners psychologically and physically. One treatment was food deprivation. They reduced my diet to one potato per day. During questioning a full meal would be brought in and placed on a table to tempt me.

"Well, this is a good way to go on a diet," I told my interrogator. Eventually he realized it would take more than hunger to make me crack.

For chronic smokers, the Germans used cigarettes as a temptation. They weren't sure whether I was a smoker or not, so they tested me. My interrogator put a pack of cigarettes just out of my reach and said, "Well, let's talk a little bit and then have a nice cigarette."

For a good cigar I might have given him the time of day, but that would have been all.

Finally the interrogator got fed up with me. "Now we'll see if you will talk," he said. "Maybe it's not warm enough in here for you."

He stormed out of the cell. I heard some clicking sounds outside the door and the little room began to get hotter and hotter.

It was a cinder-block cell about ten feet long, five feet wide and eight feet high. The door to the main hall was heavily padded and almost soundproof. There was a small peephole for the guard's surveillance and a narrow crack under the door. A window high at the other end of the cell had been boarded over and painted.

The only furniture in the cell was an iron cot with a couple of blankets and a stool. There were no internal switches for heat and light. Both were controlled from outside the cell door.

Much later, after the heat treatment was over, I found out how the heat switch operated. There were three settings, *Erster Grad*, *Zweite Grad*, and *Dritte Grad*. These were equivalent to the first, second and third degrees. Anyone who was given the third degree was supposed to talk.

When the heat switch was turned to the first degree,

the room got about as hot as a tennis court in an asphalt-lined pit at one hundred ten degrees in August in Alabama. I started loosening my clothes.

When the switch clicked to the second degree, I began to feel like a cookie being baked in an oven. I could feel my temperature rising as it had with the fever in Rome—but this was worse.

During the third degree my head started to pound. I put a blanket on the radiator to stifle the heat, but the blanket became scorched and the smoke was choking me, so I had to pull it off again. When I touched the metal frame of the bed, I burned my hand.

I said, "Lord, I need help." I prayed that my brain wouldn't get scrambled from shock.

I still believe He told me what to do. I lay down on the floor next to the door and pressed my nose against the crack so I could sniff the thin line of cool air that came from outside the cell.

The heat was still unbearable. I was afraid I might go into shock.

"Lord, please put me out," I prayed.

He did. I passed out. The next thing I knew I was lying in the center of the room, soaking wet. The Germans had pushed me back when they opened the door and had thrown a bucket of water over me.

The heat treatment was repeated several times, each time with the same results. After each treatment they dragged me back into the room and threw water over me to bring me around.

My interrogators finally gave up on that method. It was obvious to them that I was not getting any closer to telling them anything. With each treatment I only came that much closer to spitting in their eye.

The Nazis also played psychological games with

me. One interrogator would be very good to me, another very bad. The bad one would try to bully me, then the other would try to sweet-talk me, offering me various bribes if I would only talk to his friend. Though both were quite good at setting up conversational traps, this method did not work either.

After one of the heat treatments, my fever started to act up again and it didn't abate after the treatment was over. The Germans decided I still had some infection from my wounds and they took me to a hospital.

At that point I had been in solitary confinement under constant interrogation for nearly two weeks. I can still remember every step of that short walk to the hospital in the fresh air. We had to cross a street and walk through a small park. I remember how pretty the park looked. The trees were laced with frost and snow. I was grateful to be alive.

In the better bed of the hospital cell I slept most of the time, but the interrogation never ceased. The Germans would wake me up to ask me questions. By then I just automatically spat out my name, rank and serial number.

There was an advantage to being in the hospital, however. I was able to obtain reading material. One elderly worker seemed kinder than the other employees and I asked him to bring me a Bible. The next day he returned with a small edition of the New Testament in English. I read every word of it between naps, and it made me feel a whole lot better.

Chapter 9

After my release from the hospital I was allowed to join the other prisoners in Dulag Luft general camp. The camp was a kind of holding place for POWs in transit from the interrogation center to more permanent war camps.

It was great to be out of solitary at last and to be among other prisoners. Two of them, both bomber pilots, soon became good friends. Hank Burman, a big, tall, sturdy fellow with a broken tooth, was from State College, Pennsylvania. Don Stine was a Californian with a wide, ready grin; he limped slightly from a leg injury. All three of us hit it off well. We were destined to go to the same POW camp, where we shared the same mess during most of our prison life together.

At the Dulag Luft camp I also met a fighter pilot, Dick Klocko, a lieutenant colonel. On the day we met he was strolling around the exercise circuit with another American, the two of them talking about how and when they were shot down. I overheard Klocko say he was shot down on February 24.

"That's interesting," I put in. "February 24 was the day I was shot *up*."

"I was shot down just outside of Feriana, Tunisia," Klocko added. "Where were you?"

"That's where I was," I burst out.

I couldn't get over the coincidence. We had been captured within a few miles and within two or three hours of each other. For some reason, that coincidence seemed to seal our friendship.

In early April a large group of British and American POWs were sent from Dulag Luft to Stalag Luft III, a German camp for fliers. The POW compounds were on the southern edge of Sagan, a town of about twenty-five thousand in the scraggly pine forests of Silesia, ninety miles southeast of Berlin and about halfway between Berlin and Breslau near the old German-Polish border. Stalag Luft III was destined to be my home, off and on, for the next fifteen months or so. In this camp occurred the events that were to be immortalized in Paul Brickhill's book *The Great Escape,* and the movie of the same name.

The Germans were holding British and European RAF fliers and a number of Americans in what were called the East and Center Camps at Stalag Luft III. By the time we arrived, they had just opened up a third section, the North Camp, which included British and foreign fliers from the Royal Air Force (RAF) as well as many Americans.

The North Compound was a square about three hundred fifty yards on each side. Many pine trees had been cut down to make way for the new camp, but the branches had not yet been hauled away. In the northern half of the compound were long, low barracks (we called them blocks) in three rows with five buildings in each row. In this section of the compound was a fire pool—a man-made pond that held water for putting out fires—a kitchen and three or four large latrine buildings. The latrine buildings were built over deep pits, and inside each one was a twelve-hole "chick sale," a country-style mass toilet. Fastened on the walls were long urinals of bent tin, draining toward the corner pipes.

The southern half of the compound had been cleared as an exercise area, which was also used for daily roll call, which the Germans called *Appell*.

The camp was enclosed by double barbed-wire fences standing ten feet tall and five feet apart, with coils of barbed concertina wire on the ground between them. Inside the entire main fence was a strip thirty feet wide strewn with white sand. The inner boundary of the sandy area was marked by a warning rail about a foot and a half high. The guards were at liberty to shoot any prisoner who put a foot on the warning rail or stepped in the sand.

Outside the northern wire was the *Vorlager*, which contained the German guardroom, the hospital or dispensary, the "cooler" for solitary confinement and a coal shed. Like the compound itself, the vorlager was completely enclosed with double rows of barbed wire fence and barbed concertina coils. The vorlager had two gates, one leading to the compound itself and the other to the main dirt road outside.

Every four or five hundred feet around the compound were elevated guard towers which we called goon boxes. Inside each box was a sentry equipped with searchlights and automatic weapons. At night more sentries patrolled outside. Inside the fence, a hundführer patrolled with a *Schaeferhund* (German shepherd) or with a Doberman pinscher. The dogs were trained to attack on command. They went for the throat.

* * *

When we new arrivals from Dulag Luft reached the gate to the vorlager, prisoners from the North Compound ran toward us and crowded around the fence that separated the main camp from the vorlager. They all lined up to meet the incoming "purge," a word that was used to describe any movement of war prisoners into or out of the camp.

We soon learned that all prisoners in the camp were called kriegies, pronounced kree-ghees, taken from the German word for war prisoner, *Kriegsgefangener*. Though the camp was predominantly British, it included a few Poles, Czechs, Norwegians, French, Belgians and Dutch who had fled their own countries when they were occupied by the Nazis and later joined the RAF in the war effort.

The camp also included the first batch of Americans captured during the war. Some had been members of the volunteer Eagle Squadron in the RAF, while others were fliers who had been shot down out of Great Britain or North Africa. Four barracks had been set aside for the expected influx of Americans. When we first arrived, we had plenty of room, but the blocks began to fill up quickly as the months went by.

A block was divided into sixteen or eighteen rooms, each about fifteen feet square, with three more rooms, large enough for two men apiece, at the end of the building. The end rooms were for senior officers, the seriously wounded or the camp staff. One corner room held the night latrine with indoor plumbing.

When we first arrived, each of the larger rooms had four to six double-decker bunks, while the end rooms had single-deckers. In every room were a small kitchen table, a few stools and a stove in a corner on a tile base.

Each bunk was lined with hard bedboards topped

with a palliasse as padding. The palliasse was just a thin mattress stuffed with wood shavings or straw. It looked like a long burlap potato sack.

Each block had a communal washroom with a concrete floor and a lavatory where we could wash our hands and faces. In a little kitchen was a coal stove with two burners and a small oven. The kitchen was not designed to feed adequately a hundred men, and as the camp became crowded, it turned into a major bottleneck. We had to organize the mess into shifts so everyone would get to cook and eat.

The one large kitchen building outside the blocks had huge vats, but this kitchen had a secondary role in everyday cooking. The primary use of the main kitchen was to provide hot water in quantity so people could have what we called ersatz (imitation) tea or coffee, or the real thing when available. Two or three times a week our kriegie kitchen staff used the vats to cook up a thin barley or cabbage soup or to boil potatoes, when available, from the German ration.

No one got fat on a prison diet. German rations consisted mainly of bread, which came in huge loaves weighing about five pounds each. The Germans had a dark brown bread called *Roggenmehl* (rye meal). Despite its name the bread probably contained all kinds of grains, as well as potatoes and acorns and probably some sawdust. It was often moldy. We usually cut the bread into thin slices and toasted it thoroughly to dissipate the moldy taste.

Enough roggenmehl was provided for about five thin slices per person per day. The bread was made slightly more palatable with the addition of a kind of margarine and some ersatz jam consisting of boiled, ground-up sugar beets. The Germans called this pink stuff *Marmalada*.

Whatever meat we were given was ground up like hamburger, and we could never tell whether it was cow or horse. (We sometimes saw some unusual-looking animal heads in the disposal area.) Occasionally we were given what the British called Swedes or horse turnips. To me they seemed like grotesque mutations of rutabagas—gigantic, tough and pithy. We endured them because they gave us the vitamins that we desperately needed.

The vat-prepared barley soup was quite palatable, as was the occasional sauerkraut ration. Fresh vegetables were a welcome treat, but very rare.

One item the Germans liked better than we did was a creation called *Fischkäse* (fish cheese). I have no idea how they made it, and perhaps I never want to know. Its smell resembled that of dead fish combined with overripe cheese. I was so determined to keep up my strength that I held my nose, closed my eyes and ate it, but I never learned to relish fischkäse.

Another German favorite was *Blutwurst* (blood sausage). It consisted of plain animal blood mixed in a sack with some fat. Though high in protein, it was a gruesome dish to contemplate, especially when it was being sliced up raw and runny. I discovered that the best way to get a messmate's share of blutwurst was to slice it in front of him before dinner. Some men waived their rights to it promptly.

Apart from the German food, what really sustained us were the parcels the Red Cross provided. They were sent from various countries including the United States, Canada, Britain, Australia and New Zealand. We particularly relished the Australian and New Zealand parcels, which included fine butter, canned and sent to us from down under.

Canned powdered milk was a staple of the American parcels, and the tins were almost as valuable as their contents. The powdered milk was named Klim, which is "milk" spelled backward. After we finished the powdered milk, we used the Klim tins to make practically everything we needed, including cooking utensils, everyday items, and, eventually, tools that we used in preparing for escapes.

POWs were also introduced to Spam, the standard meat included in American parcels. Spam was offset by "bully beef" from England, which was quite good, and occasionally we'd get a can of salmon in a Canadian parcel. Whenever the salmon arrived, it disappeared quickly.

We were never full. It was impossible to overeat, except perhaps on those rare occasions when we had saved up for a Thanksgiving or Christmas bash. At these "feasts" our meals consisted of items that had been hoarded for days, weeks or months from our Red Cross parcels.

As we became better cooks, we learned to create delicacies from our ordinary provisions. The parcels always contained some kind of crackers, varying from hardtack to biscuits, as the British called them, which we would mash and grind up into something like cake flour. The flour grinder was made out of two cans, one inside the other, with the bottom of one can perforated one way and the other can perforated in the opposite direction to create a grinding surface. Or we would wrap the crackers in cloth and pulverize them with homemade wooden mallets.

The flour went into so-called pies or cakes. They were not always complete successes. There was one concoction we called "gedoing" pudding, so named because it was very heavy and made the sound "gedoing" when it hit the bottom of your stomach.

For flavoring we used lemon powder, Tang, or some other flavored drink powder. If we had raisins or dried prunes, those went in too. To make a cake rise we'd put in tooth powder, which had enough baking soda to make the goo rise a little. Rapid beating helped to aerate the batter and made the final product a bit lighter.

Whenever a British parcel arrived, we could create one of our favorite desserts. Instead of containing Klim, the milk powder, each British parcel held a can of Condendo, a very sweet, very thick condensed milk. We found that by stirring lemon powder into the Condendo, we could make a firm and delicious lemon pie filling that we poured into a cracker-crumb crust.

All cooking was done on a rotation basis. We had a roster that showed when each person was to cook. Usually each cook had a single general assistant called a stooge, our name for any person who served someone else. It was the stooge's job to peel the potatoes before the meal and clean up the dishes afterward, as well as perform any other tasks the cook wanted done.

Food was so scarce that every messmate watched the plates with a critical eye to make sure each person had a fair serving. The cook had to have good judgment of proportions or he would get in trouble, especially when delicacies were served.

Potatoes, for instance, were among the closely watched food items. After boiling the potatoes, we would mash them with homemade potato mashers, working in a little bit of Klim and a dab of margarine. The results were close to homestyle, and each bite was treasured. Woe to the cook who didn't put equal amounts on each plate!

The other messmates drew straws or cut cards to

establish the order of choosing plates of food, with the cook automatically coming last. If there were eight people in the mess and the cook was serving Spam, he would cut the heated Spam into eight slices, striving to make them equal. After adding a dab of horse turnips, cabbage, or any other vegetable that was available, plus a thin slice of bread with a small amount of ground-up beet jam, he would present all the plates at once to all eight men for their selection.

The desserts, too, were carefully measured. If someone had made a pie, the cook would carefully cut it into equal portions. Again, messmates drew for the first choice. The man with the high card always took what he considered to be the biggest piece, followed by each man in the order of the draw. Since the cook took the last piece, he was highly motivated to make everything equal. This rough-and-ready selection method was a just way of doing business.

Red Cross parcels also contained some luxuries. For instance, if we wanted to dress up the potatoes, we could use the real cheese that came in the parcels to make a sort of potatoes au gratin. Or we used small bars of chocolate from the parcels to vary our dessert menus. In addition to lemon pie, we would make chocolate pie or chocolate pudding by grinding up the chocolate bars and melting them down for filling.

Real jam sometimes came from America or from other Allied countries. Always better than the German issue, it was a treasured item on our menu.

Eventually candy bars became a medium of exchange. Prices sometimes ran as high as fifteen dollars for a candy bar when food was short and people were getting very hungry.

Real powdered coffee and real tea were great luxuries. When they were in short supply, our hot drinks were the German-issue erstaz herb tea and ground grain-and-nut coffee. The real tea was mainly for the British. Like most of the Americans in the camp, I always preferred coffee, which was in high demand. As with the candy bars, tea and coffee became good trading materials. In time we would use these goods to tame the German goons and buy their silence. But that came later.

When not cooking, eating or thinking about food, the kriegie could choose among a number of activities to fill the long, restless hours. The British, who had been receiving parcels for two to four years, were generous in sharing books, games, cards and other items with the newer American kriegies, and their generosity gave us the option of a wide range of activities. The kriegie could read, play cards, or when weather permitted and equipment was available, he could play sports outside. During the day, he could sleep when he wanted to, "logging sack time," or he could walk laps around the perimeter path just inside the warning rail. The perimeter became the favorite place to hold private conversations or to discuss plans for escape.

At least twice a day all activities were interrupted by roll call. The first appell was in the morning between seven and nine o'clock, when people were still sleeping or getting breakfast. We were all roused and sent out to what we called the parade ground. In actuality, it was just a big open field. On order, we lined up according to barracks in five ranks, each rank five deep, making it easy for the Germans to take count of us.

The second appell was in the late afternoon, about four o'clock. If there had been any recent escape attempts, the Germans would call an appell in the middle of the night or any time they wanted to.

The kommandant's administrative officers did the counting. One of these was Captain Pieber, an Austrian who was quite a gentle little man and extremely polite. He liked to begin by saying, "Goot morning, chentlemen!"

"Goot morning, Herr Pieber," we would reply in unison.

If we had been "good boys"—not attempting to escape recently—he would count up quickly, give a shy smile and then dismiss us.

Pieber was on the administrative side of the German hierarchy. German officers on the security side were usually far less friendly. Among them were the guards with machine guns and searchlights who manned the goon boxes and other guards who walked the fence carrying submachine guns. We were always aware of the presence of the hundführer with his sentry dog as well as the "ferrets," trained security men armed with pistols who tested the ground with long steel probes to check for tunnels. On nightly rounds, the ferrets pointed their powerful flashlights under the buildings and in every dark corner of the compound, searching for anyone who defied the curfew.

All the security men were under the direction of Oberfeldwebel Hermann Glemnitz, the most efficient security man I met in Germany.

Chapter 10

Oberfeldwebel Glemnitz, chief of the German Abwehr Security Forces (which we called the ferrets) in the North Compound, had the build of a square-shouldered light-heavyweight boxer, and he knew his business. Though he was sometimes too efficient for our liking, he had a sense of humor and was not a bully. His policies were hard but fair, and we respected him even when he threatened us and jeopardized our escape attempts.

His second in command, Unteroffizier Griese, was as incorruptible and almost as efficient as Glemnitz. Griese had a long, skinny neck and an odd way of holding his head, which earned him the name "Rubberneck."

The senior British officer (SBO) of the North Compound was initially Group Captain Massey. Still limping from old foot wounds, Massey had to make occasional visits to the hospital. When he was gone, he delegated many of his SBO duties to Wing Commander Harry M.A. Day, affectionately known as "Wings," and recognized as the real British leader over the years.

Wings was well over six feet tall, as thin as "old" kriegies always were, and he always stood ramrod straight. He was impeccably dressed in his RAF cap and blue uniform with World War I ribbons on his chest. He had been shot down in an old Blenheim reconnaissance plane over Germany in the early fall of 1939. By the time I met him in 1943, Wings had made at least five attempts to escape from various prison camps. His air of dignity and the record of his deeds commanded the respect of every one of the rugged, individualistic prisoners in that camp. But many saw that craggy hawk face light up with a gentle grin or laughter when he was in conversations with close colleagues.

When I first came to North Camp, I frequently had tea with Wings Day and two other British officers, Tom Kirby-Green and Major Johnny Dodge of the British Army. Dodge was one of the two ground officers I knew in the North Compound. The other was the Scottish paratrooper padre, Captain Murdo MacDonald—more of him later. Johnny Dodge was a big, broad-shouldered, experienced fighting man who had a genial and gracious disposition. American-born, he was a nephew by marriage of Winston Churchill.

Dodge went to England in 1914, where he was commissioned an officer. In the First World War he was wounded and later highly decorated fighting in Gallipoli and France. By the end of World War I he was a lieutenant colonel.

In 1939 Dodge returned to France as a major and was trapped on the coast when France fell. Having spotted some British ships several miles offshore, Dodge swam out to them, but the ships sailed away before he could climb aboard. So he returned to shore, a swim of several miles, and was promptly captured by the Germans.

While traveling in German custody, he broke away at least twice. On his first escape, he dived into a canal from a barge that was transporting him to Dulag Luft. Later he leapt from a train that was carrying him between camps. On both occasions he was quickly recaptured.

In the Polish block, number 123, were many fliers who had escaped from Poland and volunteered to serve for England. One of them, Minskewitz, became known as our tunnel trap genius because of his ingenuity in creating traps to block the tunnel entrances from the scrutiny of the German ferrets. Here I also met the thoughtful, bearded philosopher Kristiniak and a lighthearted younger man I knew only as Daub.

The Polish contingent also included a very strong man, Mikhail, who was a great shot-putter, somewhat handicapped by a leg stunted by war injuries. Here too were Danny Krol, a dapper fencer and expert tunneler, and Bolo Piwowarek, a very fine athlete whom I met years later working for the Americans near Paris. In Block 123 I also met Flight Lieutenant Peter Tobolski, a man so fluent in German that he traveled as Wings Day's "German" NCO escort during "The Great Escape."

Among the Americans in the camp was our senior American officer (SAO), Colonel Charles G. Goodrich, a graduate of West Point who had been dubbed "Rojo" because of his red hair and sandy complexion. After West Point he became a stalwart of the Army Air Corps and an early commander of B-25 bombers. Goodrich was shot down over Egypt on September 14, 1942, and he spent time in several hospitals before arriving at Stalag Luft III.

Another American flier was Major David Mudgett Jones, better known as Davy Jones. Tall and dark, Davy had an impressive blue-black beard and black eyes that sparkled with humor. The British called him "Tokyo" Jones in honor of his famous B-25 mission in which General Jimmy Doolittle's group of land-based planes took off from a carrier on a no-return bomb raid of Tokyo in early 1942. Jones crash-landed in China and worked his way back to U.S. forces. Later the same year he was sent to North Africa and was shot down during a bombing raid over Italy.

Stalag Luft III had its fair share of walking miracles, men who had survived the most incredible ordeals. Perhaps the most miraculous survival of all was that of Hank Burman, the pilot of a B-17 Flying Fortress who had been shot down over France. Burman was flying over St. Nazaire at nearly seventeen thousand feet when he came under enemy fire that knocked out two of his four engines and riddled his airplane. With his copilot dead in the seat beside him, Burman gave the green light for the rest of his crew to jump.

After allowing the crew time to clear the plane, Hank stood up to lift his parachute harness from its place on the back of his seat. Just then the B-17 lurched into a final spinning dive, and centrifugal force pinned Hank between the steering column and the windshield. Hank realized he could not break free. He was going down with the plane. He gave an agonized scream, "God, help me!" and then blacked out.

The next thing Hank recalled, he was crawling out of the wreckage on a plowed field. He saw some bits of metal labeled "Bendix" lying on the field, and realized those scraps were parts of his plane. A pale-faced couple and a boy were standing at the edge of the field, and they gaped at him in stupefied amazement when he called out to them. They must have thought he was a crawling corpse, or a ghost!

Hank passed out again. When he came to he was

in a hospital bed with a fractured skull, two broken ribs and a broken tooth. But after five weeks of care, the only scar from his seventeen thousand-foot fall was a broken tooth. Within a few weeks of his arrival in camp, he was the cleanup home run blaster on the barracks' sandlot softball team.

Among the other Americans in the compound was Lieutenant Colonel A.P. ''Bub'' Clark, Jr., a flier who became known in camp as ''Big S'' for his security work. A man of many talents, Clark was a West Pointer who somehow managed to tuck his six-foot five-inch frame into a tiny Spitfire fighter and went to war for the Allies. Tall and erect, with red hair and bright blue eyes, Clark was the youngest-looking lieutenant colonel I had ever seen, and one of the ablest.

In time I came to know many American kriegies very well, especially the men I ate with. There was the fine artist Don Stine from northern California, who had piloted a twin-engine B-25 bomber. Martin Plocher, a B-17 pilot in our group, was also from California. Elwin F. ''Dick'' Schrupp from Young America, Minnesota, gave me my first lessons in German and, as time went on, became increasingly valuable as an interpreter and goon tamer. Willy Wigger from Hannibal, Missouri—who had flown a B-25—was a very slight, blond, cheery lad who was popular with everyone. Other POWs in the American block included a P-47 pilot, Bob ''Ajax'' Adamina, and a bombardier named Gene Shaljean.

Each barracks was under the command of senior officers who reported to either the senior British officer (SBO) or the senior American officer (SAO). British and Polish barracks were under the command of RAF officers who held the rank of wing commander or squadron leader, the equivalent of the Americans' lieutenant colonel and major.

In North Compound the four blocks designated for Americans were numbered 105 through 108. The senior officers in these blocks were Lieutenant Colonel Bub Clark, Lieutenant Colonel Dick Klocko, Major Davy Jones and me. Block commanders met regularly with the SBO and the SAO, passing on important messages to the block personnel. We were responsible for having our men at appell for the roll call and insuring the best and fairest distribution of meals, as well as apportioning cooking time. Block commanders also supervised the issue of clothing and other items in short supply.

Initially only about eight officers occupied each large room. Those officers became the mess that dined together, and they pooled all their food resources. Each man in the smaller end rooms was invited to become a permanent member of one of the larger messes, pooling his rations and parcels with the other officers.

In my block, 108, I was invited to eat with the men I'd met at Dulag Luft and on the train. Months later when we moved to another block in the new, all-American South Compound, the members of the mess remained the same. Early messmates were Don Stine, Hank Burman, Dick Schrupp, Willie Wigger, Martin Plocher and Dominick Lazzaro, who had been Burman's navigator. Later on, Adamina and Shaljean joined us.

In the internal administration of all their POW camps, the Luftwaffe (German Air Force) and the Wehrmacht (German Army) left most of the daily duties to the kriegies. In North Camp with its British RAF majority, the experienced kriegies handled such jobs as the distribution of mail, German or Red Cross clothing, bedding and food parcels. The kriegies handled the accounting of the practically worthless reichsmarks the POWs theoretically were accumulating. They were also responsible for the issue of hot water, soap and, at those rare times when it was available, toilet paper. (Usually we had to use the propaganda papers distributed by the Germans.)

As time went on we pooled books from various sources to create a camp library, and we built a theater. Our entertainment committees organized choral groups, a barber shop quartet, a dramatic club and a debating team. In addition we had a comprehensive educational program that included both peacetime and wartime subjects. Kriegies could be found to teach almost any subject, depending on their specialties. I taught salesmanship, jujitsu, unarmed combat and Delicate Dan Fairbairn's methods of silent killing.

On our sandlot sports field we played nearly every game ever invented. At first all sports were played with homemade equipment, though we later acquired regulation bats and balls, footballs, soccer balls, rugby gear and even cricket equipment through the YMCA. My first "baseball" in camp consisted of a yarn cover stuffed with old socks. Though crude, the ball bounced pretty well when the yarn was pulled tight. Whenever I was recaptured after my early escapes, this was the ball that I bounced off the cooler walls during the lonely days of punishment in solitary confinement.

The one organization that preoccupied some of us was guessed at, but never pinned down, by the Germans. This was our secret "X organization," and its main objective was to assist us in our escapes. The X organization also supervised and safeguarded covert or semicovert activities such as transmitting radio messages to our Allies through a method developed by the British.

The X organization had various means of subverting the German cause. In addition to gathering and transmitting intelligence whenever possible, we tried to blackmail the goons into cooperating with us. We would give the goons precious supplies that were supposedly forbidden to prisoners, and then we would use their acceptance for purposes of blackmail. When they were willing to cooperate with us, we would get them to bring in tools and equipment that we needed for digging escape tunnels and to find ink, which was required by our forgers.

We also used psychological warfare to lower the morale of our guards and ferrets. We repeatedly informed them of the tremendous production of American tanks, airplanes and all kinds of war supplies. The kriegies appeared supremely confident that we would win the war, and we tried to convince the guards that they were engaged in a losing cause despite what they were being told by their masters. Sometimes we would display compassion that their country was being destroyed.

Not all prisoners wanted to escape. After having been shot down, some of the kriegies were just glad to be alive, and they didn't feel like risking their lives again. But nearly all the prisoners were quite willing to assist others in trying to make a break.

Any prisoner caught trying to escape was sent to the cooler for varying amounts of time. The eager beavers put that time to use in planning for their *next* escape. Among the kriegies I was considered one of the eager beavers, but I was not the only one.

Each of us had his reasons for wanting to escape, but there was one overriding rationale, quite apart from our personal reasons, that we all shared. We knew that every time one of us broke out of camp, we kept hundreds or thousands of Germans fully occupied looking for us, and that took their energies away from shooting our comrades at the front.

For me escape was almost a matter of professional obligation. I still felt bad about having been caught in the first place, and I knew my place was out fighting against the enemy. Still, as a well-trained OSS man I had an obligation to work against the enemy from within. Every time we made the Germans put on more guards or forced them to rouse the whole countryside to look for a missing man, it hurt the Nazi war effort a little bit more.

Rebellion was very real to me. I had loved the stories of American patriots who fought to win our independence. I loved the ringing words of Patrick Henry, "I care not what others may say, but as for me, give me liberty or give me death." I was perfectly willing to take plenty of risks to fight for the cause I believed in. Even if I never made it back to the front, I would give the Germans as much trouble as possible and keep as many people looking for me as I could. That was my duty as a guerrilla fighter.

Wings Day, the leader of the camp on the British side, and Roger Bushell, "Big X," shared an identical philosophy. Bushell, a South African who had gone to college in England, was a lawyer and a very clear thinker. Once an expert skier, he was still in excellent shape considering his long stretches in prison. A scar over one eye gave a sardonic twist to his expression, but he was not the least cynical. He had a clear, quick, incisive mind and the gift of tremendous determination.

When I met Roger at Stalag Luft III, he had already escaped two or three times and he was a marked man. He'd been out for so long and given the Nazis so much trouble that they had warned him he would be shot if he was caught again. Despite the threat, Roger, Big X, ran our escape organization.

In all the activities of the X organization we were always conscious of security. We had to make sure the kriegies themselves did not inadvertently give away any schemes in progress. All secret activities, and the existence of forbidden items like our radio, had to be hidden from the Germans. My fellow block commander Bub Clark, better known as Big S, was perfectly suited for the job. An excellent organizer, he set up a highly efficient system of internal stooges and listening posts to keep track of the activities of every German ferret and guard in the compound.

At the gate was a kriegie called the duty pilot, or DP. Each DP had a one-hour shift on a rotation system, so ten to twelve men served as DPs during the day, keeping track of every German who entered the compound. The DPs reported their observations to Bub Clark and he analyzed the Germans' activities to find out how many were in the compound at different hours of the day and where they spent the most time.

We had escape factories operating throughout the compound, where kriegies made tools, fabricated clothing, created forged documents and hammered out the other items we needed to escape. The factories were protected by security stooges through an elaborate but casual-looking system of warning alarms and signals. A security stooge would lower a window, turn a coal scuttle in a different direction or set a Red Cross parcel on a garbage container. That signaled another hut, where a second stooge was looking out a window.

At the signal the second man would blow his nose or shut a book, and the alert was passed along to people working in the tunnels or escape factories. The kriegies would close down the factories until the danger had passed.

Chapter 11

In the early days at North Compound, the new camp and its guards were tested by several individuals who attempted to escape. When we first arrived in camp, Russian prison laborers were still clearing out pine trees from North Compound. Each day branches were loaded onto trucks and hauled out of the camp. Several POWs, including me, tried to escape by hiding among the branches. Some jumped from buildings into the branches as the trucks were passing by, while others crawled in from underneath and lay on the truckbeds.

At the gate the guards jabbed pitchforks into the mass of branches, and most of the men were discovered. At over six feet two inches and two hundred pounds, I was spotted almost immediately. The only ones who made it through the gate were a couple of smaller men, Eagle Squadron pilots Barry Mahon and Leroy Skinner, who hid very deep in the branches in front of the truck.

After the other kriegies and I were discovered, we were marched off to the cooler. Though Mahon and Skinner managed to make it through the gate, they were found the next day and joined us in solitary. As the cutting and hauling continued, more kriegies tried the same ploy, but all ended up joining us. By the time the

Russians finished their job, the cooler was filled with kriegies from North Compound.

Several men attempted to mingle with the Russian prisoners when they left the compound each day. The Russians lived in the kommandantur where they had separate barracks, so they had to march back and forth from North Compound. One evening several of our men grabbed Russian hats, put on Polish overcoats and tried to walk out with the Russians when they left for the night. Spotted at the gate by Glemnitz and Rubberneck of the security forces, the intrepid kriegies quickly joined our cooler group.

A British officer, Ian Cross, attempted another method. He crawled under one of the trucks and hung from the chassis. When the truck neared the gate, Cross was spotted by Glemnitz, who commanded the truck driver to speed the truck across the rough playing field with Cross still hanging underneath the vehicle. Bumping along over holes and pine stumps, Ian hung on for dear life. We expected that he might get a bit mangled, but he survived. Glemnitz grinned broadly as he called Cross out from under and told him to go rest in the cooler.

After these first exhilarating but abortive efforts, the cooler was bulging with would-be escapees. But we were not discouraged.

Another wild scheme developed in our early days involved the use of primitive camouflage. The idea came to me one day when a fellow kriegie and I were playing ball near the outer perimeter path, and I quickly explained my plan to him. As we approached a spot midway between two guard boxes, I tossed the ball a little higher than he could reach. The ball flew over the warning wire and rolled close to the fence.

I wanted to find out if there was dead space in the perimeter through which we could pass without being seen. To test the goons, I put one foot on the guardrail. A guard swung around with a menacing gesture.

"Halt! *Gehen Sie zurück*!" (Go back) he shouted.

"I lost my ball," I yelled. "The ball is there!" I pointed at it.

Had Glemnitz been there, I am sure he wouldn't have allowed me to cross the wire. But the guard finally let me go pick up the ball, keeping his weapon trained on me all the time.

As I leaned over to pick it up, I made a couple of quick observations. At that moment it seemed to me that a man lying flat on the ground by the fence might not be seen by the goons. The guard boxes did not have an overhang. Unless the guard leaned over the box as he looked down along the wire, he probably had a blind spot. As I picked up the ball, I was certain I was standing in that blind spot.

My actual escape plan materialized some time later. Barry Mahon and Leroy Skinner, the two compact-sized pilots who had gone out in the tree branches, were in solitary at the same time I was. As soon as we got out we started to devise a plan that would take advantage of the blind spot in the perimeter. Our idea was to cover ourselves with some kind of camouflage that would allow us to crawl undetected at night across the white sand strip between the warning rail and the fence. Then we would use hand-made wire cutters to get through the wire.

It was a brilliant idea . . . if it worked. The first problem was camouflage. To cover ourselves, we would use the palliasses from our bunks. The palliasse fabric was made from a kind of wood pulp, and there was a telltale gray hue to the material. We decided to disguise one of the mattress covers with sand to make it sparkle a bit and blend in with the perimeter sand.

To manufacture glue we mashed and soaked cracker crumbs and mixed them with British Condendo milk to create a sticky gluten that held the sand. Then we built a light frame of slim laths to hold the sheet. We figured the cover should have a gradual slope on either side, rising to the highest point in the middle, over the man's back.

We rigged up a frame for one of the smaller pilots. It had to be nearly six feet across to allow for a gradual slope down to the sand on each side. This was a larger frame than we had anticipated, but even so it could not have camouflaged my large bulk. If anyone was to use the frame, it had to be Barry or Leroy. But I wouldn't let them go without first conducting a trial run.

After smearing on the gluten, we sprinkled fresh sand on our pilot model and prepared to test it. Choosing a foggy night and a time when few guards were around, we carried the camouflage frame to the warning rail, arriving there just as the hundführer and his dog entered the camp. Quickly we shoved the empty frame over the rail, leaving it in the white, sandy area of no man's land.

From inside the window of the nearest barracks we observed what happened. As long as the fog was on the ground the camouflaged frame could hardly be seen. But when the fog lessened and the traveling searchlights became more effective, we saw one light wave over the frame, then stop. The guard shouted a warning, then let loose a couple of rounds, and the sheet jerked a bit.

We scrubbed that plan.

The idea of simultaneously building three tunnels, each more than three hundred feet long, through shifting sand thirty feet underground—the idea that eventually culminated in what came to be known as "The Great Escape"—was conceived by Squadron Leader Roger Bushell when he was living in East Camp on the far side of the kommandantur.

Bushell had been toying with the idea for quite some time when we arrived on the scene. From East Camp he could see the trees being felled and huts being built in the area of North Camp. He asked the senior British officer to request the kommandant to send some prisoners of war to North Compound to speed along building operations.

That working party included a number of officers who were to play a key role in the escape. Along with Bushell there were Wally Floody, a mining engineer from Canada; a Royal Navy man named Peter Fanshawe whom everyone naturally called "Hornblower"; and Lieutenant Commander Crump Ker-Ramsey. While working in North Camp these men concluded that there was a good possibility of digging tunnels out of the camp.

Bushell's notion of building three tunnels at once was mind-boggling but brilliant. The German ferrets would never guess that we were engaged in such a vast undertaking. Even if we lost one tunnel or two, there was still a chance of succeeding with the third. For maximum security Roger named the tunnels Tom, Dick and Harry—and only those names were permitted in reference to our activities.

Tom was to go due west from Block 123, which housed the Polish RAF officers and was one of the blocks nearest the barbed wire on the west side. Dick would also go west, but from an interior block, number 122: It would be longer to dig, but less likely to be discovered. Harry, also longer than Tom, would head north from Block 104 under the vorlager and its two double fences, pass a hundred feet beyond under the road and emerge in the woods.

The Germans had built the barracks floors about two feet off the ground so the ferrets could crawl under them with flashlights to see if any digging was going on. However, the floors of the washrooms and the feet of the stoves were set on concrete blocks. Bushell, Floody and the Polish officer Minskewitz decided that the trap doors and entrances for the tunnels should go down through the concrete.

Tom's trap door was alongside a chimney in Block 123. Dick's was under a washroom drain in Block 122, and Harry's lay under a stove in one of the larger end rooms of Block 104 near the vorlager. Each trap door was thoroughly concealed.

Minskewitz was our resident expert in camouflaging trap doors. For Tom he used some extra cement left in the compound by workers, reinforced with bits of barbed wire, to make a concrete block about two feet square. He then chipped a two-foot-square chunk out of the concrete floor. The square block fit perfectly and could be removed by lifting up on the fine wires. When it was fit in place, the block lay even with the floor, the wires lay flat in the cracks, and all the cracks were covered with cement paste and dirt.

Minskewitz devised an even more ingenious trap door for Dick in 122. The trap was located in the center of the washroom. A square two-foot drain in the washroom, usually under a layer of water, was covered with a grating. Minskewitz devised a block that fit in the bottom of the drain, and he filled the cracks with sand and soap. It fit so snugly that we could fill the drain with water and put the grating on top, and the trap would be fool- and ferret-proof.

Crump Ker-Ramsey engineered Harry's trap door.

He moved the stove off the tiled floor, took up the tiles and cemented them onto a wooden frame that was hinged as a trap. It closed on a padded grille that covered the shaft below. The edge of the door around the tiles was seamless and invisible. Since the stove on top was kept burning all the time, no ferret would suspect that we moved it back and forth almost daily.

To create the passages to the tunnels below we hammered through the concrete with pickaxes or hammers. Kriegies engaged in various activities to mask the noise of the concrete workers; in plain sight of the ferrets, they hammered at tin cans to fabricate them into pots and pans—a legitimate enterprise in the sight of the Germans. Other prisoners worked in the garden outside, making a lot of noise as they dug away at rocks in the earth. We also had ad hoc rehearsals of a kriegie chorus, noisily booming out the British song "I've Got Sixpence" or the American "I've Been Working on the Railroad."

During tunnel digging two men were responsible for camp security. Bub Clark supervised overall camp security with an eagle eye. He had a nose that could sniff out ferret trouble before it happened. He was assisted by the man who was ultimately responsible for tunnel security, Wally Floody's friend George Harsh.

It was Harsh who stood by the tunnel entrance, alert to the chain of signals that started at the front gate and ended with him. When the signals informed him that a ferret was within threatening range of an open tunnel or a working factory, Harsh gave the terse order, "Pack up!"

George Harsh was well liked and trusted by everyone in the camp. I considered him a good friend, yet it wasn't until 1971, when his autobiography *Lonesome Road* was published by Norton, that I found out how he came to be there. In fact, Harsh's story was one of the best-kept secrets in Stalag Luft III.

Harsh, a well-to-do Southerner from Atlanta, had gone to Oglethorpe University. One night in 1928 he and four other college students, all from prosperous families, were sitting around a table with a gallon of white lightning when they decided to prove they could commit the perfect crime. In what was conceived as a weird sort of lark, they decided they would some day rob a big bank.

By way of practice, they decided to hold up a number of small businesses. One of these was a grocery store with two clerks. George had drawn the straw for gunman that day, and it was up to him to point his pistol and bark, "This is a holdup!"

One of the clerks raised his hands, but the other grabbed for a gun behind the counter and came up shooting. George fired reflexively and killed the clerk who held the gun. The clerk's wild shots wounded George and accidentally killed the other clerk.

At age seventeen George was sentenced to death, but his execution was delayed, and when he was eighteen the sentence was commuted to life on a Georgia chain gang. After twelve years on the chain gang he was made a trusty and went to work in the prison hospital. One night when George was caring for a patient who needed an emergency appendectomy, an ice storm struck. The hospital's doctor was delayed by the storm, and all the electricity was cut off. George saved the man's life by performing the appendectomy. For this act he received a complete pardon from the governor for "returning a life for a life."

Despite his clean prison record and courageous act of mercy, George was still an ex-con, and he could find no work when he got out of prison. After six months of disappointing searching, he went to Canada and volunteered for the most unpopular job in the RCAF, tail gunner on a bomber. Even though he was way over the age limit for an air crew job, he was commissioned a pilot officer.

After many raids over France and Germany his plane was shot down. George bailed out in an ill-fitting parachute harness, and he crushed a number of ribs in the jump.

At Stalag Luft III, there were only three men who knew of his story. Two of them lived in my block. Charlie Barnwell from Atlanta had known the Harsh family well. (Charlie was memorable because he always wore heavy wooden Dutch shoes the Germans had issued at an earlier camp. He even played excellent softball in them.) Harold Whiteman, our first-aid man who wanted to be a doctor, also from Atlanta, knew Harsh's story because it had been in the local papers for several months. Among the Canadians Wally Floody, his confidant, had heard about George's past from Harsh himself.

In all their time at camp not one of these three men breathed a word about Harsh's past. Years later, after I had read the book, I met with the two Atlantans who had known George Harsh's story. By then Harold Whiteman was a leading heart surgeon in Atlanta and Dr. Charles Barnwell was Atlanta's foremost dentist, retained by the Atlanta Falcons football team. When I asked the two men why they had kept silent, they said they both considered that George had paid his debt to society and was repaying many times over with his service in the RCAF and in Stalag Luft III.

During the day most of the kriegies kept up the normal routine of the camp with a variety of permitted activities such as sewing, cooking, washing, taking classes and walking around the circuit. Some of the activities, such as metalwork and chorus practice, had the additional effect of hiding escape efforts.

The underground workers came and went in regular shifts like worker bees in a hive. When they went underground, diggers stripped down to their long johns so their outer clothing wouldn't carry telltale traces of sand. The shaft went straight down for thirty feet, then enlarged into a room for tool storage. All the sand from the face of the tunnel was sent back to the underground room, where it was loaded into bags and then carried to the surface for distribution around the compound.

The man in charge of clearing out the sand and bringing it to the surface was Peter Fanshawe, the Royal Navy man whom we called Hornblower. Once the sand reached the surface, it was my job to distribute it around the compound in strategic locations where the Germans wouldn't find it.

As Wally Floody was digging the shaft for the first tunnel, Tom, he discovered that the dark topsoil soon gave way to a light-colored sand, yellow or golden when wet, but flat, dead white after it had dried out. In the compound that white sand would have stood out like a beacon against the dark topsoil. So every grain of tunnel sand had to be hidden, buried, or mixed with other soil to change its color.

The men in my dispersal crew were called penguins, which referred to the way they walked when they were carrying sand. Each penguin had a cloth strap around his neck, with a bag of sand attached to each end of the strap. The sandbags hung down inside the man's trousers, and each bag had a nail that could be removed when the penguin wanted to release sand through his pants legs. The penguin's pockets had been removed so he could reach into the pocket aperture and pull the pin when he was ready.

In the northern part of North Camp, near the vorlager, were some trees that had not yet been cut down. In this area our activities were screened somewhat from the eyes of the guards. We could distribute the sand almost under the noses of the guards as long as we diverted their attention with some kind of legitimate activity.

My classes in silent killing provided a perfect opportunity for the penguins to go to work. In my class I had about twenty students who came for practice and many more who stood around watching. First I would demonstrate the techniques of the day's session on my assistant, Hank Burman. As Dan Fairbairn did with me, I picked the biggest man I could find to attack me so that my smaller students would realize they too could handle a larger opponent.

Indestructible Hank, a football lineman in college, could lift a three hundred thirty-pound cake of ice in each hand and walk with the load; he was big enough to make the point. He'd attack me and I'd throw him. He'd grin, dust himself off, and come back for more. He learned fast and could do the same things to me. After our demonstrations we would pair off the students and start them practicing the holds, blows and throws.

As my students worked out, penguins wandered up to the crowd to watch. A penguin would casually adjust his trousers, then reach into his pocket and pull the pin. Sand slipped out his pants legs, and the spectators who sat or knelt nearby unobtrusively worked the odd-colored sand into the soil.

Many of the combatants also had tunnel sand in their pockets. They would pull the pins as they paired off. As they were attacking or defending themselves, bits of sand went flying through the air.

This dispersal method accompanied other sports as well. In one class men were taught how to put the shot or throw a homemade discus. The shot-putter would pull his sand pins before he whirled around the starting circle. With each stride sand dropped out of his pants legs.

Somebody else would run out with a string to measure after each throw. As the guards became interested in the sport, they watched the man measuring the distance and forgot about the spectators who moved around the starting circle, working the sand into the soil.

For a while, we put sand into the outside latrines, what the Germans called *Aborts*, but we soon put an end to that. We were clogging up a very necessary part of the camp.

In addition to the penguins I was responsible for diversionists, kriegies who could stop any of the ferrets who might unexpectedly appear in a dispersal area. If a ferret suddenly appeared, the diversionists would break into a fight or "accidentally" bump into a guard. All sorts of diversions were rehearsed so that a ferret could be distracted for a few minutes while the kriegies put their activities under cover.

In disposing of sand we surveyed the camp very carefully to find dead spots, the areas alongside the barracks where we could not be seen from the German guard boxes. Near the middle of the blocks were dead spots where we planned our gardens for burying sand.

Very early in the spring we talked the Germans into giving us some cabbage and tomato seeds. The gardening was done by my dispersal crew. Our plants were usually scrawny, but they served the purpose. To all appearances we were serious about our vegetable patches.

We alerted Hornblower Fanshawe to be ready for a "blitz job," a lot of sand in a hurry. He passed the word along to Floody, and the diggers shoved loads of sand up to the tunnel's storage area. With security stooges and diversion squads on alert throughout the vicinity, my crews in the dead-spot gardens dug up all the plants, placed them on a blanket, then removed the topsoil to a second blanket nearby.

When we were down about eight or nine inches, we gave a signal to Fanshawe inside the barracks and he started sending out loads in Red Cross boxes. (It was usual for the Germans to see us carrying Red Cross boxes containing food or odd belongings, so nothing appeared out of the ordinary to them.) Meanwhile, penguins came by and dropped their loads. As the sand was dumped, we stomped it down until we had packed about four inches in a uniform layer around the garden.

A short time before appell we closed the garden by reversing the process. We put the dark topsoil back on top of the sand and planted the little cabbages and tomatoes just where they had been before. We knew the garden was noticeably higher than it had been previously, so I used an old OSS fade-out principle. Men gathered rocks from around the camp and lined them up carefully around the newly raised garden. With the rocks in place a casual passerby would not notice any difference in level between the garden and the surrounding soil.

Occasionally a German guard would come by and say, "*Was gibt hier?*" meaning, "What's going on here?"

"Nothing," I'd say. "We're just beautifying the Third Reich!"

He would reply with something like, "Oh, baloney."

Then I'd use another old gimmick. As everyone knows, the best way to get rid of someone is to ask him to lend you five dollars. So I would say in German, "Please bring some white paint so I can paint the rocks and make them prettier."

"Ah, you're nuts!" he'd say. With that, he would walk away and leave me alone.

Chapter 12

To prepare for "The Great Escape," we not only had to build the tunnels, but also needed to manufacture clothing, forge papers, and ready the supplies necessary to flee Germany. For these preparations we set up factories where kriegies manufactured hundreds of items.

In North Compound initially all the factories were headed by experienced British and Allied artisans who had come in from other camps. When the Americans came into the camps, they added their own wealth of talent, ingenuity and hard work.

Tommy Guest, a Britisher, ran the tailoring shop where RAF uniforms and German blankets were converted into German uniforms, suits, jackets, overcoats and overalls. For dyes he used shoe polish, beets, red cabbage, tea, boiled bark, boiled book covers and any other materials that left a permanent color stain on cloth. Guest's tailors were so skillful that they could even change the texture of a fabric. For example, the fuzzy regulation RAF cloth could be transformed into a herringbone tweed simply by crisscrossing the material with a razor.

Johnny Travis, a South African in the RAF, was in charge of the metal and woodworking shop. As well as making tools for the shop, he also had to create elaborate hiding places where the tools would be hidden from the Germans. In some areas of the barracks he created false walls with items hung in between the inner and outer layers of paneling. Other secret compartments were located in the walls, under tabletops and in lockers.

The wood- and metalworkers were responsible for all the materials we used in the tunnels, including tunnel supports, carts for hauling sand and digging tools. In addition, they had to fabricate the tools we needed to make *other* tools. Using any kind of scrap metal that came to hand, they would make wood chisels, cold chisels, screwdrivers, wire cutters and saws. With drawknives and improvised planes they could shave down lumber to the sizes we needed.

In one factory a number of kriegies manufactured an air bellows for the tunnel. The bellows, shaped like a huge accordion, pumped air to the men working at the face of the tunnel. In developing the bellows Johnny Marshall worked with Travis and was helped by a Scot named McIntosh and a Norwegian, Jens Muller. (Muller was one of only three men who made it all the way home in "The Great Escape.")

In the factories numerous items were manufactured from Klim cans, including all kinds of tools, utensils and pans. To create lamps for tunnel workers, we filled small Klim cans with oleo or fat and used pajama cords for wicks.

We even succeeded in making compasses. Al Hake, an Australian, and a B-17 pilot named John Bennett were both wizards in the compass factory. Each casing was made from one of our old, sturdy phonograph records. The record was heated until it was malleable, then cut and shaped to make a casing.

A phonograph needle, sent to us in a YMCA

package, was used to hold the pointer of the compass. Hake or Bennett would implant the needle in the center of the casing, then polarize a narrow strip of razor blade by stroking it interminably in one direction with a magnet. The magnet came from a game that had been supplied by the YMCA or Red Cross. He made a tiny hole in the strip of razor and inserted the phonograph needle through the hole. Polarized by the magnet, the thin strip of razor blade always pointed due North.

If we had some phosphorescent paint, we added the final touch by painting the razor-blade needle so we could see it at night. Then we covered the casing with glass, which protected the compass and held the razor in place on the needle.

My compass was made from a hit record that Dinah Shore made at the age of fifteen or so: "The Mad About Him, Sad About Him, How Can I Be Glad Without Him Blues." Out of respect for the singer I called it my "Dinah Shore," and kept it with me at all times. In later escapes, it proved to be a true and invaluable guide.

Both the British and American craftsmen were great at reproducing any small items of German metalware they could get their hands on, such as uniform buttons, belt buckles with Nazi insignia and the metal chevrons of rank. If a guard got careless with his hat or coat in hot weather or while having a drink with the goon tamers, the item would be filched just long enough to be pushed into a pan of wet, dense sand or a soft bar of soap kept handy for molds. Then it would be wiped off and returned without the guard ever knowing the difference. The replica was poured from a small hot skillet of melted metal. The British usually melted down the "silver" paper that lined their packs of cigarettes. We Americans preferred the heavier metal, almost a lead foil, that good old-fashioned toothpaste tubes were made of. I think of those useful old tubes every now and then when I squeeze the stiff plastic tubes of today, absolutely worthless when the paste is gone.

The forgers who prepared documentation relied on either the scroungers or the goon tamers to obtain authentic German documents as well as papers, pens and ink. Their methods for obtaining these items included theft, bribery and blackmail. With painstaking care forgers duplicated the originals to create ration cards, passes, identity cards and personal letters. They even made up business letters on authentic-looking stationery, offering the bearer a job near a friendly port or near a border. With pen and ink they could create documents that looked typewritten, even duplicating typewritten strike-overs to make the documents look more realistic.

The Germans duplicated some of their less important papers on a printer very similar to a mimeograph machine. To replicate these documents the forgers jury-rigged an elaborate printer. They mixed up gelatin from the Red Cross parcels in a long, flat pan made of Klim tins, then let the gelatin set until it was firm. After printing on paper with an indelible pencil, they pressed the document down on top of the gelatin. When the original was removed, a second, clean paper was pressed down over the gelatin. The copy that emerged precisely resembled the mimeographed papers produced by the Germans.

Led by Tim Walenn, a Britisher with a huge wavy moustache, the forgers on the staff consisted of all those fliers who showed artistic talent. The Belgian Henri Picard was an expert artist who found time between forgeries to draw caricatures of many of the kriegies, showing each with a realistic face and miniaturized body.

The British forgers included the fine artist Ley Kenyon and Dickie Milne, a nephew of A.A. Milne, the author of the Winnie the Pooh books. Des Plunkett, an excellent map maker, was the forger who copied original maps for each of us to follow. Among the American forgers were Don Stine, Jim Billig and Emmett Cook, all men with outstanding artistic talent.

The men in the forgery factory were always prepared to close down their operation at a moment's notice. Within seconds of an alarm being signaled they could conceal every document in the shop. By the time a German guard appeared, the forgers would look as if they were holding a class in landscape sketching, birdcalls or an equally innocent subject. Many items were hidden in cut-out books, where the centers of the pages had been surgically carved to leave space for a compass, a tool or folded document.

In addition to preparing documents and materials for our escape, we also had to consider how we would behave when we got out. Wally Valenta, a Czech who had been engaged in intelligence work in the Czechoslovakian Air Force before the war, was a good linguist and teacher. He helped us all to devise cover stories and briefed us on the geography that lay between our camp and the border of Czechoslovakia. From Wally I learned to speak some Czech and a bit of Magyar, the Hungarian tongue. Since the Germans never bothered to learn Magyar, that language was especially useful to an escapee. If you spoke to a German in Magyar, he would just shrug and walk away.

The diggers, those who worked down in the tunnels, were experts for whom I had the utmost admiration.

Nonetheless, I did not envy them their job. Not only do I take up a lot of room, I also suffer from a touch of claustrophobia. Leaving the underground work to the experts, I contented myself with the above-ground assignment of hiding the sand.

Only a few diggers could work at one time, and none of them could stay underground for too long because of the shortage of air. Cave-ins were an ever-present danger. The tunnels were shored up with frames made from bedboards, but boards would be knocked out of place or collapse from the weight of sand, and many diggers were buried without warning.

Another nuisance was the quality of air in the tunnels. With only fat lamps or candles to light their way, the diggers persisted at their work even when there was hardly enough oxygen to feed the flames. As the tunnels grew longer, we supplied air to the diggers by using the camp-made bellows, but even that ventilating system was only partially successful. By the time the diggers came up for rest, most of them had splitting headaches.

Wally Floody, our chief tunnel engineer, kept a master list of diggers and used them in shifts. They were from many backgrounds and of all shapes and sizes. Wally considered some of the smaller fellows more efficient underground because they were more maneuverable in the confined spaces and caused fewer cave-ins. These included Danny Krol, a small, dapper, well-muscled Polish swordsman, and a New Zealander named Piglet Lamond who could cut through the ground as fast as a mole. There was also a shaggy Welshman, Shag Rees; a clean-cut young cattleman and meat packer from Arizona, Ed Tovrea; and a delightful Canadian, Scruffy Wier, who had been badly burned on the upper parts of his face when he was shot down.

Among the larger diggers were black-haired, black-jowled Henry Birkland and red-haired Red Noble, both from Canada. Another American digger, Buck Ingram, was a strong, square-shouldered, square-jawed man and a good friend of Davy Jones and Ed Tovrea.

From Norway there was a man who would have won the Mr. America contest. Blond Jan Staubo had the build and features of a classic Greek athlete. Even stronger was Jean Regis, a husky Frenchman in the RAF who kept in shape by lifting weights. He was an expert in pumping the air bellows, able to continue almost all day without a break.

Davy Jones and Wally Floody were about my size, but Wally was thinner than Davy and I, since he had been in prison camp longer and on shorter rations. Tom Kirby-Green was even bigger. He had coal black hair and black eyes, and he could beat bongo drums and speak Spanish like a native.

Most of these men had been trapped more than once in a sandfall. A careless move by the digger might displace a board or two, or some unknown factor in the sand itself might cause it to shift and cave in, trapping the digger. The others would scramble to get him out. We didn't lose any diggers, but we came close several times.

Davy Jones, the digger and Tokyo Raider, was a particular friend of mine. He had a lot of faith and a fine, dry sense of humor. Whenever a tunnel collapsed, his usual comment was "Oh, fine!" with a sardonic twist and overemphasis on the "fine!"

One day Davy himself was caught in a bad tunnel fall and had to be dug out of a few tons of sand. After he had been revived and was breathing again, he shook the sand out of his beard and spoke a line that became immortalized around camp: "The Good Book says the meek shall inherit the earth, and I just got my share!"

The scroungers and goon tamers were remarkably adept at dealing with the guards. From his conversations with the Germans, the Czech flier Wally Valenta pieced together considerable information about the local area—its roads, trains, hazards—and about the papers that we would need in order to travel. Brom Van der Stok from the Netherlands provided further information about routes across Europe and assisted in escape preparations. Bill Webster, a dapper American educated in England and an early volunteer in the RAF, was very smooth at gaining the confidence of Germans and, by one means or another, extracting needed items from them. Dick Schrupp from Young America, Minnesota, also became very adept in his dealings with the guards.

Some of the items that our scroungers obtained were fairly elaborate. We needed camera parts, tubes for the camp radio and detailed parts to perfect a tool or finish a piece of equipment.

The scroungers developed similar tried-and-true techniques to obtain the confidence of the guards and force them to cooperate. Our contact man would first offer the German guard a friendly cup of tea or coffee, a bar of chocolate, or some British or U.S. cigarettes. If the guard became genuinely friendly with the kriegie, he might be willing to provide small, necessary items out of gratitude. If he was hesitant to cooperate after receiving our gifts, we could always raise the specter of blackmail, threatening to expose him to his superiors for trading with the enemy. Such a charge was a serious offense, and the guards knew that if they were discovered, they might be sentenced to prison or death—or sent away to fight the Russians on the eastern front.

We used many kinds of diversionary tactics to screen the sounds of hammering and tunnel work around the barracks. Some musicians managed to obtain instruments from home or from the YMCA, and they augmented our tin-bashers and kriegie choruses. Tom Kirby-Green frequently had the crowd stamping its feet in time to the rhythms of his bongo drums. Tex Newton and Dusty Runner played wicked trumpets. Dusty could also play a very loud boogie base on the piano, while John Bennett from Colorado played the guitar. Duke Diamond, who had played with big bands in Hollywood before the war, could make a saxophone or clarinet laugh or cry.

A gentle lad named Lee Forsblad played Mozart (and practically everything else) on an accordion. Handlebar Hank Bryant, a musical enthusiast with a tremendous black moustache, bestowed the title "Fearless Forsblad" on Lee. When Forsblad started to play, Bryant pulled at his moustache, stomped his feet and yelled, "Go get 'em, Fearless!" In reply Fearless responded with a kind of quiet smile and played "Ochi Chornia" ("Dark Eyes") and many other accordion classics.

When we wanted to distract the attention of a ferret or strolling guard, we could turn on all sorts of "impromptu" entertainment. Slim, agile Bill Geiger and dapper Danny Krol could stage a duel at the drop of a hat. Choosing a designated spot for their fencing, they would hack away with épées delivered by the YMCA or wield their homemade swords as though murder were in their hearts.

In our midst there were also fighters who could turn hand-to-hand combat into a major distraction. Among our better boxers we numbered Heston Daniel, a former

Golden Gloves champion from Louisiana State, and a tough, agile middleweight, Jerry Ahern of Texas. When they put on their gloves and staged a lesson or fought it out in a slugging match, they quickly earned the guards' undivided attention.

We also staged many other types of fights, including wrestling, street brawls and unarmed combat. If necessary, we would steal the crutches from a crippled man who had volunteered to play the part. Suspenseful contests in any kind of sport drew the guards' attention. The fighting, brawling and noisemaking not only diverted the Germans from their jobs, but also provided entertainment for our fellow kriegies.

The tunnel preparations brought many of the men closer together and in some cases led to moments of hilarity. In an effort to shore up the walls of the tunnels we had to use every available bedboard—sometimes without a kriegie's permission. A kriegie might return to the barracks nearly exhausted after doing several rounds of the perimeter, wanting nothing more than to climb into his bunk bed and fall asleep. He would leap into the upper bunk and a moment later come crashing clear through the upper and lower bunks to the floor. That was his first indication that his bedboards had been confiscated that day by the scroungers.

While tunnel preparations were under way, my good friend Davy Jones and I would often play chess together. We set up the chessboard on a little stool outside the barracks window. Anytime we passed the stool, he or I would make a move. Davy might move a man in the morning, and after several hours—or a day or two—I would respond by moving one of my pieces. As I recall, one game lasted several months.

Each man, it seemed, had his own diversions. Perhaps the most incongruous for a prison camp was that of Jan Staubo, the digger. One day as I was passing a building, I saw Jan with a tennis racket in his hand, hitting the ball against the side of the building, pounding shots off the wall with expert forehand and backhand strokes. The sight was so familiar, and so out of place, that I stopped dead in my tracks and just stared at him. He continued to play, oblivious to the dreary surroundings of Stalag Luft III. But that brief tennis scene with Jan Staubo was a welcome reminder of ordinary life back home.

Chapter 13

There was no way that everyone could keep his spirits up all the time in the prison camp. For some it could be very humdrum, one empty day right after the other. Only so much cooking with so little food, only so many clothes to wash in cold water—clothes that had to be sewed up with yarn that we made out of salvaged socks.

From time to time there were very depressing incidents, such as prisoners receiving "Dear John" letters from home—telling that the girlfriend or wife had decided the man was too long behind barbed wire so she had tied up with someone else. The classic example was so good that the fellow permitted it to be posted on the bulletin board. It was a letter from his fiancée: "Darling, you have been gone so long that I've married your father. Love, Mother." When such sad things happened to fellows in my barracks, we all readily extended our sympathy and warmth. But when a kriegie stayed depressed, I found it useful to send him over to help cheer someone else who was in even worse shape. It always seemed that by helping some other prisoner get out of the doldrums, a man could straighten out his own attitude and have a little more faith and courage and cheerfulness to move on to the next day.

I kept very busy, as many of the other escapers did. But we couldn't escape all the time, so we helped provide the many entertainments throughout the camp. We put seats in the theater, and there were plenty of hams (good hams) who would try out for the plays. We had everything from the lightest of comedies and slapstick to Shakespearean drama. Many kept busy working on the seats, sets, scenery, and costumes. We had to resist the temptation to use the theater for escape activities so that it wouldn't be closed down. We were careful to play straight with the Germans in not using any items paroled to the theater for escape purposes. But it was true that anything we could steal that was not tied in to the theater we certainly would try to get away with.

We also had plenty of entertainment outside the theater, such as sing-alongs in the evening. Many of the Britishers loved to sing, and they would teach us such songs as "I've Got Sixpence, Jolly, Jolly Sixpence." And we'd teach them, "I've Been Working on the Railroad," and all kinds of college songs.

We got together an American chorus and a British chorus, and eventually a mixed American-British chorus. We'd usually have our sing-alongs around the fire pool. At first we had them among the pine trees of North Camp, but the Germans came in and cut down all the pine trees around our barracks to make it harder for us to mask our escape activities. Lieutenant Colonel Bob "Moose" Stillman and I decided to serenade the tree-choppers—a bit of nonsense to ease the frustration and brighten up the day. We climbed up on a big garbage container and started lustily singing, "Oh, they cut down the old pine tree/And they hauled it away to the mill/To build a coffin of pine for that old sweetheart of mine/They cut down the old pine tree." The Germans stopped cutting and watched and listened. They really had no idea what we were singing. Some smiled when we began to laugh a little. Others got irritated, believing (most rightly) that we were making fun of them. A couple shook their fists at us—to which we responded with appropriate words and gestures. We were lucky we didn't wind up in the cooler.

Moose Stillman, a B-26 pilot, was another walking miracle. The B-26 bomber has an antenna that runs straight up into the air above the airplane. When Moose was shot down, the antenna was the first thing to plow into the country road as the plane crashed upside down with Moose still in it. He was in a German hospital quite a while, but he must have been in fine shape from football at West Point; he walked into camp with only a scar on his forehead and a fine story to tell.

Once after the war Moose and I were having a drink at the officers' club on an air base in upstate New York. Some lieutenant pilots were bragging about their flying stunts, such as picking up a handkerchief with a wing tip on Daytona Beach, or zooming under the Golden Gate Bridge. Moose quietly interrupted with, "Did any of you gentlemen ever draw a line down a dirt road with the radio antenna of a B-26?"

The youngsters gasped, then took their drinks elsewhere—all except one. He came back to Colonel Stillman, looked him in the eye and asked, "Did you crack up, sir?"

Moose exploded, "I sure did, son!" And he bought drinks for all in honor of the lad's perception.

One of the evening skits that became famous involved a band of old villains tying Little Nell to the railroad tracks, to be saved just in the nick of time by Jack Armstrong.

"Who are you?" someone would yell.

''Jack Armstrong of the Royal U.S. Marines,'' came back the proud reply.

That got everybody into the act. Both the British and Americans loved the nonsense. When ''Nell'' was tied to the tracks, some would yell, ''Who'll save her?'' Others would shout, ''I'll save her!'' The first group roared back, ''Who are you?'' Then everyone sang out, ''Jack Armstrong of the Royal U.S. Marines!'' And everyone broke into cheers and laughter. The routine nearly always was a crowd warmer-upper, good for our funny bones and relaxing the tensions.

We would also have impromptu recitations, particularly with the British. They were quite hospitable about inviting us in for tea. Not the artificial herb or grass tea of the Germans. Real tea from India would come in their parcels. Afternoon tea seemed to have a civilizing effect on them. They might have been savagely playing rugby or soccer only a few minutes before, but tea was a refined gathering where we'd sit around and talk and perhaps recite poetry. The Britishers loved Kipling and Sir Walter Scott as much as I did, and sometimes we would take turns quoting ''If'' and ''The Ballad of East and West.''

One afternoon with Wings Day, I started reciting Lewis Carroll's ''Jabberwocky'' from *Through the Looking Glass*, and so help me, Wings jumped right in. We declaimed together with great arm-waving histrionics, and had a ball. Over twenty-five years later in London we repeated the act with a bit of nostalgia at a fine reunion of ''Great Escape'' survivors at the RAF club.

On rare occasions the Germans would bring in films. I recall only non-controversial ones, musicals in which the main star was Marika Rökk. I think she was a Hungarian, but to the guards she was the German Ginger Rogers—and she was a good singer and dancer. I learned all of one of her hit songs from a movie made in the Depression—"Ich habe keine Millionen." In English the song goes, "I have no millions. I have no good-luck pennies. I have just your love, and music, music, music!" Her movies were light romance and comedy with good singing and dancing, and the pretty revue spectacles modeled after Hollywood musicals. In camp they were a welcome diversion.

We had oratory contests and some great debates. The two principals in this activity were very dear friends of mine. One was Robert M. "Bob" Brown of Spokane, Washington, my home town. We had played football as rivals for high schools on the opposite sides of town and then both played for Washington State. He was a very fine center who went to law school at the University of Washington, then became a B-25 pilot when we went to war. He also had a flair for quoting poetry. We took turns reciting Robert W. Service, "The Shooting of Dan McGrew" and "The Cremation of Sam McGee" from *The Spell of the Yukon*.

The other fine friend was a Scotsman named Murdo MacDonald. I met him on the way out of Dulag Luft and liked him instantly. He was a paratrooper who had been a minister in his village, so we called him chaplain or Padre MacDonald. Even before I knew what a great human being he was, I admired him because of something he did in my own line of business. He and a doctor were captured on their airborne attack near Tunis and flown together out of North Africa as POWs in a German JU-52, as I had been. The doctor had his arm in a sling. They hid an incendiary time-pencil in the sling, somewhat similar to ours in the OSS. It was the type you squeeze to start delayed action and at a certain time later it would ignite. As the prisoners were being unloaded from the airplane at the German airport in Naples, they pressed the time-pencil incendiary and dropped it unobtrusively into some stuff at the back end of the plane. As they were driven away from the airport the plane went up in flames.

More important, Padre MacDonald radiated goodness in an unassuming and manly way. He was a Cameronian Highlander and had some association with the Isle of Skye. I once heard that he worked in a parish of Portroy. He had a lovely Scottish brogue. I liked to start quoting a poem by Bobby Burns just to get him into the act. It was as though Burns himself was speaking. Every time I'd talk with him in the morning I'd think of the delicious oatmeal porridge I'd had up in Scotland, and which occasionally would come in one of the English parcels. It was called Midlothian oats, perhaps because it came from the midlands of Scotland, and was a mighty welcome import in our prison.

When Padre MacDonald had church services and was giving a sermon, as many as could jammed into the theater and more stood outside to listen. He was a straightforward speaker, a man's man, with true love for mankind. He did wonders in this camp where one could find no more atheists than one could in a foxhole, being shot at in an airplane, or working behind the lines on a raid. When we Americans were moved from North Camp to the separate U.S. South Camp, Padre MacDonald had such an American following that we took him with us. On Sundays when appell broke up, a thousand kriegies dashed for the theater to get a seat for the Padre's church service.

While I don't recall any heavy attendance at debates during my school days, when Padre MacDonald and Bob Brown held one of their weekend debates, nearly the whole camp turned out. Their subjects ranged from the pros and cons of capital punishment to any subject thrown out by the kriegie audience. Each had a fine education, excellent command of the English language, good-natured humor, and a glib tongue. Padre MacDonald, our philosophy teacher in camp, and Bob Brown, a lawyer, matched wits beautifully. Padre MacDonald was not a large man, but he had a wealth of courage. He looked a little as I imagine Friar Tuck of Robin Hood days—lacking only the robe tied with a rope to make the likeness complete. Bob Brown looked a bit like him—another square man but bigger. In general, both had the same twinkling blue eyes, round face and big smile. They made a great team. I was happy to have Bob as my roommate in the little end room of the barracks I commanded.

Laughter and singing were great antidotes for the blues. The British taught us several rollicking Anglo-Saxon songs, some of which are unprintable. They also took to some of our American songs, which some of us sang in a medley—a sort of poor man's Fred Waring performance. It included the "Whiffenpoof Song," and often as everyone joined in on the chorus with "We're poor little lambs who've gone astray, baa, baa, baa!" someone would always boom out, "Amen, brother, we're sure lost and astray!" We also included the Notre Dame and USC fight songs, Cornell's "Cayuga's Waters," "On Wisconsin," the Maine "Stein Song," "Minnesota, Hats Off to Thee" for Dick Schrupp, and "Fight, Fight, Fight for Washington State" for Bob Brown and myself, among others.

In times when I wasn't dispersing sand from the tunnels, I tried to learn from Dusty Runner to play the piano. He taught me two or three great left-hand boogie sequences, including a rolling bass and a rocking bass. He also taught me one fine tinkling right-hand boogie melody. The only problem was that I couldn't manage both right and left hand at the same time. I thus became strictly a duet man. When I think about it, I never was very skillful at patting my head with one hand and rubbing my stomach in circles with the other.

The honey-wagon man came by the theater door one day while Dusty and I were seated at the piano. The aroma that wafted in nearly knocked us off the bench. The honey wagon was a horse-drawn tank with hoses and a pump to empty the pits of our large outdoor aborts. The driver was a skinny, lugubrious soul with a great drooping moustache, a big handkerchief protruding from one torn hip pocket and a sandwich sticking out of the other. It did our digestion no good to see him bite into that sandwich in the midst of pumping his cargo.

I'm not sure which of us started it, but Dusty and I looked at each other and began singing, "I've got the honey-wagon blues." I furnished most of the lyrics and Dusty put it to sort of a clop-clop blues beat on the piano and it came out like this: "I've got the honey-wagon blues. I'm blue as I can be. I've got the honey-wagon blues. They give me misery." Memory fails me here, but the song ended, "To the beat of the horses' feet, I've got the honey-wagon blues." I don't think it will ever sell, but it certainly pleased us.

It rains a lot in Germany, but when it wasn't raining too hard, a group of us would go out on the sports field. The North Camp's southern half was a large, rough field with plenty of space. Twice a day, during appells, each block was lined up by its block commander in five ranks for the kommandant's lager officer to count us. But we kriegies valued the sports field for more violent exercise than merely walking around the perimeter path. We were there to let off steam, relieve the boredom and anxiety, and to just plain have fun. Although little equipment had yet arrived from the United States, the Canadians had bats and balls, and with the Americans, really initiated the British into the fine art of softball.

At first thinking softball a rather poor corruption of cricket, the British eventually joined the game with enthusiasm. The British played two types of football, neither of which was the American game by that name. As we then had no U.S. footballs, the slim oval type we were used to, we started playing the British games. The one with the round ball in which no hands were permitted, only kicking or "heading" the ball, was known in America by the name of soccer, short for Association Football, the formal British name for it. It was simply called football by the British and the Allied Continentals—the Poles, Czechs, French, Dutch and Belgians in the RAF. All of them seemed to have been weaned on soccer. They could do things with that soccer ball that we couldn't, and the Allied team soundly drubbed the all-American team.

The British then got the Americans started on rugby football, played with an oblong ball that was bigger and fatter than an American football. Their game was quite different. There were no forward passes, only laterals and ball carries. Running the ball over the opponents' line, a touchdown, counted only three points, but drop-kicking a field goal was worth four points.

The British had some great kickers. I saw one of their backs running the ball across the field on the forty-yard line when he saw he was about to be tackled. With no perceptible pause in this stride he dropped the ball, and as it touched the ground, he booted it right between the goal posts for four points.

After we got a little more used to it, we Americans finally challenged the British to a game in which we assembled all the former football players we could find. We had plenty of big men like Hank Burman and Bob Hermann for linemen, who all got together in the scrum, a great, tight huddle. Everybody put shoulders together, locked arms, and pushed and kicked the ball backward with their heels to a pickup man who threw it out to the halfbacks and on to the wings.

We also had quite a few experienced backs. The British scored mainly on their fine kicking game, and we lost the ball occasionally on penalties. Blocking and stiff-arming, which we were used to, were illegal in their game. But we gained an edge on our more vicious tackling, causing turnovers. We'd knock them down and they'd often fumble, and we'd get the ball and lateral to our hard running backs.

Big Bob Menning from Iowa, a fullback type, ran like a bull, as did Ajax Adamina of California. Russell "Shorty" Kahl of Mississippi was as fast and elusive as a frightened buck deer. Don Stine or I often started a run, and as we were tackled fed laterals out to the wing position. The wing frequently made it all the way to the goal line with excellent broken-field running. Though the touchdowns scored only three points, we made enough to edge out the fine kicking game of our opponents.

As more equipment came in, softball leagues grew. Hank Burman, my buddy who had spun in from seventeen thousand feet with his B-17, was our block's home-run king. A compact, red-haired California lad named Sheriff Lynch came into camp and really slowed down the hitters. He was the fastest windmill pitcher I'd ever seen. I was a right-handed batter who tried to pull to left field. The only hit I got off Lynch was a fluke to short right field off the end of my always too slow bat.

We also had track and field meets of sorts, using

whatever we could scrounge for the shot-put or discus or hammer throw. We dug a pit for high jumps and put in sawdust. We tried to get a good vaulting pole from the Germans, but Glemnitz stopped that on the spot. "Ach, no." He wagged his finger at me. "That's too great a temptation for a try over the barbed wire and more cooler, Major Sage."

My good friend Dick Klocko, a well-built athlete and fighter pilot, might have used the pole to good advantage. He had led the pole vaulters at West Point in the mid-1930s.

Another former track man, a sprinter, was still one more of our walking miracles. Lieutenant Colonel Mel McNickle had been shot down from around fifteen thousand feet in a P-47 fighter and his plane plowed about twenty feet deep into a field. When the Germans dug out the plane they found McNickle still in the cockpit and still breathing. Although he suffered some cuts and broken bones, he came into Stalag Luft III with a scar or two but as chipper and almost as fast as ever.

Despite its great majority of British and other European Allies, the most memorable day of 1943 in North Compound of Stalag Luft III was the American Fourth of July. On a warm day in June Dick Schrupp and Willy Wigger were looking at our mess room's makeshift calendar and Willy announced, "The fourth of June, it's only a month till the Fourth of July!" Eyes lit up as light bulbs flashed simultaneously in our dulled brains and a chorus of voices sounded, "Let's lay down a brew!" Laying down a brew was the kriegie way of following the tradition of all civilizations—Chinese, Egyptian, Greek, Roman, ad infinitum—of fermenting a beverage to add luster to a humdrum existence. We learned the basic art from our RAF colleagues in Stalag

Luft III, as we had learned so many things about life in a German prison camp.

When we Americans arrived, many of the British were quite hospitable. A British mess would invite in a newcomer for afternoon tea with a cracker or two and, if the timing was right, for a small cup of kriegie brew. The first sip was the hardest, but after that it grew on you.

Basically it was a raisin wine, though we seldom glorified it by that name—we just called it kriegie brew. A mess would save up sugar and raisins or even dried prunes, apricots, or any type of fruit we could get hold of—but preferably raisins. We would hoard or trade for it from the parcels, or scrounge it wherever we could and then use any type of available container. A luxury container was a clean barrel. A keg for German mustard could be scrupulously scalded out, and if we could get rid of the mustard taste, we could lay down our brew in that. We'd take about a half barrel of water, throw in all our raisins and sugar, and then go around the camp calling, "Who's got a live raisin?" It's a funny thing, of all the times and all the different brews I was involved with, I never saw anyone start from scratch with any type of yeast. It was always a live raisin—one bubbling with fermentation. I would go around camp with my "begging spoon." I'd ask, "Who's got a live raisin?" Somebody would say, "Oh, Willy Jones has, over here," or maybe "Al Hake over there," or ffrench-Mullen was a good source.

In fact, ffrench-Mullen, an Irish flyer in the RAF, was sort of a brewmaster. You could always count on him for a live raisin.

We Americans could also always count on him to run bases for us on holidays when we were having a softball game. Someone would get a hit, then put him on first base to run. He always wore a pair of shorts and nearly always had been dipping into his brew. He'd go sliding into all the bases and he'd come off the field bleeding and scratched from his ankles to his thighs from sliding—and laughing like Ty Cobb setting his record.

So we got a live raisin from a brew that ffrench-Mullen was already fermenting and went to work. In the early days in the camp there was a brew down somewhere in the camp at all times. We figured that in cold weather it took about six weeks for it to "come off," or complete the fermentation cycle; it took only ten days in the summer.

We didn't have a barrel. I remember some of our brews were made in a big glass light bulb cover about fifteen inches across. Most of these bowls in the camp had been broken or stolen, but we kept ours screwed tight into the ceiling for safety until we needed it for a brew. We'd also use any kind of big crockery, such as a pickle jar.

As soon as we started to get things together in our mess, I wandered over to adjacent blocks to see my good friends Dick Klocko and Davy Jones, and the other American block leaders. So help me, some of them already had the same idea themselves, so we all soon had working brews getting ready for the Fourth of July. Some we started early enough so that we could try to distill it. I don't know the proper name for the product. We glamorized it by calling it brandy, but all the same what came out actually was some kind of alcohol. For that we had to have a real still.

Now there were many kinds of stills, from refined to completely jury-rigged. Al Hake, one of the metalworkers and a compass-maker as well, was very good at fashioning condensation tubes for the still. These were often made, as was so much else, from powdered-milk cans. Hake and his lads would cut a Klim tin into strips that they rolled around pencils to make the piping. We'd augment these with any copper tubing we could steal as well as trombone slides from our band. Then we'd get this devil's brew a-bubbling on the stove in the kitchen late at night with the shutters closed and blankets hung to shield out peeping German eyes. We distilled quite a bit of it. Adding the Americans' supply to that of the few Britishers who always had their own brews down, by the morning of the Fourth of July there was quite a stock available in the camp—mainly under American control.

Along with the brewing we started planning a few things we would do to start the day off right. Several accounts of this day have appeared in various books and articles. One of the best of these said I was Paul Revere, but that isn't true. I was Uncle Sam. Paul Revere was Shorty Spire in his tricorn hat, brandishing a wooden sword as he rode around on a two-man horse. I'm not sure who played the horse, but one end, I believe, was a fellow named Carlburg. Astride this horse rode Shorty Spire, yelling, "The Redcoats are coming!"

Don Stine and some Polish friends helped rig me out as Uncle Sam. For my blue top I used a British RAF shirt, which pulled over the head and split part way up the side. I tucked in the front panel of the shirt, leaving the rear panel hanging to give a frock-coat effect. One of the Polish diggers, a fine man in Block 123, let me borrow his red and white striped pajamas. I wore these patriotic pajama bottoms with the blue shirt tucked in front and a red, white, and blue string tie.

Don Stine also designed for me a great big glove made out of papier-mâché with one huge finger pointing out forward to imitate the Montgomery Flagg poster on which the fellow says, "Uncle Sam Wants You."

In addition to this nearly two-foot-long white glove, I had a magnificent hat nearly three feet high that Don made for me out of cardboard. It was decorated in water colors of red and white vertical stripes, with a broad band of blue with stars on it around the lower part. One reason I was appointed Uncle Sam was that I could grow a square spadelike goatee, which I'd shave off on every escape; it came in handy here.

In addition to Paul Revere on his horse and Uncle Sam, we also had the Spirit of '76. Three kriegies depicted the classic triad of wounded Revolutionary patriots. Here was Tex Newton with a horn, somebody with a fife or piccolo, and somebody else with a drum. Others rigged themselves as Indians and we paraded through the British blocks, throwing the British out of bed.

I took great pleasure in personally throwing Roger Bushell out of bed, yelling, "The rebels are coming, arise, arise!" and "Don your red coat and fight like a man!" They could smell the brew on our breath and they all started following us like the Pied Piper's rats to the dispensing station in the middle of camp. Everybody celebrated. The British broke out all their brews, ready or not, and general mayhem prevailed.

The Germans came in, took one good look at us that morning, and decided they wouldn't even try to count us. Later one of them told us that they thought our alliance had broken up when they saw us throwing each other in the fire pool. They were always hoping there might be some conflict to split the British and the

Americans. They soon learned that this was beyond doubt the greatest celebration of the American Independence Day by British anywhere.

I was still yelling "Uncle Sam Wants You!" and pointing my huge finger at kriegies who had already been with Uncle Sam a long time when some of the lads in my barracks decided to throw Uncle Sam into the fire pool. As I came up sputtering and laughing, I saw Wings Day looking at me, laughing too. He drained his tin cup of brew, handed it to a colleague and strode toward the pool. Wings always wore his full uniform, complete with tie, jacket, World War I medals and RAF cap. Raising one arm, he let out the clarion call of our campfire routine—"Who'll save him?" Then he answered himself, "I'll save him!" And he rapidly finished his one-man skit, "Who're you?" "Jack Armstrong of the Royal U.S. Marines!" And with that Wings belly-flopped into the four-and-a-half-foot-deep pool to save me.

He lifted me up, then we both shook hands. Looking at each other, leaning back with clasped hands stretched out across the fire pool, we both roared, "Hands across the sea!" to great cheers from the crowd. Then Rojo Goodrich, the senior American officer, joined us in the pool together with the nearby block commanders—Bub Clark, Dick Klocko, Davy Jones, followed by anyone else who looked dry—on the outside, that is. No one was dry on the inside.

The pace soon grew even more hectic. Several of us were sitting around the edge of the fire pool when suddenly we looked down and saw somebody lying at the bottom of the pool. Someone said, "My, isn't that a peculiar place to rest?"

Another said, "Yes, do you think he's breathing?"

There was some conversation about it and finally someone said, "Let's bring him up."

We brought this kriegie up and got him breathing again. He survived—I believe only through the grace of God. Shortly after this George Harsh from Atlanta said, "Don't go away—I'll be right back," and he wove his way over to his barracks. After a little while, George emerged from the barracks swathed in a white sheet and said, "To walk on water you have to have faith." And he walked right out on the pool—well, it *looked* like he walked on the pool. Actually, he took a couple of steps and then sank. He turned around looking accusingly at all of us on the sidelines and said, "You didn't have enough faith!"

The German guards didn't bother us all day. At first they rather hoped that this actually was an altercation between the British and the Americans, but our good spirits dispelled the thought. Glemnitz and Rubberneck eyed us warily, suspicious as always of escape attempts, but there were none that day. Herr Pieber couldn't understand how the British could get along so well with the Americans while we celebrated so spiritedly our breaking away from them.

The goon-box guards and the other Germans laughed nearly as hard as we did when Shorty Spire rode his "horse" into the middle of the appell ground and halted. The horse appeared to lift one rear leg, and a great stream of water poured from beneath the horse, who then whinnied and capered in relief. The back end of the horse had poured out a huge keintrinkwasser of water from under the blanket as he lifted his leg for effect.

We drank up everything in camp and then shared what we had of our food parcels in one huge picnic. Some of us sang around the pool, but many turned in early that night and woke up with big heads in the morning. We all felt a lot better after devoting one whole day just for fun alone, blotting out temporarily but so effectively the fact and feeling that we were prisoners.

Chapter 14

About the time of our historic Fourth of July celebration there was another escape attempt that I consider a classic. In the camp we started a lice scare. The Germans were very neat people. They wanted to be clean and sanitary at all times. In the early summer we all started scratching at appells and cursing the lice. Pretty soon we had some of the German guards and counters scratching themselves and believing us. So they started what they called delousing parades to the showers and "bake ovens."

There were no showers in our camp, so for any delousing showers we would have to be taken out to the kommandantur, which was between North Camp and Center Camp. Two armed guards would take out twenty-four prisoners carrying their clothes in their mattress covers on their backs. The kommandantur not only had hot showers with some soap—a rare thing—but also had a huge oven where the clothing and bedding would be dumped to roast the lice. I don't think there ever were any lice at all. We set up this elaborate lice scare ourselves just to get some escapees outside the barbed wire.

In preparation for this walkout escape attempt,

Bushell had asked Tommy Guest to create guard uniforms from some tinted RAF blues. Insignia were made by the metalworkers, and Johnny Travis mocked up rifles and pistols out of wood. He needed exact dimensions, so he sent the resident artists to get them. Henri Picard of Belgium and Emmett Cook of Texas were able to come up with quite accurate drawings just by following some of the guards along their beat. When a diversionist stopped a guard for a chat, he used folding calipers to take surreptitious measurements. These sketches and dimensions helped Travis' shop to manufacture some excellent rifles and pistols dyed brown or black, closely resembling the real items.

One day after a change of the guards at the main gate box, out from the barracks came a group of two "Germans" and twenty-four prisoners. This procedure had occurred many times before, and everything went like clockwork. The "guards" showed their passes briefly at the gate and said, "*Offnen Sie!*" The gate guards obliged by opening first the inside gate to the vorlager, then the gate from the vorlager out on to the road. Off marched this group of twenty-six men down the road toward the kommandantur. After they turned around a little bend they all disappeared into the woods and out of their bags took their change of clothes if they were going to go out by train. Some even went in German uniforms. Here we had put twenty-six men out in the countryside. I thought that was a beautiful thing, a great walkout, well conceived and efficiently and clearly carried out.

Then a party of senior officers walked up to the gate, saying they were going to meet with the kommandant. This group included Colonel Rojo Goodrich, the senior American officer; Lieutenant Colonel Bub Clark; Commander Bob Tuck, the British fighter ace; Bill

Jennens, the adjutant and a fine soccer player; and a Polish wing commander. They were guarded by Brom Van der Stok, an RAF pilot from the Netherlands and a medical student. He ran the North Camp first-aid station, but today he was a German NCO, armed with a fake pistol.

I was stationed with one of my men as a runner to make sure that no one among the kriegies made a false move or showed surprise, since many of the kriegies didn't know what was going on. As my role was a static one, mine was the perfect position from which to see the drama unfold. It was a great feeling to watch twenty-six guys walking out of the gate and then another group of five or six making their attempt.

This senior officer party got through the first gate into the vorlager all right, but the guard was questioning something on Van der Stok's pass. Evidently he didn't have the proper date on it. The guard on the outer gate at the road was still looking at the pass when Oberfeldwebel Glemnitz walked up. He glanced sharply at our fake NCO and said, "Oh, Mr. Van der Stok, you can't walk out of here. It's ridiculous to think you can walk out of here. No one walks out of our prison. Except to the cooler!" And he began escorting the group to that very place.

We were sorry the senior group was caught, but we chuckled smugly to ourselves because there were still twenty-six people loose in the forest, heading for stations to catch trains, airfields to steal planes, or toward Czechoslovakia any way they could go—on foot, motorcycle, or truck. I ran into some of these same men a little later in the cooler.

Twenty-six prisoners loose outside the gate set a new record for us at Stalag Luft III and repercussions were swift in coming. The Gestapo was called in and the camp was turned inside out. German troops were also brought in—for a day-long appell. A table was set up in the middle of the parade ground and each prisoner was checked individually against his file card to determine exactly who had escaped. The barracks searchers threw our food and belongings all over the place, tearing up the beds and other furniture, but they found little of our escape equipment. It was well hidden in false walls and false floors under the huts or behind lockers.

The kommandant was badly shaken and directed the senior British officer and the senior American officer to warn all prisoners of more serious retaliation for future escapes. Posters appeared in the compounds with the bold headline: "To all prisoners of war: Escape from prison camps is no longer a sport! They say in a captured secret English military pamphlet, the handiwork of modern irregular warfare: 'The days when we could practice the rules of sportsmanship are over. For the time being every soldier must be a potential gangster and must be prepared to adopt their methods whenever necessary.' "

Then the Nazi warning continued: "Germany is determined to safeguard the homeland, especially the war industry and provisional centers for the fighting fronts. Therefore it has become necessary to create strictly forbidden zones, called death zones, in which all unauthorized trespassers will be immediately shot on sight. Escaping prisoners of war entering such death zones will certainly lose their lives . . . URGENT WARNING IS GIVEN AGAINST MAKING FUTURE ESCAPES!" This poster concluded that escaping was now a very dangerous act ending almost certainly in death, and that the only safe place for a prisoner of war was in camp. This warning may have been reassuring to those intending to spend the war as prisoners, but it had little effect on those of us determined to escape.

One day about that time I got word that Wings Day wanted to see me. I noticed that his barracks was carefully cleared and well guarded by unobtrusive stooges to give warning of any German's presence. I noted the familiar faces of other eager beavers in the small group that Wings had assembled.

Wings began, "Gentlemen, you're here because you are people who I believe have not only the will but also perhaps the best opportunity to escape." The group contained some of the superior German-speakers and those who had some other special knowledge of or family ties in Europe. I must have been included just because I never gave up.

Wings continued, "The reason I've called you together is that we've gotten word over the canary (our hidden radio) that the Germans are developing a new kind of a weapon—some type of a rocket device. So when you are loose, look for any area that is heavily guarded and has a good railhead for heavy equipment, signs of industry, and high security."

He added that there was some such activity reported up in the Peenemunde area, but there might well be a factory south of our camp that we could report to our friends in London. We eager beavers filed it away for future reference, hoping soon to combine intelligence work with freedom. Even so, my next escape opportunity came sooner than I had expected.

Some horseplay by Al LaChasse of Glendale, California, was the first link in a chain of circumstances that led to my next escape attempt. On a sunny July afternoon Al was working out on a homemade vaulting horse, performing an impromptu half-gymnast, half-clown routine. The horse's basic wooden frame was like the ordinary sawhorses used by builders everywhere, but a bit higher. Above the two-by-fours that made the length of the frame was the top of the horse, a length of log about twelve inches in diameter to give weight and bulk to the horse. Al started attacking it like a puzzled gorilla in the zoo. His antics soon drew a crowd. After beating his chest and jumping over the horse, he finally started to wrestle with it. Suddenly the log swung loose and fell, with Al underneath, and part of the log hit Al's cheek. The laughter turned to a stunned silence. Al was dazed and groggy for a while, and we could see that the cheekbone was dented.

After some argument the Germans agreed to put Al in the vorlager dispensary that night and send him to a nearby hospital for X rays the next day. On his return from the hospital Al reported to me about his trip outside the wire. After learning that Al's cheek was healing properly, I asked him how he got to the hospital. He said they had carried him in a makeshift ambulance—a paneled truck of maybe three quarters of a ton. There was no partition between the rear area and the front cab, where two guards sat fully armed.

Al said the guards paid little attention to the rear of the vehicle because everyone in the back had broken bones—usually broken legs, broken arms, and bodies in casts. About eight prisoners were carried there on two benches, four to a side, facing the center. The two rear doors were fastened shut. The windows in the doors were rolled up and the inside handles had been removed. Iron grilles were bolted over the windows.

Al noticed that two of the bolts in the right-hand rear window seemed a little loose. He thought that maybe with the right tools someone might be able to get the window down, loosen the bolts, get the grille off, reach outside, open the doors, and get out—if he could do all that in something like twelve to fifteen seconds.

The urgency of the timing lay in a major obstacle in the route. The vehicle loaded patients from the dispensary in the vorlager and then drove through the gate out of the vorlager onto the dirt road leading to the hospital. The hospital was a little over a half mile down the road to the left, and the truck had to pass the whole length of our North Compound. But it took only about fifteen seconds for the vehicle to go the length of the compound before entering the only strip of cover—the woods. The woods were one hundred to one hundred fifty feet across there and then deepened the whole length of the camp toward the south, thus creating the best way to head out. There was no opportunity north of the road—it was the built-up town.

A good reason for getting out in a hurry was that just on the other side of the woods were the German shooting ranges. Men were out shooting rifles and machine guns every day. That wasn't a happy place to be in broad daylight. I asked, "Could one go through the truck window?"

"No one your size," Al said, "but maybe a small fellow like Shorty Spire could get through." He guessed the opening was twelve inches high and maybe sixteen inches across.

I asked Al about the possibilities of escaping from the hospital itself. He said that the chances were much slimmer than on the road simply because there were all types of guards and other security around the hospital when prisoners were brought over. It would be hard to get away in broad daylight without raising a big alarm.

So I thought over all he had told me and decided I'd give it a try. I consulted with Roger Bushell and described the possibilities. He said, "Well, I suppose you're gonna try it anyway, so have at it. It'll still be a long time before the tunnels are ready. You've earned the chance after hiding all the sand so far and your teams are well trained to keep it up without you." He added, "But how are you going to get the broken bones for the X ray machine?"

"Well," I said, "I have to have my legs to run with, my arms for strength, and my head to think with, so I guess it'll have to be my ribs."

Again he asked, "How are you going to break them?"

And all of a sudden the Lord told me, "Bill Jennens." Bill Jennens was bigger than I—my feet were size thirteen, his were about sixteen—but more important, he was an expert with his feet in both soccer and rugby. He had even played on All-England teams. So I went to Bill Jennens and said, "Bill, would you do me a favor?"

He said, "Righto, Major!"

I asked, "Would you please kick in my ribs?"

He replied with a laugh, "I'd be charmed."

Then I said, "Well, Bill, let's not go overboard. Let's just kick in a couple of them."

And so he did. You could hear them crack.

My next step was to go to the dispensary and procure a pass to get on an ambulance. On the way to sick call I pushed the bones around so they weren't exactly meeting. I could feel the bump. In fact, I can to this day. They healed a little off-center. Also on the way over there I pulled out the little demolition knife that I always kept strapped to the calf of my leg and I stuck the blade into my finger and sucked some blood back into my mouth.

When it was my turn in front of the German doctor, he looked up and asked, "*Was ist los*?"

I said in German, "I think I have broken ribs."

The doctor replied, "That doesn't mean much."

So I said, "But I have fear for my lungs," and (the Lord gave me a good gesture at the right time) just as I said "lungs" I hit myself right where Jennens had kicked.

I didn't have to do any acting. I just roared with pain and released that gore in my mouth, spitting it out over the edge of the doctor's desk. He jumped up and German corpsmen leaped to clean up his desk.

In his rage the doctor grabbed his pad of permits and I had a pass to go to the hospital to have my ribs x-rayed the very next day. Silently and gratefully I said, "Thank you, Lord."

I was just grinning about that when another good thing happened to me. For some time I had needed a bit of phosphorescent paint for my Dinah Shore compass—to mark one end of the swinging needle so I could see it at night. In the confusion around the doctor's desk I saw in the shadow from the drapes—it was getting a bit late in the afternoon—a German alarm clock, the numbers just faintly shining. It looked as though the numbers were covered with phosphorescent paint.

I turned to my colleagues there, many of them in casts, with crutches or canes. I quietly said something we often used to set up a diversion outside. "Quick, give me a donnybrook!"

Right away one of the boys shouted at another fellow and hit him over the shoulder with his crutch and was promptly hit back with the cane. Another picked it up, and pretty soon British and American prisoners were rolling around the floor in their casts banging at each other—not too hard—but just enough to make a terrific show.

When the Germans ran over to break it up, all I

had to do was very quietly walk over, take the alarm clock, stick it under my arm inside my jacket, and stroll outside. Back in camp I got John Bennett to transfer the phosphorescent paint to my compass needle so I could see it at night.

That evening I reviewed again with Wally Valenta the terrain, rivers, and routes into Czechoslovakia. I also rehearsed with Valenta the various phrases I'd learned in Polish, Czech and Hungarian, particularly Hungarian (Magyar). Since the Germans knew less of Magyar than of the Slavic tongues, I decided that if questioned I was going to be a Hungarian worker.

I went over some maps and tried to spot the rivers that would lead me south on my way into Czechoslovakia. My short-term aim was to make it down to Czechoslovakia and on into Austria, staying first in fields and later in the mountains.

First I wanted to find some friendly Czech farmers in some isolated spot to see if they would give me food and other provisions to get across the country. My long-term goal was to work my way to Yugoslavia to join the Chetniks under Draza Mihailovic. I knew he would welcome me because I had helped train the Serbs who fought with Draza against the Germans in Yugoslavia. I thought if I got up in those hills I could run into some friendly people, or at least people who hated the Germans.

I got my compass, a little hacksaw blade, and my iron ration. The iron ration was a concentrated high-calorie goo we cooked up in camp for escapes to keep people going—a combination of cheeses heavy with milk powder and oatmeal, good rib-sticking stuff. I also took a couple of D-bars, very hard, fortified chocolate. They were so hard that I think the "D" stood for dentist. The only thing I didn't take was a canteen; carrying it would have been too obvious.

My other supplies were small and flat, easy to store in the pockets of my big blue RAF coat. I knew I could pull the buttons off that when I got out. No one would find that odd because a lot of people didn't have buttons during the war.

However, I couldn't use my fine double-breasted herringbone tweed suit that Guest and his team had made in the tailoring shop. It was walled up for later use when the tunnel broke. This time there was no chance to change my looks. I had to go out in a uniform because at the hospital any other clothing would be suspicious.

At the dispensary I found that one of my American friends, Harold Whiteman, was going on the same ambulance. Harold was a B-17 navigator from Atlanta, where he later became a great heart surgeon. He had a broken leg in a cast and he sat on the left rear seat of the ambulance. He helped pass the word that I had to have the right rear seat. One Britisher didn't hear him, so I had to lift him up and push him down the bench on the right side so I could have that right rear window.

I'd brought along a copy of the big Nazi party propaganda newspaper, *Volkischer Beobachter*, and I asked the fellows up front to spread it out and talk about it to screen my activities from the two armed guards in the front seats. In my overcoat pocket I had the small tools made by the metalworkers. Al LaChasse had accompanied me to the metal shop and again described the broken window handle so they could make a tool to fit over it to roll the window down.

I also got from them what looked like a tiny tire iron to work the bolts loose. I wore an RAF blue sweater and planned to carry the coat inside out over my arm. Underneath my trousers I had to wear jump boots. I had been going barefoot a lot, trying to save my paratrooper boots. I had them fastened up under, not with my pants bloused from the tops the way we used to do when we were jumping.

Finally we were all set in the ambulance, and I was in position in the right rear seat. The fellows up front spread out the paper and, of course, everybody was talking so that my noise was hidden. The tools worked; they were good ones. I had the window down on the right side even before we'd left the vorlager.

As we turned left, I started working on the bolts and they just kept turning and turning. I felt like I was sweating blood and then suddenly I realized the bolts were just going to go around and around until I had run out of time to get into the woods. We were getting near the end of the camp and I had to get out very soon if I was ever going to go at all.

Quickly I prayed, "Lord, give me strength!" I reached up and grabbed the iron grille, tightening my whole body, then gave one big yank, expelling all my breath in a roar. Here was that iron grille free in my hands with the bolts dripping wood and metal!

As I breathed "Thank you, Lord!" I looked up and saw I was directly under the corner guard box. The guard turned, looking toward me.

I quickly slapped the grille back in its place, held it there, waved my other hand at the guard and said, "*Wie gehts*?" (How are you?)

He said something like "Oh, go to hell!" in German and turned his back on me.

I immediately reached outside and tried to get the door open. No luck. It was apparently milled steel and there was no way I could move it. I'd run out of my shot of adrenalin. With my left arm crooked outside the windows, I was not in a good position to turn the handle.

I said to Harold Whiteman, "Throw the coat after me, I'm going through!" (This was all done much faster than I can tell it.)

Whiteman said, "You'll be stuck in it!"

I just prayed, "Lord, you pull; I'll push. I've got to get through this hole."

I remember how I started. I stretched my left arm way out through the window and just kept squeezing out, making myself as skinny as I could in mind and body. The Lord pulled and I pushed, and I landed on my head in the dirt road. The ambulance kept right on going.

I reached for the coat that Whiteman had thrown out after me, but a loop on the sleeve hung it up on the outside door handle. I found myself absurdly in the position of running down the road after the ambulance in broad daylight trying to retrieve my coat. All this time Whiteman was trying to release it, and then all of a sudden three things happened at once. The coat got loose, I reached it and the guard saw me and opened up with his machine gun. I heard a sharp rat-a-tat-tat.

Up to now I had been a lineman—what would now be called a tight end—at Washington State. All of a sudden I became the fastest halfback you've ever seen. Even O.J. Simpson would have had trouble keeping up with me that day. I ran and dodged at the same time, trying to put the trees between me and those bullets.

Then I heard the dogs come out—the Doberman pinschers and schaeferhunds. I was deep among some trees, but people still seemed to be coming from two or three directions.

Wally Valenta had told me these woods to the south were part of a big reforestation project. Small roads or firebreaks ran a kilometer apart, north-south and east-west. In between there were square kilometers of low trees or brush, small trees and big tall pines.

I started running in the tall pines. I could hear the dogs baying close behind, but fortunately these dogs couldn't smell as well as bloodhounds. At least that was my conclusion because I succeeded in losing them.

Chapter 15

At first the main danger was people on bicycles or motorcycles running south on grid lines behind me. A couple bicycled right by me up to a grid corner and parked next to the crossing where I would have to pass by.

I could have stolen a bike, but I preferred the forest to the roads. I crashed off to the right on a diagonal through that square of the forest, but didn't shake my pursuers.

When they started running in to intercept me, I fell on my belly, crawled back and slithered like a snake across a firebreak into some low brush. Then I crawled and slithered across the next road where I'd get to a higher, younger stand of trees that was very dense. Branches whipped my face. Finally I had to walk with my hand protecting my eyes, but at least the brush gave me cover.

I went on through various types of woods for hours. One doesn't get very hungry in hectic times like this, but one certainly does get thirsty. When I'd get completely cotton-mouthed, I'd pray, "How about some water?" and so help me it would be provided. Though it hadn't rained there for two or three weeks, I'd come out of a stretch of forest and there in the firebreak would be a mud puddle. I would dive into the puddle, slurp it up as I thanked the Lord, keep right on crawling into the next low brush, and then get up and run when the trees got higher.

I'd lost the dogs by evening and I was climbing up over a hill, keeping in the shadow of the trees in a firebreak that had a power line strung along it. There was no one following me on bicycle or motorcycle or on foot. At least I couldn't see or hear anyone, and I was listening pretty carefully. I felt like a wolf. All my senses were heightened. I could see better and hear better; I could almost smell the enemy. That sharpening of senses made everything possible.

When I got very thirsty again, I found a big puddle in a dip on the side of the hill. It was most welcome. My feet already felt hot and blistered from going so fast in boots that I hadn't worn in so long. I took off my boots to soak my feet in the puddle, which was stagnant and all green on top. In order to get a drink I had to push aside the green stuff to scoop out water in my hands. I didn't worry about what the green stuff was. I drank it, bathed my feet in it, and shaved off my beard.

In the prison camp I had grown a beard and a moustache, not a great full beard but a square goatee. It did change my appearance somewhat when I shaved it off. Using the razor that I had in my pocket, I hacked off the whiskers after soaking them with this scummy water while I soaked my feet. I rested a little while, took another drink, and then got moving. I wanted to cover as much ground at night as possible. With my Dinah Shore compass with its dab of phosphorescent paint, plus the north-south grid lines, I had little trouble heading south toward Czechoslovakia, even in the pitch-dark. I just kept moving forward, one leg after the other.

I got very tired, so tired that I felt split into two people. I seemed to be involved in a three-way conversation. I was talking to God and God talked to me and I was talking to myself. One instant I could visualize myself walking right along above me. The fellow up above would say, "How are you down there, Jerry?"

I would say, "How are you up there, Jerome?" That's the name with which I'd been christened, but I changed it when I got a little bit older. I'd say something like, "I guess we're doing all right, buddy!"

I had to walk with my hands in front of my eyes to keep branches out of them. When a twig whipped my face fairly hard I noticed I was just sort of staggering along. I shook my head and said, "Boy, I just gotta rest." I threw myself on the ground, saying, "Please, Lord, wake me at dawn. I don't want to get caught out in the open in the morning." And I just dropped off to sleep like a babe and slept where I fell.

In an hour or two I awoke alert and refreshed, but it was still before dawn, so I could stay out of people's way. Again I thanked the Lord. Every now and then earlier that night I had heard sounds of some people rustling in the woods, but I always heard the searchers before they heard me and I managed to avoid them.

On the morning of my second day of freedom I found myself heading down a small road winding through rolling hill country. The woods had thinned considerably. I was evidently getting near some sort of wheat or grain country, and suddenly I saw a German woodcutter. He saw me at the same time. I couldn't avoid him so I merely said, "*Guten Morgen*" (Good morning), and kept on going. Nothing happened. These encounters worried me, though, because I was so big compared to most of the fellows left home to farm. Germans as big, young, and strong as I were all away in uniform. To reduce my stature I walked with a slight limp and tried to shrink myself. I carried my left arm askew as though it were twisted.

Shortly after I passed the woodcutter I rounded a bend in the road and ran into several hundred people on their way to pick blueberries. That was one of the problems of escape for all of us. The Germans were hungry and there were a lot of blueberries out in the forests. They were also picking up any twigs or branches that they could burn, so the woods were fairly clear of underbrush, making it very hard to find places to hide.

When I saw the blueberry pickers I had no choice but to keep right on walking. To those who looked rather friendly and seemed to expect it, I'd say, "*Guten Morgen*." One old lady insisted on stopping me to ask me questions; my German was not nearly good enough for me to know what she was saying. So I said in my poor German, "I'm sorry, I cannot hear you." Then I pointed to my ears and said, "A boom boom!" and ducked as though dodging a bomb. She clucked her tongue sympathetically and let me go on my way.

By now the woods had thinned out and disappeared entirely. Turning around another bend in the road, I was shocked to hear a voice call out in English, "Hello, are you English?"

I looked around, puzzled. Several men were standing nearby, looking at me questioningly. I replied, "*Nein*." I said, "Good morning," in Hungarian, and then in German I said, "I'm a Hungarian worker."

Then I switched back to Hungarian. After I had rattled off my stock of Magyar phrases, I switched to plain old double-talk as the comedians do it—particularly Danny Kaye. It was sheer nonsense to the Germans;

they just said something uncomplimentary in German and turned away. I kept on going.

Later on, in the open with no hiding places, another group of workers stopped me and asked, "Are you Russian?"

In German I said, "No, are you?" They were, and they told me that all the workers thereabouts were Russian slave laborers. I decided to take a chance and tell them who I was. They all got very excited and advised me to return to the woods and especially to avoid the towns.

As I came around a bend in this winding road, heading for the wooded hills, I met a wagonload of Germans. The driver was an older, burly man. With him were two young men, members of Hitler *Jugend* (Hitler's Youth), and a woman.

I couldn't avoid them, so I walked off to the side of the road and lay down in the bushes. They approached me threateningly and demanded to know who I was. "Where are your papers? Why are you lying in the bushes?"

I replied, "Because I'm tired." All this was in German.

The driver, who was fairly husky, was carrying a club, but he wasn't sure of himself. He again demanded my papers and I replied, more belligerently, "Not for you."

He kept yelling, "Who are you? Come with me to the police."

I continued to lie on the ground pretending not to understand this; this only exasperated him more. Finally I told him again that I was a Hungarian worker. They registered disbelief, pointing out the wool in my sweater and pants, which was far better than any German on the farm would wear, much less a slave laborer.

I then rolled over and began singing a very long German folk song I'd learned in camp from Dick Schrupp and paid them no further attention. The long repetitive song was about a pear tree. And on the tree was a limb and on the limb there's a branch and on the branch was a twig and on the twig there was a nest and in the nest a bird, feather, etc. I went on and on and finally they walked a few steps away from me. They kept looking back at me. Eventually the big German sent one of the Hitler's Youths away for the police, while he stayed to stand guard, glaring at me.

Meanwhile, as I was singing, I was also scanning the scene for the quickest route into the deeper woods. Suddenly I rose and started walking in long strides toward the densest woods. This caused an uproar from the Germans. The leader started after me with his club aloft, ordering me to stop, saying he would get the police and the dogs after me.

I simply looked over my shoulder, waved him away, and shouted, "*Auf Wiedersehen!*"

He eventually thought better of coming to grips with me armed with nothing more than his club. After following me for a couple hundred yards, he went back to the wagon, probably to wait for the police. I didn't wait. As soon as I reached the trees I began to run like mad again.

I found a small stream and walked in it for several hundred yards to throw off the dogs. Coming upon a small culvert, I squeezed back into it and hid there for the rest of the day.

That night I took to the woods again. I forced myself to keep going in spite of feeling terribly fatigued. I found I couldn't eat the D-ration; it was too sweet. The only food I'd had since leaving the camp were some wheat stalks, a few berries and some spinach leaves. I'd just pick them; sometimes the moisture on these leaves would also give me the water I'd need.

Every so often I would drop and have a cat nap. I'd say, "Lord, please wake me in half an hour," and I'd wake up again in that time. My feet were giving me a lot of trouble. I was afraid to take off my boots because I knew if I did, I would never get them on again.

At first light of the third day I was on my way; this time I was traveling downhill through woods. And then a very beautiful thing happened. As I was coming out of the forest there in front of me was a mist hanging over a little pasture in a small valley. As my eyes became accustomed to the mist and it brightened with the dawn light, I could see a little stream running through the vale, and the words of the Twenty-third Psalm gently spoke in my mind: "The Lord is my shepherd, I shall not want. He maketh me to lie down in green pastures: He leadeth me beside the still waters."

And here I was in a green pasture by the still waters, watching the most beautiful little panorama of two deer. A little spotted fawn and its mother were standing in the middle of this quiet, open field. As it grew lighter I could see them more clearly. The fawn was a soft dappled brown and the little white-tailed doe looked up at me, at first a little warily. But as I walked very slowly toward her, I was willing her not to move. Silently I pleaded, "Don't be afraid, I won't hurt you. I just want to look at you beautiful beings."

After the prison camps and the running and the shooting and everything else, this was such a beautiful picture. It gave me a lovely feeling of peace. I'd had a very different feeling as I broke out of that ambulance. I remembered yelling out, "You may get me again, you SOBs, but I'm free now!" I was exulting as I ran from them because freedom from that camp meant so much to me.

Here I was just walking very, very softly and carefully across the field. When I got very near the doe and fawn, they just walked away, sometimes in very slow little bounds over rises in the ground, but they did not run. There was no panic at all and that made a wonderful interlude. I thanked the Lord again.

The various Germans who had seen me must have passed the word by telephone that I was heading south. Every now and then I had to avoid an organized posse. Sometimes I could hear them about me, but I didn't let them see me. I'd usually walk just off the road into the woods so I could see and hear them before they could see or hear me. Every now and then I'd hear them get closer with their dogs. Then I would either go very quickly in a new direction or find a place to hide. It was very hard to find good hiding spots.

Early one morning I'd been looking for a hiding place for quite a while. I kept hearing voices getting nearer and nearer until they seemed to surround me, but still from a distance. And there were dogs again. I could hear the barking of the big Dobermans and German shepherds. I said to myself, "Lord, I think they have me surrounded."

Then I thought of an old movie starring Paul Muni, *I Was a Fugitive from the Chain Gang*. Muni ran into a swamp to escape a posse that was trailing him with bloodhounds. Breaking a hollow reed from the edge of this swamp, he sank down into the water and lay on his back, breathing through the reed. Eventually he lost the bloodhounds, which couldn't catch his scent under water.

I half laughingly thought, "Lord, how about a swamp?" knowing full well that this part of Germany didn't have any swamps; only a sandy soil covered with pine trees. But as I walked alongside the road at the edge of the trees, all of a sudden there was my swamp. A concrete culvert, a big round pipe about two and a half feet wide, ran underneath the road, and it was over half full with backed-up water.

I again said, "Thank you, Lord!" Then I took my demolition knife out, cut myself a little stick of wood and hollowed it out. I did this quite rapidly, spurred on by the voices of both dogs and men closing in on me. I scooted in on my back into this culvert. By breathing through my short hollow stick, I was actually able to stay entirely under water. My biggest problem was keeping my size thirteen feet spread out in a wide V so that my toes wouldn't show.

I stayed in that water all day. I think I might even have cat-napped. That still seems almost impossible to me, but with the Lord taking care of you . . . Every now and again I would open my eyes to see a little sunlight filtering through the water, but only much later when it was completely dark did I dare to crawl out.

Evening had fallen and the posse was long gone. There were no dogs and no men and I was on the loose again, ready to continue my journey. But I looked like a prune. I had housemaid's hands all over. I suppose I'm one of the few fellows in this world who could say he was completely wrinkled at the age of twenty-six.

It was a warm summer night, very warm for Germany, and there was a soft breeze that dried my clothes and boots in no time. I was able to keep on moving warm and dry. I made pretty good time heading south with my Dinah Shore compass, sometimes talking to myself and the Lord. When I caught myself making too little sense and stumbling from fatigue, I'd throw myself on the ground and cry out, "Please Lord, wake me in twenty minutes!" and He did.

At times it was almost completely dark in the forest. There was no moon and the stars seemed far away, intermittently blinking through the trees. Often I had to walk with my hand up to protect my eyes from the branches.

All of a sudden I felt the ground give way. I had evidently fallen down the side of a steep ravine or a cliff. I lay there a bit dazed with all the wind knocked out of me. I remembered the wisdom of the Boy Scouts, "Don't move him. He may have a broken back." So the first thing I did was to wiggle my fingers and then I wiggled my toes and then I wiggled my legs and then I sort of wiggled my whole body. I discovered I was all right when I got my wind back, but Dinah Shore was kaput. I'd fallen right on my compass; Dinah Shore was no more. Then I asked, "Lord, how do I tell which way I'm going now?"

I heard the voice clear as a bell say, "Open your handbook."

I said, "What handbook?"

"The Boy Scout handbook," was the reply.

Then came to mind a picture of a double-page illustration in the old Boy Scout handbook that shows the skies of the Northern Hemisphere. In this picture I could see the North Star, the Big Dipper and several constellations: Orion with his sword and belt, and Cassiopea, which looks like a big W in the sky.

All of that came to mind to tell me that I could keep going south if I just followed the stars. Even if clouds blew over the North Star and the two Dippers, I could use some of the larger, more visible constellations to keep on track. So I was able to follow the stars. I said, "Thank you, Lord," and kept moving. I'd find water when I needed it. I'd find food when I needed that. But evidently it was still not my time. Maybe there was more for me to learn in prison camp—because eventually I was caught.

I was too tired to keep an accurate count, but on the fifth or sixth day out, after again walking all night over hills and through forests, I felt fortunate in finding a dirt road that seemed to be heading generally south. I kept on that to save wear and tear. I didn't have to fake my limp now, and my feet were in pretty bad shape. The forest seemed to be thinning out as dawn broke and houses appeared on either side of the street. At first I saw just a single house, then a couple of houses on each side. This arrangement is what is called a *Strassendorf*, a one-street village.

Suddenly I thought, "Maybe I'd better get off this!" And I tried to, but when I started to go between the houses, although I was careful to make no noise, dogs and roosters seemed to sense keenly that I was there. Not only did dogs start barking, but a rooster broke out with a cock-a-doodle-doo. I didn't want to wake up these farmers any earlier than usual.

From a little rise in the road I looked all around. Farther down ahead of me, the sun kept rising higher by degrees. I could see some forests on the hills beyond the little valley with its road, and I decided to try to push on through this village before the good citizens began moving about.

What I didn't know at the time was that instead of a small village I had entered the suburbs of a fairly large town. The first Germans to spot me that day were a milkman on his rounds and one or two early risers. I paid no attention to them beyond giving each a nod of good morning and continuing on my way.

For some reason I began to feel tense. Suddenly, ahead of me about a hundred yards on my right, there appeared a bicycle ridden by a green-uniformed man, some sort of officer. I was hoping it wasn't the Gestapo. And then whirling behind him came more police types.

The lead man rode around me, stopped, and got off his bike with a big Luger pistol in his hand. He began to circle me about fifteen feet away. With a calmness I was far from feeling, I looked at him and shrugged my shoulders and asked, "*Was ist los*?" and kept walking.

His answer was swift and to the point. A bullet whipped by my head. The others pulled their weapons. At least one man had ridden around behind me so I figured, well, there's no sense in committing suicide right here after all this work. I'd been caught again.

The first thing I did was to reach down inside my shirt and pull out my POW disk, a small medal with the number 955, my prisoner-of-war number. I wanted to assure them that I was an escaped prisoner and to be returned to Stalag Luft III, and not a spy or saboteur to be handed over to the Gestapo. Then I realized that I was completely worn out. All the adrenalin was gone. I knew that this escape was over. I had had it for this time. Right from that point I started resting and coiling up for the next time. As in football, I would expend a rich surge of energy and then coil—get ready for the next hit or tackle.

They were prodding me to come with them, but I couldn't. I just sat down in that dirt road. My feet were really hurting. I pulled off my boots and poured some blood out of them. My heels were like raw meat. One man jabbed me in the back with a rifle butt but I just sat there, holding my boots and resting.

By this time a crowd had begun to gather. They

were getting a little excited and a few churlish-looking farmers began to shout some suggestions as to my treatment that I didn't quite agree with. One of the captors got even more excited and he kicked me hard in the lower back with a jackboot. That remained sore for a long time. The others joined in, shouting, "*Stehen Sie auf!*"

I said that I couldn't stand up, let alone move. I had run out of everything, and I realized that my intense desire to escape had by itself kept me going as long as it did. I could walk miles as a free man but not one step more in captivity. There were more kicks and rifle butt blows to my back. I'm sure they contributed to my severe back problems later. I still couldn't move and my captors finally realized that.

They called for an oxcart, dumped me on it, and hauled me away to a police building. There I suggested a call to Stalag Luft III to verify that I was an escaped prisoner. Again I showed them my prisoner-of-war identity disk and number. I then asked for a doctor, or at least some iodine. I wanted to do something for my heels since they were very raw and I wanted to prevent infection.

I was sitting there barefoot on a stool with my eyes shut, trying to recover my strength, when someone came in to the police station. I glanced up and saw he had a little bag, which he opened. I relaxed again; then I felt someone grab my feet and another my shoulders.

I looked down. The "doctor" was holding a pair of pliers, and he jerked the flesh off my heels. Then the man said in German, "Now you will not go so fast."

The men who were standing around all laughed. My first impulse was to hit the "doctor," but I had no strength. I did try to spit in his eye. All I could do was dribble down my chin. I was really at a low ebb.

They tried to interrogate me for a while, but I was too exhausted to respond even had I wanted to. They kept asking me which train I had taken, or where I had stolen a car. They were amazed—incredulous—that I had traveled so far in so few days. By their reckoning I had gone more than two hundred kilometers, one hundred thirty miles, over hill and dale, across streams and around detours.

When I finally answered, I just pointed to my heels and said, "*Zu Fuss*!" (On foot!) About that time a man came in and said something about telephoning Stalag Luft III. The prison camp would send guards for me. Then they threw me into their own cooler, a little solitary confinement cell built much like the POW ones, only a bit smaller. I was glad to stretch out on the iron cot. They also gave me water, which was most welcome as I was dehydrated. They fed me a potato, a crust of bread, and some thin soup each day, and I began to recover some of my strength.

Shortly before the Stalag Luft III guards arrived to pick me up—I think it was my third day in the cooler cell—one of the most unusual things that has ever happened to me occurred. I was sitting on a stool in this little cell with my boots off—I couldn't put them back on for about eight weeks. The door clanged open and three guards stomped in. I looked up, sort of sleepy, and asked, "*Was ist los*?"

The lead man, a husky fellow, spat out some vulgarity, strode over and smashed my nose with a big swipe of his fist. This was about the sixth time my nose had been broken.

I saw red in all directions. I saw the red blood actually spurting, and inside my head red rage and red pain. From the stool I spat out in German, "Don't hit me again or I'll break your back!"

These fellows derisively laughed at me, "Ho, ho, ho!" and the lead man pulled out a large pistol, a Luger, and pointed it right at my belly.

Then I heard the Lord's deep voice say in my head, very clearly, "Move in!"

I stood up from the stool and moved in toward the lead man, spitting out as rapidly as I could, "Shoot me, but I can kill one of you before I'm dead!"

The men again said, "Ho, ho," and then more uncertainly, "Oh ho ho," weakly fading out. They backed out of the door and never touched me again.

I didn't tell this story for many years because it was a matter too close between God and me, but I know at that moment the Lord had His hand on my shoulder. It wasn't my good looks that made them back out and leave me alone. I think they could see my faith and determination and knew that I would do what I said. And as I walked into them, I seemed to get bigger and they got smaller.

I've often thought about that later and tried to describe that moment to people who were in trouble or copping out on their problems. With kids I've used this story quite a bit to point out that anybody who gets sloppy drunk or takes drugs or tries to escape and lose himself is just a coward. If you simply have the faith and courage to face up to life, to say no to the people who are trying to push you into false things, you have to become stronger and happier. The best way to handle any problem is to face up to it and handle it directly. Nine times out of ten, if you walk into them, the problems get smaller and you get bigger. But if you turn your back and run away, the problem becomes a monkey on your back. It grows into a baboon, then an ape or gorilla, and finally drives you into the ground. Although I've continued to make mistakes, I have not backed away from a problem since that day in the German cell down near the border of Czechoslovakia.

On about the eighth or ninth day after I dived out of the ambulance, the Luftwaffe authorities came in. They were three men from the Stalag Luft III area whom I did not recognize since they were not on our regular compound staff. Their leader, a senior sergeant, was a straightforward soldier, a little bit like Glemnitz. I showed them my feet and nose. They got a doctor to put some antiseptic and bandages on my heels. Then the doctor pushed my nose back into reasonable shape and held it there with a piece of tape. I had washed the blood out of my socks in the little sink in the cooler bathroom, so I was ready to go. But I still couldn't put on my boots. The Luftwaffe guards, surprisingly enough, were really very nice to me. They treated me with respect and seemed to admire my escape efforts. Though we talked mainly in German, their leader used a typically British expression in complimenting my escape try. He described it as "a very good show!"

It took about three train changes to get back to Sagan. I suppose that's why it had taken them so long to pick me up. In the railroad station they bought me a sausage on a good hard roll and gave me a glass of beer. I don't like beer, but I appreciated their kindness. It was nice treatment compared to what I had come to expect after other escapes.

During the train ride I talked with a number of German civilians. The guards didn't seem to mind. They left me alone and I was able to put in a lot of propaganda. I told these people about the millions of soldiers and the tens of thousands of planes that America was sending to war. I added, "I don't see why you want to keep on fighting this kind of a war," and a lot of them seemed impressed. Some of them listened quite open-mouthed.

We traveled by local trains rather than expresses. At one small station a lady got on with a golden-haired daughter about four years old or so. As the little girl started chatting with me, I answered back. Then I started singing an old German song. This woman had noticed the guards weren't treating me as an inferior. The only things that were peculiar about me were that I was in stocking feet and I had tape on my nose. Since the lady didn't know who or what I was, she allowed the little girl to climb up on my lap as I sang. The girl played with my moustache and I bounced her on my knee. It was fun; I like children. Then the mother wanted to get in the act and she said, in German, "Who are you and where are you from?" Before I spoke, I thought of Hitler and Goebbels' propaganda that we American prisoners were terrible people, air gangsters, out to murder the German people. The Nazis were trying to rouse general hate against us.

So I looked her right in the eye, grinned, and said, "*Ich bin Amerikanisch Luftgangster und Kriegsgefangener*." (I'm an American air gangster and POW.)

The lady gasped and started to reach for her daughter, but then she saw the little girl looking at me and laughing, and she joined in. She slapped her thighs and said something that means roughly, "Well, I'll be darned!" She was quite surprised and pleased, and we continued our nice talk.

In addition to enjoying quiet conversation with civilians, I got some OSS work in, too. Though I wasn't out fighting with my outfit, and I'd have to heal a bit before my next escape, I could still spread propaganda to the effect that there was no way they could win the war. The quicker the Germans ended the war, the better off the country would be because they were going to be driven into the ground with all the power that was coming over from America to defeat the Nazis.

Chapter 16

When I got back to Stalag Luft III, I was immediately thrown into the cooler, which was unusually crowded, as there were people still in there from the great delousing walkout escape. Being jammed up in the cooler instead of solitary was a completely different experience for me. I was thrown in with two fellows, sharing two double-decker bunks. There was hardly any room to move around. My two cellmates were Jan Staubo, the fine-looking Norwegian tennis player and digger, and Jerry Hill of London. Both had gone out on the delousing show and had been caught in the dragnet near a main highway.

I was hungry when I came in. There had been little food on the trains, and on delivery day the sergeant had said, "Well, when you get there, they'll give you a big meal in the cooler." I'm sure he really thought they would, but when I got to the cooler and asked the guards for some food, the answer was, "*Nichts für Ihnen*!" (Nothing for you!)

My stomach was growling after the long journey, and Staubo and Hill had no food. But they had already communicated out the window to the adjacent cell, which held Welch and Morrison, also escapees from the delousing parade. So I said, "Hey, have you got any kind of food left in there?"

They had already received word that Jerry Sage was caught, so they said, "Yes, we have a crust of goon bread. Just a minute!" And they did have a solid piece of black bread, bless their hearts.

The next question was how to get it. High in the outside end of each cell was one window with solid steel bars, and beyond that was a slanting wood flange about ten inches from the wall at its top and about four inches at the bottom. It was designed so that some air and light could get in but prisoners could not see out. Welch and Morrison thought for a while and then one of them found a string wadded up in a pocket of his jacket. He unraveled the string, got it all straight, and tied the bread to it. They pulled stools under the window. I think one reached under the flange, lowering the bread end, and the other had to help. I really couldn't see their maneuvers, but they told me they were getting the bread swinging toward my window.

I got up on a stool and reached out under the flange, stretching as far toward their cell as possible. They kept the bread swinging. Once it brushed the back of my hand. Finally I caught the string with a finger and then got down to the bread and yelled, "Got it!" I pulled it back into the cell and that hunk of bread tasted like angel food cake to me. I thanked my benefactors profusely.

As I got madder about not having any chow in there, I started banging on the door. A flapper outside the door signaled the guard. I made a lot of rattling noises with this knocker and beat on the door until the guard came. I told him I was hungry, and I told him to inform the kommandant that under the Geneva convention I was entitled to some food. They fussed about it and did nothing except to say ''*nein.*'' When I repeated my requests they responded by turning off our lights. They could do that any time they wanted, but normally didn't turn off the lights till about ten o'clock at night. This time they turned them off about an hour and a half early, and that teed off all of us. I started everyone singing—I recall it was ''Pack Up Your Troubles.'' The next cell started singing and then the next cell and soon everybody was singing. I doubt if the guards enjoyed it. They just left us in the dark and pretty soon we went to sleep.

About three or four o'clock in the morning there was a lot of noise in the hall. The door of our cell clanged open and I was confronted by a big group of Germans. They switched on the light in our cell and roared, ''*Stehen Sie auf!*''

That was when I discovered that Jan Staubo was gun shy. One time after being recaptured from a train escape, Jan was being walked back handcuffed when a crazy guard shot him right through the chest. He had healed, but he had not forgotten how manic-depressive these people could be. So the first thing I heard was a loud crash. It was Jan Staubo diving against the wall from a top bunk.

I got up, still sleepy, and sat down on a stool to try to put on some felt slippers. These had been made for me by a Russian prisoner when he saw I couldn't put on my boots. The guards kept yelling as I sat trying to get the slippers on. Then I could see the kommandant shoulder his way to the front as a guard shouted, ''*Stehen Sie auf!*''

I said in German, ''In a moment.''

When the kommandant got himself up in front he said, ''Major Sage, to me you are no major. To me you are a wolf!''

The kommandant was terribly upset, and in a way I couldn't blame him. He had been thoroughly shaken up by the Gestapo and his Luftwaffe superiors after the delousing escape. He had been threatened and was given clear orders that no more escapes would be tolerated. After he had warned us clearly that there would be no more escapes, guess who was the first one to escape! And here I was back in the cooler.

The guards said that I had started so much noise that they had turned off the lights. I told the kommandant they were trying to starve me. All I wanted was something to eat, which was only proper, and then they turned the lights off earlier than they should have, which was improper. I told him, "You had better shape up this camp."

Kommandant von Lindeiner went into a rage. He pulled his little officer's pistol out of its holster. It was much smaller than a Luger, but it could be sort of nasty if it drilled you through the head or the heart. Now, I wouldn't have worried so much except that his hands were shaking with rage: That's the time a man is most dangerous.

I'd learned from Dan Fairbairn that nobody is dangerous who just tells you to put your hands up and holds his pistol firmly on you. You can finally trick him and get close enough to disarm him in a number of ways. I knew how to do that. But this man's arm was shaking so much I was afraid he'd pull the trigger accidentally and hit at least one of us. Staubo and Hill were squeezing themselves as flat as they could against the wall of the cooler.

I was still on the stool with only one slipper on. Holding the other in my hand, I stood up slowly, fixed him with my eyes, and walked very gently toward him—with no threat and no bombast. Very quietly and calmly I said, "Be reasonable." This was in my poor German but he understood me. "You would never forgive yourself if you pulled that trigger because you are a gentleman."

He said, "*You* are not!"

I replied, "That isn't the point. You can't shoot me or starve me. You must abide by the Geneva Convention."

"But," he said, "you escaped against orders."

"It is my duty as an officer to escape. You know you would try to escape too if you were in this position. I didn't make it this time," I added, "and now I'm in the cooler and I still should be fed."

By this time his rage had subsided and he put away his pistol. However, he didn't order any food. He slapped his gloves against his hand, saying, "We'll teach you discipline," and stalked out.

The door clanged shut behind him.

They weren't particularly nice to me for some time. I tried not to cause any more trouble because they had cut down all our rations quite a bit as a result of my efforts. I didn't want the others to suffer with me and it wasn't my habit merely to goon-bait. After I got over my righteous indignation, they did start adding a potato or two apiece to our watery soups.

The next day I heard Morrison and Welch's story. Tommy Guest had rigged each of them up with a skillful copy of the German Luftwaffe overall-style uniform, which was almost the same color as RAF material, but much smoother. The extra woolly nap could be scraped off with a razor blade. It was made to look like a real German uniform. They even had the little fore-and-aft German cap along with other escape materials that they pulled out of the bags on their shoulders when they got into the woods.

When they got to an airport, a Luftwaffe flying field, they found one plane they thought they could fly.

They were just winding that up, in fact they had actually started it, when along came a German pilot who thought they were ground crew who had prepared it for him. He said, "*Danke schön!*" (Thank you very much!), got in and flew the thing off, leaving Morrison and Welch on the ground, still loose but a bit disgruntled by this man taking off in their airplane. They looked for another one, but this time they were caught just as they were trying to crank it up and get it going. I don't know the sequel. However, I think they were pulled out of Stalag Luft III and might have been taken to Kolditz Castle, which was a severe maximum-security solitary for incurable escapees.

As I mentioned, this was a very unusual cooler stretch because there were three of us in the cell. We were able to con a guard out of a well-worn deck of cards and we played blackjack, twenty-one as the British call it, in the lower bunk. We had a ball. We bet great sums of imaginary money, though we didn't even have match sticks to work with.

We finally started betting in earnest—things of real value back in the outside world. I didn't have much to offer except my services for the future, since I didn't have much money, but I hit a lucky streak and wound up winning on paper. One time Jerry Hill bet a hotel and I covered the bet. His father was in the hotel business in London and they had a string of hotels, including some down on the beach. Our luck changed often, but when finished playing I had won one hotel from Jerry Hill, and from Jan Staubo, whose father was the owner of Helmer Staubo Shipping Line out of Oslo, Norway, I won two freighters.

There's a sequel to our gambling spree. Much later, when I was commanding a Green Beret outfit, the

Tenth Special Forces Group in Germany in 1964–65, we were invited to Norway to help train the Norwegian version of Special Forces in guerrilla fighting, radio work, and field medicine—the things we did best behind the lines. In turn they trained us in the finer points of cross-country skiing, at which they were such experts. Their camp was up on the great Hardanger Vita, the plateau above the Hardanger Fjord. It was a wonderful sight to view a long line of skiers, the Norwegians in their billed caps with ear flaps and my Special Forces lads in their green berets, winding across the expanse of sparkling white snow in rhythmic swoops on their cross-country skis.

One day I saw a form moving in the white distance and through my binoculars I could see it was a fox all alone in that great snowfield. A beautiful sight, flaming red. I had thought that a fox would turn silver to blend with the landscape, but this one stood out as a thing of great beauty, not to be bothered. And none of us did bother it.

I called Jan Staubo in Oslo from our camp and arranged a rendezvous after the training. Jan met me at the train and took me to his office. We laughed about our experiences in the cooler and I said, "Jan, you know you still owe me two ships."

Jan said, "Jerry, you're right." He went to his showcase of models of the Helmer Staubo ships and handed me one about six inches long and promised he'd send me another, which I received a few weeks later. Both ships have been enjoyed since by children and grandchildren. I've not seen Jerry Hill since I left Stalag Luft III, but I'm sure that if we met, he would present me with something along the lines of a small hotel from a Monopoly board.

* * *

This stretch of nearly three weeks in the cooler with Hill and Staubo, though far different from most of my cooler confinements, brought the other stretches to mind. The first one had occurred after I tried to steal the German truck between Feriana and Gafsa in North Africa. I was put in a cell on the second floor of what seemed to be a police building in Gafsa—a cell that was completely bare, cold at night, with the cold made worse by hunger. I was hungry all the time. I kept somewhat warm by prying apart the bars of a window, but when I jumped in my next bid for escape I hit some garbage cans, twisted an ankle and was promptly caught. The Germans took me back to the building.

Evidently everybody was instructed to keep a very close watch on me after that. I could hear them call me a "*schlechte Mann*," a bad man, and I was guarded closely until another guard detail arrived to take me on to the Tunisia coast town of Gabes.

Already I'd gone looking for trouble again. As I was limping around the room while the Germans were involved in some noisy discussion, I managed to slip a German fore-and-aft uniform cap under my jacket, thinking it might help me get away in a vehicle. I might look like a German behind the wheel, and now that I did know the difference between *auf* and *ein*, I figured I could probably get one of the vehicles going, given the right opportunity.

But the guards watched me like a hawk all the way into the Gabes enclosure. Once there they searched me, and when they found the cock-eyed cap, they got mad again and put me in a much tighter cell, another solitary confinement. They did give me a slice of bread, green with mold, with a little water, but they were careful to keep me a good distance from all other prisoners until we were loaded into the boxcar.

Then after the boxcar escape and recapture, when I was separated from Kimball and Southard and taken alone under heavy guard to Tunis, I endured another form of solitary. There I was put in a weird outdoor barbed-wire cell, a bent piece of corrugated metal on a wooden frame about the size of a pup tent. My only company was a vast multitude of sand fleas.

Within minutes I was covered with hundreds of tiny, itching bites. I broke up the shelter's frame and made a fire, hoping the smoke would deter the fleas, but they seemed to love it. As it turned out, I finally used the fire to burn away the green mold on a couple of slices of black bread the guards gave me.

My fifth and sixth coolers were in Naples and Rome, solitary cells that seemed somewhat like jail cells for bad boys. I was glad to get to the hospital in Rome when I was burning up with fever. There I had some rest, some healing, and more edible food than I had seen since my capture.

So I'd already been through a half-dozen solitary confinements before the three weeks at Dulag Luft near Frankfurt. This stretch was interrupted by a couple of days in the Dulag Luft hospital cell, where, although alone, I had better food and some treatment for my infected wounds.

From the North Compound of Stalag Luft III I had three stretches of solitary in the cooler. The first was for two weeks in the initial flurry of the abortive escape attempts from the new compound, which included attempts to hide in the outgoing truckloads of branches.

Another stretch followed an early night air raid near the camp. I heard the sirens, then the planes, and opened the shutters on my end-room window to see the planes. A German hundführer walked up and slammed the shutters right in my face. In an instinctive reaction I slammed them open again.

The guard glared at me and said something in German to his Doberman pinscher like, "Sic him." Like a black thunderbolt the dog bared his long, sharp teeth and leaped for my throat.

Rearing back quickly as he came through the window, I kicked him hard in his crotch and lower belly. Pivoting, I chopped his neck with an all-out blow with the edge of my right hand. I then ducked away from the window in case the guard tried to shoot me. Luckily, another guard came up, followed shortly by Glemnitz and others, and they hauled me off to the cooler. The dog was dragged off either to the vet or to the great Doberman boneyard down below. In the cooler they accused me of being unkind to dogs!

From these previous stays in the cooler I knew there were good and bad aspects to cooler life. The bad were the most obvious. Man is a social animal and rarely likes to be completely alone. The cells were usually ten to twelve feet long by six feet wide with one bare light bulb hanging from the ceiling. There was one heavily barred window high on the outside wall at the end of the cell. It was screened on the outside with boards held by a metal frame away from the building a little so some air could get in but prisoners could not see out. For furniture there was usually a wooden cot, a straw or wood-shavings mattress, a blanket, a stool, and sometimes a small table. The door was heavy. The door to the hall of the cooler had one peephole covered by a pivoted piece of wood that the guard could slide open to peer in. If one wanted to go to the toilet or get some water, one had to use a knocker device to call the guard, who was usually in no hurry to respond.

Frugal meals came at quite regular times: one or two slices of bread and artificial tea in the morning, a bowl of watery cabbage or beet soup and a potato at noon, and bread and sugar-beet jam at night. Usually prisoners were permitted nothing to read, and in my case they would not even give me a pencil. They said I might use it as a weapon—and I could have. But I did have a comb, and I would sometimes scratch verses on the plaster walls.

One damp day in summer I scratched my "Ode to a Louse."

> I've had lice in the barracks at Lewis;
> I've had crabs on the Channel coast.
> I've been eaten by fleas at Tunis,
> Where the desert sun did roast.
> But the cruelest blow to my ego
> Was dealt by mosquitos to me.
> I was bit where I sit, in the abort,
> Of the cooler of Stalag Luft III!

Another time I wrote:

> "Stone walls do not a prison make,
> Nor iron bars a cage."
> "Mind over matter," thus might read
> The script on the prosist's page.
> Now my mental prowess may be numbed
> By kriegiedom or age,
> But stone and steel seem too damn real
> To coolerized old Sage.

I caught hundreds of flies in the warm weather, but after you've learned that flies take off backward rather than forward, sideways, left, right or straight up, the game gets rather tiresome. It was cold and dank much of the time, and one survived tolerably only at the whim of the guards.

There was a good side too. In the cooler one had time to think and to rest and coil after the effort and tensions of escapes and hiding thousands of pounds of sand. Perhaps more important, when there was no other person to talk with, I talked more frequently with God. I prayed for all my folks and friends back home, for prisoners who were having a particularly bad time and those out on escapes, and it always calmed me and made me feel better.

This special sense of communication was heightened on my escapes. With thousands of miles to go to reach Allied lines and no friends near except back in the prison camp, God was almost a constant companion. He gave me extra strength when I needed it. He provided water when I was cotton-mouthed from thirst. He helped me get some sleep when I needed it and woke me when there was danger and it was time for me to move on. Frequently when I was walking at night alone across Germany, the Twenty-third Psalm ran through my mind:

> The Lord is my shepherd, I shall not want.
> He maketh me to lie down in green pastures:
> He leadeth me beside the still waters
> He restoreth my soul.

In many of the close calls with death and danger, these words helped me and kept my will strong.

> Yea, though I walk through the valley of the shadow of death, I will fear no evil; for Thou art with me, Thy rod and Thy staff they comfort me.

I talked straight and often with the Lord, and when I especially needed help, I either heard His voice as clear as my mother's over the telephone or in some other way He made me sense what to do. This faith became much stronger during those difficult days than it had been any time since my earliest childhood.

Growing up in the state of Washington, in a family that appreciated good literature, I had the great gift of a fine education, particularly from my mother. The whole family would often either lie around on the floor or sit around in chairs or out on the porch in the swing. We did a great deal of singing, but we also quoted poetry. Mother could recite all of "The Lady of the Lake," and "Marmion" by Sir Walter Scott from memory, and all of Longfellow's "Evangeline." She could also quote in Greek and Latin. My dad liked me to recite Robert W. Service's "The Shooting of Dan McGrew" and "The Cremation of Sam McGee."

We all loved Kipling, especially the great poem "If." "If you can keep your head when all about you are losing theirs and blaming it on you," and so forth. I felt that was always a good inspirational poem. "The Ballad of East and West" was also brilliant in that way. Finally a poem that often helped me, that I had loved from the first time I read it, was William Henley's "Invictus." A straightforward praise to human spirit, I scratched it on the walls of the cooler cell from memory.

> Out of the night that covers me,
> Black as the Pit from pole to pole,
> I thank whatever gods may be
> For my unconquerable soul.

In the fell clutch of circumstance
I have not winced nor cried aloud.
Under the bludgeonings of chance
My head is bloody, but unbowed.

Beyond this place of wrath and tears
Looms but the horror of the shade,
And yet the menace of the years
Finds, and shall find me, unafraid.

It matters not how strait the gate,
How charged with punishments the scroll,
I am the master of my fate:
I am the captain of my soul.

That poem did encourage me. It sustained me in difficult times behind the lines. I had said it to myself during football games. Back in high school and college, when things were really rough, sometimes snatches of it would run through my mind. But an interesting thing happened to me over a period of time in Stalag Luft III and in my many stays in the cooler.

I wrote "Invictus" on the wall very early, after I'd first been captured, but I thought about it later. There were a couple of things about it I started questioning after I had thoroughly read the Bible. And I'll tell you how that came about.

As my faith grew, whenever I'd say "Invictus," it gave me pause. That line in the first stanza, "I thank whatever gods may be for my unconquerable soul" isn't really accurate. There aren't "whatever gods may be"; there is just one God. Henley may have doubted it, but I don't. Then at the end there's that beautiful thought, when a person is strong enough to be the master, "I am the master of my fate: I am the captain of my soul.'' But I really don't believe that. I would believe that only if I were to insert the little phrase ''under God'' or if I were to say, ''I am not the captain of my soul; I'm only the first mate and God is the captain.'' That's how my faith has grown. But I do believe tremendously in faith and in the great strength of the human will under God when you're really trying to do something worthwhile or when you're trying to fight the crude, the cheap, the mean or the shoddy.

The cooler not only gave me time to think of all the poetry, it also gave me the opportunity to read the entire Bible through. It started back at Dulag Luft with a kindly old man who visited me, probably without the knowledge of my interrogators, in my hospital cell, when infection was acting up in the wounds. This little old man had a small New Testament in English that he left with me for a day and a half. I was able to read all of it before I left the hospital to go back into the cooler cell with its heat treatment. I left the old gentleman a note of my grateful thanks. Reading the rest of the Bible, the entire Bible, came about from a strange cooler sentence nearly four months after my release for the ambulance escape in July. It all stemmed from Kommandant von Lindeiner's parting words to me in the small black hours of the morning in the cooler cell. As he stomped out he said, ''Major Sage, we will teach you discipline.''

Chapter 17

After I was released from the cooler in August 1943, I returned to my sand dispersal work with the North Camp X organization. Before relating the progress on the tunnel break, and the details of the move of the Americans to South Camp in September, however, it seems appropriate to wind up the stories of my cooler experiences, in particular the one stemming from the kommandant's parting threat.

A few days before Thanksgiving two guards arrived in the new all-American South Camp. They first went to see Colonel Goodrich, the senior American officer, and then me. Without any warning or legal formality, I was ordered to the cooler under one of the most unusual sentences the Germans had ever handed out. It was in the form of a court-martial order. Major Jerry M. Sage had been "charged, investigated, tried, and sentenced in a military court-martial with having threatened three armed guards in a solitary block."

Now I believe Colonel Goodrich was one of the first people in the camp to call me the Cooler King, or the Cooler Kid, and he said that it was quite a tribute to me that the Germans couldn't see the irony of punishing one unarmed American for threatening to harm three armed German guards. At any rate, I was back in the cooler again.

We'd been saving up for a big Thanksgiving bash, during which we planned to treat ourselves to an all-out feast. We had saved up our Red Cross parcels for that Thanksgiving. Needless to say, my Thanksgiving bash that year was one potato and some watery cabbage soup back in the cell.

One of the older guards shook his head in surprise at the news of my "court-martial" and he smuggled an English Bible into my cell. Reading it through for the first time, I was greatly impressed by the wealth of terrific stories in the Old Testament—the adventure, the battles, the romance, the beauty of the Psalms and the Song of Solomon, the basic truths to be learned.

It was during this stretch of solitary that I learned a couple of Russian songs and a few words that were of help when I made my last, successful escape across Poland and Russia. I had learned the original Russian words to "Dark Eyes" ("Ochi Chornia") from Prince Serge Obolensky of the OSS on one wild evening in Washington, D.C., after a tough week at Camp B2. Serge was very popular at Two Guitars, the old White Russian nightclub, where we not only sang in Russian, we also joined the floor show and did a wild Cossack dance, circling the room, kicking from a crouch in rhythm to the balalaikas' strumming and the clapping of the spectators.

In the cooler it was a less exuberant story. Once when let out for a toilet break by the guard, I noted a small fellow in a tattered Russian uniform mopping the hall floors. The Russians, both officers and enlisted men, were kept in a bare camp in the kommandantur area and they all participated in heavy work and day-to-day labor for the Germans. They were treated as *Untermenschen* (subhumans) and were forbidden to talk with the Allied prisoners. But I grinned at the

Russian and waved to him when the guard wasn't looking. Later I heard the scratching of the peephole cover moving on my cell door and I looked up to see an eyeball filling the peephole. The eyeball disappeared and a finger came through, crooking a couple of times in the universal "come here" gesture. I went up to the hole and peered through, and there was the little Russian backing off so I could see him.

Evidently the guards had everyone safely locked in and were busy in the guardhouse. The Russian grinned at me, pointed to himself and whispered something like "*kapitän,*" or maybe "*hauptmann*," both of which mean captain in German, and we continued the brief conversation in German. I asked him to teach me some Russian or a Russian song. He then started singing every time he cleaned anywhere near my cell and he taught me all three verses of the Red Army song "Tachanka." I learned it phonetically, just like a parrot; within a few days I had learned all of it. ("Tachanka" is about a machine gun mounted on the back end of a four-wheeled cart drawn by horses to the fight, swung toward the enemy, and rapidly put into action—"all four wheels rolling.")

I started to learn other Red Army songs such as "Polushka Pola," "Meadowland" in English, and "Katusha," about the artillery rockets fired in barrages by the Russians.

One day I heard the Russians singing in the kommandantur, out near the German billets and headquarters of the camp, to a sort of a chopping noise. I smashed one end of the outside board blocking my vision, jumped up and hung on the bars just to see the activity. The Russians sang as they chopped cabbages on a rude table outside their barracks, and they dropped the pieces into what looked like empty mustard barrels. I figured they were making sauerkraut.

In the cooler, any time I looked at, smelled, or heard about food of any kind, I was hungry. In fact, if I looked at a rock or a fence I was hungry. So I thought I'd ask for a little bit because it looked like there was a whole load of cabbages there.

The next time my Russian friend came by, I pointed to my water pitcher, pointed out the window and said in German, "*Bitte, bringen Sie mir etwas Kohle.*" (I had heard *kohle* used as the term for cabbage.)

After repeating the last word a few times the Russian said, "Ah, *kohle*, da, da." He nodded his head, yes, grinned at me and left.

Later on I heard a knock on the door and saw the little peephole cover move. There was his eyeball looking at me and then he gestured for me to come look. I went over to the door and looked out. There the Russian stood in the hall, pointing toward the bathroom, and beside him was a water pitcher. He said, "*Kohle.*"

I thought, "This is great!"

As soon as the Russian soldier was safely out of the way, I rapped for the German guard and told him I had to go to the abort, and he let me out. I went inside the abort, looking forward to a cabbage feast that afternoon. When I looked inside, I was dismayed. Instead of cabbage there were two briquets of coal. Then the light dawned on me. I had asked for *kohle*, coal, instead of *kohl*, cabbage.

So, when the Russian came back the second time, we started a new charade. I said, "*Kohl,*" and kept pointing at the window, adding the chopping gesture, rubbing my stomach and putting my finger in my mouth to indicate hunger. Again the little Russian nodded, "Ah, da, da, da. Oh, *kapusta*!" And he left again.

Some time later I figured I'd go out and get a pitcher of chopped cabbage and sauerkraut. When the Russian did come back, he gestured, pointing again to the pitcher. Again after he'd gone, I called the guard and went to the bathroom. There in the pitcher were two little heads of cabbage.

Well, it wasn't the sauerkraut I had expected, but those two cabbages I greatly appreciated and I told him thank you in every language I knew. He just kept nodding his head and grinning, feeling very good about helping me.

In later stretches of solitary I did have time for some philosophy, to try to figure out what was going to happen after this war. I knew the war couldn't last forever and I had planned just to do my job, defeat Hitler and the Japanese, get the war over with, and go back to civilian life. But as time went on and my faith grew, I had this feeling for service. I said to myself, "When this war is finally over, what should I be doing? Maybe business isn't really what I want." And I thought, well, I do want to help other people. I had learned in prison that when you're really feeling bad, one of the best ways to get over your gloom is to find somebody feeling worse and try to make him feel better. I wondered what the best occupation would be and where I really could be of value to my fellowman.

I didn't consider myself any better than anyone else. I was weary of seeing the inhumanity close up. Later, after the Nazis, I would see the same thing under the communists, and I didn't like it any better.

Thinking of ways to make my contribution, I realized how much I admired the doctor who heals people. However, I didn't want to go through school again to become a doctor. I also thought of being a lawyer who really searched for justice, but I didn't want to be a lawyer. I started thinking maybe I could be a minister, but then I said, "No, I'm not good enough."

Finally I thought about teaching. Right away I realized that ever since I was little, I had always respected my teachers, got along fine with them, enjoyed learning and liked to help others in their teaching. Back in college I had been a tutor. My sister taught me even before I went to school. She was a natural-born teacher. And I had loved it! So I said, "Maybe what I'll be is a teacher."

I did become a teacher. I taught in the Army before the Korean War and again before the Vietnam War. I taught at West Point and at the Command General Staff College in Kansas and at other service schools. When I retired, I became assistant to the president of the University of South Carolina, as well as a teacher in the Columbia, South Carolina, high schools. I found that I liked teaching at high schools even better than at colleges.

Helping the youngsters was a rewarding experience, and I felt particularly honored to be chosen Teacher of the Year for the State of South Carolina in 1979. My teaching career really started back in the cooler when I was deciding what I was going to be when my warrior days were over. By the time I became a teacher, I was in my late fifties, with many years of war and peacetime experience behind me.

There was a rather sad incident in one stretch of complete solitary confinement. One morning I heard a banging against the wall of a cell in my cooler block. The banging didn't stop, and I knocked for a guard and asked what the noise was.

He said in German, "A kriegie sick in the head," indicating with a circling motion of his finger around his ear that a prisoner was mentally ill. Then he pretended he was knocking his head on the wall.

I asked the guard to put the poor fellow in with me. I said, "I just want to hold him and try to ease his worries and calm him down."

The guard refused to comply with my request. He told me there were orders from the higher-ups: No one in solitary gets together.

Later the knocking stopped and the next day I asked the guard about that prisoner. He told me the prisoner had died of a heart attack. Shocked and angry, I cursed the guard for not letting me help with the prisoner. I certainly didn't believe that he had died of a heart attack. I'd seen too much evidence of the Nazi superman myth and the idea that "lesser" people—Jews, Slavs, the retarded, the weak—should be purged, including even the aged. I never did learn how the man died—nor his name, his nationality, or the prison compound he was from. The guard couldn't, or wouldn't, tell me anything.

Even with events such as these, I must say, quite honestly, that I never hated the Germans for what they did to me. I deserved most of the punishment I received, and of course I did my darnedest to cause them great trouble and cost them time with my escapes. But I did thoroughly detest the Nazi system and the Germans' treatment of other people, the *Untermenschen*, under that system.

On my first entry into Germany through Brenner Pass from Italy, we had changed trains in the Munich *Bahnhof* (railway station). There I first saw the great indignities that "lesser" people were made to suffer. Groups of people in tattered clothes, each with a yellow star on the back and a jacket marked with a big J for

Jude, were prodded and herded like starved cattle into filthy boxcars. The phrase "Man's inhumanity to man" frequently came to mind. I recall an incident involving a young Hitler Youth soldier of the Afrika Korps in a jail in Gafsa. Another prisoner, a black soldier, perhaps Senegalese, was wearing a crucifix. The young Nazi tore the cross from the prisoner's neck and hurled it across the room, shouting in German, "*Gibt es keinen Krist!*" (There is no Christ!). And I remember saying to myself that such bastards could never win the war.

On other occasions, usually when traveling under guard in Germany, I saw German overseers whipping and beating Slavic prisoners and slave laborers, both men and women, in the fields. Some of my POW friends told me of incidents far worse.

When I was finally let out of the cooler in August 1943, after my ambulance break, I returned to receive a warm welcome from my messmates. Dick Schrupp and Hank Burman made a cake from Red Cross goodies and iced it with sweet, thickened Condendo, and Don Stine decorated it with "Welcome Back, Major Sage!" They said they had great fun watching the ferrets who came to search my room after I escaped.

They were amused at the welcome I had prepared for the Germans. With almost worthless German scrip I had bought a stack of cardboard insoles for use as boot soles. The night before I went out in the ambulance, I tacked insoles, alternating left and right footprints, from the door of my room a few feet across the floor to the wall, then diagonally up the wall, across the ceiling, and down to the top of the window on the outside wall. There I wrote a note in both English and German, with an arrow pointing to the window that read, "He went that-a-way!" My messmates said the ferrets almost turned blue when they read it.

Another bit of comic relief was awaiting me in my small stack of mail, which had built up a little during the escape and my seventh stretch of solitary in the cooler. There was an official letter for Mr. Jerry M. Sage from the draft board in San Francisco notifying me that I was late in reporting to my draft board and that Uncle Sam wanted me and that if I didn't respond in thirty days they'd come and get me. By that time I'd been on very active duty for well over a year, plus six months on and off as a prisoner. I wrote the draft board to hurry and come and get me, and I'd be waiting for them!

After eating the welcome-home meal and reading my mail, I met with Roger Bushell, Wings Day and other X organization leaders to give them a report about what I had seen and heard on my travels. I told them that I had looked for the carefully guarded factory where the Germans were supposed to be making some kind of a rocket, but had seen no sign of it.

Again I took up my old tunnel job of providing diversion teams and final dispersal people for hiding the sand. By then the sand had already mounted to close to a hundred thousand pounds.

In this period of July and August 1943 there was another noteworthy escape by an American, with many similarities to my ambulance escape—but more successful, in my book, because he stayed out longer. Lieutenant Alvin Vogtle of Birmingham, Alabama, was a Spitfire pilot forced to crash-land behind German lines by a weather and fuel crisis in early January 1943. I had always heard him called Sammy Vogtle by his colleagues. When I asked him how he got the name Sammy, he told me that in radio communications among the planes, nicknames rhyming with the pilots' home towns or states were often used. Vogtle was identified as "Sammy from Alabamy."

Vogtle was a genuine eager beaver. He was first sent to Oflag 21B from the Dulag Luft interrogation center. In March he and a Captain Oliver tried to cut their way through the thick coils of wire at a spot that was shielded from the goon box. They worked only half an hour at noon each day, when most Germans were eating. On the fourth day they were about to reach the last layer of wires. By coincidence there was a thorough inspection of the fence that day, and the guards found the hole cut nearly through. Immediately the hole was sealed off and the blind spot eliminated.

When he got to North Compound of Stalag Luft III, Vogtle immediately tried to find an escape route. He soon hit on the ash and trash cart as the best way to get out. This wagon was driven by an old German civilian and loaded with emptied Red Cross boxes, tin cans and ashes by the British orderlies. When he took his plan to Roger Bushell to get help from the X organization, he learned that a British prisoner had come up with a similar plan. They got together and agreed to cooperate. They then got Big X's permission plus some good information from Roger Bushell from his earlier escape in Czechoslovakia.

They two had decided to walk south to Czechoslovakia, the nearest non-German area, then called the Protectorate of Czechoslovakia by the conquering Nazis. There they hoped to encounter Czechs willing to aid them.

This was the same route that I had come up with quite independently for my own ambulance break. I didn't learn the details of Vogtle's experiences till much later, however. Vogtle made himself a cap from some old trousers and carried a homemade compass, maps from the forgers, and a small identification form saying he was a Spanish farm worker.

On the morning of July second, while some British officers diverted the driver's attention, the two escapees climbed up on the wagon and lay down. The orderlies hastily covered them with ashes, boxes and cans. After a short wait the wagon moved to the first gate of the vorlager and stopped for a brief inspection, then moved on to the outer gate. Here the gate guard climbed up the side of the wagon and began to poke into the ashes with a long, thin metal probe. On one stab the probe went right through the leg of Vogtle's companion, and Sammy heard the guard pull the wounded kriegie out of the cart.

The guard then probed on Sammy's side of the cart, but he was considerably deeper under the trash than his friend, and though the probe poked him several times, it did not penetrate. Much to Vogtle's amazement, the guard quit his probing and the wagon moved on out of the camp.

Vogtle put a box over his head and looked out over the top until the way was clear. He then jumped out and ran through the woods to the north of camp.

Though he had slipped out of the cart without attracting the driver's attention, he had to take evasive action because a civilian was walking down the road. Forced to run into the north woods, he then turned west a half mile or so, returning back across the road to the south at a dead run.

I enjoyed Sammy's own words about that run. "I thought someone was right behind me because I could hear loud footsteps. But when I ducked into a bush to look back, I realized it was just my heart pounding." He also said the aroma of the cart was evidently still with him: A trail of insects streamed behind him like the tail of a meteor. At a small stream he took off his jacket and washed up to reduce the insect menace. Then he rested in a thick wood until evening.

At dusk he started walking south, steering by the stars, following a route quite similar to the one I followed a few weeks later. He detoured around towns. During daylight hours he would hide either in the woods or in the middle of the grain fields.

One evening, he awoke to find that the grain around him had been cut to within ten yards of his hiding place. He came upon small deer, as close up as I had, and ate berries he found growing wild in the forest. They must have been blueberries, called *Blaubeeren* by the Germans, the same ones I fed on. They had both good and bad aspects. They were good to eat, but they were bad because the Germans also liked them, and in daylight wandering pickers were always a threat to escapees.

Vogtle got farther than I had. He managed to get out of Germany proper. He first noticed that road signs were in Czech rather than German. He crossed the border into the protectorate, and on the edge of a small town, he heard two women talking in what sounded to him like Czech. Having memorized a few Czech phrases, probably from Wally Valenta in camp, he told one of the women who he was and asked for food.

The woman gave him food, took him to friends and told him which towns to avoid because of the Gestapo. Then she showed him the best routes to his destination, Prague.

Sammy stopped at several farmhouses and small villages, always finding the Czechs friendly and willing to give him food. But he found no underground network that could really safeguard him and move him on toward freedom.

American prisoners of war in Stalag Luft III. From left to right: Lieutenant Colonel Mel McNickle, South Camp adjutant; Lieutenant Colonel Richard P. "Dick" Klocko, education officer; Colonel Charles G. "Rojo" Goodrich, senior American officer; Lieutenant Colonel Albert P. "Bub" Clark, security officer of North Camp and chairman of escape committee, South Camp.

The daily early line-up for hot water or ersatz tea. Most of the cans are out of sight against the wall.

The service for Corporal Miles, who was shot dead by a guard while standing in a South Camp kitchen doorway. Chaplain Murdo MacDonald stands left of center. Behind "Padre" MacDonald, saluting, is Colonel Goodrich.

A typical day in the washroom—scrubbing clothes or washing up.

A skit by kriegies over the "radio station" in South Camp. At other times we would hear the mellifluous voice of disc jockey Bill Nance (not shown) over the loudspeakers as he broadcast news, comedy and music.

Alvin W. Vogtle, Jr., "Sammy from Alabamy," was an avid escaper and a dependable scrounger for South Camp escape materials. This sketch is by Carl Holmstrom.

Britishers in North Camp: Major Johnny Dodge; Wing Commander Hetty Hyde; H.M.A. "Wings" Day; Squadron Leader Williams.

The Luft Bandsters, a South Camp band led by Duke Diamond (reeds) and Dusty Runner (trumpet). The band's name was a play on the German label for kriegies, who were called the Luft Gangsters (Air Gangsters).

My messmates from North and South Camps: Willie Wigger, Dick Schrupp, Martin Plocher, Hank Burman, Don Stine, Gene Shaljean.

In the North Camp barracks. At top is Wally Floody, the Canadian tunnel engineer, resting after his digging shift. Sam Sangster, at lower left, scans the Nazi propaganda sheet, the *Volkischer Beobachter.* Beside him on the bunk is Mike Wood. At right is Ivan "Pop" Collett.

Colonel Charles G. Goodrich, senior American officer, Stalag Luft III.

The author, just home, in March 1945.

Alexander Kramerenko, "the Mad Russian," and Robert Hermann. Both were on B-17 crews.

Bob "Maxie" Menning wins a bet, and Bob McCormick forfeits his hair. Standing next to them (at ease) is Martin Plocher. Jerry Ahearne, Gene Shaljean and another kriegie look on.

Donald A. Stine, fine artist and master escape forger, from his German POW identity card.

Bob Hermann, weightlifter and one of “Sage's Storm Troopers.” He was among the thirty last-stand commandos who trained in South Camp.

Squadron Leader Bill Jennens, North Camp adjutant, was the man who kicked in my ribs for the ambulance escape. Here he discusses matters with Major Davy Jones.

In center, bearded Davy Jones, a head tunneler, has his arm around Hal "Shorty" Spire. Shorty was an avid escaper who could conceal himself in containers as small as a cabbage crate or a toolbox.

In South Camp, left to right: Ralph Johnson, Allen Karstens, the author and Dick Kimball. Kimball, Southard (a South African), and I escaped together after wrecking a boxcar window en route to Tunis. Karstens and Johnson were in a second group of three who jumped out of the hole in the boxcar.

Davy "Tokyo" Jones, in shorts, with Buck Ingram. Both were diggers of the tunnels Tom, Dick and Harry.

With my mother, Ruth Myers Sage, at the Christmas in April party, 1945.

With my father, E. Howard Sage, April 1945.

"Judge" Bob Brown of Spokane and Padre Murdo MacDonald of Scotland could be practicing for one of their famous debates or "liar's contests" but it's really a fish story!

John Bennett, master compass-maker, also coordinator of all escape factories and of procurement in South Camp.

Charles C. "Hupe" Huppert, South Camp manufacturer.

Beginning second from left (standing): Tex Newton, Major Huston, theater officer, Pudge Wheeler and Irving Biers, a play director.

Gene Shaljean, Dave McCorkle, the author and Hank Burman.

A goon box with searchlights, high above the barbed wire. The guard is armed with a machine gun. In the background, the forest where I escaped from the ambulance.

Constructing sets in the South Camp theater.

A "keintrinkwasser" can and "best china."

Oberfeldwebel Hermann Glemnitz, chief German security ferret, looks as though he's waving me to the cooler. In fact, Glemnitz and I had an arm's-length respect for one another.

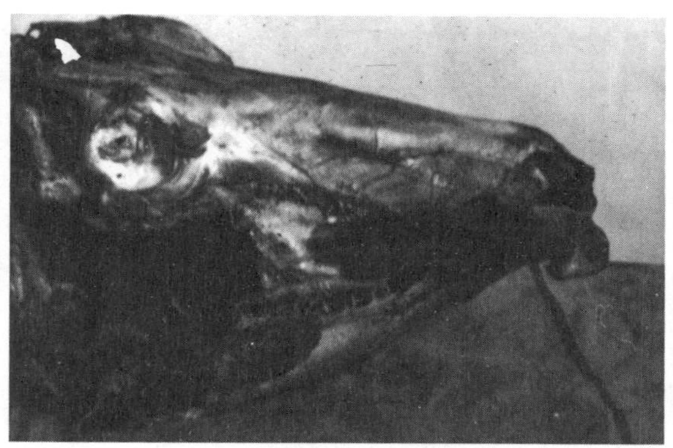

A surprise treat from the German ration—soup bone.

Chipping away stumps in South Camp to make firewood.

A typical kriegie room.

The author's letter to his sister and family, July 14, 1943, describing the great Fourth of July celebration.

JULY 14, 1943

DEAR SIS + ALL:

OH, HAPPY DAY! FIRST MAIL TODAY— MOM'S ISN'T HERE YET. WHEN DID YOU HEAR I WAS CAPTURED BEHIND GERMAN LINES? HAVE YOU WRITTEN BEFORE? GENE SOUNDS FINE— WILL TRY TO BRING HIM A GRADUATION PRESENT FROM HERE. CONGRATS, LAD! BELOW IS TEXAN FLIER'S CONCEPTION OF HOW I LOOKED IN TUNISIA IN FEB. HOPE YOU ALL "GET THE POINT" AS I DID. JOANNIE + TREE LOOKED FINE. HAD BIG FOURTH WITH RAISIN WINE BREW, SERPENTINE THRU BRITISH BARRACKS WITH REVERE + HOSS + ME IN TOPHAT AS UNCLE SAM WITH NATURAL BEARD, "SPIRIT OF '76", ETC. PLAYED BALL, SANG, AND THREW ALL SENIOR OFFICERS IN FIRE POOL. BOB B. + PALS THREW ME IN FIRST + WE CHUCKED IN THE REST. GENE, I'M PLAYING BALL, TOO. PITCHED 9 WINS TO LEAD LEAGUE HERE. BROKEN RIB IS ABOUT WELL NOW + AM PLAYING BACKFIELD IN RUGBY. EXERCISE + STUDY KEEP MIND OFF THE BARBED WIRE! PLEASE SAVE THIS "DISGRUNTLED DONALD" FOR ME. WILL RUSH WEST AS FAST AS I CAN WHEN THIS IS OVER.

LOVE,

Jerry

"GOOD TO THE LAST DROP"

In front of the greenhouse, Oflag 64. From left: Carl Hunsinger, Clarence Ferguson, John Creech, George Durgin, John Slack.

Standing: Tex Newton, B. W. Meyer, Buck Ingram, Bill Geiger, M. D. Draper. Squatting: I. G. McDaniels, Robert Ries, Lieutenant Colonel Bub Clark, Ed Tovrea.

A vista from South Camp toward West Camp, then under construction.

The winter exodus from Oflag 64 on January 22, 1945.

In the background, Bob Hermann and Cy Widen check supplies as an aide unwraps goods.

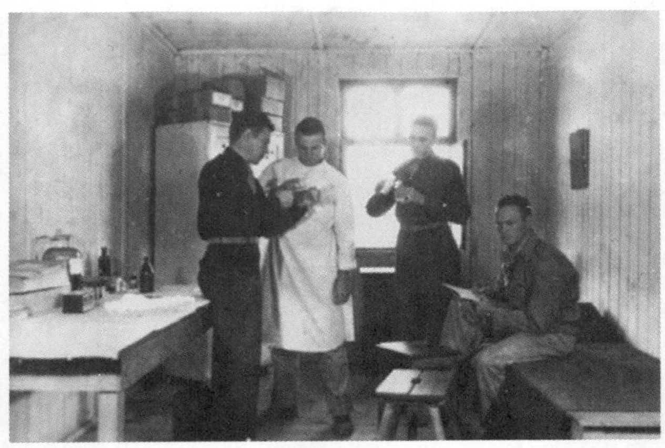

First aid staff. At left is Heston Daniel, a Golden Gloves boxer from Louisiana State University. The man in white is Luther Cox of Baltimore. Harold Whiteman of Atlanta stands by the rear window.

An evening game of cards. Mel McNickle is in the light-colored sweater, looking on. The escaper "Shorty" Spire lies on the bunk in the background.

Typical mess table. Dick "Wings" Kimball is second from left.

This painting of the author by Don Stine won the Stalag Luft III art contest in December 1943. Stine named the portrait "Stille Tod" (Silent Death). Note the two skulls looking down from the background. (I grew several beards in camp, but I always shaved them off on escapes.)

A portrait of the author in the late 1950s.

H.M.A. "Wings" Day, a great RAF leader and an indomitable escaper. The painting is by Henri Picard, a Belgian RAF flier who was executed during the "Great Escape." The inscription for Jerry Sage is from Wings Day.

Major David Mudgett Jones, of the Doolittle Tokyo raid, was an expert tunneler. Portrait by Don Stine.

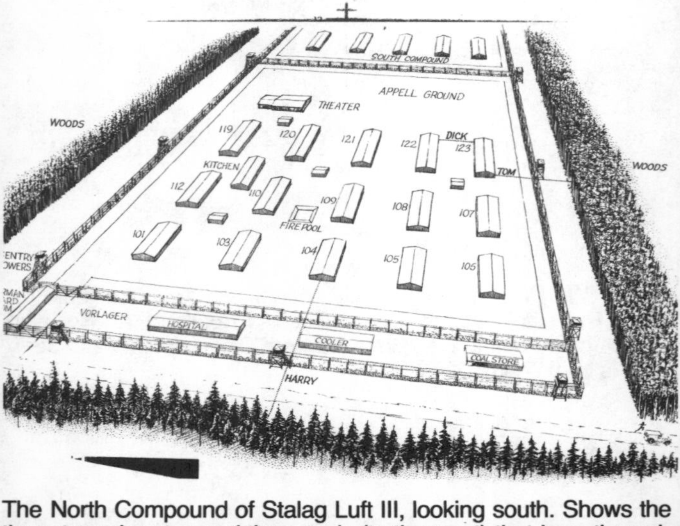

The North Compound of Stalag Luft III, looking south. Shows the three tunnel routes and the woods (to the west) that I ran through after I escaped from the ambulance. Drawing by Don Stine.

A quick pencil sketch by Don Stine of the area along the fence between North and South Camps.

View of a guard box, with kriegies trudging along the perimeter walk inside the warning rail.

Liberation day at Moosburg. Three of my friends are aboard the tank. Seated, second from left, is Lieutenant Colonel A. P. "Bub" Clark. Blowing a smoke ring from his victory cigar is Lieutenant Colonel Bob "Moose" Stillman. Seated at right, my former messmate and camp interpreter, Dick Schrupp.

In Oflag 64. From left to right: Lieutenant Colonel John K. Waters, Colonel "Pop" Goode, a YMCA visitor, Lieutenant Colonel Schaefer and Colonel Millet.

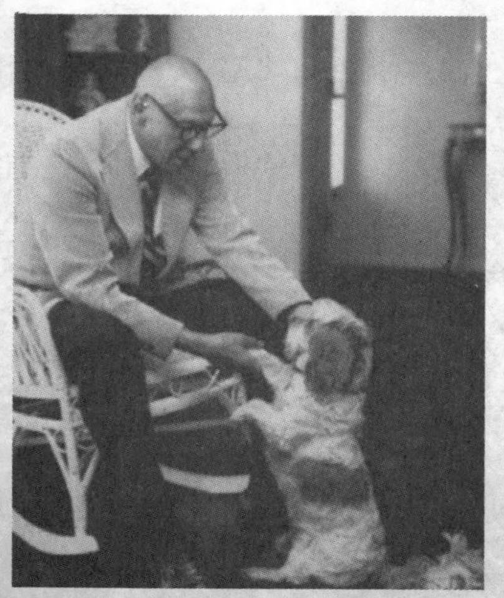

The author, Retired Colonel Jerry Sage, discussing the book with his dog Buddha at his home in Enterprise, Alabama.

Photograph by Doug Paramore, *The Enterprise Ledger.*

Colonel Jerry Sage, 1983

Photograph by John Chew

Vogtle was finally suspected when he tried to get help in the town of Bakov. Local police asked for his papers, checked on the address of his employer and telephoned the company to confirm Sammy's claim that he was a Spanish workman. It didn't take them long to expose Vogtle as an impostor. The policemen fed Vogtle, then held him until guards came to take him to the local civilian prison at Jungbunzlau, a short distance northeast of Prague.

The prison was run by the German SS, who provided SS guards for half of the prisoners, leaving the lesser prisoners to the Czech guards in the other half. For eleven days Vogtle was placed in solitary confinement in the Czech half of the prison. The Czechs treated him kindly and sometimes gave him extra food to augment the meager regulation meals. He also was allowed thirty minutes of exercise in the courtyard each day with several other prisoners. On the eleventh day Vogtle was transferred to a cell in the German half of the prison with a Yugoslav who had escaped from his work camp in Germany.

As a military prisoner Vogtle was not treated so harshly as many other prisoners under the SS. Every day he could hear the cries of men being beaten. After twelve more days Vogtle was interrogated by the officer in charge of prisons. Vogtle stuck by his name, rank, serial number and POW status.

Shortly, guards from Stalag Luft III appeared to take him back by train. He spent another fourteen days in the same cooler that I had just left. On the trip Vogtle lost about thirty pounds and his feet were sore, but he had traveled south a total of about one hundred fifty miles. He was free for ten days and in Czechoslovakia for nearly a month.

* * *

Another of our colleagues who had gone out on the delousing parade was returned to North Camp that summer of 1943 with an amazing story.

Soon after the group broke up in the woods, Johnny Stower, the tough little Spanish-Britisher from Argentina, was stopped by a guard near the camp. When he showed his forged pass as a Spanish worker, he was let go. He walked across country, following about the same route toward Czechoslovakia that Sammy Vogtle and I took on our separate ventures. In a Czechoslovakian town Stower found a friendly Czech bartender who gave him better civilian clothes and some money and helped him get a train ticket to a town near the Swiss border. He walked across the border at night, not knowing that he was crossing a narrow strip of Switzerland that stuck out into Germany. He was caught by a German border guard as he walked back into Germany on the other side. After some weeks in prison he was sent back to Stalag Luft III.

Later it seemed a double tragedy that he should have been temporarily free on Swiss soil and then recaptured by a fluke of geography. The next March he went out through tunnel Harry and was one of the fifty officers caught and executed.

Chapter 18

During my weeks on the road and in the cooler, the tunnels progressed well. Each one was at least seventy feet long and was equipped with wooden trolleys for hauling both the diggers and the sand, the latter in detachable boxes. Each wheel was made of three disks of the toughest bedboard wood, screwed tightly together with the inner disk slightly larger to serve as a flange on the rail. Travis used metal stove rods for axles. They turned inside hard wooden wheel bearings that were greased with margarine.

The rails were made of inch-wide strips cut from barracks moldings and nailed parallel to the tunnel floor about a foot apart. The trolley was pulled each way by handwoven ropes anchored at each end.

The diggers worked mainly in four-man shifts. One kriegie worked the bellows, a contraption of tough kit bags sewn together. The bags could be stretched and collapsed on a movable frame to force air up the tunnel through Klim-can pipes buried under the floor.

At the start of a shift, two men stripped and put on gritty woolen long johns, the uniform for digging. One lay on his belly on the trolley and paddled himself up to the tunnel face with his hands. The other pulled back the trolley with the rope and followed on up to the face. The fourth man, back in the roomy shaft beneath the trap, hauled the trolley back and hooked the empty sand boxes on it. Then the second man, who lay facing the shaft, hauled it up to the face. The lead digger cut at the face and pushed the sand back to the second man, who loaded it into the boxes on the trolley and jerked the rope to signal the shaft man. After the shaft man hauled it back, he emptied the sand boxes into bags in the storage area, replaced the boxes on the trolley and signaled the rear digger to haul back the trolley. When another wooden frame was needed for shoring up the tunnel, the second digger sent a note back on the trolley. The man in the shaft would load needed items from the stacks of preslotted and tongued bedboards and send them to the face.

Pieces of air pipe and fresh fat lamps were also sent forward to the tunnel face as needed. The diggers hated the lamp fumes, which were never completely cleared from the tunnels by the air pump. The diggers often had headaches and intermittent coughs, and they would sometimes spit black.

Eventually the fat lamps were replaced with electric bulbs. An electrical engineer did some rewiring, and after splicing together all the pieces of wire he could save, he hooked into the power line and put electric lights down into the shafts. Later, kriegie scroungers walked away with two coils of wire that German workmen had carelessly left behind, and lights were added farther up the tunnel.

As the bags of sand were pulled up from the trap, the penguins strolled in and out, their trouser bags filled with sand. They casually wandered in to one of the dead spaces where my teams were gardening or to one of my silent killing classes. While Hank Burman and I made spectacular attacks to rivet the guards' attention, the onlookers worked the penguins' loads of sand into the topsoil with their feet. Still other penguins dropped their sand in the midst of other diversionary groups—the boxers, fencers, debaters, shot-putters, volleyball players and just plain squabblers.

Meanwhile, the tailors were designing, sewing and storing away a wardrobe of German work clothes, suits, and uniforms for the tunnel escapers. The forgers were hand-printing beautiful copies of documents obtained by Valenta's goon tamers or by straight theft. Hand-carved from boot heels, the most realistic stamps of the Nazi swastika or the German eagle were used to authenticate the papers. Scores of maps were drawn and reproduced in indelible ink by the gelatin process. Our crude but efficient compasses were stockpiled. Things seemed to be going almost too well.

It was then that a crew of half-starved Russians started clearing the forest just to the south of our North Compound. The trucks with building materials began to arrive after the foliage had been hauled away. Senior British and American officers questioned Kommandant von Lindeiner, who told them that the Russian crew was building a new compound where the Americans would be separated from the British. The news was a real blow. It meant that if the Germans had the compound ready before we could break a tunnel, the Americans would miss out completely.

Wings Day and Bushell decided to go all out on Tom, the most advanced tunnel, and close down Dick and Harry. Floody picked three shifts of the best diggers, mainly Americans, and the smaller, more maneuverable tunnelers of the Allies. Work on Tom was rapidly moving forward when a ferret, possibly looking for an odd radish, stumbled onto some golden sand in the garden.

The next day Glemnitz and Rubberneck brought in all the ferrets. Turning over the gardens, they found more yellow sand. From then on, the ferrets intensified their searches of the barracks and drove huge heavy wagons around all the barracks near the fence, trying to collapse any tunnels. But ours were safe at thirty feet down.

We became even more careful in our routing of penguins. I rousted out every dispersal and diversionary team available. As the Germans usually left alone for a while any area they'd already searched, I could route more sand into the gardens the ferrets had just uncovered. They didn't think to check them again until Glemnitz found some fresh sand several days later, the equivalent of several feet forward for Tom. Glemnitz then brought in soldiers with picks and shovels and had them dig a trench about four or five feet deep along the barracks on the western row. The trench ran between the barracks, including Block 123 where Tom began, and the barbed wire that surrounded the perimeter. The ferrets probed the bottom of the trench with thin steel rods five or six feet long, hammering them down and hoping to hit the top boards of a tunnel. Eventually, their steel rods clanged against something hard and immovable. That discovery got them temporarily excited, and we enjoyed their discomfiture when they found out they had hit only rocks.

My dispersal crews were stretched to their limit in mixing topsoil and creating diversions. The ferrets watched the gardens like hawks. In order to continue our blitz of Tom, we decided to put the sand down tunnel Dick. We sent loaded penguins on carefully worked out systems of routes to the Block 122 wash-room shaft of Dick. Dick's diggers then took over, trolleying the sand to the tunnel face and bringing out the bedboard frames and rails as they filled in the tunnel. All salvaged material was moved to Tom, which now extended well under the barbed wire. Again things were going all too well.

One day workers appeared in the woods to the west of our compound, armed again with axes and saws, and began felling trees right and left. Within a few days nearly forty yards of forest had been cleared. We learned that still another compound was to be built for the ever-growing stream of American airmen. Tom was at least one hundred feet short of the trees and we had to dig on, though sand dispersal had by that time become a real problem.

Tunnel Dick was now full and we didn't want to fill Harry because we had to hold it open in case Tom was found. Ferrets were digging every day in the dirt of the camp, in the gardens and at nearly every activity site.

We resorted to storing sand in Red Cross boxes that kriegies usually kept under their bunks. We started in the barracks that had most recently been searched and got away with it for several days, adding another precious fifty feet or so to Tom's progress. Glemnitz found boxes of sand in a surprise search of Block 103 and again ruined all the gardens around it with his heavy anti-tunnel trucks.

When we heard that the Americans would be moved to South Camp in about two weeks, Bushell decided to seal Tom as it was. It was not yet to the woods, but it reached well beyond the circle of light thrown from the goon boxes. He figured we'd probably be able to get out there and crawl in the dark the rest of the way to the tree line. This wasn't ideal, but Bushell didn't want to run any more risk from sand dispersal.

Roger asked me to set up a giant fake dispersal to

throw the ferrets off the track and give us a breather. I rousted out forty or fifty "volunteers." I worked them into Block 104, then sent them walking in groups of two or three across the camp to Block 119. A ferret noticed and sent another ferret running out of the camp.

In came Glemnitz and a squad of guards. They chased everyone out of Block 119 and searched it for hours, finding nothing but kriegie junk and the Red Cross boxes. One of Valenta's "honest-faced" men told Glemnitz later he was being ribbed by the whole thing. The man said we wanted to keep the ferrets busy looking for sand that had really been dug right from under the gardens the searchers had gone over and that there had never been any tunnel at all.

Glemnitz was only half fooled and he kept up a search of all huts next to the wire. Eventually persistence and suspicion paid off. One day a ferret was idly tapping his probe on the concrete floor by the chimney of Block 123 when the point stuck in the concrete and a chip of cement came out. Closer inspection revealed the outline of the trap door.

The Germans were ecstatic as they smashed Minskewitz' carefully concealed trap, which had served so many so well for so long. They then called in engineers, and with Teutonic thoroughness, blew up the tunnel with explosives. In their enthusiasm they also blew the roof off Block 123, resulting in a long and costly repair job.

With Tom's undoing, morale in North Compound plummeted. The ferrets were so hopped up that Roger decided to leave Harry sealed until things cooled down. A few days later, in early September, we Americans were marched over into the new South Camp. So many of us had given so many hours and so many buckets of sweat to the tunnels that Wings Day and Bushell led the Britishers in thanking us most warmly at a farewell party. We had enjoyed the camaraderie with them, but we mainly regretted not getting out of the tunnels together. Later we would learn that we were more fortunate than we realized.

George Harsh of Atlanta, the former tailgunner with the Royal Canadian Air Force, and a few other Americans who had lived many years in England, like Bill Webster, remained in North Compound. Murdo MacDonald, parachuting padre from the Isle of Skye, had such a church following of Americans that on his own volition he came with us to South Compound. It was a great asset to our mental and spiritual health, and a lift to our collective sense of humor to have him along. Some of us entered South Compound grimly determined to leave it as soon as possible. Glemnitz was sent with us to see that we didn't!

On September 8, 1943, we Americans from North Camp, under the leadership of Colonel Rojo Goodrich, marched between double rows of armed guards out of the vorlager and down alongside the camp on the kommandantur side and entered our new home, the South Camp of Stalag Luft III. The overall area was quite a bit smaller than North Compound. It had fourteen barracks buildings, and a much smaller sports field that needed destumping. It was pretty rough playing ball on an obstacle course with the tree stumps as a constant hazard. An additional shower hut had been built, but never completed. It was still not ready at the time I was purged out of South Camp much later on. During my entire stay in the Sagan camps, we either had sponge baths or used a hose and a punched-can shower at the basins in the washroom in each block.

There was also a large cookhouse and later we built a theater. The new camp buildings had ample space when we first moved in, but we were able to spread out for only a few days because the population kept growing as the American raids got bigger and bigger and as more and more planes, both bombers and fighters, were shot down. The Germans opened a new camp for the British at Belaria in January 1944, and they built the new West Compound for American prisoners right where tunnel Tom should have broken for us in April of that year.

I later heard that in Center Camp and East Camp the Americans were kept pretty well clean-shaven. We entered South Camp with quite a carry-over of beards and moustaches and had come to look much like the British in North Compound. The handlebar moustaches were at their best on Lieutenant Colonel Dick Klocko and Ed Bryant. In fact, Bryant came to be called Handlebar Hank after the great wavy appendage under his nose.

In the whiskery area, Davy Jones had a huge, almost blue-black beard, a prize item. Joe Boyle, an artist and poet in our camp, had a blonder one, as did Don Eldridge, one of the men who worked on the news flow in the camp and who lived in one of my blocks. I grew at least four beards; I'd shave them off on each escape. My usual style was a squared-off goatee with a moustache. Though my natural hair color is blond, the goatee grew in with a distinct reddish tinge, a heritage from my red-haired Virginian grandmother.

Some people became quite professional barbers. Kriegie Hall, so called because he was the first American shot down from the Eagle Squadron in the RAF, eventually set up a regular barbershop in South Camp. But I had first-class barber treatment from one of my messmates, Don Stine, the fine artist, and I greatly appreciated it.

Since there were no real showers, the basins in the washrooms were used not only for bathing, but also for washing our clothes. Doing the laundry wasn't bad in warm weather, except when we had to wash our heavy outer pants and jackets. But in wintertime it was miserable trying to wash the standard-issue long johns. These long winter underwear, made of wood fiber, were nearly unmanageable. When you washed them, they got bulky and heavy with water. They felt like they were made of slippery elm.

We were short of many necessities. We had very poor brooms and mops for cleaning, and most of them wore out after about two sweepings of a barracks. Also we were short of that prime necessity, toilet paper. I learned to treasure it. From that time on, in later wars, excursions and camping trips, I always carried an extra roll of that lovely luxury.

We had to use cut-up squares of German propaganda newspapers. We enjoyed this in a way, when out of the *Volkischer Beobachter* we'd cut or tear out Hitler's or Göring's or Goebbels' picture for our daily ablutions. It seemed to serve an appropriate end.

We got our toilet articles either from the YMCA or in personal parcels from home. I was given my double-edged Gillette razor by a kindly Britisher who had an extra. I carefully sharpened the blade on the heel of my hand every day and made it last for months. The habit persisted long after the war and people stared in amazement when I carried out that procedure in a washroom stop while traveling.

Although some clothing came from the YMCA, we had to use British clothing for a long time. The British did a better job than the Americans in getting clothes to us in our early prison days. However, the YMCA got us other extras, including educational and recreational materials. They sent in the oil paints that Don Stine used to paint the portrait of me that won for him the 1943 kriegie art contest. The cardboard he painted on also came from the YMCA. (He later carried that portrait all the way home for me.) The YMCA sent in musical instruments and religious and educational supplies, some of which we used for entertainment.

Fortunately, the YMCA also sent light bulbs, which were always in short supply. The light bulbs would be installed in the halls by the Germans and they'd be almost as quickly removed by the kriegies and put in our rooms to allow us to read in the evenings. There was one sixty-watt bulb or two forty-watt bulbs for an eight-, ten- or twelve-man room, fifteen by twelve, and this just wasn't enough light to read by.

It was even worse in the washrooms and the latrines. The bathrooms at the end of the building were for night use only, and each had only a fifteen-watt light. When the camp opened, each overhead bulb was encased in a big sphere of white glass about fifteen inches across, but the covers disappeared one by one.

The bowl-shaped covers made ideal containers for our brews. We put our concoction of raisins, prunes or other dried fruit in those big light bulb covers and allowed them to ferment. Eventually our brews caused us problems with the camp command and they were outlawed. All the light bulb covers were taken away, including those we hadn't used. So we wound up with just plain bare bulbs, when we had any at all.

One cook stove in the little cooking room of the barracks, with only enough space for two cooks at a time, had to feed fourteen rooms full of kriegies who were hungry all the time. The stoves were fueled with coal briquets, each about half a kilogram—that's a little over a pound for each briquet—but the little chunk of charcoal already had most of its energy extracted.

The German conversion plants produced margarine, synthetic oils and other materials from the coal before the residue was pressed into a briquet. What was left was the grayish-black block, capable of producing only a tiny bit of heat. In a way it was a good thing that the stumps were left in the playing field. With great effort we were able to hack them into smaller pieces with axes and saws, and use them for fuel.

As you can imagine, there was never enough of anything good in camp except good will and a sense of humor, but sometimes even the sense of humor ran thin. Since everything was in short supply, under Colonel Goodrich's direction we developed quite a chain of command on the administrative side.

In North Camp, the key positions in both the X organization and in daily camp administration were held by the British, although Americans assisted considerably. In South Camp, where we were running the whole show ourselves, we had to fill all the key positions of supply, logistics, and other administrative operations with American officers.

Lieutenant Colonel Bub Clark was Colonel Goodrich's executive officer and chief administrative assistant, as well as chief of X organization. Lieutenant Colonel Dick Klocko, our pole vaulter and one of our many philosophers, was put in charge of all education and entertainment. We built up a fine library. We got some books from the British at first, but then we started receiving a great number from home, both from the YMCA and from other organizations. The libraries were used by students for reference work and by all for the simple pleasures of fiction. At first church services were held in any available empty room, but Padre

MacDonald had so many people attending his services that the room became crowded.

We built a kriegie theater before winter settled in, and Padre began holding his services there even as it was being built. His classes were always jammed, even after the theater was finished. On Sunday men ran right from appell to get a seat. The overflow stood outside and listened at the theater windows.

There were classes in religion and well-schooled choirs that put on Handel's *Messiah* and other cantatas at Christmas and Easter. Our kriegie college, Sagan U, was in full swing in South Camp. Padre MacDonald, Bob Brown, and Dick Klocko taught philosophy and psychology.

At Sagan U, Padre MacDonald and Dick Klocko ran several successful experiments in hypnotism. As word got around the camp, they were called on to demonstrate for larger audiences in the theater, providing some evenings for hypnotic entertainment. Klocko taught Spanish, and we also had classes in German, French and Norwegian. Many aircraft subjects were taught, including aeronautics, dynamics and air engineering. To satisfy broader interests we had economics, drama and public speaking. I taught salesmanship, self-defense and unarmed combat. Later on we were to use these skills in dead earnest.

Major Harold Houston was general supervisor of many and varied theater activities. Each show had its own director, and there was a great range to the repertoire, from Shakespeare to slapstick. One of the funniest shows was an old vaudeville routine billed as "Crowley and Shea," put on by Ralph "Bud" Gaston and Dick Coffee. They were truly funny. And in addition to plays we had lots of music. Major Duke Diamond, Dusty Runner, Tex Newton and many other artists were all skilled performers.

Chapter 19

A very important part of camp life was, of course, the kitchen. We were always hungry, and it was especially important to morale to have everything distributed on an equitable basis, which was done very well in that camp. The kitchen or cookhouse was under Captain Jack Shuck and A.J. Burton. Our meals in South Camp were still based primarily on the one or two slices of *Roggenbrot*—that's rye bread made of coarse grain plus potatoes, sometimes plus sawdust. About three days a week, the kitchen staff would boil up some barley soup. It was just German barley boiled in water, but it helped keep body and soul together at noontime. The soup was issued in pitchers to each mess. Each mess's stooge for the day got in line with his pitcher to get the ration, bring it back, and serve it.

Before POW days I'd never heard of kohlrabi, had never seen a sugar beet, and would never have thought of ordering a dish of rutabaga. But in Germany these items were easier to get than anything else, perhaps because nobody else wanted them. Kohlrabi is a mis-shapen bulge in the stem of a peculiar turnip. Young rutabagas are not bad, but the ones we got must have had overactive pituitary glands. They were huge, heavy, dried-out things that the British called horse turnips or Swedes. Both these vegetables are extremely pithy, sometimes even leaving splinters in the gums.

The German issue was so scanty that we were really grateful for anything. Our captors gave us barrels of a pink jam they called *Marmalada*. It was made from ground sugar beets, boiled slightly.

When cabbages were available and if the kitchen staff told us they were clean, it meant that we could eat them raw as a slaw or a salad. But if they were wormy, not clean, we had to cook them first to kill the worms.

I really think the best food we got from the Germans were the potatoes, good white ones. We didn't get nearly enough of them. We had only one or two small ones each day, but they were a staple and we relied on them.

The cookhouse also issued hot water, the main ingredient in ersatz tea and coffee. The tea was made with mint leaves or other herbs and the coffee of ground grain with acorns. The Germans had a hard time getting coffee and tea themselves because of the Allied naval blockades. But good or bad, we drank the ersatz beverages basically because they were hot. Sometimes if we didn't have hot shaving water, we used this weak tea stuff to shave or wash.

Lieutenant Colonel Mel McNickle, one of the miracle boys who crashed in a fighter plane, was our adjutant. He assigned rooms, kept up the camp roster and daily report, and got from each block adjutant the total number of people who were sick or ready to stand appell. He would then swap figures with the German lager officer in charge of counting prisoners.

Another officer, R.E. Williams, did a superb job of supervising the issue of parcels from home. When the Germans opened these parcels and looked in them,

Williams would stand by to see that items were not "mislaid" or destroyed. Captain Carmichael had a similar job. As the mail officer, he received our mail in bulk from the German censors and then sorted it and handed it on to the block mailmen to deliver. Great day! Mail from home was one of the best of all morale boosters.

There were always people who needed medical attention. We had all the cases: battle wounds, illness, broken bones and injuries incurred playing sports. Given our poor camp diet, bruises were slow to heal and our teeth deteriorated until they were in terrible shape. We did have a medical first-aid room run by Captain Heston Daniel, the boxer from Louisiana State University. He had two fine assistants, Luther Cox and Harold Whiteman, from Baltimore, Maryland, and Atlanta, Georgia. Carl Holmstrom, another of the fine artists in camp, was in charge of issuing art supplies, and he made sure that both artists and art students received sketching materials.

Cy Widen and Bob Hermann issued camp property such as the water pitchers. The pitchers, made from a fragile porcelain-type material, would often break, but we also had a metal pitcher, called a *Keintrinkwasser*, which means literally "no drink of water." That's because the can was made of zinc, which could be poisonous. The zinc from the pitcher would make you ill if you drank from it over a period of time. The keintrinkwasser, which we sometimes shortened to the kein, would carry the water to wash in, which was not potable. It provided the hot water for washing ourselves and our clothes.

If you received something that you didn't particularly want in your Red Cross parcel or a parcel from home, you would trade your item at what was called the

Foodacco. We picked that up from the British abbreviation for "food account." The American Foodacco was run by Quentin Burgett and Al LaChasse, the latter my California friend who told me about the loose bolts in the right rear window of the ambulance.

We had a news room and bulletin board outside the kitchen shack and some of the people who worked on that were Ed MacMillan, Frank Saunders and Don Eldredge. We would digest the news over the German radio together with the items we got very quietly from elsewhere on our own—over our radios and from other sources. From these divergent sources we would then try to develop the truest possible estimate of what was happening in the war effort and disseminate that information through the camp. We even had a sort of "radio station" that gave us broadcasts over a loudspeaker. I remember Bill Nance with a deep resonant voice was one announcer. Eventually from that station came news about an invasion only a couple of weeks before I had to leave this camp. That was a great day.

We were allowed to send out only three brief fold-up letters per month and four small postcards, just about half a normal postcard size, with room too scant for the message. You had to be very careful about what you chose to say or it would be blacked out by the censors, particularly anything derogatory or offensive about the Germans. When it arrived nearly all blacked out, your letter or postcard was pretty much wasted.

While the mail was in general a good morale booster, not every letter was a good one. We certainly had some classic Dear Johns besides the note from the kriegie's fiancée who had married his father and signed her note, "Love, Mother."

Another was a first letter from another fiancée: "You were listed as missing over a month ago, so I got married." We did our best to cheer each other up—actually, there were so many of those letters that they got to be quite a common occurrence. Still, it was pretty devastating to many of the men.

The camp had a newspaper called *The Circuit*, our name for the perimeter walk around the camp. *The Circuit* printed a lot of news: the sports scores, humor, and even Dear John letters if they were submitted. While it also attempted to keep up on the news of the war, most of the newspaper consisted of homey stuff concerning what went on in the camp. Most of it was written in a humorous vein; it reviewed recent entertainment and listed what was coming up.

During my time there the theater improved quite a bit. The Canadian food parcels were packed in large wooden crates; with the crate boards we were able to make quite comfortable seats for the theater, with everyone working together. In addition to plays the theater was the stage for radio programs and concerts. Some of our bands were very good. One of them, Dusty Runner's band, called the Luft Bandsters, was excellent. Duke Diamond had a truly great band, in the Glenn Miller mold. He had been with the big bands and played a marvelous saxophone.

Not long before Christmas 1943, Duke was allowed to take his band from South Camp over to North Camp to play for our British friends, then on to Center Camp for a concert. On the way back, outside the kommandantur, he played "America" so loudly that everyone could hear it. This, of course, is the same tune as the British national anthem, "God Save the King." Americans and British alike popped to attention, saluted and sang their own country's lyrics. But the kommandant didn't like this display of patriotism by the enemy; for this outburst Duke's band practice was banned for a week.

I'll never forget three good old American holidays in 1943. One, already described, was the unforgettable Fourth of July. Next was Thanksgiving; everyone in the compound tried to hoard food for that, saving the best things from their Red Cross parcels so they could have a really big bash. Even if we couldn't have any turkey, we could eat as much as we wanted on Thanksgiving Day.

That, of course, was the time the Germans chose to pull this court-martial on me for having threatened the three armed guards. Thanksgiving found me in solitary, eating one potato with weak barley soup. Nonetheless, I was glad my buddies back in camp did have a good Thanksgiving. Padre MacDonald gave a wonderful church service and everyone gave thanks for their loved ones, safe and well at home, for being alive and relatively well themselves, praying that all would be reunited before the next year.

For Christmas we again saved food and were able to have a huge bash. We laid down many brews again—kriegie wine, some of which was distilled. Wassail bowls graced many of the messes. We started socializing among the barracks, sharing each other's liquid refreshments and edibles. By Christmas night many were feeling no pain and decided to see their friends over in North Camp.

The fence between South and North Camps was double-barbed wire, with white sand borders and warning rails. The goon boxes were only at the extreme ends, but their weapons could fire the length of the fence between the camps. When some of us started climbing over the wire both ways, Colonel Goodrich called in a couple of us and asked us to start collecting our boys before some German got trigger-happy, so we went along the fence and brought some back.

Now, Willie Wigger didn't hold his liquor too well. He'd get a little bit pixilated after a couple of sips of kriegie brew. Fearing that he might fall into the wire, Hank Burman and I took turns carrying him home wrapped around our necks like a blond mink stole. Next morning, when they took the appell, I think there were about four Britishers in our camp and thirteen Americans with the British. Actually there were a few shots fired, but only a few and clearly over everybody's head, so no one was hurt as a result of this visitation.

At some of our kriegie reunions I've heard other men talk about taking a parole walk outside the barbed wire. "Parole" means word—you give your word not to try to escape. Nobody even asked me to give my parole because they knew very well that I would try to escape. Sometimes when I thought about all the shortages, the very hungry days, and all the time spent alone in solitary, I wondered which was real and which was fantasy: my life back in the States or in camp as a kriegie.

At the very start of South Camp, Colonel Goodrich called together Bub Clark, Davy Jones and me. In his own colorful way, Rojo said, "You gentlemen will be the X committee, the Unholy Three, and in charge of all nefarious activities." He explained that this included all escape activities, secret communications with our home country, communications across the wire with the British and the security required for all those activities. The three of us certainly had extensive experience.

Bub Clark was chairman and continued to be director of security and communications, as he had been in North Camp under the British. Davy Jones was the expert in all types of tunneling activities and had of course brought with him his two able lieutenants, Buck Ingram and Ed Tovrea, also fine diggers. I was to concentrate on the barbed wire and the vehicular jobs, and what the British called hard-arse travel.

We three worked well together. Entering a new camp, one always looked for oversights or mistakes by the Germans to make possible a snap escape. Such oversights had been apparent when North Compound was opened. The Germans had actually permitted some of the British to go over ahead of time and help build it. By doing so, the POWs were admirably situated to steal and hide materials for escapes. They had purposefully left a lot of trees standing to give us cover and conceal us.

Also in North Camp they hadn't taken very careful note of just how everything was before we entered. When we started to alter things in our tunneling and dispersing, it was easier for us to move things around without being noticed.

But South Camp was tougher. Glemnitz, the Germans' best security man, was sent over to direct the ferrets and all anti-escape activities. Long before the prisoners moved into South Compound, Glemnitz checked everything, leaving nothing to chance. South Compound was made as neat and clean as a pin, free of vegetation. All the trees were cut down and all the white sand was spread neatly between the guardrail and the fence so that any movement would stand out. The sand under the huts had been carefully raked so that any digging would be clearly visible. All loose objects, all carpentry implements and any other extras had been cleared away.

We saw, as we always did, that all those restrictive measures simply created more problems to be solved. We started working very quietly. The factories were started up under people who had gained some experience in the North Compound. Bub Clark made sure that our communications stayed open. Although communications between North and South Camps were strictly forbidden, one way to get messages through in a hurry was with Padre Mac. A Gaelic speaker from the North Camp would walk around the circuit yelling, "Say hi to Chaplain MacDonald for me." Padre Mac would come stroll on our South circuit parallel to the North Camp path. By chatting in Gaelic, their mother tongue, they could pass along information not meant for German ears and too foreign for our German keepers to decipher. In another subterfuge we threw messages over the fence in weighted four-ounce coffee cans. But we could do this only after both sides checked the perimeter to make sure no guards or goon-box sentries were watching.

We also used visual code signals. A man standing inside his barracks in North Camp holding some signal, a flashlight by night or a flag by day, sent messages to another man standing in one of our barracks in South Camp. You could use either the Boy Scout semaphore signal alphabet or just a wave to the right for dot and a wave to the left for a dash to represent Morse code. With some skill and luck we managed to keep communications open. Colonel Goodrich and Colonel Clark kept the activity of the coding messages under tight control. The little radio that we were able to carry with us from North Camp was also under maximum security.

Still another way we were able to communicate among the various compounds—East, Center, North, and South—was through the Catholic chaplain. There was only one, so he was allowed to visit his flocks in the various camps and could convey messages wherever he went. Occasionally there were meetings between the kommandant and the senior officers of the compounds, providing an opportunity for the officers to speak to each other.

Davy Jones, Ed Tovrea and Buck Ingram surveyed the camp very carefully, looking for likely spots to start a tunnel. They studied the innards of the aborts—the outside latrines, about twenty-holers. They also surveyed the cookhouse, though both that and the aborts were a long way from the fence. The situation was even more difficult than in North Camp, but even so they soon started coming up with plans. Meanwhile, I walked the circuit inspecting the barbed wire with Hank Burman, the home-run hitter and college football lineman who was my right-hand man.

To avoid confusion among individual escape attempts, escapers put up their proposals through their block X representative, who passed it on to the X committee to ensure that one try wouldn't detract from another and that we could all help each other. If it was a wire or a vehicular job, their ideas were given to me as their representative on the escape committee. I also asked the kriegies in each of the barracks to keep a close watch on every vehicle that moved in and out of the camp and to get all the details they could—its dimensions, a description of cargo, its schedule, comings and goings, plus any special tips, such as the one about the ambulance. You never knew when you could make a snap escape from a vehicle.

One of the first propositions that came to the X committee was from a couple of lieutenants who wanted to do a wire job involving two ladders. The ladders had to be constructed from materials taken from the buildings themselves and hidden in the walls of the barracks. One ladder was to go up the wire to the overhang, and the other would be placed across the two inner and outer top wires above the coiled barbs of concertina. The man would climb the first ladder, go across the second, and then drop down on the other side to freedom—given sufficient training, a dark or rainy night and good diversions.

To minimize wasted motion at the fence itself, we practiced inside one of the larger rooms, going up to the ladder and then up against the wall. The horizontal ladder was placed between two double bunks. Our escapers would practice scooting across that ladder and dropping down to the other side, moving as quietly as possible all the time. As our plans and practice improved, I thought we might get several men over the wire, so I assured the two lieutenants who brought in the scheme that they'd be number one and two to go, and that we'd be ready with four more trained men, including me, if all went well.

We knew we were just faking the conditions and it would be different out there at the wire, but we had planned a major diversion. We had to wait for a foggy night. We already knew we couldn't carry out the ladders and conceal them with those powerful searchlights moving. We knew that we needed diversions at each end to direct the beams of the goon-box searchlights away from the exit point. In addition to the Germans in the goon boxes, there were the strolling night guards who patrolled between each guardhouse.

We finally got a foggy night. The men had been prepared with all their escape materials and the whole escape committee was ready to run the diversion. Davy Jones on one side and Bub Clark on the other side, each with some well-trained assistants, went to the extreme right and extreme left of the escape point to attract the attention of the right and left goon boxes. They each had a grappling hook with tin cans attached to throw onto the wire. By pulling on the wire on these two sides, they would attract the attention of anybody on the extreme flanks of the operation. I was to draw the attention of the strolling guards right at the escape point itself and divert them away from that point. Then I'd circle back quietly to join the other three men after the two primary escapers got away. At my signal, the two diversion teams were then to go into action and the two lieutenants would tackle the wire. We couldn't use any visual signals in the fog, so my yell was to serve as the signal.

Moving noiselessly so as not to draw fire, the two lieutenants and I approached the wire in the fog. I particularly watched the nearest strolling guard. Just as he passed the point I'd selected for the job, I ran to the right and let out a yell. The guard immediately opened fire at me and ran in my direction, away from the escape point. Far to the right and left Clark and Jones slung their hooks across the wires and tugged on the long lines, drawing the attention of the goon box and strolling guards. While all this was happening, the two lieutenants raced to the wire and raised the first ladder. One man scrambled up and laid the second ladder across the top. In split seconds the leading escaper, the smaller one, crossed the wire, and quickly dropped down on the other side.

The second fellow was not so lucky. The ladder cracked and tilted when he was midway between the two rows of wire and he fell into the barbed concertina wire. He was caught a few minutes later. The other kriegie was able to stay out only a few hours until he was also caught in a dragnet that surrounded the camp.

After drawing the attention of the guards, Clark, Jones and all the second-wave escapers raced for our barracks. The fellows inside opened the windows for us. We were found happily "sleeping" a few minutes later when the Germans routed us out to see who was missing.

So we weren't completely skunked on this first escape attempt from South Compound. We did get one man loose. The guards had to turn out a lot of people to find him, and we'd have gotten both out if the top ladder hadn't somehow given way. In fact, four others of us would have been right behind.

These efforts were not a total failure. We had accomplished part of our escape mission, which was to keep the Germans busy, using up their time and materials chasing us so they couldn't devote so much to fighting at the front.

One of the next escape attempts was interesting to me because again history repeated itself—through Sammy Vogtle, the Spitfire flier. Sammy and Lieutenant John D. Lewis each came up independently with the same idea that Barry Mahon, Leroy Skinner and I had experimented with and discarded in North Camp in the spring. They decided to make a frame for a sand-covered sheet as camouflage for crawling up to the wire. Maybe we had made too elaborate a contraption that stuck out too much. After we were spotted by the Germans on a test exposure, about the end of April 1943, we had dropped the idea. Now this same idea was coming up independently in October in South Camp. Again, inside the main barbed wire, there was a thirty-foot stretch of pure white sand between the outside fence and the small wooden fence that was the warning guardrail.

It was shooting time if ever one of us got over that warning rail, or even stepped on it. The guards kept a sharp lookout in the daytime and they used the goon-box floodlights continuously at night to see if anyone was trying to run or crawl across the sand. The daylight shift of guards was in among our barracks until ten o'clock at night, when they locked us in. Then they left. Usually, at twelve o'clock a German hundführer or two came into the compound with sentry dogs. Vogtle and Lewis decided, as on that earlier try of mine, to disguise themselves with burlap. They got some burlap sacking and glued sand on it using Condendo.

The two men went out of the barracks between ten and midnight, slipped under their burlap disguises and very slowly worked their way across the ground toward the wires. They used no diversions. They wanted to draw no attention whatsoever, hoping to succeed by stealth alone. They knew that in addition to the guards in the goon boxes with the spotlights there were also the walking guards outside the wire. They chose a rainy night so as to disguise the sound of the cutting. The wire cutters were homemade out of metal strips taken from the buildings.

Lewis left the building first under his sand-sprinkled sacking. As he had already been practicing cutting wire, he carried the cutters. Vogtle followed at a short distance. They crawled flat on the ground for sixty yards or so and arrived at the guardrail. Lewis then went on ahead to the wire and Sammy went about halfway between the wire and the guardrail to a low spot in the sand. Later on Sammy said the camouflage had worked perfectly. The lights had continually flashed over them but never hesitated, showing that the guards had not been alerted.

Each had a small supply of sticks to prop up the concertina wire between the fences. John began to cut the wire. To Sammy the noise sounded deafening. In the meantime the rain had stopped and after a while the stroller outside the wire was attracted by the noise. He came up to the spot and turned his flashlight on Lieutenant Lewis. He brought down his rifle and aimed it at Lewis, who immediately surrendered.

The alarm was sounded. A hundführer went in to pick up John Lewis. The dogs ran right by Vogtle. In the excitement the guard did not even notice Sammy lying under the camouflage on the ground quite near Lewis. After about thirty minutes the commotion died down and the guards escorted Lewis from the camp to the cooler. Sammy then managed to worm his way back to the block from which he had come. He knocked on the window, his friends inside opened it, and Sammy scooted inside.

Sammy was lucky to avoid another two weeks in the cooler. Though this attempt didn't work, it did better than ours earlier in the year. Again the kriegies almost made it. Perhaps if the rain had kept up they would have succeeded.

At one of our escape committee meetings Bub Clark, Davy Jones and I came up with the idea that a wire job, an escape through or over the wire, might be a lot easier and more successful if we could short out the perimeter lights and goon-box searchlights. The electric wires were strung on poles about forty feet high running above the outer barbed wire fence and connecting the goon boxes. We figured the safest place to short out the wires would be between North and South Camps, where there was more space between goon boxes.

The spot we selected was near the end of a barracks in South Camp. We started our metalworkers making a metal grapple consisting of three hooks fastened to about ten feet of bare wire, which would, of course, conduct electricity. Attached to the bare wire was a long section of insulated wire. We were going to slip out on a dark rainy or foggy night, hold the end of the insulated wire and throw the metal grapple over the power lines midway between the guardboxes, then pull the wires together to short them out.

Preparations were going well when one night just before lockup, Bub sent a message for me to meet him along the perimeter path outside the end barracks next to the wire. He just said, "Look at the lights." The lights between North and South Camps had gone out.

We saw that around the corner toward the woods to the south and west, where our escape would begin in earnest, the lights were still shining brightly. So the two sets of lights were on different circuits! We never found out why the lights went out where they did, but we were very grateful to learn about the two separate systems before we put escapees in jeopardy.

Chapter 20

In the mild winter of 1943–1944 we had one of our most successful individual escapes from South Camp. Hank Burman and I had been keeping our eyes on all vehicles that moved in and out of the camp, just as I used to do routinely in North Camp. We paid particular attention to a truck that delivered vegetables to the cookhouse. From time to time this truck was left unattended for a few minutes. We looked for a chance to put a smaller fellow out and get him completely hidden under what was left after the truck had been unloaded. Sometimes there would be some scraps left, or a piece of tarpaulin that a man might be able to hide under.

In early February 1944 I spotted this truck in the kitchen yard. The driver was in the kitchen having a cup of coffee and a little talk. I grabbed Hank and said, "Hank, meet me at the cookhouse, wagon job!" and just kept right on walking. Then I went to Shorty Spire's block and said, "Shorty, pack up your gear."

Hal Spire was always ready, an eager escaper who could speak German very well. He always kept a little kit of papers in his room behind a false board so he could travel by train, and he was thoroughly briefed and checked out. All I had to say was, "Shorty, let's go—

cookhouse truck,'' and Shorty was on his way. Hank and I got him aboard the truck and by sheer luck no one saw us, not even another American.

I didn't even have a chance to tell Bub Clark or Rojo Goodrich that Shorty was going until he was gone. Then I had the happy privilege of reporting that he had made it.

Hank and I had watched carefully, prepared to divert the guard at any second, while Shorty scrambled aboard. He lay flat right behind the cab in the bed of the truck, squeezed in the corner under a flap of canvas and some cabbage leaves. The small lump he made didn't look at all suspicious.

Hank kept his fingers crossed and I did a little praying as the wagon rolled out with no problem whatsoever and Shorty was gone. I immediately went to Bub Clark and Rojo Goodrich to prepare a cover for Shorty for the afternoon appell. I told them where Spire was headed. He was trying to go across Czechoslovakia into Austria and then to neutral Switzerland. We were able to cover up for him for some time by shifting men within the ranks, with a little horseplay and milling around while the guards were counting. It gave Shorty plenty of time, as there was no network out looking for him.

Later on Colonel Goodrich heard from the kommandant that there was a fellow insisting he was from Stalag Luft III, South Camp, and that he was an Amerikaner; his name was Spire and he was trying to convince the people down in Vienna, Austria, that he was a prisoner, not a spy. He had been caught when they found some error in his working papers and discovered he wasn't the worker that he was pretending to be. We hastened to assure Kommandant von Lindeiner that

Harold Spire was indeed an American POW from South Camp and not a spy or agent.

You can imagine the embarrassment and rage on the part of von Lindeiner and Glemnitz when they found that the man had been missing for a week from the camp and they didn't even know it. But Shorty did get the official okay and was brought back to the camp for his two weeks in the cooler and then back into camp with us.

About the same time in January, Sammy Vogtle started thinking up another plan to escape. This one involved going out to pick up personal parcels in the vorlager, the camp's front office, and bringing them back into the camp. From time to time a group of twenty men was sent outside South Camp along the eastern wire to the vorlager of North Camp, where the personal parcels came in from the United States to be checked over by the German parcel censor. After picking up those parcels, the men would carry them back to South Camp. Sammy planned to dress civilian, but cover his civvies with a greatcoat. On his return from the parcel room, he planned to shed the overcoat and walk casually away from the group posing as a civilian. He hoped to manage this in such a way that the guard wouldn't see him until he was several yards away and by then would think that he was just a civilian passing by.

Sammy assembled all his equipment and briefed the other members of the party on procedure. At the last minute, when the party was all ready to go, they found that the party was one man short. The usual party consisted of twenty men, and the Germans wouldn't move until everybody was there.

With hardly a second thought Sammy ran over to

see Hal Spire, who lived nearby, knowing Hal was ready for anything at any time, and asked Shorty to fill in for him. Hal had just returned from the cooler after his long trek to Vienna. When this whole group arrived at the parcel room, one of the Germans there recognized Shorty Spire and he warned the guards, who had been very lax on the way over, that this Lieutenant Spire had just escaped and might well attempt to do it again. The guards were ordered to watch the American group very closely. They did that with great efficiency and Sammy's plan came to nothing.

There was still another individual escape try in the winter of 1943–1944 in South Camp. Joe Bell had the idea of getting outside the wire in a laundry wagon. He explained his scheme to Bub Clark, Davy Jones and me, and obtained the official escape committee approval for the attempt. The plan was for Bob Hermann and Cy Widen, our supply officers for German items, to help get Joe Bell out in the horse-drawn German laundry wagon when it was loaded with sacks of dirty sheets and pillow cases. The break was planned for somewhat warmer weather for traveling, but the colder winter weeks were used to establish a pattern of conditions to aid the break. With frequent invitations Bob and Cy conditioned the walking guard and wagon driver to have hot tea or coffee and cigarettes with them in the South Camp supply room.

One day in March, as the guards were enjoying our hospitality inside, Joe Bell buried himself among the laundry bags in the wagon. He was to jump from the vehicle after he felt it make two turns in the road, then dive into the nearby woods. Still chatting as they left the supply room, the driver, Cy and Bob climbed aboard the wagon seat and started out the gate with the walking guard alongside them. As luck would have it, the plodding guard happened to look across the wagon as Joe slithered over the opposite side and dropped to the ground. The walking guard instantly gave chase.

The armed driver covered Hermann and Widen on the wagon. They heard crashing through the woods, then a shot. A bit later they were relieved to see Joe Bell walk out of the woods in one piece, with his hands up, the guard behind him. The walking guard was faster than he looked. He had gained rapidly on Joe and fired a warning shot past his head, ending the try. All three kriegies spent the next two weeks in the cooler.

In the meantime Davy Jones and his diggers, trap men and other craftsmen had not been idle. Davy started one tunnel in his own block near the south fence of the camp. The concrete base for the stove in one of the end rooms was not truly squared off, so Davy had the craftsmen Jack Bennett and Carl Cook tidy it with a neat rectangular addition to one corner of the base, which aptly concealed the tunnel trap door Carl Cook constructed. Carl had considerable experience in woodworking. He had built many a hideaway hole for escape goods into the walls and in the floors of lockers. Davy and his oldtime digging mates, Buck Ingram and Ed Tovrea, dug a vertical shaft, starting the tunnel toward the southern woods. The excavated dirt and sand were dispersed carefully under the cookhouse to escape the evil eye of Glemnitz. As I recall, Willy Wigger and wooden-shoed Charlie Barnwell were among the sand-carrying penguins.

Jack-of-all-trades Bennett asked Charles "Hupe" Huppert if he could come up with a better pump than the air bellows Jens Muller had contrived in North Camp. Hupe was a mechanical engineer from Evansville,

Indiana, who seemed to be able to design machinery in his head.

Huppert was sometimes called the Manufacturer. He commissioned about twenty kriegie craftsmen around the camp to make the more complicated components. After Bub Clark or Jack Bennett told him what was needed, he'd design the product or device and then farm out the components to each craftsman. When each piece was ready, he'd pick up the parts and assemble them into the complete product under the protection of the stooges who shielded him from the evil eye of the ferrets. One of Hupe's designs was a new device for developing pictures taken surreptitiously in the camp for intelligence purposes. But much of their work was for the tunnels, such as the air pumps, and later, slow-speed blowers. They also repaired radios from time to time.

Robert Spurgin III from Indiana did most of the metalwork. He used a forge to make wire cutters that were hardened in the fire with sugar. The same process was used for a series of saws. He also cut the molds for the gears used in the blowers. Huppert melted Victrola records and poured them into the molds to make the gears. These were lubricated with mutton fat. Carl Cook did most of the carpentry that went into this machinery and Dad Beckham became the expert in molding small items from lead foil. Bennett made compasses and other small mechanical items. Otis Pritchard and Lloyd Hicks worked on grappling irons, plaiting ropes from bits of string and cloth. Bob Lacey and others would come up with wood or metal cams for the devices.

The tunnel was progressing well, but in March, when Harry's trap under the stove in North Camp was exposed, the ferrets went over every stove base with sharp probes. The trap in Davy's block was discovered, as well as Huppert and Spurgin's new pump.

Our American craftsmen proved themselves as ingenious as the Pole Minskewitz of North Camp in the trap they designed for another tunnel. In the washroom of Block 130, in the row toward the western fence, Jack Bennett and company "accidentally" pulled a sink down from the wall and asked the Germans to put it up more solidly. They were hoping the goons would build up a brick base to hold the sink. The Germans obliged with a neat square pile of bricks and mortar. As soon as the German bricklayers were gone, our crew went to work and carefully moved the entire pile of bricks before the mortar could harden and stick to the floor below or to the sink above. (In the washroom in the chill of winter, the mortar didn't dry very rapidly.) Soon they had a large movable brick plug that would disconnect from both the floor and the washbasin and slide out. Then Carl Cook cut a tunnel trap directly beneath the plug. Band practice outside the barracks drowned the sounds of hammers and picks. After Davy, Buck and Ed got the shaft down and the tunnel started west, our craftsmen cut a small ventilation shaft through the concrete block under the washroom stove. The penguins hid the sand at the other end of camp under the band room in the cookhouse. After Carl Cook put a trap in the wooden floor, Bennett's team scraped back the dirt directly beneath it so that sand could be dumped into the hole in a hurry and the trap closed. The operation was going along fine until a ferret accidentally spotted the air hole in the washroom by noticing a bit of steam rising from under the stove. But we never gave up.

Other kriegies, such as Dale Bowman, a wizard at building and repairing tiny radios, did yeoman service in communications. Hal Decker of Auburn, Alabama, also deserves much credit for his outstanding work with secret radios. Not only did he know how to get the best possible reception from the BBC in London, he was also skilled in shorthand. Many nights he'd listen through a headset in the small hours of the morning and take notes by the shaded light of candles or fat lamps. Sometimes the broadcast contained a coded message for us kriegies. A man named Finnigan was one of those who helped him with the decoding.

Bub Clark later told me that on the long march from Sagan to Moosburg in southern Germany in late January and February 1945, Hal Decker kept the senior officers continually informed on the progress of the war by receiving BBC news through earphones sewn into his winter cap. The earphones were attached to wires that led down the back of his neck. Hidden by a muffler, the wires were attached to the radio secreted in his pack. The radio was so compact it could fit into two empty cigarette cartons—batteries in one, receiver in the other. Hupe Huppert also carried a radio.

Willard Heckman worked in the "fudge factory" making a high-energy, high-protein mixture of oatmeal and chocolate that he packed in pocket-sized tins or in stiff cardboard packages of Canadian Sweet Caporal cigarettes. These condensed calories were of great value in escapes and during the long evacuation march to Moosburg.

After Christmas 1943, our relations with the Germans went from medium-bad to worse. Perhaps they were losing faith in Hitler's ability to win. The Battle of the Bulge turned in our favor and the great German counterattack of December failed. Allied bombing increased as B-17 Flying Fortresses added deep daylight bombing raids to the night raids of both the British RAF and the U.S. Army Air Corps.

The Germans were getting touchy. The night guard's Doberman had almost torn out my throat on the hundführer's order.

A Britisher who was going round the bend or wire-happy back in North Compound cooler was shot by guards. After an abortive escape attempt, when he was being given his fifteen minutes of walking in circles in the cooler yard, he suddenly went for the fence and was shot dead. Another kriegie was shot running across a roof—whether trying to escape or courting death we never learned.

We escapers were used to the chances of being shot if we went over the warning rail, or if we were caught in the barbed wire in an actual escape. But some shooting occurred in South Camp that was not prompted by escape activities.

A few days after Christmas 1943, Lieutenant Colonel John Stevenson was sitting in the end room that he shared with Dick Klocko. The air raid alarm sounded. A few minutes later a bullet ripped through the barracks and tore through both of Stevenson's legs. The bone and muscle of one leg were so severely wounded that he was in the hospital for about six months. ("Big John," about six feet four inches tall, dark, a good-humored West Pointer, walks tall with a friendly grin but with a permanent limp.) There was no valid reason for the shooting. A strolling guard had fired twice into the barracks area and later gave the lame excuse that he had seen "some shadows" moving near the barracks.

In March 1944 two shots were fired into American Block 130 late in the evening. The rounds passed through two rooms full of kriegies and lodged in the far wall of the second barracks room. The good Lord must have been really looking over the kriegies that night; incredible as it seems, neither bullet touched anyone. Again, there was only the lame excuse that a guard saw some sort of "disturbance" at one of the windows. The kriegies present denied any such activity.

On March 25 we got word from North Camp that there had been a mass breakout from tunnel Harry the night before, and that even though the tunnel had been exposed before all could get out, about eighty men were now loose on the outside.

The chronicle of worsening relations with the Germans took a steep downward turn. A couple of days after the North Camp tunnel break, the Germans seemed to flex their muscles to show us they were still the bosses. (No doubt this was also to deter us from following the example of the North Camp escapers.)

A heavily armed contingent of Germans called an extra appell to make a thorough head count and search for contraband. They kept us out on the cold, wet parade ground for about five hours. They also ordered that all Red Cross food must be cooked in the central kitchen to cut down on the hoarding and hiding of food for escapes. This order was soon rescinded when it became apparent that the kitchen facilities were grossly inadequate for feeding the entire camp.

On April 6, Colonel Goodrich, our senior American officer, read orders from Kommandant von Lindeiner indicating that the Luftwaffe could no longer be responsible for the safety of officers outside the wire. In a choked voice he announced the killing of forty-seven British and Allied officers who had escaped from North Compound. This number was later amended to the final total of fifty dead.

On April 7 we held a memorial service for our RAF colleagues on the appell grounds. By a prior resolution of our senior officers, not one American spoke or looked at a German during this memorial ceremony. We stayed at rigid, reverent and disdainful attention, honoring our dead and dishonoring the Germans with a silent hatred they could feel. Our tribute to our dead was intended to shame the Germans.

Then, on Easter Sunday, April 9, 1944, Corporal C.C. Miles of the U.S. Army was shot when on duty in the main South Camp cookhouse. In this case there was no way possible to interpret his actions as an escape attempt. An air raid alarm had sounded. Prisoners had returned to their barracks per German orders. They stood inside, near their open doors and windows on that sunny spring day. One guard pointed his weapon at several such prisoners. Corporal Miles was leaning against the doorway and talking with two other men in the cookhouse. He had been standing that way for several minutes, a clear two hundred yards inside the barbed wire fence, making no move to escape. Without warning the guard lifted his rifle, aimed at Corporal Miles and fired the fatal shot.

No such action had ever before been taken toward prisoners standing in doorways or leaning out windows. Despite this incident, two days later we all stood at windows and cheered for the first formation we had seen of daylight raiding U.S. B-17 Flying Fortresses. A lot of us were praying for one tail-end Charlie, who seemed to be lagging behind the formation, looking like a perfect sitting duck for German fighters.

It was about this time that Colonel Rojo Goodrich summoned me for a tightly secured talk in his room. When we were alone, Rojo said, "Jerry, it's getting so we don't know what these crazy Nazis are going to do next. They just might give orders any day to liquidate us to get us off their hands." I nodded agreement as he asked, "Old Silent Death buddy, do you think you could train a group of men to take over the camp, or get everybody out—if push came to shove—as a last-resort measure?"

I said, "Yes, sir, it can be done. There'd be lots of loss possible—but if we could break the majority out, they'd be better off than being shot down like rats in this barbed wire trap."

He asked, "How many men do you want?"

"I'd start with about thirty, hand-picked for strength, speed, athletic ability and guts. Then I'd add on as our planning might require."

Rojo said I could have the pick of the camp and wished us Godspeed. I started recruiting that afternoon, beginning with such trusted colleagues as Hank Burman and Don Stine, who with my students in silent killing contributed to the nickname I acquired, "Silent Death."

An art contest was announced for South Camp in the fall of 1943, and one day Don came into my room and said, "Major, would you sit for me?"

I said, "Well, that's pretty easy—what do you mean?"

He said, "I mean pose for a portrait." He had a piece of cardboard from the YMCA that had been sent in with some art supplies, including paints and brushes. With these materials and his own native talent, he did a fine job of painting my portrait. On the back he lettered "Silent Death." He also wrote in German, "Stille Tod." There I was with a moustache and square goatee that I'd shaved off on each escape. And up above me, one in each corner of the painting, were two faint skulls looking down. For this portrait Don won first place in the art contest.

I can't recall all the people in that group of thirty but, as usual, Hank Burman was my number-one assistant, and Don Stine and a few others who had taken courses with me were at the head of the class. We were soon called "Sage's Storm Troopers," a name obviously derived with the Germans in mind. Many of the troopers were athletes, including Hank, Don, fullback Bob "Maxie" Menning, halfback Shorty Kahl and weightlifter Bob Hermann. We had Shorty Spire too, one of the smallest men in camp. You never knew when you'd need a well-trained fellow to get through a small place to accomplish some specialized mission.

One average-sized man who took to silent killing like a duck to water and learned very rapidly was Dave Pollak. (Dave is now retired from the steel business in Cincinnati. He has performed a tremendous service for the alumni of Sagan U by organizing, for well over twenty years, reunions of Stalag Luft III POWs.)

I have always liked his brief story of being captured. A second lieutenant fighter pilot, he was shot down in 1943 over Holland. He hid his parachute, got out of the immediate area and kept walking west. Dave said, "I was two days on my way to Spain and was crossing a road when a convoy of Germans came around the bend. I dashed across the road to the nearest house, dived into a basement window, lit in a couple of feet of water, unhurt, and felt even safer thinking I'd probably get help on my return home from the friendly Dutch folks who lived in the house. When the 'folks' came down the stairs, I found I was in the basement of the local Gestapo headquarters!"

We made all types of weapons—fighting knives, hatchets and spears—and kept them hidden away. We also started collecting bits of wire and pieces of rope for certain jobs like getting rid of the sentries. I really do believe our storm troopers could have taken over the camp, but I was purged from the camp after I had trained them only a few weeks. Some German had evidently seen me teaching them how to break somebody's back in a hurry or how to use the Japanese strangle. The Germans evidently added that footnote to my record of escapes and pretty soon about five guards appeared in camp to move me out.

Before I left South Compound, however, I participated in two or three more incidents that broke up the general monotony of prison life. In early March Hank Burman, Dick Schrupp, Don Stine, my other messmates and I laid down a brew. We went around and got a live bubbling raisin from a colleague, threw it in with our raisins and sugar, some prunes and a whole lot of water, and watched it gently bubbling in a couple of huge light bulb bowls during late March and early April.

You may recall the rule of thumb in the prison camp brewery: in winter a brew or a kriegie wine takes about six weeks to become as drinkable as it ever would be, but in the heat of summer, the process takes about ten days. We reckoned that it would take four or five weeks in the cool weather of March. At any rate, we figured it was about ready on the weekend of the nineteenth and twentieth of April.

As I recall, Davy Jones' mess also joined us with a brew they had going and we decided to distill the stuff. We made our own poor man's brandy, some kind of alcohol that came off through a makeshift still—another Rube Goldberg contraption of rolled Klim tins, a trombone, some teakettles with raw potato corks in them, assorted pans and tin mugs for sipping. We usually didn't drink the first half-cup that arrived drip by drip from the condensation tube. One had a tendency to go at least temporarily blind drinking the first cup that came off; it was mainly wood alcohol.

We were just starting to drain off the pure stuff,

the so-called sipping white lightning, when we heard the warning call, "Goon in the block!" In came a ferret called Phil, sniffing as he walked. Phil hadn't been a particularly bad type—in fact, I think Dick Schrupp was trying to tame him. But he came in saying, "Aha! *Verboten! Verboten!*"—"Forbidden! forbidden!" When we tried to move him out, he started acting thirsty. We jollied him along a little bit. Then we gave him the first cupful of stuff we had drained off.

The son of a gun deserved the fate he got because he gulped it down like a pig. There went a lot of our precious Red Cross parcels in that hooch. There also went Phil. In no time he was feeling no pain. In fact, he was close to dead. The first thing we did, of course, was to take off his belt buckle and insignia, and relieve him of all his papers. Even though we'd had a bit to drink ourselves, we were still primarily in the escape business, so we sent the forgers the documents to work with and had the metalsmiths make soap or sand impressions of his buckle and insignia, to be poured the next day. Then I said, "Well, look what's fallen into my lap to start my storm troopers if we ever have to take this place over." I had Phil's pistol, belt and holster.

Someone asked, "What do we do with him now?" We decided we'd leave him in the abort, the big outside toilet with the many holes. When we got him in there, a few of us repeated, "What'll we do with him now?" We were having trouble keeping him propped up, so Davy and I decided to shove him down one of the holes. We were just sending him toward a redolent repose when in walked Bub Clark, who had gotten wind of our activities.

Bub, in his six foot four, red-haired, reasonable manner said, "Now that isn't exactly the thing to do with him. We might regret it tomorrow. Let's just leave him here and let them find him.'' Then he added, ''And Jerry, you'd better leave the pistol there too, or they'll turn the whole camp upside down.''

On semi-sober reflection, Davy and I decided that was the best course of action. The next day, Sunday morning, when we went out to appell, we saw more ferrets coming in. Soon we saw them hauling poor old Phil out of the compound, and that was the last time we saw him. We don't know what they did with him; at least I don't. He might have been shot or just sent to the eastern front, where he was also quite possibly shot.

Chapter 21

Then there was one sunny day on which Don Stine and I had a whole lot of fun, just for ourselves. Our plan had no practical purpose whatsoever. The sun was shining brightly and we decided to eat our bread and stuff at poolside.

We hauled out a table and two chairs, and put them down by the fire pool—a sidewalk cafe at the beach. We kept moving the table closer to the pool and finally we decided, sober as judges, to have a tea party in the pool. We threw the table into the pool, threw the chairs in after it, and jumped in ourselves, holding up the sandwiches and cups of ersatz tea. We laughed our fool heads off for no good reason except in sheer animal spirits and relaxation—one of the craziest tea parties that ever happened.

When the kriegies saw us in there, they asked, "Good Lord, what are Major Sage and Don doing? Something must be going on. Looks like they're creating a diversion." They always suspected us of some escape activity.

Our messmates still remember another day Don Stine brightened by combining his humor with his talent. Don had a loose cap or two on his front teeth from dental work after a football game back in school. When he lost a cap, he'd carve a replacement out of an ivory-colored toothbrush handle, sand it till it fit, then glue it on with some concoction he worked on with his buddies among the craftsmen. One day he got a new toothbrush in a parcel from home. Its handle was a glistening ruby red. Later in the day he wandered off out of the room, taking his tool kit with him. In the forging shop he got out his carving tools and from the new brush made a bright red cap and glued it on.

That evening he walked into dinner very quietly, sat down with the one lamp that we had in the mess room shining full in his face—but saying nothing. The room gradually got quiet and Hank Burman exploded, "Don, what in hell's the matter with you?"

Don opened his mouth and said, "Nothing!" He sat there with a grin like a ruby highlighted Cheshire cat. His new red tooth scintillated and brought down the house!

A little later there was some excitement when a ferret whom we called Schnozz, because he had a big nose, stumbled upon our forgers working on some documents. He usually wasn't too nosy, despite the size of his proboscis, but that day he was. Our men didn't have time to close down or use a hideaway. As Schnozz burst into the barracks, the men burst out of the room with their documents in their hands. It became a foot race as he chased them in and around Block 129 until the kriegies wore him out and enough people got in the way that poor old Schnozz was winded. In the end he lost them, a very angry ferret.

The next day the administrative officer came in and announced that the theater was closed until further notice as a punishment to the compound for winning that race with Schnozz. A couple of days later the Germans turned out the whole camp for another five-hour appell out on the parade ground, where they searched everybody individually, stripped them, checked every man against his picture in their card file and shook down all the barracks. Some items were hidden on the parade ground, and when the Germans raked it with a fine-toothed comb, they hauled away from the field and barracks a load or two of contraband.

Near the end of May we saw another great flight of B-17 Flying Fortresses. It always lifted our spirits to see our planes flying overhead.

The sixth of June was the great day when the compound went crazy. The first word about the D-day invasion came from Padre MacDonald through the wire when a fellow shouted to him in Gaelic. It was confirmed over the compound loudspeaker by the Germans, who were saying the Allies were being killed on the beaches. From then on, our people spent a lot of time trying to plot the progress of our armies across Europe.

In June the theater opened again, but the harassment continued. All of a sudden the Germans confiscated something like sixty thousand cigarettes from the barracks. They pretended to have a reason. Someone in German intelligence had figured out that there were some numbers on the inside wrappers—messages to the kriegies in code. That wasn't the case, of course, but this excuse allowed the Germans to grab quite a few smokes.

All this time, we in South Camp had kept up pretty well with the progress of the tunnels in North Camp, and of course we were able to fill in the gaps with later post-war conversations. Through Padre MacDonald and Colonel Goodrich's senior officer meetings, we would get word of just how the tunnel was progressing. Our escape committee—Clark, Jones and I—stayed quite current with what was going on. Perhaps to let the Germans think that the Americans had been the prime movers in tunneling, and to let Rubberneck, now the head ferret of North Compound, and the other ferrets simmer down a little bit, Roger Bushell stopped all tunneling for several months after Tom was blown up. The factories—Tim Wallen's forgers, Travis' metalworkers, Al Hake's compass men and the map makers—kept on working to ensure adequate equipment for a really big breakout. The fudge factory also continued making emergency rations of concentrated oatmeal and chocolate.

In January 1944, when the air was frigid and the ferrets were less active, Bushell and Wally Floody started the digging again. Fanshawe had hit on the idea of hiding sand under the floor of the North Compound theater. At first we had stayed away from the theater so as not to jeopardize the programs that were put on for the entertainment of the entire camp, but Wings Day made the hard decision to use the compound theater to finish the tunnel. The sand was put under the floor through a hinged seat near the rear of the theater. With dispersal assured, the digging moved forward rapidly. Using the penguin system my dispersal crews had used earlier, they took the sand outside by normal kriegie traffic or made random additions to sand already under the theater.

Evidently Rubberneck was still suspicious. He marched thirty extra guards out to the appell one day near the end of February. He suddenly called out a list of about twenty men who were then surrounded by guards, marched away, searched and taken immediately out of the camp to another compound at Belaria, about five miles away.

Wings learned that the ferrets had picked the ones

they suspected of escape activities from identification photographs, just going through the files. Some of these people had nothing to do with the tunnels, but most of them did, including such key men as Wally Floody, the chief tunnel engineer; Hornblower Fanshawe, the penguin sand dispersal chief; and George Harsh, tunnel security.

I can imagine the frustration and disappointment of these three. Having worked so hard for a year, fully earning a place on the breakout list (as had Bub Clark, Davy Jones and I before being moved to the American compound), now these three were yanked completely out of the picture. But they felt differently about it two months later—as did I. When I learned of the tunnel's tragic end, I thanked the Lord for not having been one of the fifty who were shot after recapture.

The tunnel progressed rapidly in March and soon was nearly three hundred fifty feet long as measured by running off a spool of string alongside the trolley. According to a surveying estimate from within the camp, it would reach several feet into the northern woods. So Roger picked a moonless night, March 23, a weekday, for the break. That was always a consideration: The train schedules changed on Sunday, so a Saturday night break wouldn't do much good. All the identification documents had to be dated and ready to go and train hops planned for the normal weekday.

In Europe after the war I was able to visit Wings Day in London. (I was coming from Germany, where I was commanding a Special Forces Group, Green Berets, in the Bavarian Alps.) When I was visiting in London, Wings threw a big party for me. He passed the word to all points of the British Isles. About twenty former colleagues from Stalag Luft III showed up for this gathering. There, from a few of the other survivors and later with Wings alone, I heard the fantastic odyssey of Harry and Block 104 on that long-awaited night of the break.

I was fortunate enough to be able to visit all three men who made it all the way back to RAF duty in England from tunnel Harry. I visited Brom "Bob" Van der Stok in Amsterdam when I was stationed at the headquarters of the European Command just after the war. Later, when I was commanding the Tenth Special Forces Group, I went on an exchange training mission in Norway. In Oslo I visited Jan Staubo, who had been with me in the cooler. He in turn brought in Jens Muller and Rocky Rockland, whose real name is Per Bergsland. These were the two who worked their way to the North Sea, hopped a Swedish coaling vessel and made it across to Sweden. Hence I was able to hear their stories firsthand.

After the signal "go" was given in late morning of March 23 at the X-committee meeting, Crump Ker-Ramsey and a couple of other diggers headed right for the trap in Block 104 and chipped it open. They opened the tunnel and went below to prepare for the exodus. Crump took down some extra light bulbs and hooked them into the wiring system. Then he took strips of blanket and muffled the rails on the first and the last parts of the track so the noise wouldn't be heard above ground as the men rolled down the tracks with their suitcases. After the second appell of the day, the diggers started opening the escape end of the tunnel. There they ran into some trouble.

They had hoped to get it open by eight-thirty at night, but it took longer because the boards covering the exit had swollen. Several factors created delays in getting out of the tunnel, but not through any fault in planning. The thoroughness of the planning and the skill of the factories really paid off because that night over two hundred men filtered into Block 104. The normal occupants had moved elsewhere earlier in the day to bunk for that night. Each escaper had been interrogated by monitors to ensure that he had his cover story down pat. Each had enough money to move according to the way he was going, whether across country or by rail. Each had appropriate maps from Des Plunkett's shop and documents from Tim Wallen's forgers stamped with the proper date by a rubber boot-heel carving of Hal Hake's. Each carried one of Al's compasses, fortified fudge rations, a cardboard or metal suitcase or worker's pack, a tin canteen made by Travis' metalworkers and appropriate clothes from Tommy Guest's tailor shop. The train travelers had business suits and hats. The cross-country men, called hard-arsers by the British, wore worker's clothes and could afford to be dirty and crumpled.

The first few men into Block 104 that evening almost had heart failure when they saw a Luftwaffe corporal stomp into the barracks. Some dived into the nearest room while the head stooge rushed toward him to try to get him out. After a terrible moment he saw the big grin spreading on the "German's" face. It was Peter "Tob" Tobolski, the Polish flight lieutenant who was going with Wings Day. He was in one of Tommy Guest's remade RAF uniforms complete with hand-molded insignia, eagles and swastikas. Tobolski, with typical Polish courtesy, apologized for causing the panic and went into the room where he would wait for Wings—and caused another royal flap among the men waiting there. (Tob had been a pilot in the Polish Air Force. He escaped to England when the Germans overran his homeland and flew Spitfires in the air battle over Britain in 1941.)

Wings was going out posing as an Irish colonel who, in resentment over Britain's failure to free Ireland, had been converted to Nazi leanings during his years as a POW. On parole to Berlin, he had a fictitious mission to see the devastation of civilians by the "bestial" British and Americans. Wings' Luftwaffe escort would be Tobolski, who spoke excellent German and had acquired first-class Luftwaffe documents. He would explain that Wings was a friendly prisoner who spoke only English. So Wings didn't have to put on an act or even try to speak an unfamiliar tongue. Tobolski also had a sister married to a German in the port city of Stettin, where they hoped to catch a neutral ship to Sweden, probably as stowaways.

Bushell was all togged out in a gray suit, black overcoat and dark felt hat. He carried a little attaché case. He was going out as a French businessman with a good set of verifying papers, and he looked the part. His traveling friend was a Frenchman in the RAF named Scheidhauer, who hoped to get the two of them into an escape organization by way of his friends in France.

Before Bushell gave Johnny Bull the go-ahead to open the boards in the top of the shaft of the exit, several people got into position. They were Bull and Marshall opening the tunnel itself and Wally Valenta the Czech, Bushell and Scheidhauer. Sidney Dowse was helping haul the cars from one of the halfway houses, a little indentation in the wall of the tunnel. It was very cramped quarters. Bull started working on the boards, but they were so warped he had Marshall get up to help him. They finally got one board loose and pulled out the rest. Bull dug out the top dirt and sod.

When Bull put his head out of the tunnel, however, he was stunned to discover that they were in the clearing over ten feet short of the edge of the woods. They were out in the open surrounded by white snow, with the goon box only fifteen yards away. He ducked his head back in and explained the situation. After more delay, considering the alternatives, the decision was made to hide a controller in the nearest clump of brush at the edge of the woods, holding the end of a rope anchored to the top of the ladder in the shaft. When the coast was clear, the controller would yank the rope, and the man on the ladder could feel it, come out as fast as possible and run into the woods.

The goon-box guard was no great problem, as his attention was always directed inside the camp within the sphere of his searchlight. The strolling guards outside the fence were the threat. They met at the goon box, turned and walked away again. After they turned, Bull yanked the rope and that was the signal for Marshall to snake out. Marshall followed another rope from where Bull was to a meeting place well into the woods. Men could wait there for their partners or form up into a hard-arsers group going through the forest toward Czechoslovakia.

The escape was already an hour behind schedule when the trap was opened. Then there were further delays as escapers tried to move up as rapidly as they could on the trolleys with their suitcases. Some of these suitcases were just too big or too hard to manage on the trolley in the narrow two-and-a-half by three-foot square of tunnel space.

There were some falls that had to be repaired. But soon one man was going right after another with just a few delays waiting for the tracks to clear or the next person to get out. Valenta, Bushell and Scheidhauer led the way, and once out they started moving more people up through the tunnel. Next came Tobolski and Wings Day.

Our expert tunnelers, Red Noble, Shag Rees and Henry Birkland, were hauling people on carts from the halfway station. All three could fix minor sand falls and make repairs as needed, but they kept gradually falling further behind schedule. Some men knocked out frames or derailed the trolley. Then a hauler would have to crawl up and ease the weight of the man on the trolley so that the wheels could be fitted back on the rails. Rockland and Muller, whom I saw later in Norway, went through very smoothly. Actually, it was one of the diggers himself, Tom Kirby-Green, who caused a bad fall. With his big shoulders and wide suitcase he knocked out a prop, and added another delay for repairs.

A little after midnight the sirens sounded. It was an air raid the escapers hadn't planned on. All the electricity went off. Wings Day wheeled himself forward with some fat lamps, dropping them off to light up the tunnel. They figured that was a good time to keep right on moving because the outside lights would also be off. With this unexpected cover, they did manage to get quite a few people out.

Eventually the air raid ended. More than eighty men were outside the tunnel or in the mouth of the exit when, just as dawn was starting to break, a strolling guard came upon some prisoners hiding in the snow. At first he didn't see them and almost walked into them. When he did spot them, he jumped, pulled up his rifle and let go one round in the air that brought people on the run from all over the kommandantur.

By that time some kriegies had already succeeded in reaching the railway station in Sagan, the nearest town, and were well on their way. Others were on their routes north to Stettin, east toward Hirschberg station or south toward the Czech border.

Others started moving very rapidly through the

woods when they heard the shot. Three or four people were held at gunpoint near the exit of the tunnel until reinforcements arrived. By that time those in the tunnel had quickly reversed direction and were trying to scurry as fast as they could back into Block 104. Everyone started burning papers and getting out of civilian or German military clothes and throwing them out the window. There were so many small fires of documents burning up and down the corridor and in the rooms that it looked at first glance as though the whole barracks was on fire.

When the last kriegie had dashed back out of the tunnel and up the ladder, Crump closed the trap door from above and put the heavy stove back over it. He later heard scratching and pounding at the trap door but Crump figured he hadn't invited the ferret so he'd leave him there.

The Germans couldn't find the trap readily from up in the barracks and they appealed to the kriegies to let the ferret out. The man under the trap was a quite innocuous little fellow named Charlie, the only ferret brave enough to crawl into kriegie tunnels.

Red Noble was noble enough to let him out, but Rubberneck was in a rage. Noble was an old adversary of his in and out of the cooler, and he started to manhandle Red, who naturally resisted. Then Noble was ordered to the cooler. Kommandant von Lindeiner had already lost his temper at the four who had been caught at the tunnel exit, now already in the cooler. He sent several more to the cooler right from the doorway of 104 because the kriegies appeared to be baiting or laughing at the Germans. He said he would shoot if such actions continued, and the kriegies believed him.

A number of guards came in with the identification card file, ready to work. For the next few hours the prisoners had to stand in the snow while each man was searched, some almost stripped naked. Each man in camp was checked against his photograph to see who was missing. Von Lindeiner's face became a death mask when he learned that seventy-six men were loose outside his camp. He stalked out of the compound.

Later, the hundred-odd kriegies caught in Block 104 were marched to the gate of the vorlager where the cooler was, halted there for a long time in the snow, and then dismissed. The kommandant had wanted all of them in the cooler, but he simply didn't have enough room.

Chapter 22

Meanwhile, delays and difficulties continued far beyond the tunnel for the escaped kriegies. After Wally Valenta and Johnny Marshall missed the train from Sagan to Hirschberg, they tried to walk across country to Czechoslovakia. It was such tough going in the slushy snow that they seemed to be going one foot forward and two feet back, so they were forced to use the main roads that night. After hiding in the woods all day, they went on in twilight and shortly thereafter were caught in a one-street village that sounded much like the one where I was recaptured near Czechoslovakia after my ambulance escape.

The three Germans who spotted them were definitely looking for prisoners, and our men had little chance to bluff their way out of the situation. Valenta might have gotten by longer with his fluent language, but Marshall, who knew a little French and was trying to pass as a French worker, was tripped up by a German who spoke much better French. They were taken to a jail that already held several kriegies, caught in much the same way. Evidently every police and home guard unit of every village and city throughout Germany was alerted, as well as all the Nazi armed forces and their version of a coast guard. One of the kriegies heard a German captor talking over the phone, saying that groups of prisoners had been caught all the way up at the port of Danzig on the North Sea as well as at Hirschberg and other nearby towns.

Major John Dodge, the Artful Dodger—the only other ground officer I knew of in Stalag Luft III except for paratrooping Padre MacDonald and me—got on a train to Hirschberg along with several other "workmen" heading for Czechoslovakia. They left the train about dawn at a station before Hirschberg and started moving across country. Having for some time made extremely slow progress in the slush, they returned to the Hirschberg rail station, bought tickets and boarded; they were picked up just after they got on the train, following a very meticulous examination of their papers by the police. At the jail they met more old friends, both British and Poles. The Poles were treated particularly badly as part of Nazi policy; it turned out that no Poles at all came back alive.

Hundreds of people other than kriegies were also being jailed in this great nationwide dragnet. This included German deserters, criminals, slave laborers and many more "suspects."

Wings Day and Tobolski were safely ticketed for Berlin at the Sagan station near our camp. In Berlin they found a Danish contact man whose name had been given to Wings by another prisoner a long time before, and they asked him for help. The Dane's German girl friend seemed hostile, however, so Wings and Tobolski left and hid in bombed-out cellars for a couple of days. Then they took a train to the Baltic port of Stettin, where they contacted some Frenchmen in a labor camp. The Frenchmen took them into their barracks, fed them and gave them a bunk to sleep in. Their hosts said they would help the escapers find some Swedish sailors who might get them aboard a neutral vessel, perhaps as stowaways. But they were betrayed by one of the Frenchmen and arrested the next morning.

Wings and Tob had four days of interrogation at the police headquarters at Stettin. One interrogator was a high-ranking officer who was particularly enraged when he read Tob's pay book and other documents, which had been franked with very authentic stamps all the way up on the various train trips. The officer could hardly believe that a Pole could get away with that much in the German Reich.

Then he turned his attention to Wings Day's identity card for a Hungarian laborer, his fallback position in case his cover as an Irish colonel didn't work. As it turned out, neither cover worked. The officer began shouting at Wings Day and Wings just out-shouted him; eventually they moved Day back into a cell.

On about the fourth day they were taken by train back to Berlin, where two cars with several guards were waiting for them. Tob was put in one car and Wings in the other. Wings told me that he asked, "Where are you taking my friend? He's an officer of the Royal Air Force and I'm not going without him."

The guards seemed embarrassed, but they said, "He's probably going directly to Sagan. As a senior officer, you're needed for further interrogation." It didn't convince Wings at all, nor Tob, who well knew what the Germans thought of free Poles who resisted them. Wings remembered that Tob gave him a last salute as he entered the car, quite sober-faced. Wings never saw him again.

Wings was taken to the Albrechtstrasse police headquarters where a senior SS police officer told him they had had enough of his leading mass escapes. Evidently the Luftwaffe couldn't hold him, they observed, so he would be sent to a place from which there was no escape. Wings said he thought it was a roundabout way of telling him he'd be executed.

He was taken north out of Berlin to a small compound next to a large camp behind a very heavy barbed wire gate. Inside this small compound was Johnny Dodge, who told Wings he was in Special Compound A of the Sachsenhausen concentration camp.

Wings found his new camp mates quite interesting. They included a collection of Russian generals and colonels, Polish RAF pilots who had been dropping agents and supplies to the resistance movement of Poland, some Irish-British soldiers, some Italians and Captain Peter Churchill. Churchill was of course a magic name to the Germans. Peter had been captured in the French Resistance movement in 1943 as an agent of the British Special Operations Executive (SOE), the outfit I had worked with in the OSS in England and North Africa.

Two prior residents of this special lager in Sachsenhausen had been the sons of the top men of the Soviet Union. One was the son of Stalin himself, Jakob Djugashvili. The other was Vassili Molotowski, the son of Molotov of the Politburo. The story was that Stalin's son had been so upset by German claims that the Russians had massacred thousands of Poles in the Katyn Forest that he protested for days and kept dwelling on the massacre. Djugashvili must have finally lost his mind because he tried to climb the fence and was caught in the electric currents of the barbed wire at the top of the wall, then was riddled with bullets by a guard. Wings reported that Molotov's son was transferred out of that camp shortly thereafter.

Soon two other Stalag Luft III kriegies, both British, joined Wings and the Dodger. First came Jimmy James, then Sidney Dowse, who had broken out with Dapper Danny Krol, the Polish digger and fencer. Krol, like Tobolski and the other Poles, was separated from his partner on capture and was among the fifty shot.

As I have mentioned, all this was told to me by Wings during quite a few meetings in London many years later. Needless to say, I was fascinated by his story. He told me with his rather shy grin that the electrified wire on the top of the wall, combined with "very trigger-happy guards" in the goon boxes, persuaded him and the other three alumni of Sagan to try tunneling.

Though the guards on the walls were alert and efficient, there was no Glemnitz or Rubberneck looking for tunnels out of Sachsenhausen. The usual "liberation" from SS control was death through overwork, disease, malnutrition, punishment or simply liquidation. A saying among the SS guards and the old inmates was that the only way to freedom was up the crematorium chimney.

But Wings, Dodge, Dowse and James were an experienced team. They made saws from SS-issue table knives by rubbing them on the concrete floor to make jagged teeth in the blades. Then they cut a trap door in their end of the cell block and started digging.

From the same propaganda newspaper we were issued at Sagan, the *Volkischer Beobachter*, Wings first learned of the D-day invasions on June 6, 1944. Not long after that he was shocked to read in a later issue a paragraph-long German rebuttal to the British Parliament's protest of the murder of RAF prisoners after their mass tunnel escape. He called his group together, but after bitter discussion of this horrifying news they decided to press on with their tunnel. Dowse and James did most of the digging, pushing the sand back tightly under one end of the barracks.

In mid-summer the group was joined by Jack Churchill, a tough Commando officer captured on a Greek island. Wings said, "He reminded me of you, Jerry, so we gave him the sand dispersal job."

Churchill had managed to keep his steel helmet with him; he made good use of it to scrape together the loose sand and carry it deep into the space below the barracks. The tunnel was ready in September and broken on a dark rainy night. Wings Day and Dowse caught a train to Berlin. James and Jack Churchill set out to find a freight train going north to a Baltic seaport. Dodge went off alone across country to the west, hoping either to meet the Allies or to hide out until they reached him.

A trusted fellow inmate in Sachsenhausen had given Wings the name and address of an anti-Nazi black marketeer living in a small town near Berlin who might leap at the chance—for a reward—to assist senior British officers as the war was drawing to a close. But the houses at and near the man's address had been gutted by incendiary fires. Police picked them up as they sought shelter in the rubble.

At Gestapo headquarters they were separated and Wings soon found himself back in Sachsenhausen. But this time he was sent to the death block, handcuffed and with his right ankle chained to a hasp cemented in the middle of the cell floor. After weeks of interrogation and solitary, he was moved to a cell block called The Bunker. He was no longer chained, but here he was not allowed to sit or lie down during daylight hours. He said later that he paced his six-foot cell, trying to remember details of past good times in his youth and to recite poetry learned long ago. He laughed as he told me he could still recall all of Lewis Carroll's "Jabberwocky," which he and I used to recite in unison accompanied by grand sweeping gestures and a lot of laughter around a fire back in the Sagan camp.

In November the RAF inmates were allowed a half-hour of morning exercise in a small courtyard. There Wings learned from Jack Churchill and James about their attempt toward the north. After ten days of alternately jumping freight trains and hiding out, they were caught—about twenty-five miles from the Baltic coast. Churchill, James and Dowse had all received treatment much like Wings': switched from cell to cell, occasionally chained to the floor. In November Johnny Dodge too was back after more than four weeks on the loose.

On Christmas of 1944 the Sagan men got a bit of meat in their stew, passed around a homemade Christmas card, and listened to Christmas carols over the Sachsenhausen loudspeaker, mingled with the sobs of a man in a nearby cell who was sentenced to die the next day. Wings said that in January the Sachsenhausen kommandant received orders to cut down the population. Many Russians, Poles and groups of underground resistance fighters were shot or gassed. Even SS men convicted of crimes were killed—usually hanged—including a general who was involved in the July plot to assassinate Hitler. They sentenced him to die slowly in a noose of piano wire.

In February Dodge disappeared from The Bunker, but not through violence. He was taken to Berlin to meet with "officials of Germany's Foreign Office." Wings said that the Germans had known since Dulag Luft days back in 1939 or 1940 that Dodge was a nephew of Winston Churchill by marriage. Through Dodge the Germans hoped to get a message to the prime minister.

Soon after, Wings and his remaining three companions were pleasantly surprised at being moved from The Bunker back to their much earlier compound, Sonderlager A, where they had much less rigorous treatment. There they found their colleagues—Russians, Poles, Italians and Irish—waiting for them, standing at attention with Peter Churchill as their spokesman with the agreed-upon welcome: "We salute four brave men!" Wings said he had trouble with a frog in his throat as he went down the line shaking hands with his old colleagues.

Within a few weeks the *Prominenten* (leading figures) kept hostage at Sachsenhausen were all moved by train four hundred fifty miles south to the Flossenberg concentration camp between Nuremberg and the Czech border. They were told their transfer to southern Germany was to avoid falling into the hands of the Russians, who were now quite rapidly approaching the Sachsenhausen area.

Flossenberg was crowded with evacuees from camps farther east and the crematorium was kept burning nearly continuously. Wings said that along with foreign laborers who had been starved to death, the bodies of several Germans were carried to the crematorium in April. They included men involved in the July 1944 plot on Hitler's life, among them Admiral Canaris, the former chief of German Intelligence; his chief of staff, General Oster; two other German generals; and the prominent Pastor Bonhoffer.

Wings' group of *Prominenten* were kept moving south, spending a few days in the notorious concentration camp of Dachau. They were then taken by bus to a small camp at Reichenau in the foothills of the Bavarian Alps. Here the Germans seemed to be assembling the surviving ranking hostages from many prison camps. They included the famous Pastor Niemöller, who had been Hitler's prisoner since 1933; Dr. Hjalmar Schacht, former president of the German State Bank; industrialist Fritz Thyssen, an anti-Hitler plotter; General Franz Halder, former chief of the German General Staff; Leon Blum, former prime minister of France; Kurt Schuschnig, once chancellor of Austria; and General Garibaldi, the grandson of the liberator of Italy, along with similar prominent officials of Hungary, Greece, and other countries. Wings said it was a Who's Who of European politics. Altogether the prisoners totaled about one hundred fifty people, including some women and even a few children.

In a few days this number was again loaded on trucks and buses and driven through Innsbruck, Austria, and on through Brenner Pass to Italy. Here in northern Italy, the various groups of Italian and Austrian resistance groups were in control of more territory than was the German Army. The SS guards were eventually disarmed in a friendly village and the threat of SS liquidation was lifted. Wings teamed up with an Austrian, Tony Ducia, and they worked their way south through the mountains and the tenuous German lines to join a surprised U.S. infantry outfit.

Wings then worked his way back to higher headquarters, which sent a relief force to assist the *Prominenten* they had left behind in the Italian village to the north. Soon he, Dowse and James were flown home to England. Wings' saga of escape came to a grand finale nearly five and a half years from the day he was shot down.

As he finished his tale, Wings smiled a sort of proud yet diffident grin and said, "It took over five years, Jerry, but I finally was able to get through the German lines in Italy and report myself back to the Allies."

All I could say was, "Wings, you dearly earned it."

* * *

In 1947, when I was on staff of Headquarters European Command and dealing with the problem of displaced persons, I was able to discover Brom Van der Stok's address in Amsterdam. I visited him on a short leave and met his wife and child. Brom was completing medical school. I thanked him again for taping up the ribs that Bill Jennens had kicked in for me to set up the ambulance escape. Then Van der Stok told me his story.

He had been among the first twenty out of the tunnel. The German soldiers stopped him near the railway station, told him to take shelter—there was an air raid on—and then helped him into the station. Van der Stok bought a ticket to Breslau and, recognizing several other escapees standing nearby trying to be inconspicuous, he thought it best to talk with a German girl. She told him she was a censor from the camp on the lookout for escaped prisoners! Van der Stok was delighted when he could finally board the crowded train for Breslau. At Breslau he bought a ticket to the Netherlands by way of Dresden and Halle.

During all the police checks on the trains and one at the Dutch border, Van der Stok's papers prepared by our forgers passed readily. Friends sheltered him for six weeks until the Dutch underground took him to the south of the Netherlands and across the Maas River into Belgium by boat. He then rode a bicycle to Brussels, where he lived another six weeks with a Dutch family.

The underground then took him by train, disguised as a Flemish employee of a Belgian company, to a stop near Paris. During a train change in Toulouse he sold his watch to pay a guide to take him over the Pyrenees. But before they set out the guide was killed in a clash with German sentries.

Van der Stok soon made contact with a band of Maquis, French underground resistance people, in the foothills. They took him to a pass on the frontier and pointed him into Spain. He hitchhiked to Madrid, called the British consul, and was back in England four months after the tunnel break. When I next made contact with Brom, he was Dr. Van der Stok, a ship's surgeon on the Matson Line sailing out of California.

The other two of the three who made it all the way home from the tunnel without recapture were Norwegians. Jens Muller, the craftsman who had worked with Travis, and Per Bergsland, who went by the name Peter "Rocky" Rockland in prison camp. (He changed his name to avoid any reprisals to his family in occupied Norway for his escape attempts.) I met both of them in Oslo during my Green Beret exchange training visit with the Norwegian Army in the winter of 1964–65. Jan Staubo, my old friend from the cooler who paid me with a small freighter for my blackjack winnings, arranged the reunion at Oslo's Grand Hotel.

It was a terrific blast as we exchanged highlights of our adventures over several glasses of aquavit and had a fine dinner of saddle of venison and some delicious salmon. Jens and Rocky had been able to catch one of the early trains from Sagan after the tunnel opened, and they changed at a small town station near Frankfurt an der Oder to a train for Stettin on the Baltic. This they reached less than twenty-four hours after leaving the tunnel.

At that Baltic seaport they fortunately met some sailors from neutral Sweden about to sail home. The sailors took the Norwegians aboard and hid them securely. Though they could hear the German inspection party, no alarm was raised and the ship sailed without a hitch.

They landed in Sweden the next day and sent messages through the British embassy to the RAF. They were soon on a plane back to England. At the time of my visit, both Jens and Rocky were pilots on civilian airlines and Jan Staubo was running the family shipping line.

Looking back, I believe the tunnel achieved its objective of costing the Germans time and effort. The entire nation was alerted to find the escapers and many weeks later remained searching for the ones not accounted for. But the cost to us was also high. The fifty who were shot were fine, courageous men, and we missed them.

Of course I knew some much better than others. Al Hake had made my Dinah Shore compass. Tim Wallen, master forger who made papers for me, had shaved off his prized handlebar moustache for the tunnel break. Others were Henry Birkland, expert digger and a fine man from Canada; Henri Picard, the artist and forger from Belgium; Wally Valenta, who taught me phrases in Czech and Magyar; Tom Kirby-Green, who welcomed me in North Camp with a cup of tea and a tattoo on his tom-tom; Dapper Danny Krol, a fencer and digger; and all the other fine Polish officers who died with him.

I remember Johnny Stower, who walked out on the big delousing parade, got all the way into Switzerland, and by a quirk of geography walked out the other side of a narrow tongue of that country's map and was caught walking back into Germany.

Among the escapers were the Australian Cat Catanach and, of course, Roger Bushell. I occasionally argued with Roger, but he was some sort of genius. It was hard to win a debate with Roger. I always respected him and I believe the feeling was mutual.

I didn't find out what had happened to Roger Bushell and Scheidhauer, the Frenchman who had traveled with him, until after the war. But Brom Van der Stok in Holland told me he had seen Bushell buying train tickets in the Breslau station, evidently for Saarbrücken, as they were both trying to get to France. So they had caught their train in good order right out of Sagan and from Breslau to Saarbrücken. I have no details on their capture, but evidently it was in or near Saarbrücken. After the war, investigators established that the Gestapo chief in Saabrücken was told in a top-secret order that the two prisoners were to be shot. Gestapo people took Bushell and Scheidhauer out on the autobahn and shot them. Their bodies were cremated at Saarbrücken.

All fifty kriegies who were killed were great people with tremendous will, courage, perseverance, faith and patriotism.

The Germans also paid for the killing of this group. The Gestapo tore up the kriegies' rooms and all the compounds. Finding little, they went to the kommandantur and arrested von Lindeiner for court-martial. We never saw him again.

After the war ended, Great Britain, still enraged by the Nazi butchery, organized teams of interrogators under the lead of an ex-Scotland Yard detective, Wing Commander Bowes of the RAF Special Investigation Branch. These teams went the length and breadth of Europe to determine what had happened to the missing fifty. After months of painstakingly and doggedly following dim trails—as described in Paul Brickhill's book, *The Great Escape*—the details of every murder were learned. And nearly everyone who had any part in the crimes was arrested. All the perpetrators were tried and convicted in a war-crimes court in Hamburg in 1947 and 1948. Some received long sentences in prison, but most were hanged by the neck till dead.

In the spring of 1969, twenty-five years after the tunnel break, contingents of both Canadian and U.S. officers were invited to England by the RAF for a great reunion and memorial service at the RAF chapel. The families of all those killed were invited to the ceremonies. I met Roger Bushell's niece and nephew, Peter Tobolski's son Paul, and Henri Picard's little sister from Belgium. Others from Australia and New Zealand were present for the tribute.

The memorial church service was conducted entirely by ex-kriegies: Padre MacDonald, John Casson, Dickinson Hennessey, and the Reverend Mr. A. ffrench-Mullen. (The latter was rather a surprise since ffrench-Mullen's main preoccupation in North Camp was as brewmaster. You could always count on ffrench-Mullen for a live raisin.)

On the plane from the United States were Colonel Rojo Goodrich, Lieutenant General Bub Clark, Lieutenant General Dick Klocko, Major General Davy Jones, Major General Moose Stillman and Major General John Stevenson from North Camp, plus later POW arrivals General Jake Smart and Major General Del Spivey, all in the U.S. Air Force. Among these was also Jerry Sage, Infantryman, paratrooper, OSS and Special Forces from the U.S. Army. From Canada came another planeload headed by Wally Floody, Red Noble, and Scruffy Wier.

When our plane landed at the RAF airfield we had a nice rush of nostalgia. There on the tarmac waiting to greet us, much older as we all were, was our old camp's adjutant, my rib-kicking old buddy Bill Jennens, who'd been sent out by Wings Day to meet the plane and to escort us into the airport. Wings had arranged cars for everybody. Helping to welcome us was the widow of Johnny Dodge, an absolutely lovely lady with many years but tremendous and overriding charm. She certainly was a fine and appropriate partner for such a grand gentleman as the Artful Dodger Major Johnny Dodge.

The Service of Remembrance was in the RAF chapel at St. Clement Danes, London, on the afternoon of Saturday, March 22, 1969, dedicated to "Those members of the Royal Air Force and Allied Air Forces who lost their lives while prisoners of war in German hands 1939–1945." After the date on the program was *Twenty-five years after the Great Escape when fifty officers were shot*. The service was solemn and reverent, and the families of the deceased warmly expressed their gratitude in turn for this touching tribute to their loved ones.

In the evening there was a great reunion party at the RAF Club, where refreshments and nostalgic anecdotes flowed freely. Wings and I did our old "Hands Across the Sea" routine in the middle of the dance floor. We recited "Jabberwocky" at the top of our lungs and then did a Russian Cossack dance to great stomping and clapping of hands. We were feeling no pain until we tried to walk the next morning.

After closing the RAF Club, we visited other night spots. There was some reversion to past habits. As we were walking down the corridor of a fine hotel, Wally Floody suddenly reached up, unscrewed a light bulb and put it in his pocket. We accused him of thinking about tunneling under Claridge's. After one meal at a genteel restaurant, Wings arose and quietly collected all the rolls left in the baskets on the table, putting them in his jacket pockets. He never got over the habit, and I'm afraid I haven't either, of never leaving any food. In the wee hours of the morning, at one unsavory place reportedly run by gangsters, Wings sent me ahead to ensure that we had a corner table with our backs to the wall, and then I went out to the kitchen to check a "bug-out" route in case of trouble or a raid. These were all things that we expected of one another.

The book *Wings Day* by Sidney Smith was published just before our arrival in London. We Americans all bought copies and passed them around for signatures at a farewell party thrown by Americans and Canadians for our British friends. That too was a memorable evening of songs, pranks, and a bit of mayhem, but no serious casualties.

That was the last time I saw Wings Day. We occasionally corresponded until he died a few years later. I'm glad he finally put his story into print—a great saga of courage, persistence, devotion to duty, and concern for his fellowman. And I'm glad that young people have the opportunity to gain just a little inspiration from the great story of Wings Day.

Chapter 23

In the spring of 1944, the pressure on the men in South Camp increased considerably. Having seen what had happened to the men in North Camp who tried to escape, each of us knew that we might well share the same fate.

The stress of these times made each man turn to his inner resources. There were two elements in my background that helped give me strength. The first was the superb training I had received under Donovan; the second was my faith in God.

As I've mentioned, Donovan was one of my heroes of World War I. So was Sergeant York. (I also had a hero in Charles Lindbergh in 1927, when I was ten.) I started reading very young and I liked heroic tales. I liked the idea of men fighting for what was right and what they believed in.

I used to make lists of things that I wanted to do. When I was very young I wrote down several things—from the gentlest ones like writing a song and publishing a poem to flying an airplane and parachute jumping. Then in 1940 I added blowing up a bridge, an idea I got from Hemingway's *For Whom the Bell Tolls,* about guerrilla fighting in the Spanish Civil War. I could even then see the value of guerrilla warfare and believed in it. It made sense to go to the heart of the enemy. What did not make sense to me was to sit in trenches shooting at each other as they did in World War I; to me that just dragged out the killing.

Then Donovan said, "I'm going to carry the war to the enemy." His idea was new, it was big and it was powerful. I liked the idea of trying to win the war fast, hit them where it really hurts. Donovan was certainly a persuasive man. His was a great job and it seemed to me that I was really getting into the war and doing what I was getting paid to do as an officer in the Army.

Donovan also said, "We have an unusual job for some very special people . . . who are not only going to expose themselves along the front facing the enemy, but they are also going to expose their rear to the enemy from behind the lines. So they have to be really dedicated and be able to learn, to be in good shape to do a very important job." I thought that was fine and I was very willing to do it. I always knew I would be in a dangerous position, and I accepted the risks.

The other thing that kept me going during this time was my faith in God and love and respect for the precepts of Jesus. All the while I was in prison, my faith was growing, and I had reason to reflect on the early influences and conditions that later made my beliefs so strong and vital to me.

I was from a Christian family. We believed in Jesus, we believed in God, and we children started praying when we were very young. I particularly remember that God made sense to me because He was always there: He was big and strong, and He answered my prayers.

As a youngster I always had a dog when we lived

close above the swift Spokane River. I very frequently lost my dog; he'd go chasing off after another dog and I'd go running out to find him. I was always very much afraid that my dog would fall into the river. As I ran along I would pray, "God, help me find my dog!" And He always did. I would say, "Thank you, Lord." He had a fine record of answering my prayers and I just plain believed in Him.

During high school I went to church quite a bit. I also played on several church league basketball teams and sang in young people's church groups. But then in college I did not go to church as much. I never stopped saying my prayers at night, but I got more exploratory, as one does in college, taking philosophy courses and reading the classics.

College teaches humanism rather than respect for God, so I less overtly practiced my faith, but I certainly resumed my practice when I started being shot at behind the lines—and sometimes hit. When I was a prisoner, everything about my faith seemed to solidify. It made sense and got me through. I was very grateful to the Lord, Who talked with me, walked with me, and gave me strength and water when I needed it.

Sometimes I've been questioned about my belligerence toward my captors. I had nothing but contempt for the Nazi system and the myth of Aryan superiority. The whole thing was rotten to me—their persecution of *Untermenschen* for their accident of birth.

Beyond politics my pride was wounded by being shot up and captured by such people, and I did my darnedest to keep escaping. I know that I deserved the punishment I got for these attempts. Even the occasional brutality to me, such as the Doberman attack, the pliers on my heels, and the Dulag Luft heat treatment, did not affect me so much as what the Nazis did to other people just because of accidents of birth.

When I was growing up, my parents taught me to deplore bullying, not to tolerate it, never to bully anyone and not to stand for bullying by anyone. The Nazis, of course, were experts at bullying. They did that with all the *Untermenschen*—Jews, Slavs, Gypsies, the disabled, even Christian Germans—anyone not an "Aryan superman."

It was also drilled into me at a very early age not to go along with the crowd, to resist what is now called peer pressure. My mother always said, "Do the harder right rather than the easier wrong." She was the scholar in the family. Both parents trained me never to be a sheep. Mother told a story about one panicky sheep who started a stampede of the whole flock off the cliff. If you must be a sheep, I was told, be a strong one, the bell sheep, and lead the rest to safety.

My dad did not have such a literary background. He graduated from the second grade and that was as far as he got in school. But he had a lot of practical knowledge, a lot of natural kindness and strength, and he was an excellent salesman. We never had much money, but we were always fed and clothed and had school supplies and a little family movie fund.

Those were Depression times, and what money we had we couldn't waste. My older sister and I used to argue, scuffle and play practical jokes on each other. When we broke things in such doings, we either paid for or fixed them. Sometimes we'd throw things at each other and break a window; that sort of damage came out of our hides as well as our meager earnings.

Dad had dual values on broken windows. He gave me two pairs of boxing gloves. One day he came in to find a window broken in the ground floor den. With a stern look, Dad asked, "How'd you break it this time?"

I said, "I was boxing and knocked Paul, the neighbor boy, through the window."

He paused a bit, then said, "Well, we can afford a new window." After another pause, he asked, "What did you hit him with, a left or a right?"

Both my parents worked when I was young, so it was a great treat when I could get out on the road with my traveling salesman dad in his little John Morrell Meat Company car. I had spent many of my younger days with my red-haired grandma, Lula Myers, who was a Victorian Virginian with flashes of humor. Most of all she was clean, and she insisted everyone else be. I had to wash my hands before, after and in between everything to do with the bathroom, and before and after I ate.

I began to feel like a raccoon, which washes everything meticulously before it eats. One had to whisper, "Grandma, I have to go to the bathroom."

She'd say, "Wash your hands!"

I was out on a country road one day with Dad up by Kettle Falls along the Columbia River in old Colville Indian country. Early-morning orange juice and milk began to press on my bladder.

I said, "Dad, I have to go."

Dad just put on the brakes, waved toward my door and said, "Well, go, son."

I opened the door, but before I stepped out I thought about Grandma's warnings and said, "But Dad, what do I do if someone comes along?"

And almost with disdain, he said, "Shake it at 'em, son, shake it at 'em!"

That phrase later came to mean much more to me than it did along the Columbia River.

Whenever I've been in trouble or danger or halted by embarrassment or fear, that phrase helped me to face up to the problem—that heritage from Dad. When Germans or Russians started bullying me, I'd figuratively "shake it at them"—stand up to them and with faith meet strength with strength, or laugh it off or bluff through or press on with a devil-may-care outlook. That's part of the reason I did some of the things I did to the Germans. I made all those Arbeits Korps people change their route by leading the kriegies in singing, "Heigh-ho, heigh-ho, it's off to work we go!" the work song from "Snow White and the Seven Dwarfs." That was just doing my part to keep the enemy off balance.

I believe that something under five percent of the kriegies in North Camp or South were true escapers, eager beavers whose primary thoughts were escape plans. These were the ones who would take every opportunity, at almost any risk, to get away. They were willing to work hard each day on tunnels, cut wire at night within range of ready machine guns, get their bones broken to get out in an ambulance or be buried in ashes or garbage or—even worse—in the honey wagon. These were the hard-core escapers. Perhaps another ten to fifteen percent would escape if a fairly safe opportunity arose in the milder weather of spring or summer.

Some kriegies thought that they were lucky to be alive after being shot down. Their expertise had been in the air, not on the ground, and they didn't want to push their luck a second time. Probably well over half just felt that they weren't equipped to get very far and were worried about knowing enough language and local lore to get by. Friendly lines were a long way off. (Much of our escape activity took place well before the Allied invasion of D-day 1944.)

Nearly all kriegies were ready to help in group escape activities, to help out in the dozens of specialized jobs needed for a tunnel escape, to be on the stooge-alert forces or diversionary detail, or to craft things in the shops and factories. Many hundreds of kriegies worked on the large North Camp tunnels, Tom, Dick and Harry. The severity of the punishment, the massacre of fifty colleagues in the spring of 1944, the attempt on Hitler's life the following summer with its ensuing reprisals, and the mindless shooting into the barracks gave some potential escapers second thoughts. But many kept scheming and trying, and some of us made it.

Alvin W. Vogtle, Jr., Hal Spire and John D. Lewis were among the Americans who kept on trying. I left South Camp in June of 1944, so I didn't witness their activities after that. However, I learned of some of their plans and adventures through the unpublished memoirs of Sammy Vogtle, to which he graciously gave me access when we got in touch many years after the war.

One good scheme of Sammy's was foiled by the summary evacuation of the camp in late January 1945. Sometimes cigarette parcels meant for other camps found their way into the South Camp storeroom. After a half-dozen or so large sacks of misdirected items accumulated, they were sent out to the vorlager, reclassified and sent to their proper destination. Shorty Spire and Sammy planned to get into two large burlap cigarette sacks, be carried to the vorlager, spend the night among the parcels, and the following day be loaded onto a wagon going down to the Sagan railroad station with parcels destined for other compounds. They intended to cut their way out of the sacks, jump off the wagon before it reached the station, steal bicycles from among the large racks at the station, and cycle to Switzerland.

By that time they were both well provided with good maps, money, forged passes, ration tickets, bicycle repair gear, fine new civilian suits, including felt hats, and all the food they could carry. The senior Americans okayed the plan but urged them to wait until the winter weather improved, possibly in March. The plan was scrapped when South Camp was evacuated on thirty minutes' notice on the night of January 27, 1945, and the kriegies were moved out to a camp at Moosburg, a Bavarian town in southern Germany. During that trip the men were subjected to untold miseries on foot and in boxcars. I learned about them later, as I myself was by then heading east across Poland.

In early February, as the freight train neared Moosburg, Colonel Rojo Goodrich passed the word through the boxcars that a few men from each car who desired to escape might attempt to do so. Sammy and John D. Lewis, who had tried the unsuccessful camouflage wire-cutting job six months before, decided to team up again and head for the Swiss border, now less than two hundred fifty miles away. They got their gear together and at night, as the train shifted from the Moosburg main station to a siding, they pried open a window and climbed out to lie down beside the train until it pulled away from them.

Vogtle and Lewis, wearing overcoats and carrying a blanket apiece, walked south through the crusted snow to find a rail line heading west from Munich to Switzerland. It was bitter cold. They walked at night and hid in the woods when there were woods or buried themselves in the snow if dawn found them in more open places. After about four days the snow turned to rain, the slush was difficult to struggle through and both men were soaked to the bone. In order to dry out they hid in a barn under several feet of straw with their clothes spread out under the straw to dry.

That afternoon workers started binding the hay and eventually uncovered the kriegies. They tried to pass as Spanish workers, but someone sent for the police and the Germans locked them up. Sammy said the German people brought them brandy, soup, bread, coffee, and a bag of apples and were quite friendly in their conversations. The police arrived and turned the POWs over to army guards, who also treated them well, fed them, and took them back to Moosburg by train.

On his return to camp Vogtle learned that several others had also jumped from the train. All were recaptured, but they also reported kindly treatment by civilians. This was good news. The senior officers had been reluctant to permit escapes because of the shooting of the fifty officers who had tunneled out in "The Great Escape."

After a couple of weeks of rest and scheming in the Moosburg camp, Sammy came up with another plan, this time with Hal Spire. Early each morning a group of fifteen or twenty British orderlies would bring hot water in large jugs to the main gate of the camp. Since these men came into camp at other times during the day, Sammy and Shorty were able to obtain British sergeants' uniforms.

On the morning of February 23, the Americans and the obliging British orderlies all arrived at the gate while it was still dark and only one guard was present. In the milling about Vogtle and Spire managed to infiltrate the group of orderlies and return to the open lager of the enlisted men. That day they traded their British clothing for French uniforms because Frenchmen had more freedom to move about in Germany than any other nationality.

At five o'clock the next morning they joined the usual party of two thousand enlisted men who were taken the fifty kilometers into Munich to work, fifty men to a boxcar. In Munich the fifty were split into groups of ten, with each group under one guard. Vogtle and Spire were put to work chopping wood in an apartment basement. They found a door ajar behind a huge pile of debris, and when an old woman entered the building to ask the guard some questions, the escapers fled through the back basement door and hid themselves among the crowds on the streets of Munich. They walked out of the city on a main street toward the southwest and no one paid any attention to them.

Vogtle and Spire were looking for a French camp where they might obtain help in getting into Switzerland. Occasionally they were stopped by police, but they were always able to tell a convincing enough story in French or German either to get help from the official or to confuse him enough to escape again.

Eventually they met some friendly Frenchmen who fed them and brought them French civilian clothes complete with berets, ration tickets and train tickets to another town near Switzerland. They had no passes and were not asked for any on that particular train, but Vogtle thought the train too great a risk without a pass and decided to walk to Switzerland, then less than a hundred miles away. Spire said he'd chance the train as he was extremely fatigued and had a bad cold.

They split up their equipment and Vogtle walked on, mile after mile. Eventually he found a bicycle and cycled to the border area near Lake Constance, worked his way across several streams and canals, caught a boat across the Rhine to the Swiss bank, and finally walked into a small town. After making certain it was indeed a Swiss village, he entered the police station. The Swiss police gave him food and a bed and then sent him to the U.S. military attaché at Berne.

There he was surprised to find Hal Spire, who had come partway by train. When he found he would need a pass to buy his ticket to the next town, he also decided to continue on foot. He was given good directions through some woods to the border by a German civilian and had little trouble reaching the Swiss town of Ramsen, where he called the military attaché in Berne.

Spire and Vogtle were taken to Geneva, then to Paris, and a week later flown to New York, arriving in March, the same month that I made it back to the same city, though by a completely different route. I was delighted to get the happy ending of the story from Sammy.

Alvin W. Vogtle, Jr., is doing extremely well. He recently retired from his jobs as president and chairman of the board of the large Southern Company, based in Atlanta, Georgia. At every kriegie reunion I've asked for the whereabouts of Hal ''Shorty'' Spire, but no one has yet been able to help me. The last word was that he made it home to California in March of 1945.

Chapter 24

According to Major Gustav Simoleit, the deputy kommandant of Stalag Luft III, the German staff grew from seven officers and one hundred guards initially for the smaller east and center compounds to about thirty-five officers and twelve hundred guards for the four or five compounds in operation by late 1944. Simoleit estimated that the ratio of German personnel to prisoners fluctuated somewhere around one to ten. Some prisoners estimated that the proportions of Germans working at or for the camp might have made this ratio as high as one to four. Whatever the actual numbers, the prisoners at Stalag Luft III kept plenty of Germans busy.

The largest group by far consisted of the guards who manned the goon boxes and the strolling posts outside the wire, and who watched the movement of prisoners anywhere between or outside the compounds. Though many were very young or old or otherwise unfit for combat, which is the only reason they were with us and not the German army, they were all armed for the sole purpose of preventing escapes. The guards, as well as other camp staff, knew that if they failed in their duties they would likely be sent to the Russian front, a fate equal to or worse than death.

It was the men of the Abwehr who had the job of monitoring camp security and preventing escape preparations. They conducted the personal searches of prisoners, of the barracks, of all other buildings—even probing the dirt on the appell grounds for contraband items and signs of tunneling, wire cutting and tampering with German security measures.

One officer, accompanied by six or seven NCO ferrets in their dark blue overalls, was assigned to each compound. The ferrets could go anywhere unannounced, probe thoroughly with their long sharp rods, eavesdrop from under floors or in attics, and search and arrest anyone they considered suspicious.

Meanwhile, hundreds of Germans were engaged in administrative work. They supplied us with food, clothing, fuel and water, managed the cookhouse and distributed YMCA and Red Cross parcels. Over a hundred Germans censored the mail and books sent to and from kriegies. Others maintained an intricate file system of one card for each prisoner, each card including photograph, fingerprints, and as much other data as could be collected. There was also a small German medical and dental staff.

Two of the lager officers who often took roll at appell were the Austrian Hauptmann (Captain) Hans Pieber and Hauptmann Golodowitz, who sported a shiny gold front tooth. Pieber was a rather gentle soul hoping to keep both Nazis and kriegies on his side. He seemed to be happiest at appell, when he'd sing out, "Goot morning, chentlemen!" and we'd shout back, often quite mechanically, sometimes derisively, "Goot morning, Herr Pieber!" I thought both Pieber and Golodowitz rather innocuous.

Glemnitz was the only German at Sagan I had much respect for. He tried to do a professional job without fear or favor. The kommandant, von Lindeiner, was probably better than most German camp commanders. Colonel Rojo Goodrich said von Lindeiner avoided me and would not walk within twenty feet of me. He occasionally called me a wild wolf. Goodrich also said that he occasionally saw von Lindeiner lose his temper, but that he believed I had the distinction of being the only American von Lindeiner had pulled his pistol on and threatened to shoot. That had not endeared him to me, nor had the two extra cooler sentences he gave me, one for zapping a Doberman as he was trying to devour my throat and the other a "German court-martial sentence" for "threatening" three guards in a previous cooler cell.

When I came back into the camp from one of those cooler stretches I was thinking no good thoughts of any German. I met up with Oberfeldwebel Glemnitz. He greeted me, paused and looked at me long and quietly. Then he said soberly, "Major Sage, you're vun man I'm not sure I vant to meet after the var!" (As it turned out, we did meet many years later and had a good conversation, not warmly as buddies, but as a couple of old pros from different sides.)

One cannot describe a prisoner-of-war camp in a single word, but one adjective that comes close might be "grayness." For much of the time the average kriegie's life was one dull, empty, monotonous routine played out against a background of gray. The kriegie lived in a landscape trimmed with unfriendly barbed wire, dotted with watchtowers, manned by unfriendly armed robots with even less friendly machine guns, under dark clouds on a perimeter walk that went in a squared-off circle to nowhere. He was forever hungry, a state that sometimes prevented sleep.

As the war dragged on, some prisoners fell into fits

of depression. There were a few who went around the bend, a barbed-wire psychosis resulting from too much privation, too little mail, and too long a war, accentuated by increasingly crowded living conditions, too much worry about the future and too much self-pity.

In some cases, the suffering ended quickly and tragically. The first I recall was in North Camp in late June 1943. A young RAF officer named John Kiddell was so affected by this psychosis that Wings Day, on the advice of British POW doctors, asked the Germans to send him to a special hospital. Instead, Kiddell was sent to the vorlager infirmary. He tried to escape from there, but was caught in the barbed wire, and shot and killed by a guard. There were other such kriegie fatalities—and of course many POWs returned home with serious mental scars.

Those of us who were wholeheartedly engaged in escape activities or who kept mentally busy with our studies, books, arts, and crafts were much better off.

In wintertime no one could be truly comfortable. There was too little food and too little heat. There was no way to keep dry in the sudden showers at appell. And sometimes appell lasted for hours on a rainy day as the barracks were searched. It was hard to dry out afterward because no place offered enough ventilation or warmth. There was never enough of anything—clothes, food, hot water, utensils, fuel, blankets. Many kriegies stayed in their bunks to keep warm. Being in bed was warmer than being outside. They were better off not moving at all, burning up fewer calories because they weren't getting enough food. Even in the bunks, though, cold was a problem. The too-thin blankets were enough only when sewn together with layers of the Nazi propaganda newspaper *Volkischer Beobachter* in between as insulation.

As the rooms became more crowded, privacy became increasingly rare. Card games were often played after lockup in the evening, to keep minds occupied and men busy until it was time for bed. But the only approximation of privacy a man could find was out on the perimeter walk or in the abort outside the barracks. To ensure a small measure of privacy after lockup it was an unwritten law that a man's bunk was his castle. He could retreat there without fear of interruption to read, sleep, draw pictures, write letters or just dream of home. No one would sit on a man's bunk without his express permission.

But as the men per room increased to twelve or fourteen, nerves frayed more rapidly and on less provocation. Occasionally I'd have to break up a flap or rumble in the barracks stemming from what would have been under other circumstances only a minor irritation.

I was better off than most in this regard because as a block commander in Stalag Luft III I had a small end room with only one roommate. When things seemed too congested, I could go to my room to study, read, write or sleep, but I had deep sympathy for all who had to live cheek by jowl with so many others. Usually even though cold, damp and gray—except in the brief but quite beautiful German summer—the days were better than the nights. Except in the worst weather one could walk or jog around the perimeter, stop to throw horse shoes, or play catch or join a game of softball, soccer or football.

Some kriegies had to haunt the cookhouse for hot water. They were the room stooges or cook's assistants for the day, who carried over crockery jugs for drinking water and ersatz beverages. Still another kriegie would be scheduled as cook of the day for his room. He sliced the rough bread as evenly as possible, and tried to make palatable for himself and his roommates the German issue and the Red Cross parcel items.

I guess one of the greatest aspects in all prisons is waiting, the big "W," for the end of the sentence. In our case the length of the sentence was unknown and almost completely outside our control—unless we could manage the very risky long-shot route of escape. The end of our term in prison had not been set. The end of the war depended on a great number of elements far beyond our influence, and though we made numerous bets that the war would be over by such and such a time, at least half the bettors lost every time a date came up. Being primarily a cock-eyed optimist, I always bet on the quicker ending and kept having to revise my bets each time I lost. I paid off several fifty- and hundred-dollar bets after the war.

We waited for nearly everything except monotony! We waited for hot water, and for imitation coffee or tea at the kitchen in the morning. We waited impatiently for each meal because we were always hungry. We most eagerly waited for letters from home. We waited on lists to see the dentist or doctor or to get a shoe or a new coat repaired. (We repaired all cloth items ourselves.) Or we waited for a better blanket or more of the sad German coal briquet fuel because we were cold nearly three fourths of the year. And if we needed to use the one indoor commode, the only toilet for nearly a hundred men after lockup at night, we had to wait.

Thinking of shoe repair reminds me of a problem with my boots and shoes. It was very hard to husband clothes; I was pretty big and pretty hard to fit. Shoes were even harder to find. As I've mentioned, my feet are size thirteen. My paratrooper boots had hollow heels to soften the landing, and the Germans tore them off through every search because they always suspected I had something hidden in them. I never did. The heels were pulled off and on so much that eventually the rubber just slid off and on the nails. I had a hard time gluing them on or finding bigger nails to hold them. At last I was able to draw one pair of British medium-topped boots or high shoes. They were black with steel toes and heel plates, but too big. I was almost swimming in them and I got some calluses in uncomfortable places.

The best way to beat the frustration of boredom and to add color to the long gray days was to keep busy. Helping someone else was really the best way. I looked for someone worse off than I was. If I was hurting, I would go help someone in worse shape. The escape work, studies, arts and crafts, reading, sports, exercise, and walking the perimeter—all helped pass the time.

It helped to have a library, but even that involved waiting. A popular library book such as Lloyd C. Douglas' *The Robe* was always in demand, but it was well worth waiting for. The book had beautiful things to say about faith and it was a good inspiration.

The worst days were the long, frigid, gray days in winter and the cold, dank, gray days of driving rain in spring or fall. At those times nearly everyone was cooped up inside. The smell of wet wool and soaked shoes and socks blended with the rotten-egg smell of boiling kohlrabi, horse rutabaga or wormy cabbage. These were mingled with the varied odors of twelve or fourteen men with no shower facilities, and a gray cloud of cigarette, cigar and pipe tobacco smoke added to the claustrophobia.

Sometimes nerves would get rubbed so raw that a fistfight would brew from an argument over the number of men who could use the nearest abort after breakfast.

The best way I could find to break up this argument was to send one of the debaters out to count the holes. I used the phrase "count the holes" so often that it came into general usage to break up senseless disputes. We had a dictionary in the library, and when there'd be doubt about the pronunciation of a word, we didn't say, "Look it up in the dictionary." Somebody would shout out, "Count the holes!" In our barracks that meant go to the trouble of finding out the facts and cut out the arguing.

Though some of the tomfoolery in camp was specifically designed for the ferrets or guards to further some camp escape activity, much of it had to do with escapism of a different kind. It was often quite spontaneous, comic relief in reaction to the pervasive cold, hunger, frustration, and boredom. A bug-eating contest even broke out in my barracks one day. It started with flies and got more bizarre as competitive spirits rose. I think some youngsters—two, I recall, called Gus and Shadrack—won mocked-up trophies for their consumption of spiders and yellow jackets. On days when we could get outside, we were able to work off lots of tensions on the sports field with games, track meets and field events.

From right after the war till the present time I've intermittently given many speeches. In the question period after the speech someone usually asks, "What did you think about mainly in the prison camp? Girls?"

I look at my questioner very solemnly and reply, "I am perfectly willing to debate with any of the adherents of Freud, Jung, or Adler that sex is not the prime motivating factor in life. The prime motivating factor is *steaks*. When you're really hungry all the time, you're not thinking about sex, you're thinking about food."

A grown man who is fairly active needs about three thousand calories a day. We received from the

Germans only a little over half that. The heavy brown bread was the main item issued to us. Each kriegie was supposed to get twenty-one hundred grams, about four and a half pounds a week. The Germans were generally good about getting the bread to us, though sometimes not the full allotment. We also were to receive about four hundred grams a week of potatoes. That isn't enough of a diet by itself and we very often did not get even that.

In 1943 there was a potato shortage in Germany, and there were hardly any potatoes issued for many weeks. About three days a week at noon we were served some kind of starchy soup—oatmeal, barley or "green death" pea soup—a few grams of sugar-beet marmalade, and a few grams of sugar and salt plus a bit of fish cheese or blood sausage. We obviously couldn't subsist on that diet. Fortunately we also received Red Cross parcels.

The American Red Cross parcel was designed to help sustain one prisoner for one week. Supplies included one can each of corned beef, salmon, pork luncheon meat, liver paste, a pound of oleo margarine, a can of orange concentrate, one can of powdered coffee, and one of powdered milk, a small can of jam, a box of raisins or prunes, a box of sugar cubes, a little box of biscuits (large K-ration crackers), a chocolate D-bar, a small package of American cheese, one bar of soap, four of five packs of cigarettes and a few matches.

The Canadian parcel was very similar to the U.S. parcel, and we would occasionally get that too. The Canadians sent butter instead of margarine, a treat that proved particularly useful for some of the desserts that we dreamed up. The British parcel contained greater variety and it was fun to receive now and then. There was no coffee in it because the English preferred tea or cocoa, but in place of Klim there was a can of Condendo, sweetened condensed milk, excellent for mixing with lemon powder or ground-up chocolate to make pies. The English parcel also included one can each of meat roll, meat and vegetable, vegetable (or bacon) and sardines, corned beef and salmon. It also had a small can of dried eggs and one of oatmeal.

Parcels did not come in regularly, and the German issue was erratic as well as inadequate. When these parcels did arrive on time, if we ate everything given to us, we had a more or less adequate diet. Remember that in general the kriegies were in good health when they arrived in camp. Most of the fliers were hand-picked crews, and we were certainly in wonderful shape in the OSS. I'm glad we started out in decent health because we would never have lasted so well had we not been.

In order to keep in shape for the rigors of escaping and maintain our strength and morale, we tried to get as much exercise as possible; yet to keep putting out energy we had to put in fuel. I taught myself to trade very carefully. I read books in the camp library on nutrition and tried to trade lower protein foods for those with a higher protein count. I'd trade my sweets for less tasty but more nutritious foods. Sometimes people were willing to pay thirty dollars for a candy bar. I would trade that to them for cheese or a meat product or even Klim, simply because I believed these would keep me in better shape.

A typical daily menu might be something like this. Breakfast was two slices of the German bread with a thin spread of the sugar-beet marmalade, washed down with powdered coffee, if available, or the ersatz tea or coffee drawn from the cookhouse made from minced herbs or ground-up nuts.

Lunch at noon would be soup from the main camp

kitchen served three or four days a week. On other days we sometimes had some boiled cabbage or root vegetables, with one slice of German bread, and coffee or tea.

The evening meal, between five and six o'clock, would be potatoes—served au gratin if we wanted to use some of our cheese or with Klim to really fancy it up—the potato special could be a delicious dish. Added to that was about a third of a small can of meat, Spam, or corned beef. About twice a week there'd be vegetables, again with one slice of German bread and coffee or tea.

In our mess, we always mixed up the Klim to make a sort of cream to put in coffee or tea, which seemed to make it more palatable and give everyone a fair share. We'd often save the dessert to eat before bedtime between nine and ten. That might be the Condendo lemon or chocolate pie or cake—or it would turn into gedoing pudding, depending on how it happened to come out. Sometimes we made cocoa at night before sleeping.

Every so often, of course, we'd save up our parcels to give ourselves a big bash for Thanksgiving or Christmas or for a messmate's birthday or the Fourth of July. We also saved our sugar and prunes to go into the kriegie brews made in the big light bulb covers. All in all, I was still in good shape when I was finally purged out of Stalag Luft III in June 1944.

Chapter 25

Per Colonel Goodrich's orders, I had been training thirty hand-picked kriegies in my storm-trooper group to take over the camp in case the Nazis ordered our liquidation. The men were well trained, quite well equipped with makeshift weapons, grappling hooks, and other assault gear, and ready to charge the goon boxes with me if worse came to worst.

Then on a late June morning Colonel Goodrich told me that I was to be purged from the camp. He had just received a message from the kommandant that I was to be ready to leave that afternoon. The messenger told the colonel that he didn't know where I was going. When he asked the ferrets about my destination, he could get no reply. Rumors spread rapidly through the camp. The top two guesses were that I was going to be either shot or sent to Kolditz Castle, the *Straffelager* or punishment camp, a maximum-security prison for prisoners the Germans deemed to be incorrigibles.

My messmates brought out some extra items from the Red Cross parcels and they whipped up a midday feast, sort of a "last supper." Dick Schrupp even made a lemon Condendo pie, my favorite.

Don Stine asked me, "Are you going to take your portrait with you?"

And I said, "No, Don, that's your portrait."

He insisted. "No, it's yours, sir. I painted it for you."

So I said, "But I can't take it with me. I'm not going to wherever they intend to take me, and I don't want it lost." Don then accepted custody of the portrait and said he'd get it back home to my folks.

And he did. He carried it all the way to Moosburg on the wintry roads. En route he had to burn the frame to keep warm, but he kept the painting under his shirt. Though the painting was done on nothing more than YMCA art cardboard, it came through in fine shape. He carried it across Europe and the Atlantic Ocean to the United States and delivered it to me on the West Coast in Long Beach, California, nearly a year later.

After our farewell meal in the mess, a five-man band that included Dusty Runner, Duke Diamond, Tex Newton and Fearless Forsblad serenaded my block. Friends dropped in with little farewell gifts they had stashed away for future use. A small can of peaches, some cigars and even a couple of small bottles (like vanilla bottles) of kriegie brew were dug up from a garden hideaway.

About five or six guards came for me. A couple came to the barracks and the rest waited outside the gate. Right up to my departure Colonel Goodrich tried to learn where they were taking me, but without success. Padre MacDonald and I had a quiet prayer together. As I walked with Colonel Goodrich from my block to the gate, kriegies lined each side of the path. There were hundreds of them shaking hands and shouting, "Good luck." By the time we reached the gate, I was pretty well choked up by the kindness of these friends.

When I got outside the gate, however, I was able to shake it off and get back into character. I gave them a jaunty salute and shouted, "I'll be home before you are." They all cheered and the guards marched me off.

We didn't walk far that day. I was surprised to be escorted right back to one of my old cells in the cooler. I still could learn nothing from my custodians. They evidently had been told to watch me carefully, as they kept opening the little peephole cover in my cell door every few minutes to peer at me. I knew that the chances of breaking away were better on the road than in the cooler, so I relaxed and tried to rest. My old term "coiled" came to mind. An Abwehr security man came in and gave me a thorough search, possibly the reason for the cooler stopover. (Or, maybe the kommandant still wanted to shoot me himself.) In any case, their search uncovered nothing.

One of the old guards brought me a plate of cabbage and potato soup, a piece of bread and a mug of some kind of herb tea. After supper I rearranged the meager belongings I was carrying, which had been tossed about in the shakedown. I then had a long talk with God and slept well to be ready for whatever was coming tomorrow.

Early the next morning the guard woke me with room service, another mug of ersatz tea and a couple of slices of goon bread smeared with sugar-beet jam. A little while later a team of four guards escorted me to the Sagan railroad station. Bub Clark had said, on an optimistic note, that maybe they'd send me north to the Oflag in Schubin rather than to an execution or Kolditz prison. I was rather hoping he was right. At the station I listened carefully to the senior guard getting the tickets. The first city names I recognized on the route were Leipzig and Nuremberg deep to the southwest, exactly the opposite direction from Schubin, two hundred miles or so to the northeast.

The route we were taking led toward Hitler's redoubt area in the Bavarian Alps, and concentration camps such as Dachau. I was determined to take any opportunity to break away. Meanwhile I tried to present a relaxed and unthreatening attitude for the guards, talking with them in a mixture of German and English about the scenery we passed by. Their attitudes ranged from pleasant to merely civil, but they did not relax their vigilance.

At every stop one guard got out and stood outside my window. At least two watched me at all times. When I had to go to the bathroom, if the train was rolling, one stayed in the aisle at the door and one went in with me. If the train was stopped, the guard usually posted outside my window moved to the bathroom window as I did. The guards gave me a bit of sausage and bread and ersatz coffee in Leipzig and we took the train south to Nuremberg. I still could learn nothing of my destination, but wherever it was I knew I didn't want to go there.

Just after we pulled into the Nuremberg bahnhof it seemed like all the sirens and alarms in the world went off. People started dashing like mad for the *Luftschutzskellar,* the air raid cellar. My guards grabbed me and hustled me down the stairs to a large concrete bunker. At the foot of the stairs stood a burly character in SS uniform with a proudly displayed Nazi swastika.

He halted our group and asked, *''Wer ist er?''* (Who is he?)

The guard said, *''Amerikanische Major—Fallschirmjäger. Sehr schlecter Mann.''* (American major—paratrooper. Very bad man.)

The SS character said, *"Nicht für ihm—oben!"* (Not for him—upstairs!)

The sergeant said, *"Ja wohl!"* And they turned around reluctantly and started arguing among themselves.

At the foot of the stairs the darnedest thing happened. The guards pulled out *Pfennigs* (pennies) and matched out to see which two would take me up to the attic and which two could remain a bit safer in the air raid shelter. The two who lost hustled me up the winding stairs to a heavy locked door at the very top of the big bahnhof building. A guard there unlocked the door and they pushed me into a room already quite crowded with other people who had to be secured, expendable though they might be. The room was obviously a transit cooler, with bars at the window set in concrete. It had thick cinder-block walls and a heavy reinforced door.

Though I had managed to retain a tiny hacksaw blade through all the searches over the last couple of years, the window bars were so thick it would have taken hours to cut through them. Then there was the sheer drop of about sixty feet to the concrete below. My cell mates were a mixed lot—French, Belgians, Dutch, Russians, and even a couple of Italians. I gathered that some had been enlisted prisoners who refused to work.

The alarms seemed to become even louder and I heard a man near the window shout, "*Avions*!" (Airplanes). I elbowed closer to the window and saw in the distance a cloud of little specks like a swarm of mosquitoes. The specks kept getting bigger and bigger, and eventually we could hear the deep hum of the motors in the distance. As it was still light, I knew it had to be a raid of B-17 Flying Fortresses, which could defend themselves best in daylight. I had never seen so many airplanes in the sky at one time before.

The sight threw panic into many of my cell mates.

Some dropped to their knees and started praying. There were shouts in many languages. I recognized some words such as "*Aborte*," "*Ausfall*" and "*Gehen avec!*" all meaning roughly the same things—stop, go back, fall down, get away! I was praying too, grimly, earnestly, but differently. "Dear God, please let these planes do their job, hit their targets and really hurt the cock-eyed Nazi war machine and its railroad. But if you see any future value in this pointed-eared son of yours, you might please just save this room."

That's just about what happened. The noise swelled to a roar. Great booms sounded. From the window we could see fires starting in the city, and the building itself seemed to rock. Bits of plaster and cement showered over us, but no one in the room was seriously hurt. The part of the city we could see through the window was soon a shambles.

Some time after the all-clear sounded the door was unlocked and guards started picking up their charges. The first guards to arrive came for their group of French, Belgian, and Dutch prisoners, which included some quite big men. I quickly asked one of them with whom I'd been talking earlier if I could borrow his beret. He whipped it off and handed it to me and I slapped it on.

I tried to shrink a foot or so and limped down the stairs with that group. The two guards who had taken me upstairs earlier passed right by me as they went up to the attic cooler. At the foot of the stairs our group turned left; the outer door about fifty feet away looked very inviting. Just then the sergeant and my other guard came striding up. I eased toward the far edge of the group, but they spotted me and let out a shout. I sprinted for the outer door, a shot rang out, everyone except guards dropped to the floor and I slid to a stop as two guards at the main door stepped out, blocking my way with their pistols drawn, and the other guards closed in. No one seemed too trigger-happy except for one of the guards who had not seen me on the stairs. He was red-faced, fingering his pistol unnecessarily, and shouting invectives at me. The sergeant soon cooled him down.

Then a peculiar thing happened. The sergeant seemed to be asking questions of his companions about my papers. They showed their empty hands and shrugged. The sergeant stood and thought for a while and walked up to a nearby information booth, which a man had just re-entered after the raid. I heard the sergeant ask, "*Wo ist den nähest Kriegsgefangenerlager*?" (Where is the nearest POW camp?) The man pulled out a map and obviously gave some directions. He also said that all train travel was "*kaput*" (disrupted).

The upshot was that the sergeant obtained a truck from an officer, loaded the guards and me aboard, and drove south an hour or so to what was obviously another POW camp at a place called Eichstadt. There the guards were just going off their daytime shifts. The officer in charge listened to the sergeant somewhat impatiently, then directed some Eichstadt guards to take me to the cooler—where else?! The sergeant and the guards from Stalag Luft III drove off in their truck without even giving me a fond farewell.

I found quite a talkative guard at the Eichstadt cooler and learned that this was Oflag 7B, a camp for British Army officers. I felt a wave of relief. It did not sound like an execution or a Kolditz Castle. And it might offer opportunities for escape. That night before I slept I thanked the Lord over and over for safekeeping during the bombing and for whatever led the sergeant to dump me at an ordinary POW camp. The next morning after the usual slice or two of goon bread with pink jam and ersatz tea, tasteless but hot, I was taken to see the kommandant.

The officer who had received me from the Stalag Luft III sergeant was also there. They were both officers of the Wehrmacht (army), not Luftwaffe (air force) as at Sagan. The kommandant looked at some notes on his desk and then looked up.

"You are Major Sage?"

I replied, "Yes, Herr Kommandant."

He said, "It seems the Luftwaffe sergeant who brought you told my hauptmann here that you have escaped many times, that you tried again yesterday, and he asked that you be locked up." The kommandant then raised his voice, "But ve don't vant you here!"

I looked him right in the eye and said, "I don't want to be here. Why don't you just send me home?" And I grinned at him.

At first I thought he'd blow his stack as I stood grinning at him. Then a sort of a smile came over his face and he said, "Maybe you are a good soldier, but a bad prisoner. Now, you go back to the cooler for a while till I decide what to do with you."

I was in the cooler only a couple more days, then released into the main camp. It was a former school of some sort with one big gray building at the top of a small slope, a sports field at the bottom, and about six low-lying barracks and several aborts around the edges of the field. The security system of double barbed wire with concertina wire in between—goon boxes and walking fence guards plus ferrets—seemed just as tight as at Sagan. The German guards handed me over to the British adjutant inside the camp, who in turn took me to a welcoming committee. Their aim, of course, was to ensure that I was not a German plant put in camp to spy on them.

We had a similar process in Stalag Luft III where newcomers were checked out to learn if they were the people they pretended to be. We asked about their flying comrades, checked home-town data or asked questions about sports that only a real American or limey would be able to answer. Here, I thought, they had to take me a bit on faith as there was no other U.S. prisoner in the camp. But so help me, up popped a Canadian captain from British Columbia, right across the border from my state, who had gone to Washington State University and remembered me from my football days there. A small world!

The camp was full of ‘‘old’’ kriegies, all from the British Commonwealth—English, Scots, Welsh, Australians, New Zealanders, South Africans and Canadians. Many had been there since the fall of France—the ones who didn't make it back to Britain from the evacuation of Dunkirk—and many of the later kriegies, particularly Canadians, were from the Dieppe raid of August 1942. They were eager for any scrap of fresh news and though I had very little, they were as hospitable as the RAF men of North Camp had been when I first went in there.

Soon I was settled in a room in a block down along the sports field. I was invited out to tea. One of the first things I asked for was a map. I was still curious as to why I was deep in Bavaria. A geography professor, I believe from Oxford, had been able to obtain an atlas from the library of this former boys' school shortly after it was made into a POW camp. I found that Oflag 7B at Eichstadt was about halfway between Nuremberg and Munich, and the second stop from Eichstadt on the way south was the infamous Dachau. I wondered aloud, ‘‘Could von Lindeiner have been sending me there?’’

I never did find out, but I thanked the good Lord over and over for His protection during the Nuremberg air raid and for whatever caused the guards to drop me off at Eichstadt.

When I asked about escape activities, the senior kriegies told me that they had a couple of tunnels started, but they had been closed down after the news of the execution of the fifty from Sagan. They said that these tunnels might be developed for possible use later if the Germans were to give the rumored orders for liquidation. Several messes had me in to tea. They frequently asked me to tell them about the camp life and escape activities at Sagan.

This camp was still getting Red Cross parcels plus some personal supplies from their homes in the far-flung corners of the earth. Tea and biscuits and New Zealand butter seemed plentiful. The Commonwealth kriegies were most hospitable and I had tea with them nearly every day of my brief stay, interspersed with a full-time sports schedule.

The Canadians had plenty of softball equipment and a decent backstop. There was even a tennis court plus the large soccer field. From brief notes in a tiny Swiss YMCA appointment calendar book that I carried all the way home with me, I find that I played tennis, basketball, softball, or cricket nearly every day of my short stay at Eichstadt. I can't recall the faces, but I do remember the names: I played tennis several times with Tony Field-Fisher and Brian Phillips of London and Mac McCormick from Sydney, Australia.

On July 2, 1944, my entry reads, ''First cricket—caught out one in slips and made nine runs and fourteen runs in my two times at bat for third high on team.'' I won't try to explain the game of cricket here—it's the British forerunner of baseball—but I will say I was lucky with the bat. Their bat is about the length of a baseball bat. Flat on one side, round on the other, it is swung vertically to protect a wicket of three vertical sticks. The opposing bowler (the pitcher) attempts to knock the wickets down with a ball that he can throw with a spin at these sticks. I merely defended by fouling off the ball until the bowler made a mistake and threw the ball too far in front of the wicket. It then bounced about waist-high—just right. This looked quite familiar to me; I shifted to a baseball horizontal grip and knocked the ball out of the park. I received big hurrahs from the ordinarily reserved Englishmen. This happened twice—and I could have enjoyed free tea for weeks from my cricket teammates for my bit of beginner's luck.

The next day, the third of July, maybe to warm up for the Fourth of July, I pitched a thirteen-to-two one-hitter in a Canadian softball game. These people were obviously sports nuts and I joined in with them.

One of the best athletes I've ever seen in my life was a big fellow, a very dark Maori from New Zealand. He made me think of Jim Thorpe. Of course he had played a lot of rugby, cricket, and soccer in New Zealand, but he seemed to pick up all games easily. He was tremendously well coordinated: He played excellent basketball and softball, and I'm sure he would have excelled at tennis as well if he had taken it up. He was at least six feet two and at normal times would have weighed around two hundred pounds of bone and muscle. He was thinner then, as were we all.

Then on the Fourth I dressed up in the best I had or could borrow for Independence Day, a one-man Yankee Doodle among a thousand or so Redcoats. We played basketball in the morning, then cleaned up again for lunch. John Majors in my mess surprised me by baking a very tasty and professional-looking cake decorated with "Jerry" printed in bright red strawberry jam from his latest food parcel from home. Later I had a "rebel tea'' with another friendly mess group, followed by tennis. This Fourth was far quieter than the gala camp-wide blast at Sagan the year before, but these hospitable British and Canadian officers made the day very pleasant for the lone Yank.

At Eichstadt I saw one of my most unusual sights. I was walking toward the big house on the hill in camp to visit a friend when I saw on the hard surface road that led up to the house a big man roller-skating toward me. He appeared to have a large bright wool afghan billowing about him—an incongruous sight on this hot July day. As he got closer, he gave me a big grin, called out, ''Hi, Sage!'' and waved a knitting needle at me.

It was a Canadian brigadier from the Dieppe raid, already preparing for winter. The brigadier was knitting at a rapid clip while he flew along on his roller skates. When I remarked on it during tea at the big house, the officers said knitting was quite a hobby in camp—and they showed me some examples of knit afghans and blankets made from any kind of old wool that could be unraveled.

Another memory of my brief stay at Eichstadt was the worst thunderstorm of my life. It blew up at the end of a hot July day, perhaps the fifth. Huge black clouds rolled up into a twisting, almost blue-black mass. Great flashes seemed to split the skies in to huge ravines of yellow followed by grand rolling booms of thunder and torrents of rain. I walked to a corner of a perimeter walk, reveling in the pure power display above. I had a notion to see if I could make it over the fence in the tumult, but having no escape gear ready and not knowing how wary the guards were, I let the idea drop. I remember throwing back my head and letting the rain soak my face as the lightning flashed across the sky and yelling, "Look at this, you Nazi bastards! This is a blitzkrieg that makes yours seem puny!" When I went in to dry off, I felt purged of some pent-up frustrations and slept like a log that night.

In the next day or so a guard came to escort me to a talk with the kommandant, who said that I seemed to be adjusting well to the British prisoners and participating fully in the sports activities. He still didn't quite understand why I was there, but he asked if I might like to go to a camp of American officers, Oflag 64 at Schubin, over five hundred miles to the northeast. I thought about it a minute or two. Schubin was even farther north and east than Sagan was and much closer to the Russian armies than Eichstadt was to the Western Allies. So I said, "Yes sir, I'd like that."

He then ordered his adjutant to arrange the trip and me to be ready to leave the next morning. That afternoon and evening I visited as many of the Britishers, Australians, New Zealanders, Canadians and South Africans as I could. These people had been extremely kind to me, including me in their teas, their kriegie brews, their celebrations and a terrific sports program. Near the end of my farewells I visited the big house up on the hill where one of the captains of the cricket team lived; he also happened to be one of the skilled knitters. When I admired a large afghan he was just finishing, he said, "Ah, Jerry, I have a parting gift for you." And he handed me from his bunk a long cot-sized afghan that he had finished earlier.

Over my protest he said he was well fixed for the winter and that I'd especially need a warm afghan way up north where I was going. I thanked him profusely, and there was many a frigid night I thanked him again during the next winter in Schubin and going across Poland and Russia. When three guards came for me the next morning, I had rolled the afghan around my few spare clothes and tied it into a tight horseshoe I could wear over one shoulder. Thus attired, I was taken to the railroad station.

The guards were neither friendly nor unfriendly, but businesslike and very watchful. They were particularly wary every time the train slowed down or came to a halt. So I relaxed and tried to spend the time profitably spreading propaganda about the thousands of planes, ships and tanks that were pouring out of American factories. I added that for their own sakes I hoped the Allied armies came into Germany from the west before the Russians came in from the east.

One German lady with a small boy had a basket of tree-ripened cherries; she gave some to me and to the guards. We stopped briefly at Treutlingen, then went on to Nuremberg, where the tracks in the station had already been completely repaired. Train traffic seemed to be moving just as well as it had before the huge B-17 raid I'd been caught in not too long before.

We continued north through the famed Wagnerian opera town of Bayreuth, then on through Hof, reaching the southern bahnhof in Leipzig just as it was growing dark. There we debarked and trudged through the debris of the recently bombed-out city of Leipzig to a substation at the northeast corner of the city. We picked our way through the rubble, the fires, and the angry glares of homeless German people who guessed I was a prisoner and a comrade of those who had bombed their city. I was rather glad it was dark when we came to the more heavily populated areas, as I believed I could feel the bitterness of those seeking their loved ones and their belongings in all that devastation.

We reached the substation without serious incident and soon moved out on a train toward the northeast.

The car was less crowded than the previous one and I was able to get some sleep.

In the morning we arrived at Cottbus. After an hour or two we continued on in a northeasterly direction, traveling all day until we reached Posen in the evening. By then the guards and I were getting along quite well. They bought me a delicious meal of salt herring and other fish snacks with a hard roll and beer—weak but necessary to wash down the salt fish. The guards set up their schedule of vigilance, as we had a long wait before catching the local train that would eventually get us to Schubin. I stretched out on a bench and so did a guard. Two guards always stayed awake in rotation while one took time out to sleep.

The third day we chugged through fields of rugged barley and rye and great mounds of freshly dug sugar beets, giant rutabagas, turnips and the inevitable potatoes. In one small town I even caught a strong scent of sauerkraut curing, a scent that seemed to linger long after we had passed by.

Chapter 26

Eventually we reached our destination. As we entered, I read the larger sign on the station, which had the new German name, "*Altburgund*." In small print beneath was "*Schubin*," from the old Polish name before the German invasion. I put my afghan horseshoe roll over my shoulder and began the two-mile walk northwest to the camp, Oflag 64. For thirty or forty minutes we hiked along a cobblestone road and heard both German and Polish spoken by the bystanders, most of whom showed little interest in our passing. When we came within sight of familiar double rows of barbed wire, concertina coils, and tall goon boxes, we knew we had reached the camp. There was one very large whitish stone house, several smaller square houses and a half-dozen long, low brick and concrete barracks.

I saw a large arched gateway, but we didn't enter. Instead we went into the German administration building on the other side of the road. As I half expected out of habit, the Germans put me in a cooler alongside the administration building while they decided what to do with me. After that train trip I rather welcomed a chance to stretch out for a nap before moving on. In the evening the guards brought me weak potato and cabbage soup and a piece or two of goon bread and left me there overnight.

The next morning the camp kommandant gave me a stern warning that no escapes would be tolerated and he repeated a few more of his rules. Then he had the guards take me across the street.

There in the big house I met the American senior officer, Colonel Thomas Drake; his executive officer, Lieutenant Colonel John K. Waters; and the adjutant, Major Merle A. Meecham. Colonel Drake assigned me to one of the barracks as executive officer to the barracks commander, Lieutenant Colonel Max Gooler. Major Meecham gave me a quick tour of Oflag 64, now under the control of the Wehrmacht, the German armed forces.

I had heard quite a bit about this camp when it was run by the Luftwaffe and designated Oflag 21B. Wings Day had once led a tunnel out of there; it was there too that he and Colonel Rojo Goodrich met. Sammy Vogtle had tried to cut through the wires there. Charlie Barnwell, Bob Brown, and the fine artist Carl Holmstrom had also been among the large group that was brought in to Sagan's North Camp in the late spring of 1943.

The camp was about two hundred by three hundred yards overall. The large stone building, called either the "White House" or the "Big House," had been a school in earlier days. The small square buildings housed about fifty enlisted soldier orderlies. There was a linen and utensil store, the cookhouse, a three-story hospital, a combined library and theater, a storehouse for Red Cross parcels and a small shower house.

When I arrived, only three of the six long barracks buildings were being used to house the five hundred to six hundred U.S. officers. Three others were opened one at a time as the camp population increased in the fall and winter to well over fifteen hundred prisoners.

Each barracks, one hundred twenty feet long by forty feet wide, was a huge open bay with cold stone floors. There were no built-in partitions. Lockers were used to form a hallway the length of the building and double-decker bunks divided each side into a semblance of cubicles about seven by ten feet, each housing at least eight men. Each kriegie had a straw mattress, a pillow, one sheet and a pillow case. The Germans supplied only two thin blankets, woefully inadequate in a latitude less than a hundred miles south of the Baltic Sea. The aborts were in separate buildings next to the barracks. The barracks lay along the sides of a large sports field with a bigger latrine building at each end of the playing area.

Lieutenant Colonel Max Gooler and I lived in the end of our barracks with some of the other older kriegies as messmates. Max had been on the U.S. military attaché staff in Egypt and was doing his job as an observer of the war between Rommel's Afrika Korps and Montgomery's Eighth British Army when he was captured at Tobruk by the Afrika Korps in 1942. We made a good pair, rather complementary. He was the more calm, reflective and conservative in his words and deeds. He said my normal enthusiasm and relatively violent activities tired him out—but he was smiling as he said it.

We had some good quiet evenings of bridge with a philosophical Texan, Clarence Ferguson, puffing on his pipe, and a math teacher, a quick-witted professorial fellow named Phil Foster. It was a fun group with lots of good humor and friendly banter, but we played tough bridge. We even got some duplicate bridge going, passing around the unchanged hands in trays made from

Red Cross boxes to see how other sets of partners in the barracks would bid and play the same cards. Actually, the three quieter men may have been wise to forego the strenuous sports program. They lost weight somewhat more slowly than the athletes as fewer and fewer Red Cross parcels came into our camp.

The German ration was even worse in both quality and quantity than at Sagan. The German ration for one man per day was officially listed at 318 grams of bread for a total of about one kilogram loaf or about 2⅕ pounds a week; 353 grams of potatoes; 200 grams of cabbage; 35 grams of meat (that's a spit in the eye); 9 grams of oil; 25 grams of barley; occasional issues of turnips or carrots or a dab of sauerkraut; a few grams of margarine, beet jam, cheese and sugar; and only a gram or two of ersatz tea or coffee.

The Red Cross food parcels were the real means of subsistence in the camps, and as no parcels were delivered from October through December, you could almost see the flesh fall off the more active prisoners. A weight check of all men maintained for about three weeks in late October and early November of 1944 showed the average loss across the entire camp population to be about ten pounds per man.

There was no clothing issued by the Germans, and as more prisoners came in, the Germans collected all uniform items except one set per man—to pass on the "extras" to those with even less to wear. Bedding was even more scarce. Sometimes officers slept two to a bunk during the coldest weather in order to pool their thin blankets. I scrounged a needle and some thread, placed German newspapers between my two thin blankets, and sewed together a sleeping bag topped off with the afghan given me by the friendly Britisher at Eichstadt.

Within a couple of weeks of my arrival at Schubin

Colonel Tom Drake was repatriated. He was succeeded as senior American officer by Colonel George "Zip-Zip" Millet until the more senior Colonel Paul "Pop" Goode arrived in mid-October. Colonel Goode remained as SAO throughout the rest of the Schubin period and on the marches to Hammelburg and Moosburg. Lieutenant Colonel John Waters remained the camp's executive officer under all three SAOs until he was quite seriously wounded by a guard during the raid of the Fourth Armored Division on Hammelburg the following March.

Johnny Waters was an excellent choice for executive officer. He immediately impressed everyone as an efficient, dedicated and level-headed officer. I could readily believe it when told he'd been first captain at West Point in the Class of 1931. He was the commander of the First Armored Battalion at the landing of the First Armored Division in North Africa in late 1942. One of the initial jobs of this battalion was to attack a German airport. In a quick strike he captured about twenty German airplanes. He was then promoted to executive officer of the First Armored Regiment.

In February 1943 he was in Combat Command A under General McQuillan, whom I was sent to find for General Ward, the First Armored Division commander, when Rommel counterattacked at Sidi Bou Sid and Casserine Pass in Tunisia. That was just a week or two before I was captured in February 1943.

I also learned that John Waters was a friend of Bub Clark, whose father, a medical major in the late 1920s, helped get John Waters into West Point. Johnny Waters was also General George Patton's son-in-law. Soon after the war ended, in the fall of 1945, I met John Waters in Washington and he invited me to the Pattons' home, where John's wife Bea had stayed while he was away at war. There I was to meet Mrs. Patton, Bea

Patton Waters and her sister—all lovely people. (The gathering occurred about two months before General Patton was killed in Europe in an automobile accident near the end of 1945.) About three years after this occasion, both John Waters and I were stationed at West Point, where I was on the social sciences faculty and Colonel John Knight Waters was Commandant of Cadets.

In late August 1944 we formed about eight intramural softball teams and had a tournament that was a lot of fun for both the players and spectators. I can't recall all the players on our team, but I know that Waters was second base, I pitched and the catcher was Poteet. Our first baseman was a left-handed doctor who never wore a glove, even though the softballs certainly weren't soft and many of the infield throws were pretty hard. As a pitcher I showed little variety and not much speed, but I had good control and could put a bit of spin on the ball. One day in a seven-inning quarter-final game, Poteet and I noticed that my high and inside ball with a spin was working well in the early innings, so we stayed with it.

We were putting most of our opponents out with pop flies or easy grounders off the upper part of the bat. At the end of four innings, when we were ahead about 3–0, as we went back out on the field Johnny Waters said to me, "Jerry, I'm not sure I need to mention this, but the other team hasn't even reached first base yet." I hadn't been conscious of it, but he was right: There had been twelve opponents up and twelve down. Poteet and I passed the word that I'd try to keep pitching the ball to spin high on the inside corner of the plate so they would pop up some more. We hoped for the best.

The fifth inning, and then the sixth, ended the same way. A strikeout or two—but the outs were mostly easy fly balls to the outfield—and the tension kept building. By the seventh inning we led 6–0 and everyone wanted a shutout. By now eighteen opponents had batted without reaching first. Then the first batter in the seventh inning tried too hard and struck out. The second hit a pop fly to the shortstop. The third batter was a big left-hander.

Waters turned and waved our left and center fielders a bit farther to their left. That brought them a little closer to our weakest fielder, an eager but rather uncoordinated youngster named Meyers. During the tournament Meyers had muffed more balls than he had caught. All right fielders had to watch their step. The right field at Schubin sloped up the hill toward the barracks and presented a liberal sprinkling of trees and stumps.

I may have been extra tense when this last man came up, or maybe a little tired, but whatever the reason, I gave him a pitch he liked. He pulled the ball in a high fly to right field and we all groaned. It was going toward our boy Meyers. Our shutout game was riding on Meyers' next move. He had been playing well up on the slopes—wisely, because it is easier to run downhill after a ball than uphill. He saw the ball coming and started racing down the slope, dodging trees all the way. Near the foot of the slope it looked as though he'd lost his balance. He dived forward with his arms outstretched and caught the ball neatly in his glove.

Rolling over, Meyers looked at his catch in disbelief and jumped up with a wild whoop and a tremendous grin. "I caught it!"

We all mobbed him. Our lad Meyers had caught the shutout ball, the only one in his direction all day.

We never forgot that perfect game, twenty-one up,

twenty-one down—no hits, no runs, no errors. Later I reflected that maybe malnutrition affects batters more than pitchers.

As more Americans came into camp, the empty barracks were put to use one at a time. I was made barracks commander of one of them, with Major Jack Dobson as my executive officer. Jack had been commander of the First Ranger Battalion; he and several of his men had been trapped out in front of the Anzio battle, badly shot up, and captured. These included James Bond; a light, tough boxer named Pat Teal; and a big lad, Jim Dew.

Dobson had been a rangy end for the West Point football team and was a great asset on our barracks soccer team as that league opened. Playing goalie, he could stop just about everything. After the opponents had tried a goal that he blocked or caught, he'd look for me and I'd always be off on one flank, usually the right one. He'd throw the ball out to me upfield. He could kick long, but his throwing arm was strong and more accurate. Having played my share of soccer with the British, I could get Dobson's pass under control and start our new attack rolling.

We had some pretty good games. Though at that time we were getting no Red Cross parcels and were continually hungry, we kept in shape at our sports and at least stayed lean and mean.

Lieutenant Colonel James "Gentleman Jim" Alger was in charge of security and escape activities. He had been the commander of the Second Armored Battalion in the same tank regiment as Waters. Alger, Drake and Waters had all been captured near Sidi Bou Sid in mid-February of 1943.

Alger's security committee screened all newcomers to make sure the Germans had not planted a spy in the camp. There had already been some progress on a couple of tunnels, but when Colonel Goode learned of the murder of the fifty "Great Escape" tunnelers in March and April 1944, he discouraged any more mass escape attempts. In fact, I knew of no escape activity at all when I arrived in late summer. The advice from camp headquarters seemed to be that the war would soon be over, so we shouldn't rock the boat. I didn't entirely agree with that philosophy, but I did resolve to wait until the Russians were closer to make my next move for freedom.

Though I had little to do with the German administrators, I quickly developed an antipathy to the camp security officer, Hauptmann Zimmerman. He acted like a true Nazi, a Heil-Hitler type, a petty bully. In the summer of 1944, four U.S. officers were being marched under guard to the hospital in a nearby town for treatment. They were ordered to walk in the streets rather than on the sidewalks. When they protested to the guards that this was humiliating and violated the Geneva Convention, the guards finally let them onto the sidewalks.

The incident was reported and Zimmerman brought the four men to trial in October 1944 for "obstructing the functions of the German Reich." They were acquitted, but in December 1944 they were informed that they'd be retried on charges growing out of the incident. At the retrial in January 1945 all four officers were sentenced to death, though fortunately they were liberated before sentence could be carried out.

Another example of the Nazi mentality occurred in late September 1944. Lieutenant Schmitz, the American assistant adjutant, was in the office of the White House alone when two unteroffiziers came in to tack up anti-escape posters. Schmitz considered the posters insulting to American officers because they accused our government of "resorting to gangster warfare up to and within the frontier of the Fatherland." He asked the Germans to wait until he could talk with the senior American officer.

Unable to reach the SAO, he brought back another senior officer, Lieutenant Colonel Schaefer, who discussed the posters with the unteroffiziers. As they were leaving, Lieutenant Schmitz stood in the doorway in, as he said later, a token protest. When the leading German touched Schmitz, the prisoner promptly got out of the way.

Later Schmitz was accused of blocking the doorway and Schaefer was charged with the catchall crime of "obstructing the functions of the German Reich." They were tried in December 1944 and both sentenced to death. They also were liberated one way or another before sentence could be carried out. Colonel Schaefer was sent to Kolditz and finally made it home safely when the camp was liberated.

As for Schmitz, the Germans must have forgotten about him in the confusion when we were marched out of the camp in January. He was hustled along with a lot of the others; the guards paid no special attention to him on the move. Johnny Waters told me later that when the kriegies arrived at Hammelburg, they bandaged Schmitz's head, said he'd been hurt in a hassle there and kept him in the hospital. The Germans forgot all about him. Schmitz also made it home.

Nevertheless, Lieutenant Colonel Schaefer might well have prompted the German ire. He could be very explicit at times, and he probably told the Germans what they could do with their posters when he was trying to assist Schmitz. He had no more love for Nazi tactics than I did. On earlier occasions, if a German guard shouted too loudly at him or bothered him in some way, Schaefer would swiftly pull out his set of false teeth, point them at the German offender and snap those teeth with amazing ferocity and speed.

I hadn't been many weeks in Oflag 64 when I had trouble with a wisdom tooth. It grew in crooked, its cutting edge canting sideways. I seemed to spend twenty-four hours a day trying to bite my cheek. The cheek was constantly bleeding, the tooth hurt, and it was hard for me to eat even the meager amount of food I was getting. But it was difficult to get help. Our one American dentist was up to his ears trying to help people with worse problems, painful cavities and rotting gums.

As few people trusted the camp's own German dentist, I was able to get in to see him one morning. He noted with glee, "Ach, this *is* a problem!" and told me to open wider. Then he related macabre stories of the everlasting pain that could come from extracting roots as big as mine evidently were. When I suggested some Novocain, he snorted, "A big man like you doesn't need anesthetics."

He laid out drills, hammers, picks, chisels and a huge pair of pliers, stuck one knee in my stomach, and went to work. He eventually got the tooth out in pieces and wiped the sweat off his forehead and the blood off his hands. As I rinsed with hot salt water, he chortled, "I zink today you vill not eat your *Mittagessen* (lunch)!"

Spitting out bloody saltwater, I said, "Like hell I won't, you S.O.B.!" Then I added, "*Danke schön!*" with what I thought might be taken for an evil grin and left for the mess hall. I half-chewed, half-drank the usual big cup of cabbage soup. Before I was through my soup was a dark pink and looked more like borscht than cabbage soup, but I ate it all anyway.

As in other camps, we tried to break the monotony and forget the hunger by setting up special events. We had all-star basketball games such as I played in Eichstadt, a rough touch football tournament, and a great track meet in which we got hundreds of POWs competing in a great variety of races. The events we set up included relays, high and broad jumps (the Germans wisely wouldn't allow us a pole vault), shot-put, discus, hammer throw and comic contests using all types of balls and implements. One of the outstanding contestants was Eddie Berlinski of New Jersey, a fine track man and football halfback. Looking back, I don't see how we kept going as we did without Red Cross parcels to keep up our strength.

The officer in charge of the athletic program was Herb Johnson of Camp Hill, Pennsylvania. Only recently I learned from him that D-day, June 6, 1944, was the occasion of a tremendous track meet in Schubin. It had been planned long in advance without any thought of an invasion, but according to both Max Gooler and Herb, the Germans had the idea that the Americans had some foreknowledge and planned this tremendous track meet in advance as the celebration. I was still back in Stalag Luft III on D-day and knew nothing of the June track meet.

The subject came up while I talked with Herb Johnson not too long ago. I recalled one track meet in which I ran a third lap and passed the baton to Eddie Berlinski to win the relay race. He said, "What do you mean, you guys won that relay race? *I* ran the last lap for the winning team of that race." Then we realized we were talking about two quite separate days. He was talking about the sixth of June; I was talking about a meet held later, in September of 1944.

We tried to think of some others who had played a lot of basketball, tall fellows in our all-star basketball exhibition game. Among them were Bill Farrell, Jack Dobson, Carl Hubbell, Bill Farber, and probably Herb Johnson, all good athletes. We ran ourselves into the ground, kept fit and stayed hungry.

Sometime in October we had wonderful news—a train of boxcars such as carried relief agency goods had been pulled into a siding near the camp at Schubin. Someone reported that it was loaded with Red Cross food parcels. When volunteers were called forward to help unload the train, everyone in camp volunteered.

A detail was selected to go with the German guards and trucks. It turned out that only one boxcar actually held supplies for us, but a boxcar can hold a lot of eleven-pound Red Cross parcels. We believed what we wanted to believe, that it was full of food. The trucks came back full, but the kriegie detail seemed greatly subdued. With most of the camp standing around salivating, their hungry tongues almost hanging out, the detail announced that the entire shipment was from the YMCA and it contained complete uniforms for several football teams—no food, but plenty of cleated shoes, padded pants, jerseys, shoulder pads, helmets—the works. So we kept on starving. When we did set up an exhibition game to provide some entertainment for the troops, the game sent over half the players to the hospital.

The hospital, *Revier* to the Germans, was in a tall old building with unpainted floors, very undependable plumbing and some thirty beds. Despite the hardships caused by insufficient and sometimes spoiled food, impure water supplies, and poor sanitation facilities, the public health in camp was surprisingly good, perhaps because we had a pretty tough young population, many of whom had been introduced to hardship early, in combat. However, the revier was ill-equipped to handle the badly wounded or seriously ill. Such cases were sent to a hospital in a nearby town. Most of the patients in the revier had stomach problems. Some seemed to be getting ulcers from eating the acidic black bread.

In the late fall of 1944 things seemed to go from bad to worse for me. I was losing weight rapidly and I would become unusually tired playing ball. Then, of all things, I lost my appetite. I could hardly look at food, and in particular fat, without nausea. When my eyeballs turned yellow, my friends insisted I see a doctor. The medics weren't sure what it was, but something seemed to be wrong with my liver. At the minimum I had a severe case of jaundice. Most agreed I had hepatitis, though one or two thought it might be some weird form of malaria (hard to believe up in the bitter cold of the Baltic winds). I stayed in the revier only a day or so, but meanwhile I was put on a diet of white bread that the doctors received in special Red Cross parcels for invalids. The doctors sent along some white bread and medicines when I returned to camp and I slowly got better.

But what a change in my general attitude! Before, I had always been full of optimism, pep and encouragement no matter what the circumstances—always saying the war would soon be over and cheering up others the best I could. This illness thrust me into a gloom period. No pep, little enthusiasm, and more than this, I began to think that the war would never end. Then I remembered something I'd read in a book of essays by Will James back in Stalag Luft III. One of these essays was a fine dissertation on the intimate relationship between mind and body.

One example was what James proposed as the direct correlation between a sound liver and an optimistic personality. He cited cases of liver malfunction such as hepatitis and jaundice as inducing deep pessimism. He was perfectly correct as far as I was concerned. I definitely was looking at the world with a jaundiced eye. In the four weeks or so it took me to recover, I still couldn't eat much of anything fatty, and even now the blood banks will not accept my blood. I guess they think it may still carry hepatitis or malaria, but I managed to recover my optimism in full measure.

I fondly remember a great guy who needed quite a bit of help from the doctors when he arrived in camp. Wright Bryan, a war correspondent for *The Atlanta Journal*, went too far to the front covering an attack and was shot in the leg and captured. He was a true southern gentleman, never complaining of his unusual status of wounded POW and ready with a helping hand or sympathetic ear for others. We were glad for him when he was repatriated in 1944, but we also missed him.

We've seen each other several times since. Among other things, he left the editorship of *The Atlanta Journal* for that of *The Cleveland Plain Dealer*, then became vice president of finance for Clemson University in South Carolina, where he remained until retirement.

Lieutenant Colonel Charlie Jones from Northwood, Iowa, was another upbeat, jolly person. And I enjoyed talking with Father Stanley Brach, our only Catholic chaplain, who maintained a beautiful little chapel in Schubin for two and a half years. Several Protestant chaplains came and went, and they were all good men, but I didn't get to know them anywhere near as well as I did Murdo MacDonald, our parachuting Scottish padre of Stalag Luft III. Strong interdenominational Protestant programs were maintained at Schubin, just as they were at Sagan.

There was also a good theater program dubbed by the leading Thespians the "Little Theater of Schubin College." Frank Maxwell, Wilbur Sharpe, Bob Rankin, Russ Ford, Bill Farrell and John Carpenter were some who did a fine job of bringing us hit Broadway plays and musicals from scripts and scores sent in by the YMCA. They also presented several one-act plays.

Mail was always great for morale, but mail service got slower in late 1944 as Allied bombers increasingly disrupted transportation. The best morale boost after the great D-day invasion celebration was any big advance on the western front by the British and Americans or on the eastern front by the Russians.

After I got over my liver affliction and my spirits were back up, I composed another song to encourage our Allies. The Russian field marshals whose army fronts were making the most progress after they had finally turned back the Germans at Stalingrad were Rokossovski, Zhukov, Konyev, and Malinovski. On the western front I was counting most on General Patton's Third Army and General Patch's Seventh Army, but my main hope in Poland was to get loose and join the closer Russians. So as morning broke over Schubin and we went out for appell, I'd burst into song to the Russian tune "Ochi Chornia," the lovely ballad "Dark Eyes."

My song went:

"O Rokossovski, bring your Russkis!
Come and get me—
I'm kaputski!
Marshall Stalin, hear me callin',
Keep high-balling—
Don't take roots-ski!
Zhukov, Konyev, Malinovski,

Patch and Patton,
Rokossovski—
Come and get me—
I'm kaputski!"

One of two of my colleagues started joining in on this song, and our little group soon grew from a trio to at least an octet and we got a bundle of applause. Everyone in camp agreed with the sentiment, whatever they thought of our doggerel or voices.

Chapter 27

The camp newspaper, a monthly publication known as *The Oflag 64 Item*, was also good for morale, with summaries of the sports, theater programs, new acquisitions in the library and other news, all in an upbeat, good-natured vein, highlighted by some excellent kriegie humor cartoons. *The Oflag 64 Item* had a long life and was revived after the war, thanks to the work of our colleague kriegie John Slack, a Schubin alumnus living and working in Gladwyne, Pennsylvania.

For about twenty years he has published a newsletter for the former Schubin kriegies that he calls *The Post Oflag 64 Item*. This serves as the glue that holds together the fine spirit of camaraderie among Schubinites and keeps everybody informed of the dates, places, events, and responsibilities for Oflag 64 reunions, which have been held every two years across a span of nearly forty years. John Slack is a warm, generous guy who has given hundreds of hours of effort to keep the reunions alive and full of fun.

Dave Pollak of Cincinnati, Ohio, with assistance from Willard Heckman, of the North and South Camps of Stalag Luft III, has also kept up the reunions of groups for over twenty years. The Stalag Luft III reunions were initiated by Major General Mel McNickle, the camp adjutant of South Compound, while he was at Wright-Patterson Air Base near Dayton, Ohio.

The last reunion I attended was in Chicago, Illinois. It was run by Bob Weinberg of the Center Camp and Dick Schrupp, my old messmate from North and South Camps, who did an outstanding job.

Among the important people in the prison camps, Henry Soderberg must be cited. I saw him in all the regular German POW lagers I was in. Soderberg is a Swede who has been with the Swedish Air Service, SAS Airline for the past many years. In World War II he was the representative of the neutral Protecting Power as set up by the Geneva Convention. He would visit the camps about six times a year to talk privately with the camp's kriegie leaders with no Germans present. He reported his findings to the Protecting Power and lodged POW complaints or requests with the German authorities. Although his requests were often disregarded, Soderberg's visits and transmissions to the Free World did much to ensure that our stay in captivity was no worse than it was.

We also owed a great debt to the International Red Cross for food parcels and clothing and to the YMCA for athletic and recreational material, including many books for our well-used library. As the weather grew too cold for outdoor sports, we increased our reading of all sorts of titles, including a variety of texts for the many classes at Schubin U.

Hobbies also flourished. Many kriegies found they had hidden talents in sketching, painting, cartoon work, sculpture, knitting, embroidery, and wood and metalwork.

When my RAF blue jacket issued way back in North Camp finally wore out, I received a British Army battle jacket—designed like an Eisenhower jacket—as a replacement. In fact, the Eisenhower jacket was modeled after the British Army battle jacket. I could find no gold major's leaves to put on the shoulders, and Major Ed Haggard helped me out. He found some goldish-yellow yarn in a YMCA hobby kit and used it to embroider a fine set of gold oak leaves on my jacket.

One item of metal manufacture far more prevalent at Schubin than at Sagan was the "smokeless cooker" (not a completely accurate term). There was even less stove space available in Schubin than at Sagan, and hardly any fuel. So by necessity we invented our own miniature stoves. These consisted of a small can punched full of holes wired into the top half of a larger can, also punched, which had a good-sized door cut out of the lower side. We burned scraps of paper, cardboard or bits of kindling wood in the lower half, and the top half burned the residue of combustible gases left in the smoke from the bottom. I did not make one of these, so my description may be a bit off—but the smokeless cooker could heat a cup of water or barley soup in a matter of minutes and was just right for a bit of cocoa or bouillon before going to sleep on a frigid night.

The winter of 1944 set some sort of record for being frigid. We stayed indoors wrapped in everything warm we had, going out only to visit the bulletin board at the White House, where we learned the best news we could glean about the progress of the war. "Where's Rokossovsky?" "Where's Zhukov?" "Where's Patton?"

The only thing that could really cheer us, after the almost negligible mail from home, was news of solid advances by the Allied armies, or the welcome word in December that our Red Cross parcels had finally arrived. Even these had to be issued sparingly. Jack Dobson and I set aside some of the most favored items from ours, determined to celebrate Christmas with a real bash. On the important day we spread out all we could eat of Spam, cheese and pancakes we'd made of big round flat crackers soaked in water, fried and colored with sugar-beet jam. We topped off our feast with a huge gedoing pudding of cracker crumbs, prunes, raisins and orange powder. Within an hour we were both sick as dogs. Our shrunken stomachs just couldn't handle the sudden rich traffic!

As the Russians came closer and closer, the Germans of Schubin grew more and more nervous.

At seven o'clock Saturday evening, January 20, 1945, Pop Goode called all camp staff and barracks commanders together and told us he had heard we would be evacuated deeper into Germany the next day. The Germans had given permission for those who were wounded or too ill to march to remain behind in the hospital. The remainder were to start marching west to some nearby railhead and take a train for another prison camp in Brandenberg.

The standing order not to escape was not rescinded at that time. There was a great deal of anxiety about Nazi SS troops following our column out and more than a little apprehension about the treatment an escapee might receive from the Russians. I kept my own counsel, resolving not to go deeper into Germany, but to take my chances going east at the first favorable opportunity.

I alerted my barracks to the situation and everyone started packing, distributing all the food and blankets each one could carry over all his clothing. I rolled up meat, cheese and bread into my afghan horseshoe roll, this time with another blanket inside. In the morning I put on two pairs of my least tattered and best mended socks, long johns, two pairs of pants, a heavy shirt, a sweater, my battle jacket, overcoat—and a knitted balaclava, which covered all my head, neck and face with holes in front for my eyes, nose, and mouth.

We marched out of Schubin's gate Sunday, January 21, in swirling dry snow, and turned west. At the edge of town a posted sign read "Exin" (the Polish town of Kcynia) followed by "24 KM." So it was twenty-four kilometers, fifteen miles, to this first town where we were to expect the train. As we plodded along in the buffeting wind on that icy road, loaded down with food, blankets and clothes, the twenty-four kilometers seemed like one hundred twenty-four.

I had not realized how my strength had fallen off in the preceding three months, during which my exercise was curtailed by hepatitis, malnutrition and cold. Much of the muscle seemed to have evaporated from my legs and I felt as though I were inching along on pipe stems. Several men stumbled and fell and had to be helped along. I also fell, but was able to get going again by myself.

At Exin we learned that no train was waiting for us, and we were then marched to a large dairy farm at or near a town sign for Siernicki. By now it was fairly dark. The temperature was below freezing and the ground was covered with icy snow. We headed toward two or three huge barns with what strength we had left and there took refuge from the bitter wind and cold.

The barn I entered was truly an unforgettable haven. The first impression was the smell—the sweetish fragrance of hay mixed with the aromas of old spilled milk, urine and cow manure, all suspended in a steamy vapor, but wondrously warm after the wintry blast outside. Smell or not, we nestled against the warm cows, ate a bit of our cold food and slept awhile.

As I recall, I awoke some time during the night to Jack Dobson's shaking me. It was fully dark and he whispered he was bugging out and asked if I wanted to go with him.

I started to get up, but my legs wouldn't move. They seemed to be frozen stiff or paralyzed, so I told Jack, "Go ahead. I'll have to make my move when my legs start working."

I massaged my legs for a long time, wrapped them in everything I could and stuck them into the hay between two big old cows. Every now and then I moved my legs to keep blood circulating. Before dawn I was able to hobble around slowly. I crept out of the barn and found a loose cellar window in the big farmhouse.

The guards were evidently completely fatigued and drowsy, or else they were standing watch somewhere around the corner. No one bothered me. I slithered through the cellar window and landed in a big pile of vegetables. As the day grew lighter, I found I was in a root cellar half filled with mounds of rutabagas.

Before full daylight I dug myself down into one big vegetable pile. Only part of my head stuck out. I had lots of hair then, and so did the rutabagas. It was a fairly good disguise, though I was certainly the only rutabaga in Europe with pointed ears! I stayed there until I heard the column of kriegies and Germans moving out, around the crack of dawn. The last German words I heard from the panicky guards were "*Mach' schnell! Mach' schnell!*" (Make haste, hurry!)

As the sounds of the column moving away finally faded, I went to the window and cautiously scanned the farmyard and as much of the road as I could see for any German or SS uniforms. None could be seen. Again I was free from German custody, but this time I felt sure my security would last. This final escape was by far the easiest of any I had attempted.

And then, wonder of wonders, my legs started feeling better. I gradually stretched them and walked in place, working them up and down as I paced round and round in the cellar, recalling my recapture after the ambulance breakout. I remembered how I had been walking vigorously, though limping, as a free man, but when I was caught, I could not walk a step as long as I was surrounded by my captors. Here the reverse was true. The legs that had become almost paralyzed walking deeper into Germany regained strength with a sudden rush when I realized I was free to work my way east toward freedom and I said, "Thank you, Lord!" over and over as I began to inch my way out of the cellar window.

As I limped across the farmyard, I saw heads poking out of the other cellar windows, barn doors and haylofts. Quite a few other kriegies had hidden out during the night, and the Germans had been in too much of a hurry to make a thorough search before leaving.

Mindful of a rumor of SS troops between the prison column and the advancing Russians, we all stayed inside the farmhouse and barns the rest of that day. The Polish people were generous. They provided a huge pot of tasty vegetable soup, ladling it out for the many of us who were hungry. We kriegies reciprocated by giving them chocolate and some real coffee. As they had not had such items for over five years, the Poles were delighted.

The Poles were glad to see the Germans go, but they seemed equally nervous about the Russians. At the farmhouse I kept alternating leg exercises with rest and applied heat to my legs. I ate good farm vegetables and started learning some practical phrases in Polish. I asked the Poles if they knew any Russian, but they did not.

That evening a Pole came in to report that a Russian patrol was heading west on a nearby road. We heard some gunfire, but it was intermittent and still some distance away.

The next morning we heard the definite rumble of tanks approaching from the east. The Poles asked who would go out to greet them. The American officers looked at one another, but most eyeballs seemed to fix on me. So I asked the Poles how to say, "I am American Major Sage, senior officer here."

They taught me phonetically to say, *"Ya yestem Amerikanski Mayor Sage, starsha officera tuti."* As the Poles had heard that the approaching troops were a prong of Marshal Zhukov's forces, I learned to say, *"Gdjeh Marshalli Zhukov?"* (Where's Marshal Zhukov?) It probably was very crude Russian, but I thought it might work.

As the first big Russian tank came up the road toward the farmhouse, I went out to meet it. I rapidly considered what gestures to use. I knew I'd be dead if I gave a straight arm salute like the Nazis, with an open hand. I thought the communists used a clenched fist, but I didn't want them to think I was shaking a threatening fist at them. So I approached them waving both arms in a friendly arc over my head and giving them a big old Joe College grin and saying, "Hi there!" That was the start of my travels across Poland and east into Russia.

What happened to the other kriegies of Schubin was told to me much later by colleagues when we met after the war.

When the Germans pushed the column out of Exin, there were more than fourteen hundred tired and hungry POWs. Theirs turned out to be a grueling march of forty-five days before they finally reached a railhead that could operate. Even then there were only enough boxcars to take the first four or five hundred men with Colonel Goode and Johnny Waters to Hammelburg. Throughout this long march, no advance preparations had been made for quartering the kriegies at night. When the column arrived at some village or farm or factory at dark, the kriegies had to stand around on frostbitten or wet feet while the guards made some allocation of space in barns, stables, cow sheds or warehouses. Often, no fires were allowed for preparing meager meals or drying socks. Some who had carried their Klim-can smokeless cookers surreptitiously heated scrounged potatoes or water for ersatz tea or coffee. Drinking water was often inadequate and there were usually no washing or shaving facilities. Baths were impossible the entire way.

The daily ration was a bowl of turnip or cabbage soup, a few potatoes, half a slice of goon bread and a cup of ersatz ground coffee or mint tea. While the POWs were in former Polish territory, the kind Poles gave the kriegies vegetables from their own paltry stores along with whatever medical supplies they could find to help those who were ill or hurt. Farther on, kriegies occasionally traded with the German farmers, exchanging soap, fountain pens, and cigarettes for eggs, apples or anything else to eat.

Occasionally the kriegies came upon corpses of Russian POWs, evidently shot by their SS guards for straggling from an earlier column being marched west. Once the kriegies plodded by an outdoor latrine on which sat a Russian, frozen to death. The German guards would not even allow the kriegies to cover or bury the body. Such evidence of callousness could not have done much to foster compassion for the retreating Germans as the Red Army rolled into Germany from the east.

The American column gradually stretched out in the long march, and kriegies were loaded by groups into boxcars as they became available. The first group, with Pop Goode and John Waters, had about a five-day boxcar trip to Hammelburg. The second group of about four hundred boarded a train a day or so later for a camp near Brandenburg. Another similar group walked all the way to Moosburg, which was becoming the final German destination for all.

I heard more about the Hammelburg group as I talked with Johnny Waters and other colleagues from that group shortly after the war. The kriegies arrived in Hammelburg on March 9, 1945. On March 27 the German kommandant told Pop Goode that the camp would be evacuated that afternoon. The Germans seemed panicky and rumors started around the camp that an American tank column was approaching. The rumors proved to be true. A small tank and armored infantry column from the U.S. Fourth Armored Division had punched through about sixty miles of enemy territory to liberate the American POWs at Hammelburg.

The German kommandant surrendered the camp to Pop Goode as the U.S. tanks moved up to the barbed wire. As the battle continued, John Waters volunteered to go out to meet the Americans and tell them the camp had been surrendered. He took with him an American flag carried all the way from Schubin. A German captain interpreter and three junior American officers accompanied Waters. After they walked through the gate, a German soldier, from some accounts an SS soldier, appeared from behind a house, raised his rifle and shot Waters. The bullet smashed Johnny's right hip, chipped his tailbone and passed on through his left buttock. The soldier then came up and threatened the German captain, but finally the captain was able to make the private understand the new situation. The Americans carried Waters back to the hospital on a blanket.

Two POWs carried the American flag over to the flagpole, pulled down the Nazi insignia and ran up the Stars and Stripes. The tanks then knocked down the barbed wire fence and were greeted by hundreds of hysterically happy American kriegies. Pop Goode pushed through the crowd until he found the task force commander, Captain Abe Baum. Baum told Goode that he had expected to find fewer than three hundred Americans in Hammelburg; Goode replied there was actually a total of about five times that number. The elation of the POWs turned to bitter disappointment as they learned that the column had no immediate backup, could not stay and defend the camp, and could carry only two or three hundred men out. Even if they could do so, they would probably have to fight their way back through to the U.S. lines. They did understand that all the rest of them were invited to escape across country on their own if they wished.

Many climbed on the tanks and the armored personnel carriers. By this time the Germans had been able to position some good armored fighting outfits at strategic places to block all the exit roads, and in the last analysis, none of the vehicles made it back to the U.S. lines, though some soldiers and POWs did get back on foot. Most were rounded up by German reinforcements and returned to the prison camp, again under German control.

In another two days all the Americans except those in the hospital at Hammelburg were evacuated to Moosburg. Some went by train with a stopover in Nuremberg and some went by foot. It took the last group a full fifteen days to march the ninety miles because of the almost continual Allied bombing and their own weakened condition.

Only a week or so later Hammelburg was surrounded by the Fourteenth Armored Division of the Seventh Army and this time truly liberated. Johnny Waters was evacuated to the U.S. Army Hospital at Gotha, Germany.

Bub Clark, who had arrived at Moosburg earlier with the South Camp kriegies of Stalag Luft III, told me later of meeting Pop Goode as the Hammelburg group arrived. Bub said that Pop Goode was still carrying his bagpipes, as he had all the way from Schubin.

In the early months of 1945 there were many columns of prisoners being marched west across Germany. One axis went across the northern plains, another across the center and a third deep into Bavaria. Most of my colleagues from previous camps had been in the latter group, which ended up in Moosburg near Munich. From reports of my friends who were in Moosburg, there was little good to say about the camp except that it became the place of final liberation by U.S. troops.

The camp at Moosburg was crowded with well over thirty thousand prisoners of many nationalities, plus vermin, lice, bedbugs and filth. Many prisoners preferred to sleep outside in tents or lean-tos rather than endure the unsavory barracks. Security was lax near the end. A man could bribe a guard to take him out to trade cigarettes or other items for a chicken, eggs or other food.

The great and final day was April 29, 1945. American tanks rolled up, the gates were flung open and kriegies joyfully mobbed their grinning GI rescuers as they climbed out of their tanks and personnel carriers.

The thin but happy kriegies were POWs no longer; they were now ''Recovered Allied Military Personnel'' (RAMPS) awaiting transportation home. Home—what a wonderful word!

Chapter 28

Meanwhile, back at a farmhouse near Exin, Poland, in January 1945, a tall, lean major is approaching a Russian tank. Waving both hands, he is grinning and shouting in a language incomprehensible to the Russian tankers.

Those Russkis were certainly security-conscious. As the tank came to a halt, its entire turret swiveled toward me and the main gun, at least a 105 and probably bigger, was trained right on the farmhouse I had just left. Then a double bank of .50-caliber machine guns swung around to point across my belly. They throw slugs bigger than my biggest middle finger, and I didn't want those in my stomach! I made a decision right there to stop. Then and only then did the tank turret bang open. Out climbed a big man in a greasy overall uniform. This first fellow was probably the tallest Russian I would see all the way to Odessa.

We looked at each other for a moment and I stated my case. "*Ya yestem Amerikanski Mayor Sage. . . .*" The big tanker poked a finger at my left upper arm, where I had sewn the little two- by four-inch silk Stars and Stripes the OSS had given me so long ago—the identifying insignia I had kept in the lining of my clothes no matter where I went.

He asked, *"Shto etto?"* which I figured meant "What's that?" It made me a little hot under the collar.

I said, "That's the American flag—flag, Amerikanski." Finally the light dawned and he said, waving his big hand, "Ah, *flahk*!"

I said, "Da, da."

I told him there were several of us who had escaped. I had learned the word in Polish that sounded like *"uchekli"*—that meant escape in Polish—and the *"Niemetski"* for German. So I was able to get across to him that we were escaped American POWs. Then I asked him again, *"Gdjeh Marshalli Zhukov?"* He just waved way back to the east, where he'd come from.

By this time a passing Pole had joined me to help interpret and the tanker said there'd be an officer along soon to ask about these higher headquarters matters. He said he had to get going *"Do Berlina!"* (To Berlin!) Giving me the first grin (and a broad one) I had seen since I met him, he got into his tank and roared off.

More tanks came by, and soon a Russian lieutenant in a jeep stopped to talk to me. I asked him if he could help us get some transportation. We wanted to get to a higher headquarters and on to Moscow to get back home. He said he'd see and turned around and drove back toward Exin. We waited the rest of the day and saw unbelievable numbers of refugees struggling along the icy road or in the crusted snow of the barren fields whenever the Russian units pushed by. People were moving in both directions—most, I believe, toward the west.

Certainly any Germans who had moved in to occupy Poland were trying to get away from the Russians and perhaps from the Poles; and some Poles too were heading west, while others were working their way east, trying to return home from Germany to find their families and friends.

These initial sights—of people bent under heavy packs with haggard, drawn faces or with all the clothes they owned on their bodies or with goods heaped high on any kind of car, truck or animal-drawn vehicles—were repeated day after day all the way across Poland. Some of the vehicles were recognizable as handcarts, sledges or sleighs, but anything that would move seemed to be going in either direction on all the roads in Poland.

Back at the farmhouse I teamed up with Lieutenant Colonel Charles Kouns of Ardsley-on-Hudson, New York. He was a paratroop officer, the commander of the Third Battalion of the 504th Parachute Infantry Regiment, who had been captured in Sicily in 1943. As no word had come from the Russian officer all that day and no Russian transportation had showed up for us, Charlie and I started walking toward Kcynia (Exin) the following morning, joining the two-way traffic of refugees that had evidently kept moving all night. Abandoned vehicles were scattered between the Siernicki farmhouse and Kcynia.

One sight in particular seemed to summarize all the unholy ravages of war. We walked around a bend in the road—and there was an ancient hearse half covered with snow beside the road. Its motor was evidently long gone, but refugees were riding in anything on wheels; two horses had been hitched to the hearse and had been pulling it along the frigid road. This horse power had apparently just worn out, and the horses were lying as they had fallen, in the traces with bloated bellies and legs jutting out stiffly toward the horizon. The riders were also frozen. Looters had pillaged their belongings, even stealing the shoes and socks off every person. I told Charlie it reminded me of Tolstoy's gruesome description of Napoleon's winter retreat from Moscow in *War and Peace*.

In Exin/Kcynia we met a Russian lieutenant who spoke some English. He said there might be transport back at Schubin and took us to the old camp in his three-quarter-ton truck. As yet we had no word about transportation to Moscow. We picked up a Red Cross parcel from our old stores in Schubin, divided the parcel between us, and decided to try to hitchhike to Moscow, over a thousand miles to the northeast. Our first objective was Warsaw.

Looking at a map now, I see that a straight line from Schubin to Warsaw would be under one hundred fifty miles by air and not much over two hundred miles by country road. But the way we traveled it took us two weeks to reach Poland's famous capital.

I don't claim to have a clear memory of just where we went and when, but fortunately I had with me my little 1944 YMCA appointment calendar. I had not used the calendar for the early months of that year, but I started using it for 1945 when we were alerted for the move on January twentieth. My notes are brief, in tiny writing or in a print sometimes too cryptic to reconstruct. Entries are missing for many days, but some entries can still be deciphered. On Thursday, January 25, we "Walked to Exin, then were taken to Schubin by a Russki Lt. Caught truck to Mogilno."

We were left off in the town square in the small village of Mogilno and soon were surounded by curious townspeople. When they learned we were American officers, they practically jumped for joy—but by doing so made us feel mighty humble and impotent. To them

Americans were far different from the hated Germans and Russians who had ravaged their country; they welcomed us as heroes. Some had relatives in the States. All believed our country would insist on a free Poland. They asked where our troops were, hoping that we would turn out to be part of a force that would ensure a truly free Poland after the war.

When they learned that we were just escaped POWs or "displaced persons" with no official powers, they were disappointed at first but quickly recovered and displayed the gracious hospitality all Poles showed to us in those tough times. They took us to a small hotel on the village square that had been turned over to the Polish Red Cross.

A lady named Maria took us under her wing and showed us to a neat room on the second floor. There we had two single beds with spotless sheets, pillow cases and plenty of blankets. Wonder of wonders, there was an adjoining bathroom with good plumbing, a shower over the bathtub, plenty of hot water, and a small bar of good soap. We took turns bathing and washing our clothes. What a treat!

Then Maria knocked on the door and took Charlie Kouns and me down to a small dining room off the kitchen. There we were served delicious soup and good Polish bread and sausage. We then gave everybody the Nescafé and chocolate we had brought from the Red Cross box and divided before we left Schubin.

The next day, Friday, we talked with many of Mogilno's townspeople. Some told us they had relatives in the United States. A Mr. Jacob Kraut of both German and Polish descent said he had become a naturalized citizen of the United States in Milwaukee in 1913. Mrs. Edward Przymusinski said she had a son in Buffalo, New York.

Another lady, an elderly one, who lived in the same apartment as Mrs. Przymusinski, warmly insisted that we have a cup of tea with her. She brought out her best china and poured us each a cup. She had a hide-a-bed in her one-room apartment; she pulled back the mattress and under it was a little flask of brandy. She insisted on pouring a little of her brandy, perhaps the last she had, into the tea for us. Then she said a prayer for our safe journey home, leaving us with a most touching memory.

While Charlie conversed more with the English speakers, I used with the others a combination of German and the new Polish words I was learning as rapidly as possible. All were glad that the Germans were gone, but they were also most apprehensive about what would happen under the Russians. Mogilno was a small town off the main axis of the Soviet thrust across Poland, so no Russian troops had yet appeared in the town. By evening, however, we learned what the first Russian troops' treatment of Mogilno would be.

We learned much in Mogilno from all our conversations that day. First we heard about the Russian betrayal of the Poles at Warsaw in the fall of 1944. We didn't learn all the details on that day; as we marched east we learned more and more of what happened in the summer and fall of that year.

During five years of subjugation under the Germans, the Polish underground resistance had lost many good men and women, but it had never been completely destroyed by the invaders. The underground's strength grew as the Germans suffered defeats after Stalingrad, and by July 1944 two hundred thousand men and women were secretly organized into the National Home Army under the command of General Bor, sometimes called

Bor-Komorowski. (His real name was Komorowski: His cover name in the underground was Bor.)

Of this two hundred thousand total about one fifth were armed and ready to fight the Germans in Warsaw itself, which had a population of well over a million before the war. By mid-July the Russians had taken the old Polish city of Lublin, a little over a hundred miles southeast of Warsaw. There they promptly set up the Committee of National Liberation. This committee comprised Polish communists, brought to Russia years before and given complete indoctrination and training for the governing of Poland. Operating under Moscow and backed by the huge Red Army, the committee was nothing more than a puppet government backed by the Russians.

Within a week the Russians were within ten miles of Warsaw. The Poles could hear their artillery and see Russian planes flying overhead from nearby advance bases. General Bor expected the Russians to attack the German-held city at any moment. He tried to coordinate efforts with Marshal Rokossovski by radio, but he received no reply.

Then in late July, Bor picked up a Polish-language broadcast direct from Moscow, authenticated by Molotov, the Soviet foreign minister, plus a Polish member of the Lublin Committee. It announced that the time for liberation had arrived and called all Poles to arms. The next day London monitored another broadcast in Polish from Moscow urging the people of Warsaw to rise up and help the Red Army cross the Vistula River and take Warsaw from the Germans.

London also radioed Bor that Polish Premier Mikolajczyk, head of the Peasant party and three fourths of the Polish electorate, had gone from London to Moscow to confer with Stalin at this same time, the end of

July. Stalin told Mikolajczyk outright that the Russian troops would enter Warsaw within the first week of August.

During the day of the planned assault, small groups of Polish people entered every building with windows commanding street junctions or facing German barracks, offices, and supply or transportation points. The Germans had a strong mechanized garrison in Warsaw, including tanks and artillery. The Poles had no heavy arms, only Sten guns, rifles, grenades and explosive charges for blowing up buildings—and bottles of oil and gasoline for fighting tanks. Only a few could be armed, but all pitched in and helped.

Precisely at five o'clock windows and doors all over town flew open and Germans were mowed down. Unarmed Poles brought their furniture to build barricades. Polish women became couriers, passing messages between fighting units in different sectors of the city. When the streets became impassable, these gallant messengers went underground, crawling through the filthy water, stench and slime of the sewers. Small boys darted through the streets putting up Polish flags. Boy Scouts delivered *Free Warsaw*, the newspaper that hit the streets the first day and kept going to press until the whole thing was over.

Teenagers became adept at destroying tanks with bottles of gasoline. Each group suffered many casualties, but never quit. The Germans lost so many tanks in the early days, about fifty or so, that they soon began using Polish hostages for protection. Dragging men, women and children from buildings, the Germans herded them along in front of their tanks so the resistance fighters would hold their fire.

Within two days General Bor's heroic forces held

two thirds of Warsaw, all without one word from the Red Army or from Moscow about the uprising.

The Russian planes, which had been bombing German positions nearly every night, suddenly stopped flying, and the Luftwaffe attacked General Bor's forces in Warsaw with no Allied air opposition. The Russians also stopped firing their *Katusha* rocket batteries and all the heavy artillery barrages they had been showering on the German garrison.

Though the Polish premier and Allied ambassadors in London appealed to the Soviets to move into Warsaw, the Soviets double-talked and stalled until the mechanized might of the Germans prevailed.

The Russians were repeatedly urged to attack the Germans, as they had promised they would do if the Polish Home Army would arise. But when the time came for action, the Russians either didn't reply at all or washed their hands of the matter, saying the insurrection was premature. Their earlier calls for the uprising were "forgotten" or denied.

British and American planes could not drop arms, ammunition or supplies to General Bor, as the distance was too great for nonstop round-trip flights. The Soviets refused permission for aircraft dropping arms in Warsaw to land in Russian territory.

The Poles fought on much longer than anyone expected. They had to start making their own weapons and ammunition. Ordinary garden hoses and fire hoses were converted into flame throwers. Tin cans were turned into grenades and unexploded German bombs became a source of explosives. The Poles were able to get five hundred to six hundred pounds of explosives out of each one of these bombs; there was quite a risk in making them, but every hour was itself a risk at that time.

Bor's forces fought on until a desperate lack of ammunition and food ended the resistance in early October. Still the Russians did not enter Warsaw. The German commander announced to the whole world that in reprisal for the uprising of the Poles the Germans wouldn't leave a single stone standing in Warsaw. He ordered every building not occupied by Germans to be blown up or burned. Meanwhile, the Russians across the river waited until the Germans had destroyed the city completely.

The Russians had achieved their purpose: to discredit Mikolajczyk and the Polish government in exile in London by blaming them for a "premature uprising" that the Russians themselves had started. But even more important, they were able to achieve destruction of the Polish Home Army so that it could not hope to provide leadership to challenge the authority of the Lublin communists and resist the ultimate control of Poland by the Soviet Union.

Later that Friday, back in our room, Charlie Kouns and I reviewed the story that we had gathered about Russian activities in Poland over the past few months, pieced together from conversations in the square, in the streets of Mogilno, and in the small lobby of the Red Cross hotel. In addition to the betrayal of Warsaw and all Poland by our ally Russia, there were many stories of raping and looting by Red Army troops as they moved east across Poland.

Late in the afternoon a boy dashed into the hotel and shouted in Polish, "The Russkis are coming!" We looked out the window and all the Polish people seemed to have evaporated from the streets except for two individuals—the young lad on our side of the street and another across the way—each shouting into a door or window of the houses as they ran along. Soon we heard troops coming down the street from the east.

These were not armored columns but foot soldiers unlike any I had ever seen before except in the movie *Genghis Khan*. They were dressed in thick quilted pants, wearing coats and round fur caps with ear flaps and a red star or hammer and sickle on the front of each cap. Their high boots appeared to be made of some rich material that I later learned was felt. They all were armed with rifles or automatic submachine guns.

Several had draped down puffs around their shoulders—at least that was what we called such feather-stuffed quilts back in the state of Washington. The down puffs are quilted and embroidered bedcovers stuffed with goose or duck feathers. They had obviously been taken from Polish homes along the way and probably were treasured keepsakes of the family because each was handmade, a labor of love. (Many of them are made for the bride's hope chest.) One puff slid off a soldier's shoulders and fell off into the street. Those behind walked right over it, leaving it in a muddy tangle in the road. A sad ending for this local treasure created over a period of many months or years by some young Polish lady, possibly for her trousseau.

The Russians carried other "souvenirs" of their travels. One fellow with dark skin and eyes like a Mongol was wearing a toilet seat draped around his neck. He seemed to be enjoying the new toy.

The majority of the column plodded on through town, but some must have been quartered nearby. As night fell, we heard shouts and shots; the ladies who operated the Red Cross hotel became increasingly uneasy. They hurriedly served soup, bread, and sausage and started closing up for the night.

The noise and unrest seemed to grow like a living

thing, sending waves into the town and its hotel. Even levelheaded Maria was panicky. So I suggested she bring the hotel staff along with a deck of cards and come into the room with Charlie and me. Four other ladies came in. One dived under the bed, two went into the bathroom and one sat down at the table. Having put four chairs around the table in the center of the room, we had Maria and another lady sit across from each other while I sat nearest the door with Charlie facing me.

I asked Maria and the others how to say a couple more sentences in Polish or as close to Russian as they could come. If they knew any Russian words, I asked for them, so I would be ready to use them when the time came.

Sharp barks of weapons, yells, and screams seemed to punctuate the low noise of town more often and more closely than before. We heard banging downstairs; then suddenly our door burst open. A young lady who worked in the kitchen dashed in. Without stopping she ran to the large wardrobe in the room—a separate piece of furniture like a closet with a rack for hanging clothes—and squeezed herself in.

A beautiful woman about eight months pregnant, she had long blonde hair, huge blue eyes now glazed with fright, and pale translucent skin like Dresden china. I was afraid she'd hurt the baby, so I pleaded with her to come out. She was hysterically begging me to shut the door, so I did. Maria told her through the door to keep quiet.

Then Maria and the other lady made a valiant effort to teach Charlie and me a Polish card game. Intermittently the women were praying in Polish. I think Charlie was praying and I know I was, fervently. "Lord, please help us to avert whatever bad things might happen here. Just keep everyone safe."

We heard banging doors downstairs, then closer up

on the second floor. I kept rehearsing my phrases in a mixture of Russian and Polish; Charlie maintained a grim glare. When our door burst open, I was ready. I turned to the door, pointed my finger between the eyes of the Russian soldier standing there, glared at him, and barked my memorized Slavic phrase, "Get out, these are ours!"

The leading Russian stood there a moment, swaying a bit in his shabby quilted uniform and felt boots, uncertainly fingering his automatic rifle with a puzzled and truculent expression on his face. Again I ordered him out, loudly and clearly, as I swept my pointing hand toward the hall and put my other protectively on the shoulder of the nearest lady. The soldier paused another moment, shrugged, mumbled something I didn't understand, and lurched on down the hall, pulling his companion along with him.

Quietly I said, "Thank you, Lord!"

Charlie added, "Amen!" and the women bobbed their heads, crossed themselves, and gave thanks in Polish, quietly and reverently.

We had no more intruders that night, but the ladies were still afraid to leave. All six of them stayed, taking turns napping on the beds. Charlie and I stretched out on the floor in front of the door. Everyone had a little rest by the time morning dawned quietly over the village.

The next morning the grateful Red Cross ladies gave us a special breakfast of bacon, eggs and fresh bread. Afterward we went out, picked up a Pole who could speak some Russian and searched out a Russian officer. We met a friendly first lieutenant, a *starsha leytenant*, Constantine Nazarkin. I must have been impressed with his friendliness because I found his full name jotted down in my little YMCA notebook for Saturday, January 27. We told him of the roaming troops and all the disturbances the night before and the reported incidents of rape and pillage.

He apologized, saying that some troops had celebrated with too much vodka and whatever else they could find, but that they had been rounded up during the night and moved out of town. We told him we were trying to get to a higher headquarters and on east to Warsaw and Moscow. Lieutenant Nazarkin arranged for a Russian truck to give us a ride in the early afternoon. We thanked all the Red Cross people, re-rolled the horseshoe packs with our few belongings, boarded the truck and headed east that afternoon.

Dry snow was swirling again and it was quite cold, but at least we were on the move. In less than an hour the truck sputtered a few times and stopped dead, out of gas. The driver waved down a few other trucks on the road, but none could or would give us any gas. It was getting colder, so we decided to take any transportation available in any direction.

The next vehicle to come by was a two-horse sleigh (in Polish, *dva koyni shlanki*), heading back the way we had come. The driver, a Pole, offered us a ride to Mogilno. We looked at the large fur lap robe and hopped aboard. Warm under the robe, listening to the muffled clop-clop of the horses' hoofs, the jingling bells on the collars and the swish of the sleigh runners, I found myself humming ''Jingle Bells'' and recalling happy boyhood sleigh rides in the winters of Spokane.

The helpful Pole pulled up his sleigh at the Red Cross hotel in Mogilno and we went in to have another delicious bowl of soup made by the pregnant Dresden china blonde who had hidden herself in the wardrobe the night before. We were glad to learn that the ladies there had not been bothered again.

After a good night's sleep the man who had been

naturalized in Milwaukee in 1913, Jacob Kraut, came by the hotel to ask if we could come and have a drink and a bite with him. We went with him to his home, where in the front parlor his wife fed us *canapskas* (very close to canapes) and a Polish sausage thin-sliced on brown bread, washed down with a small glass of a mild orange-flavored Polish vodka. Kraut was very rusty in English and I knew very little Polish, so we talked mainly in German.

Suddenly the front door burst open and a Russian soldier bounded in, leveling his rifle at us and shouting, ''*Niemetski!*'' (Germans!) Jacob Kraut quickly started explaining in Polish and I yelled ''Amerikanski,'' fixing him again with my eyeball as fiercely as I could and pointing to the flag on my arm as I drew myself up to my full six feet two. He didn't shoot, but he seemed itching to—until a Russian lieutenant came in, listened to our explanation, and ushered the soldier out.

Chapter 29

My visit to Jacob Kraut was representative of most of our travels in Poland. The Poles, who had very little for themselves, were consistently kind, helpful and generous to us. The Russians varied tremendously, perhaps just as much as human nature in general. On several occasions the Russians almost shot us. They were very trigger-happy. At other times they were quite helpful. And there were some occasions when they were not hostile, but not helpful either.

That afternoon Charlie Kouns and I met two of the friendlier Russians, a major and a captain. They invited us to a Polish home where they seemed to be quartered. We had a congenial polyglot conversation about how bad the Germans were, discussing their faults as we ate Polish doughnuts and offered vodka toasts to Stalin, Roosevelt, and Churchill.

There were a couple of discordant notes that jarred me amid the prevailing rough camaraderie. After several toasts the major said in Russian, "To Soviet victory in Berlin next week, in the world next year."

That has an ominous cast to it, but that's what he said—he was loaded enough that it came out spontaneously. When this was translated for us I wondered how many other Russians were feeling so imperialistic. I certainly had the impression that at the top level the feeling was operating full tilt.

Still later the Russian captain looked up at the picture of Christ on the cross over the door, as displayed in most Polish homes. He waved his hand at it contemptuously and said, *"To yest nyeh Bogu!"* (There is no God!)

When this was translated for me, I felt much as I had when the Afrika Korps Nazi threw the Senegalese prisoner's cross into the dust. Again my thought was, "These godless so-and-sos *can't* win!" The Polish family members turned pale, looked at one another and seemed to draw closer together in spirit, maintaining a stubborn silence that affirmed their faith.

When we parted that night, the Russian major said he had two trucks going to his artillery headquarters the next morning; they would stop and pick us up at the hotel. The next morning, after again saying our thanks and good-byes to the Polish Red Cross people, we waited several hours for those trucks. Since the Russians didn't show up, we finally took a ride in another two-horse sleigh with two Polish men from another town that had been under Russian control for several days.

One of the men was in the Home Army there. He told us that some colleagues of his in the underground who had come into town to visit family and friends and celebrate the "liberation" had been rounded up by Polish communists with the help of local Red Army units and were hauled away to the east. He said bitterly, "Freedom fighters are not wanted in Poland by the new communist masters."

The Poles dropped us off outside the gate of a Russian artillery headquarters at Parlin, then whipped up their horses and moved off even as we were shouting our thanks to them. After we got something to eat, we went to sleep at the artillery headquarters. In the morning we asked for transportation to Warsaw. An artillery officer told us he had heard that transportation for ex-POWs was being arranged back at Schubin.

The first ride out was again via sleigh. The Polish driver took us to the town of Znin, where he was stopped by some Russian trucks. A Red Army major seemed in charge, so with assistance in interpreting from the Polish sleigh driver we asked him for a lift. The major had a small old American Willys with a driver. When he told us he could drop us at Schubin, we crammed ourselves into the back seat and the Willys took off.

Back at Oflag 64 we learned that a number of American kriegies who were left behind in the hospital under Colonel Drury on January 21 had been moved out by Russian truck a week later. The destination was given as Rembertow, a Russian refugee processing center east of Warsaw. Colonel Millet took charge of the camp, a tough job, since by now the camp held a wide variety of nationalities and the refugees showed little discipline. Throughout the camp there was poor sanitation, many cases of disease, and the same perpetual hunger.

Millet told us he had asked for more transportation and not to go off on our own. He said that two senior Russian sergeants, the Russian liaison in the camp, were billeted in the White House at the old camp administrative headquarters. We went over to meet them.

Sergeant Kutsi was a strong, tough man from Byelorussia (White Russia), nearly six feet tall with a quiet, reserved demeanor, steady brown eyes, and dark hair. He was the leader on split decisions; his comrade was more of a communicator.

Sergeant Kachenko was a Ukrainian, almost as tall

as Kutsi but more slender, and had wavy blond hair, blue eyes, and an engaging grin that sometimes made him look as crafty as a con man. We used a mixture of Polish and German, adding sign language or charades, and a few words of Russian, English, and Ukrainian to spice up the stew.

The Russians had two extra bunks in their good-sized room in the old administration building and they invited us to bunk in the two empty cots. The room was clean, and as Charlie and I figured we'd learn more by staying there, we gladly accepted the invitation.

Kachenko and I passed on the gist of our exchanges to Charlie and Kutsi, who talked less. Kutsi and Kachenko were not communists; maybe that's why we liked them. They seemed to be good country lads doing their job the best they could and getting along with others while doing it.

The next morning, January 31, Colonel Millet appointed me mess officer for the camp. The store of Red Cross parcels left behind at evacuation was dwindling rapidly and we needed to add fresh meat and vegetables to feed all the Allies who had wandered into the camp. A Polish man from Schubin had volunteered to assist Colonel Millet as interpreter. Through him I was able to learn of nearby farms evacuated by Germans as the Red Army came through. For a foraging party I recruited some farm boys—a pair each of Serbs, French, British, Czechs, and Americans, plus one Russian, our volunteer Sergeant Kachenko.

We rounded up some carts that were drawn by anything that could pull: a horse, an ox, a donkey, even a goat, plus us. I wouldn't let anyone touch Polish property because the Poles had already been hurt enough—first by the Germans and then by the Russians—and they didn't have much. We made our way to the former German farms and took everything edible we could find, filling the carts with potatoes, rutabagas, kohlrabies, cabbages, sugar beets, turnips, even some frozen carrots. We also rounded up thirteen head of cattle and herded them with us back to camp. Most of the animals were thin and one was a tough old ox.

We set up a corner of the camp as a butcher shop. One big Serbian ex-prisoner stood on a chopping block and clobbered a couple of the animals in the head with a huge sledgehammer. A Frenchman slit their throats and cleaned them. The Serb promptly grabbed the liver of the first beef killed and passed around slices, raw and still warm, to his colleagues. It didn't taste bad at all!

We doled out the meat and vegetables as fairly as we could to the groups in the camp. Even the menu of our Russian roommates was brightened. They had quite a bit of their Red Army issue of canned goods, some of which was lend-lease from the United States: dried sausages and kasha—ground barley—and other grains that they ate boiled, as we would cereal at home. They enjoyed the switch to fresh meat and vegetables.

After dinner Kachenko taught me another Red Army song. I think it was either "Meadowland" or "Katusha." We asked if they had heard anything more about transport to the east, to Warsaw or perhaps even to Moscow. They said no; what they wanted to do was to get their orders out of this administrative job and on to Berlin. Kachenko said with a twinkle in his eye, "For raping and looting!" I had a hunch he was only half joking; the Ukraine suffered terrible treatment by the Germans and many Russians were vengeful.

Then we went back to talking about vehicles. They both were familiar with what they called "Shtootebekker," "Dotzsh," "Fourt," and "Gay-Em-Tsay," his way of naming the new American trucks. Then Kachenko told me that when they were first issued these new trucks, Red Army recruits asked where they came from. On instruction from the communist commissar always placed in each unit to make sure communist views were followed, the officers said they were from a "*Bolshoy Fabrica z Uralli*" (great factory in the Urals). When the recruits pointed to the three letters painted on the truck they were told that spelled the name of the factory in the Urals, "Oosa" (USA). Kachenko laughed uproariously at the punch line; even Kutsi grinned.

Kachenko said some Russians were aware of the great quantity of goods coming from the United States. He put his finger alongside his nose and said with a wink in Russian, "I wasn't behind the barn door when the brains were passed out!" He added that the government took credit for all the material received and the Russian people took credit for most of the suffering of the war and nearly all the fighting. I still think Kutsi and Kachenko were the two most honest Soviet citizens I've met.

The next day I was grateful for their comradeship. A young American officer came running to get me, saying that the Russians were taking our Red Cross parcels. I loped over to the storeroom, and sure enough, three or four soldiers were loading Red Cross parcels onto a cart under the direction of a Russian officer. I roared at them a word I'd learned the hard way from them, "*Stoy!*" (Stop!) (You learn it the minute someone pulls a tommy gun off his shoulder, pulls back the slide, points it at your stomach, and yells, "*Stoy.*") When I informed the officer in charge that these were American parcels from the Red Cross, he evidently told the others to continue their loading. I again roared "Stop!" moving in among them. Again the Russian soldiers halted. The officer glared at me, shouted in

Russian, picked up a parcel, and started to hand it to a soldier.

I knocked the parcel out of his hands; it dropped, hitting his feet. He hissed in rage and reached for his pistol, which was nearly out of the holster when I broke his jaw. I ordered the soldiers, who were fortunately unarmed, to dump the parcels off the cart and then dump their own officer onto it. He looked as though he'd have a long sleep as they trundled him out the gate.

I then went straight to my room and told the tale to Charlie, Kutsi, and Kachenko, who were all there. I was still angry—and, to top things off, the cock-eyed Russian had left part of a tooth sticking into a knuckle of my right hand.

As I cooled down, I said, "I don't want to cause any more trouble, so maybe I better be on my way out of camp."

Charlie, of course, said he'd go with me—but Kutsi told me, "Stay." He spoke rapidly to Kachenko and then hurried out.

Kachenko said Kutsi had gone to see his big boss. When Kutsi returned, Kachenko related the story.

There had recently been an order against looting in Poland, and Kutsi learned that the looting party I'd broken up was from a transient outfit in Schubin. He convinced his colonel that the officer had refused to stop taking parcels from the refugee camp and had suffered a broken jaw in the confrontation. The colonel advised that I lie low in camp awhile; he'd take care of the matter. So I rested in my room for a day or so, soaking my hand, which had become infected from that lousy Russian tooth, in hot saltwater. When Kutsi learned from friends that the transient outfit—broken jaw and all—had left town, he was inspired to arrange a celebration for us all.

That night Kutsi came riding up to the White House in a three-wheeled gig or light phaeton drawn by one of the biggest horses we had seen in a long time. Kachenko and several other Russians, some of them Cossacks, were mounted on horses from a Cossack cavalry outfit. Kutsi beckoned Charlie and me aboard his rig. He cracked his whip and the rig lurched forward. Shouting like wild Indians in Russian, the riders booted their horses down the road, then took off across country. Kutsi grinned like a happy gorilla, yelled something like "Hold on!" and made the phaeton fairly fly. It pitched, rolled, and yawed, but we managed to hang on to draw up with a flourish and a cloud of dust at a large farmhouse about five kilometers from Schubin.

The Cossacks had evidently brought plenty of food and vodka there earlier in the day, as the Polish people didn't seem to resent this intrusion. We guessed they had been invited because they genuinely seemed to enjoy themselves. It was a spirited evening. Here were just plain Russians—no war, no politics. They were just being themselves, having a party. They drank the vodka and afterward we toasted all kinds of things, some of which we understood and some we didn't.

I noticed that they would dip one hand into a platter on the table, and as I looked closer I saw that this was just a big platter of lard. They dipped their hands into the lard and slapped that into their mouths. It seemed to help them drink more. We had some sausages and rolls, and all that eating was mixed with singing and dancing.

When the Russians started singing their songs, they reminded me a lot of the Irish, who either sing great wild songs like "Have You Ever Been into an Irishman's Shanty" or very sad ones like "Kathleen Mavourneen" and "Danny Boy." The Russians also switch from sad to happy songs and back again. And could they sing! We felt like amateurs among them. One of the Russians had a high tenor voice and the others all listened while he sang "Meadowland," a bittersweet, mournful plaint. Then they all went wild singing "Tachanka," about the four-wheeled machine-gun cart. I joined in on this one.

Soon the Russians started dancing a wild Cossack dance. They would lower their tails almost to the floor and then their feet would go shooting out in front of them. Well, I could do that too. I'd learned that from Serge Obolensky, but I didn't tell them my teacher was a prince chased out of Russia by their Bolshevik fathers. I could keep up with them fine in the dancing, but wasn't up to their singing; they were very good.

They took turns jumping up on the table, singing a song, then dancing; they urged me to jump up too. So I danced an Irish jig for them up there on the table and sang some Irish songs. For lively numbers the best I could do was "The Rambling Wreck from Georgia Tech" and my old football song, "Fight, Fight, Fight for Washington State." The only thing I could get Charlie to join me in was "I've Been Working on the Railroad." We got them all shouting "Dinah, von't you blow!"— Russians, Poles, and all. We really had a lively evening, but I still don't know why we weren't killed as Kutsi drove us back to Schubin in the three-wheeled gig with that huge horse charging down the road and across the fields at full tilt.

As we were getting ready to retire for the night, Kachenko evidently had some happy thought. He broke into an elfish grin and said something like, "Wait. I have a surprise for you," and careened out the door. Shortly he returned holding the hand of a Russian woman soldier, almost as tall as Kachenko, but much rounder.

He brought her over to me and said, "For you, Tovarich major" (Comrade major) and gestured to my cot.

I said, "Thanks a lot, but no thanks," and then added, "I'm too big for my cot as it is," to soften the turndown.

Kachenko then turned to Charlie, "Tovarich pulkovnic (Comrade colonel), for you?" Charlie also demurred with polite thanks. Kachenko was only slightly crestfallen. He thought a moment, shrugged, grinned, and then said, "*Doshtvedanya*, for tonight," and left with the woman himself.

The next day was Sunday, February 4, and I went to church in downtown Schubin. It was a moving experience to watch the joy of families openly worshipping together for the first time in five long years. Under the Germans the Poles had been forbidden to assemble for church. Schools had likewise been curtailed and monitored. Then, even after "liberation" by the Russians, freedom seemed to last only a couple of weeks.

Under both Nazis and communists, the Poles were forbidden to listen to British or American radio broadcasts. Two or three weeks after "liberation," people could legally listen only to the amplified loudspeakers in the town squares of the villages and these gave only the news acceptable to the Lublin provisional government and the Red Army—most of it, of course, from Moscow.

When I wanted to beam out to my old OSS outfit a message that I was on my way out, I had to go to a radio kept well hidden by the Polish underground beneath a trap door under a big desk in an office building. I did not trust the Russians to forward my message. I sent out the following message via the Polish underground: "Jerry the Dagger is on the loose and coming home." After I finally came out, I learned that my words were picked up by OSS monitors in at least Italy, England, and Egypt.

On January 5 we learned that Colonel Millet, who had forbidden us to leave camp, had himself gone, leaving us feeling free to move on as well. Again we got a ride in a Polish sleigh, this time heading northeast to the old Polish town with the tongue-twisting name of Bydgoszcz, which the Germans had changed to Bromberg during the war.

It was snowing again; on the way we saw a Russian soldier trying to hitch a ride. The Polish driver asked if he should stop. We said sure, and the youngster said, *"Spasibo"* (thank you) and stood with both feet on the sleigh runner and one hand each on the front seat and the rear, for balance.

Over one shoulder of the hitchhiker's quilted coat was a rifle with a sniperscope on it. I asked the soldier about it and the grinning response was "Da, da, over thirty Germans dead." I gathered this from a show of fingers, with help from the Polish driver. When I said that was admirable shooting, the soldier proudly opened his coat to show us his decoration, the Red Star of Stalingrad.

To our surprise there was ample evidence from the well-rounded and well-filled blouse that our soldier was a woman, not a man. She laughed at our surprise, pulled off her fur chapka cap, and shook loose long blonde hair. She looked a little like Sonja Henie, the figure skater and movie star, but she described lining up her German victims like a professional assassin. When we neared her unit, she told the driver to slow down a bit; waving a cheery good-bye to us, she hopped off and trudged away.

Our driver left us off at another Polish Red Cross station in Bydgoszcz. There we met a Pole who took us home for the night. We had a bit of supper and some good conversation about affairs in Poland, expressing ourselves again in a mixture of sign language, Polish, English, German, and some French, of which the Polish couple spoke a little. Charlie was able to join in with some learned at West Point.

The highlight of the evening was saying good night to their beautiful one-year-old baby. It was a homey touch that Charlie and I both enjoyed.

The next day we did almost as much hiking as hitching, getting short rides with both Russians and Poles through the city of Thorun and on southeast to Brzesc Kujawski, in the heart of Poland's sugar-beet country, where a Polish driver let us off at the town hall. On learning we were Americans, a tall man, neat but threadbare, very courteously asked us if we would spend the night at his house. Several others also made the same invitation, including a big man who seemed to be the town's mayor and who said he had a house with plenty of room for us. But the first man seemed so afraid we'd go elsewhere that we decided to accept his offer.

We stayed on long enough to talk with all the others. With obvious pride they reported that Brzesc Kujawski had been the place where the Poles rallied and stopped the invading Swedish army under Gustavus Adolfus in the seventeenth century. This time, as the Germans retreated, they tried to get the Poles to sabotage the sugar-beet factory in their own town; the Poles refused. Gravely they added, "And we will outlast the Russians, too."

We accompanied the tall man to his home, a very modest one, and met his shy wife and three small children. As neighbors kept dropping in bringing sausages, bread, pastries, and other morsels, we didn't feel so bad about eating with those folks, who we knew had so little. One man brought some maps to show us the way he thought best to go to Warsaw. The neighbors told us that Warsaw was destroyed, that their real government was still in London, and that the new provisional government was farther east and south in Lublin. When the last visitors finally left, we stretched out on the floor by the small stove and slept.

We were not asleep very long when we were awakened by the sound of small-arms fire. The man of the house also awoke, telling us this was probably the local home guard shooting at looters violating the curfew. The home guard took turns serving as curfew keepers, protecting the village at night from stragglers and looters. Our host kept a watch out the window and soon beckoned us to come look at the guardsmen returning to their homes. They were in ordinary farmer clothes topped by distinctive armbands. We had seen them in other small towns without knowing just what the armband signified. As we moved east we saw several more.

Somewhere in our trek, neither Charlie nor I remember just where, we came across a scene that we both recall all too vividly. We were passing a swampy area in a truck when we saw a big tank foundering in the morass with some burned-out overturned vehicles, one or two still exuding wisps of smoke. There was a Polish truck parked off the road, evidently commandeered by a Red Army unit; Russian soldiers were picking up corpses and stacking them onto the truck like cordwood. Our driver stopped his truck—all three of us must have been gaping wide-eyed.

After tossing another corpse onto the gruesome load, one Russian soldier reached into his coat pocket, pulled out what looked like a bottle half full of vodka, and took a long pull. He wiped his mouth on his sleeve and was putting the bottle away when he noticed us. He shouted something with a mean look, shaking the bottle at us. Shouting again, he started for a rifle standing against a tree.

Another Russian in a long wool officer's overcoat started moving toward the soldier. The angry man's weapon was pointed at us, almost ready to fire, before the officer got his attention and stopped him. Our driver was so rattled he couldn't get the truck started, and there we were, sitting ducks for a rifle shot in the crowded cab. I again breathed, "Thank you, Lord." Later I also gave silent thanks to that Russian officer. He made the soldier throw away his vodka and then gave him what looked like a royal chewing-out.

I fast tired of being threatened with extinction so frequently by our Allies. I thought back over the last several days: the security-conscious tankers with their huge gun trained on our Polish farmhouse; the two .50-caliber machine guns aimed right at my belly; the soldier with the tommy gun who broke into the Krauts' Polish home as we were having tea and nearly started firing before we could convince him we were friends; the armed drunks in the Mogilno hotel; the Russian officer trying to shoot me over the Red Cross parcels he was stealing.

Now this soldier was getting ready to shoot us for no good reason. It would have been ironic to be shot by our own Allies after so many months of taking risks in the hands of our common enemy.

Chapter 30

One indicator of the omnipresence of the Red Army was the change in route and city signs. These were originally printed in Polish, then changed to German during the five-year Nazi occupation, and they now read in Russian. We saw a big sign pointing east as we came to a road junction. I read the big letters aloud, "BAPWABA."

The driver laughed and said, "Warszawa," pronounced "Varshava." That's the Polish word for Warsaw in their own alphabet. The Russian sign, printed in their alphabet, is also pronounced "Varshava." Though I can sing and speak a bit in Russian, Warsaw still remains the only word I can print in the Cyrillic alphabet—and it still looks like BAPWABA to me.

Another vivid memory was the last lap of our hitchhike to Warsaw. We were in the back of an open-bed truck and the driver stopped to pick up another hitchhiker wearing an old patched Polish army uniform. He was nearly six feet tall, and thin, as we all were after prison or labor camps, with tired but alert blue eyes and a square face under his old Polish officer's cap. He had been hurt and walked with a slight limp. He was very glad to learn we were Americans—then disappointed, as others were, to find that we had no official basis for helping the Poles against the Russians. But mainly he was excited because we were nearing his home town of Warsaw.

As we entered the city, Charlie Kouns said, "Oh, my God!" We all gasped, then were as still as the city. Rubble was everywhere. It seemed that no brick or stone belonged where it lay. The German commander, in collusion with the Russians, had truly destroyed the city. Farther along we saw men and women clearing the streets. The Polish officer, tears streaming down his face, kept repeating, *"Moja wadna Warszawa!"* (My beautiful Warsaw!) He peered around intently as we went along one street, then gave a start, pointing to a deep pile of rubble. He cried in anguish, "That was my home!" Then he turned to Charlie and me, and from the depths of his pain flung out, "What will you men do about this? What will America do?"

I believe he could feel our deep sympathy for him and for Poland, but only we know how impotent we felt, having no immediate power to change the situation. It was then that I resolved I'd report the whole truth about the USSR's treatment of Warsaw and Poland to Wild Bill Donovan and to anyone else in the American government who would listen.

The Polish officer asked to be let off nearby and we wished him Godspeed in finding his family. Our driver headed east to cross the Vistula River into the eastern section of Warsaw, called Praga, which was less damaged; that was where some of the Red Army waited for the old city of Warsaw to be leveled by the Germans.

When we reached the Vistula, we saw the jagged remnants of an old bridge that had been destroyed, and we directed our driver to detour about a block. There we learned how the Russians had managed to make river crossings when the Germans had air superiority and could bomb any bridge in progress. Posts with bits of cloth attached on top stood up out of the water to show the lanes of a new underwater bridge. Following these subtle but effective signals, our driver drove recklessly right into the river. Water came up to the truck's hubcaps but no farther. The Russians had built a deck bridge completely submerged by eighteen to twenty-four inches of water, probably at night back in the late summer of 1944, ready for use when ordered to enter Warsaw.

I have no notes to help me recall just where we rested that night in Praga, Warsaw, but I believe it was in a building used as a Red Army headquarters. I do have a brief note for the next day, the ninth of February. "A.M. walked Praga—met Russki pilot, a major."

In the morning I asked several Poles in Praga if any Polish government remained in Warsaw. They said that the true Polish government was still in exile in London. The only other men they trusted who might have been in the government were survivors of General Bor's army, but they were still in hiding to avoid being sent to prison or worse by the new regime. The only government tolerated in Poland was the communist provisional government in Lublin, to the southeast.

I was sure that my boss Bill Donovan would want to know all he could about this government, so I decided to slip back into my OSS role, go to Lublin, and learn all I could. I figured it would cost the OSS many thousands of dollars to put an agent into Lublin now. Here I was right on the spot, by the grace of God, with a chance to save Uncle Sam a pot of money.

We met a Russian flying officer who made me believe the Lord was in solid support of my decision. This major had a tiny car he had commandeered from somewhere, as well as a truck loaded with soldiers and supplies. He was taking them to Lublin that afternoon. The Russian major was very curious about American officers, and he was, besides, a generous soul. He took us to a small café and bought us vodka, rolls and some delicious Polish ham.

It was late in the evening by the time we reached Lublin. At my request the friendly major escorted us to the main administration building of the Polish provisional government. There were only a few staffers on duty, but they managed to dig up from someplace a bit of soup and then let us sleep on the big table in a conference room.

I slept like a log until sometime before dawn, when it grew colder and the table seemed to get harder. I remember lying on my back and wondering again about the vagaries of life. Which life is fantasy and which real? Back home? At peace? The OSS job behind the lines? The grayness of prison? Escapes and coolers? Or this cold, exhilarating trek across Poland?

I was better prepared for the bestiality of the Nazis than for the intimate revelations of the ugliness of the communist machine run by our ally the USSR. I chuckled grimly as I thought, "War makes strange bedfellows, but we better not marry them."

I recalled the many contradictions to the hard times—the fun with Kutsi, Kachenko, and the Cossacks. And the vignette about boots.

My Russian sergeant friends thought my old parachute boots were too cold for winter in Poland and Russia; what I needed was a pair of long gray felt valenkas. On ice and dry snow the thick felt was far better insulation than leather. Late one afternoon at Schubin, after I had taken off my jump boots and was warming my feet at the stove, Kutsi and Kachenko had a brief animated conversation, pointing at my big feet with knowing nods and exclamations of "Da! Da!" They gestured they'd be back soon and went out the door.

In less than an hour they were back, laughing and slapping each other on the back, knocking off snowflakes. They proudly dropped a huge pair of valenkas in my lap. Though cool on the outside, the boots were warm as toast on the inside—and an amazingly good fit. When I asked where they got them, they laughed uproariously. I kept querying them and they finally said that a "Bolshoy Russki," a big Russian, had "donated" them. They would say no more but chuckled a lot. Charlie and I figured they had found a Russian about my size, clobbered him, and taken his boots. But we couldn't get Kutsi or Kachenko to admit it.

But with such camaraderie at the soldier-to-soldier level, I also remember two stark realities. First was the terrific uprooting of peoples, the roads packed with refugees going in both directions, dropping their pitiful goods as the loads grew too heavy for underfed animals and malnourished people, and the frozen corpses of these animals and people by the roadside.

Second was the callous denial by the Russian authorities of the rights of Polish people. If a Russian horse fell, a Russian soldier would take from a Pole the first healthy horse he could find. Occasionally he'd say, "We'll trade. You take my dead one." If his horse was lame, it was the same trade. The Russian attitude was clear: The Red Army had all the power and the Soviet Union would brook no governing authority other than communist. Polish patriots who were even a potential threat to the new regime were shipped east to Siberia, imprisoned, or eliminated.

In Lublin I wanted to check on these impressions to learn who were these new communist leaders of the

Russian puppet government for Poland, to get my best feel for what they were doing—and then get on home as fast as possible.

As elsewhere, Poles in Lublin were happy to see Americans and very helpful to us. One Pole who spoke some English took us to Polska Radio, a radio station near the new Polish headquarters. Our interpreter told us that the station was under the communists now, and its main program was to relay items from Moscow in Polish. I asked them to broadcast another message for me—an innocuous one, saying only that Charles Kouns, Jerry Sage, and several other Americans had escaped German custody and were working their way out of Poland.

Then Charlie and I got ourselves billeted with a delightful little old lady on Marie Curie-Skladowska Ulica—the street named after the talented Polish scientist who married Curie of France and did such great pioneering work in radioactivity.

The tiny gray-haired hostess showed me into a neat little room with a single bed. She asked me to try it to see if it was big enough. I took off my boots, stretched out, and said the bed was just fine. Then the little lady spread a down puff comforter over me. I pulled it up to my chin and she giggled, pointing to my feet, which were sticking out at least eighteen inches. She pulled the down puff over my feet; the top then came to the bottom of my chest. We laughed again. Then we slid the puff up and down a couple of more times, both laughing. Finally she put her finger beside her nose, thought a minute, opened a big wardrobe and pulled out another puff, which she laid over me to overlap the first one covering my feet. That night the bed was truly warm and comfortable, particularly compared to the cold hard table in the office building the night before. It was my warmest, deepest sleep in a long time.

After a good night's rest under the combined down puffs and a bit of breakfast, I went out with Charlie Kouns to see what could be learned about the new rulers of Poland, the Lublin provisional government. We picked up an English-speaking Pole at Polska Radio, then walked to the main administration building on the town square. I had asked several people that day and the day before the name of the most influential Pole in the new government; the answer, by consensus, was Jakob Berman.

He was a Polish Jew and communist who had been trained for many years in Moscow and brought in behind the Red Army with the new provisional Polish government. His official title in mid-February 1945 had the tone of minister for foreign affairs.

We waited a couple of hours to see him. When we finally got into his office, Berman greeted us most courteously. He was not a large man, but he had an aura of quiet power. He had alert, deep-set, dark eyes that gave us a thorough once-over as we shook hands. His hair was gray-black, receding sharply from a high forehead.

We asked Berman if he could help us with transportation to Moscow. He replied that he'd look into it, reminding us that the Red Army had priority on all movements east and west. We told him that many Western Allies were in Poland, with quite a number right there in Lublin, and asked if any provisions could be arranged for them. I mentioned all the lend-lease goods from America that we had seen with the Red Army. He agreed that these were under Red Army control.

Two or three times we were interrupted by telephone calls. In each instance Berman answered the phone with "Da! Da!" He evidently was talking to Russians, possibly in Moscow, since the Polish word for "yes" is *"tak."* Other Polish government officials who dropped in seemed to defer to Berman's decisions.

We were convinced that he was a leading member of the new Polish politburo and the prime tie to the Soviet politburo. Charlie even asked Berman if he could advance us some Polish money. Berman seemed sympathetic but told us, "There is no provision for such an action." We left the office convinced that Berman was a real power in the current government, which had only the power that the Kremlin in Moscow authorized and the Red Army enforced.

That night we had dinner with a Polish family. I started to write their family name here, but on further reflection I decided against it. Although it may seem inconceivable to some readers, communist secret police, Soviet and Polish, have long memories, notebooks, and files, and I will not endanger the families of the wonderful Poles who helped us on the way out and who hated the guts of their communist oppressors.

However, I can certainly use the father's first name, since it was a common one—Jan. Charlie and I enjoyed a simple but delicious meal with Jan and his wife and baby. Then, what a treat! Jan took out a well-used violin and played beautiful compositions for us. Some were of course by the great Polish composer Chopin (Szopena in Polish). Some of our friends in Lublin lived on the street named for him, Szopena Ulica.

Jan had been in the underground army and detested both the Nazis and the communists. Some days later, just before leaving Lublin, we learned that Jan was one of the many arrested by the secret police in the middle of the night and thrown into a castle dungeon in Lublin. As freedom fighters, these men were considered very active threats to the new communist regime.

Chapter 31

Much effort in the succeeding few days in Lublin was devoted to trying to get food for the increasing numbers of Allies who turned up in Lublin: escapees, former prison laborers, liberated personnel and a few airmen who had been shot down and had hidden out with the underground. One of the fairly large public buildings on the town square was converted into a makeshift dormitory for some of these ex-prisoners or displaced persons, and we used the lobby of one of these buildings as an informal information center.

That's where we would greet newcomers and where we put up a bulletin board to post news about food as well as progress reports on travel out of Poland. Realizing we would get no help from the Polish provisional government and wanting not to take any more food than necessary from the generous but hungry Poles, I began haunting all the Russian supply points I could find, but with little success.

I finally located the main supply depot and some time later ran down the chief quartermaster officer, a Russian major. He said he was sympathetic but spread his hands, saying he could give me "*nietchievo*" (nothing). He added that he could issue nothing to anyone outside the Red Army. I offered to enlist, but he only laughed and disappeared into his paperwork. I then asked around until I learned the name of the commanding officer of the area. The *kommandant miasta* (city commander) was Soviet General Major (Major General) Senchillo. It didn't take me long to find his headquarters building, near the main square of Lublin. I tried twice to see the general, reporting through their channels as soon as I learned the network. It took me a while even to locate the adjutant of the outfit, but I did. I was told once that the kommandant was too busy to see anyone that day and twice more that he was not in.

The next time I came in I was dragging a somewhat reluctant Polish interpreter with me. I made it clear that I intended to see General Major Senchillo *today*.

"Now, where is his office?" I demanded.

The adjutant blurted, "He's not in." But his eyes shifted momentarily toward the stairs to the second floor.

I said, "*Spasibo,*" led my interpreter rapidly to the stairs, and started climbing two at a time.

I knew I was right when I saw the sentry at the top of the stairs. He stepped forward and started to pull his submachine gun off his shoulder.

I kept coming and yelled at him, "*Do General Senchillo!*" As I reached him I knocked the weapon aside and asked, "*Kokdula? Hurasha? Dobra!*" (How are you? Fine? Good!) I slapped the guard on the back and kept moving, pulling my interpreter along past him.

At a desk in an anteroom sat an officer whom I recognized as another of the adjutant types who had given me the runaround before.

I demanded, "*Gdjeh General Senchillo?*"

He replied, shaking his head, "*Nyeh tuti.*" (Not

here.) But his eyes flickered slightly toward the double doors to the right. Still guiding along the interpreter by the arm, I pushed open the door.

There at a huge table was obviously a staff meeting in progress. At the opposite end of the long table, facing me, was just as obviously the boss. I didn't glance at the others but popped to attention, threw a sweeping salute, and held it tight until the general acknowledged it.

I almost broke out laughing. Running unbidden through my mind were the score and words to Gilbert and Sullivan's "He was the very model of a modern major general/He's everything that's animal and vegetable and mineral."

At the end of the table was a huge man. His unbuttoned tunic was covered with braid and medals, and he was holding the longest cigarette-smoking apparatus I'd ever seen. He was smoking a Russian Popurosa, a cigarette of about three inches of black tobacco rolled in paper and manufactured together with a cardboard holder about four inches long. That total was stuck in an ivory holder another six or seven inches long. He held this exaggerated cigarette tilted upward in the Franklin D. Roosevelt manner.

As soon as the "model of a modern major general" returned my salute with a quizzical look, I started my spiel, looking him straight in the eye. In a mixture of Russian and Polish I told him I was Major Jerry Sage, senior American officer here with many loyal American and British allies, mainly escaped POWs who were going hungry. I said, "Everywhere I look in the great Red Army I see American trucks: Studebaker, Dodge, Ford, GMC. Americanski *miemsu* (meat), Americanski *mahswa* (butter)!" Whenever I needed a Slavic word I'd glance at the interpreter and squeeze his arm. He'd fill in.

I continued, "I've asked at your supply depots for food and socks for these men and was issued none. I would not like my uncle Franklin Roosevelt to hear of this. We need some of those U.S. supplies issued to us today. And we need transportation to rejoin our forces."

When I finished, the general looked down both sides of the table, spread his hands and asked something to the effect of, "Why has this not been done?"

The quartermaster officers I had talked with before flushed slightly and seemed to draw their heads into their tunics.

The general snapped out some orders, turned to me, and said, "What you ask shall be done."

I said, "*Spasibo*!"

Throwing him another sharp salute, I did an about-face and left. The interpreter needed no prodding; he was close on my heels. As we shut the door behind us, I breathed as usual, "Thank you, Lord."

I grinned at the adjutant type and the sentry, slapping him on the back as we went down the stairs. Then I got Charlie and went for a walk while we waited for the general's conference to break up.

When the senior quartermaster officer returned to his office, we were waiting for him. He didn't seem happy but did make out an authorization for the issue of some food. I asked about quantities. With a wink he said, "This is enough for you two," meaning Charlie and me.

Oh, that made me mad! It was obvious that he thought if he could satisfy the two senior officers his job was over. The rest could fend for themselves. This is all too typical of the Soviet system, which takes care of the top five percent in the Communist party who hold the power and doesn't worry much about the rest. I told this major, "*Nyet*!"; we wanted enough to feed the nearly two hundred men sleeping in the homes and public buildings around the town square.

The quartermaster added something to the paper he had drawn up and gave it to me with instructions for getting to the warehouse. I told him many men were without stockings, including me. Again he added something to the paper and handed me what looked like a roller bandage. It proved to be a long strip of heavy cotton material about two inches wide wound up into a short, thick cylinder similar to our old wrapped leggings of pre-war days. That night I started unrolling that cloth at my toes; I mummified my feet in those crude socks. They worked best in the valenkas, the felt boots. In my parachute boots they caused instant blisters.

From a friendly Pole I borrowed a horse and buggy, which I'd never driven before. I rehearsed with him my directions to the warehouse and set out, a woefully inexperienced Ben Hur in a childhood chariot. But even Polish horses are friendly, and with their help and the Lord's, I got to the warehouse and back. Despite my pleas for enough food for all, I was able to bring back to my colleagues enough food for only a day or two. It included canned goods from the United States, a big sack of mixed grains, a large bucket of sausages, another bucket of lard, and about twenty loaves of bread. Charlie and I took only a couple of tins of vegetables and some sausage wrapped in heavy paper to give to our next Polish benefactor.

As I look through my little YMCA notebook, trying to pronounce correctly the names printed there by me or written by others in a European hand, I have great memories of the kindness and hospitality of these wonderful Polish people, most of whose names are very long, ending in "ski" for men, and "ska" for women. As I said earlier, in order to protect these Poles from reprisals, I will not spell out their names. The princess is an exception because she was of a highly respected Polish royal family; the communists left her alone.

Our meetings with some of the leading families of old Lublin started with a chance encounter on February 14, 1944. Charlie and I had already wished each other a happy Valentine's Day and we were walking along the street trying to find someone who spoke English to ask directions to some of the Red Army installations we needed to visit. All responded to the effect, *"Nyeh muvium po Engelski,"* (my poor Polish for "I don't speak English").

Then we noticed a young lady coming toward us. She looked like a picture on a Valentine card. She was a small girl in big boots trimmed with white fur, and a red coat with a white fur collar. She had a red and white scarf at her throat and a round white fur cap, chapka style, perched jauntily on curly blonde hair. She walked up to us and said, "You are Americans, no? I speak some English. Perhaps I could help you."

She told us her long name, then quickly shortened it to Lucy. Looking just as charming close up as she did coming down the street, Lucy had dancing blue eyes, a turned-up nose, and an expressive mouth that smiled readily.

She gave us the directions we needed and invited us to tea with her family that afternoon. After our chores were done, we followed Lucy's directions. It turned out to be a spacious apartment of friends of her family on the great composer's street, Szopena Ulica. Lucy's folks, whom I'll call "Ski" and "Ska" for brevity and security, had lived on a large country estate outside Lublin, but their house had been taken over by Nazi bigwigs in the German occupation. Now it was occupied by Russian officers.

Mr. Ski was quite elderly, a small, dignified man who had been a local official in the pre-war government. This quiet gentleman was comfortable only speaking Polish and left most of the talking to his wife and three daughters.

Mrs. Ska seemed considerably younger than her husband, and she was completely devoted to him and her three blonde daughters. She was of medium height and slender, with patrician features and hairdo. But her regal appearance was relieved by a generous smile. She spoke little English but was fluent in French, so Charlie and I used that tongue with her. When I'd known her for only a short time I became very fond of Mrs. Ska, and when I learned the words, I started calling her "*Pani Kochana*," which means roughly little Mrs. Sweetheart. That name would always make her laugh. The three girls had all learned English in school. Lucy was about eighteen, an obvious leader and the spokesman; Hanya, perhaps fifteen, and Putsya (I believe that's a nickname), twelve or thirteen.

We had several afternoons and evenings with the Skis. Other couples, friends of theirs, had us over for dinner on two occasions and we had tea at the home of the social leader of Lublin, Princess Theresa Czartoryska, a true princess in her gracious hospitality as well as in name and lineage.

Once at the Skis', Charlie and I played bridge with Mrs. Ska and Lucy. We used Polish cards, which had some unfamiliar features. We were bidding and playing in at least four languages: Polish, French, and English plus the fourth—which all of us were weary of but which we all could speak—German. Occasionally we used it to clarify a meaning in another language. We would mix the languages, using Polish numbers with French suit names and English verbs. Everyone got into the act with different linguistic combinations. I doubt if Culbertson or Goren would have thought much of our bridge, but it gave us a lot of laughs.

On the more serious side, Charlie and I acquired a tremendous respect for the Polish people. Most had lost nearly everything they had to the Germans and were by this time used to privation. All were staunch supporters of the Home Army and of the underground. Even the girls of Ski's family had smuggled arms to the underground fighters in the forest around Lublin. Hanya, the second oldest, had flowing blonde hair, charm, and courage. From the age of twelve she had helped support the underground by smuggling weapons. One day she was carrying a loaded pistol with an extra clip of cartridges in her canvas zipper bag of schoolbooks. At a bridge leading to the forest she was stopped by a German soldier who asked where she was going. She gave him a big grin and said, "I'm carrying guns to the secret army, see?" And she whirled her zipper bag in his direction as she danced across the bridge, laughing.

The guard laughed with her and waved her on down the road. Hanya's quick wit and humor averted what could have been a tragic situation.

The Poles talked about the heavily loaded boxcars, horse-drawn carts, trucks, and other vehicles moving east to Russia across Poland. The boxcars carried entire factories from industrialized areas of Poland. The smaller vehicles carried equipment and supplies from Polish farms and shops. One Pole said with a sigh, "We thought everything of value had been taken west by the Germans, but some must have been left for the Russians."

The Lublinites estimated that no more than five percent of the Polish people supported the communist provisional government. It was maintained in power only by virtue of the Polish secret police, the *Urzad*

Bezpieczenstwa, or UB. This organization was augmented in the early stages and trained completely by the Soviet agency for state security, the old NKVD, now KGB, who were in there by the hundreds, backed up by the total might of the Red Army.

We also learned from these people that Poles claiming American citizenship could not get exit visas to leave Poland. In fact, we met many Poles who wanted to go out with us. Sometimes their original documentation—birth certificates, and so forth—were burned or destroyed by bombing, and many of them were arrested for the alleged crime of having been members of the underground army that was secretly fighting the Nazis. This of course made no sense, but as I said before, the communists wanted no freedom fighters left. The logic was that if they would fight for their freedom against Nazis, they would fight just as readily for their freedom against communists.

Chapter 32

After my talk with General Major Senchillo, we kept in close touch with the Red Army transportation office as well as with the food supply staff. At the same time we were also trying to keep tabs on all Americans and British in the area, compiling and updating a list of names so that we could use it without much delay when we finally did get transportation out of the country.

Around the nineteenth of February we got word that there were quite a few U.S. and British military men at two camps outside Lublin. We decided to go visit them the next day. It was snowing that next morning, so we borrowed a sleigh. We found the farther place, Grottgaia, a big warehouse and some outbuildings, being used as a transit camp. To our surprise there were one hundred seventeen American officers and enlisted men and forty-nine British there, all eager to get out and to get moving home.

At our next stop, Majdanek, we found twenty-six Americans and fifty British. We had heard some awful tales about the concentration camp at Majdanek; the people there were eager to show it to us. Some of the bigger camps in Poland such as Oswiecim (Auschwitz) were dismantled or demolished by the Germans before they moved west. But the Russians advanced so fast on Lublin that the Germans had no time to destroy the Majdanek camp on the edge of town.

I will never forget the first room I entered, with huge bins on each side piled nearly to the ceiling with shoes: There must have been over two hundred thousand. Many were baby shoes. The Pole who showed us around lived nearby and said when the shoes filled the building clear to the ceiling, they were sent to Germany for use there.

We saw the disrobing room, where people stripped "for a shower." We looked through a thick, round glass window in the massive steel door to the "shower room." Our guide pointed out the hole in the ceiling through which the cyanide gas was released for the shower of deadly vapor. In a smaller room we saw large canisters still full of the murderous cyanide gas. We saw the cremation ovens where the corpses were burned. The ashes were shipped to Germany for fertilizer. Everyone was pale, grim-faced and silent as we left this too-tangible reminder of Nazi horrors.

On the night of February 20, when we added the two hundred forty-two names of Americans and British from Grottgaia and Majdanek to our rolls, we about doubled the number of men who would need transportation. The next morning we got the word we were waiting for. Boxcars were being brought in on a rail siding. We were to get everyone ready to leave by the afternoon of February 22 for Odessa on the Black Sea.

The officials of Lublin and the Red Army seemed glad to be getting rid of us. They provided trucks and drivers to bring the people in from outlying camps and buildings, and loaded aboard food, water, and clean straw for the floors. They even added a few cases of lend-lease DDT disinfectant powder from the United States.

Charlie and I rapidly made the rounds of all our new-found friends in Lublin, saying good-bye and leaving with them our heartfelt thanks and warmest regards and prayers for their future. We knew they would need them.

We left for Odessa in a long string of boxcars the evening of February 22, 1945, so glad to be moving on toward home that we didn't grumble too much about the wintry cold and discomfort of the crowded boxcars, our mobile home for the next five and a half days.

We crossed the new Russian border that legalized the Soviet appropriation of eastern Poland, including the ancient Polish city of Lwow (or Lvov) the first night. I rather hoped that we would go through Kiev, the old cathedral city of the Ukraine, but we turned south short of there, at Zhitomir. In fact, on February 24, 1945, in a boxcar on a frigid siding outside Zhitomir, I celebrated the second anniversary of my capture. I recalled the same day a year before, when Dick Klocko and I—who were shot down and shot up, respectively, precisely on February 24, 1943—celebrated our first anniversary with our buddies Bub Clark and Davy Jones over a kriegie brew or two in Stalag Luft III.

Another memory of that trip was of the immense white flatness and emptiness of the Ukraine in winter, which reminded me of Kansas as it might have looked a century ago. Occasionally the train stopped between the far-flung stations out in the middle of nowhere so we could stretch our legs and relieve ourselves, but no one strayed too far from the train. All we could see was mile after mile of ice and blowing snow; when the whistle blew for departure, we reboarded the cars in a hurry.

Looking back, I again recall the movie of Pasternak's novel *Dr. Zhivago*, showing the hero walking across Russia in winter with ice and snow in his moustache, hair, and eyebrows, trying to follow the railroad track through a long blizzard. That's the way I think it would have been had we failed to get back on that train.

At some stations soup kitchens had been set up by the Russians, and the hot soup was most welcome. Their soup was mainly cabbage or beets and potatoes. They also operated one or two delousing stations. Whenever we Americans or British struck up any extended conversation with the local townspeople, however, an ever-present grim-faced Russian, obviously from the secret police, would walk up to us and the talk stopped abruptly. The Ukrainians wanted to be friendly but the officials didn't want them getting any Western ideas. It's the old Russian xenophobia—the fear of the stranger, which seems to be part of the permanent Soviet character.

I remember singing Russian songs and leading a group in our full boxcar in a sing-along as we rolled through Vinnitsa (or Venessia). I had forgotten about the poetry, but John Slack, editor of the *Oflag 64 Item*, recently sent me a copy of a letter he received from John Sutherland in 1981 with some nostalgic comments about the trip out, and among them was this: "Memories of Jerry Sage, declaiming 'Lochinvar' from memory, with heroic gestures in a straw-filled boxcar while I dusted him with a precious can of DDT powder!"

According to my little YMCA notebook, we reached Odessa at three a.m. on February 28. When the sun was high that day, we realized how far south Odessa was for a Russian city. The sunshine and breezes off the Black Sea seemed to thaw us out with a hint of spring. A few American officials from the embassy in Moscow and many Russians scurried around on administrative errands, promising that we'd all be leaving within a few days. We were notified that anyone seriously ill or hurt could be sent to a hospital in Poltawa, about three hundred miles northeast in the Ukraine. But no one volunteered to go back into Eurasia—a ship home sounded too good.

We were billeted right next to the port of Odessa, and though we were not permitted to roam through the city itself, we enjoyed the sights and sounds of the great harbor and found the Russian administrators quite friendly. One young Russian officer with whom I'd worked quite a bit even gave me a chapka, the Red Army winter fur hat complete with ear flaps and a red star insignia. He said he'd worn it in the battle of Stalingrad. At the port I enjoyed, as I always have, seeing and hearing the ships, observing the antlike activity of the stevedores and smelling the sea breezes. We kept busy enough filling out forms, washing and mending our clothes and making final preparations to board a ship out.

One night, we received a treat. The Russians showed us a lend-lease movie, Robert Taylor starring in *Tribute to Russia*. It was made when Hollywood was trying to glue us to our ally, the Soviet Union, which was greatly glamorized. I'm not sure who the leading lady was, but she was charming enough to win the heart of every ex-kriegie present, and the music was beautiful. The movie told the story of Mother Russia's scorched-earth policy as the Nazis advanced in the early 1940s; the scenes of the great grain fires started by Russians in their own fields were most impressive.

My last breakfast in Odessa was an unusual one. My bowl of boiled cracked grain, or kasha, was accompanied by a lettuce leaf stuffed with Beluga caviar. I guess I could have had a shot of vodka to wash it down if I had asked, but I didn't.

It was a great morning, March 7, when we loaded on the British steamer *Moreton Bay*. It was a converted freighter, but to us it might have been the *Queen Mary*. The food was probably quite ordinary, but it seemed like banquets. White bread tasted just like angel food cake.

We sailed at one in the afternoon, south into the Black Sea, which the Russkis call "*Chornia Mer*." By evening we were off the coast of Rumania with the land to our right. Many leagues to our left the Crimean Peninsula, with Sevastopol and Yalta, jutted south into the Black Sea. We steamed past Bulgaria during the night and were off the coast of European Turkey by morning. I rose early and watched the ship being piloted through Istanbul Bogasi, the narrow strait of the Bosporus. It was great to look from European Turkey on the starboard side to the hills of Asiatic Turkey on the port side that lay only a few hundred yards away.

We entered the Sea of Marmara and anchored off Istanbul. As I saw the shining minarets of the great mosques of the ancient city, I couldn't resist bursting into a song of the late 1920s or early '30s—"Constantinople." It went like this:

"Constantinople,
C-O-N-S-T-A-N-T-I-N-O-P-L-E;
Constantinople,
Just as easy to spell as say your ABCs
Show your pluck, try your luck, spell it loud with me
Constantinople, C-O-N-S-T-A-N-T-I-N-O-P-L-E!"

After getting that off my chest I savored the antiquity and history of the city. Istanbul has been the name only since 1930. For 1600 years it was known as Constantinople, built in 330 A.D. by the emperor Constantine I on the site of ancient Byzantium, with its roots deep in the centuries before. Constantinople served as the capital of the eastern Roman Empire and later as the capital of the Ottoman Empire.

Istanbul stands today as it has for centuries at the crossroads of Europe and Asia. The spires of the cathedrals and minarets, with the many-colored houses on the hillsides, called me to explore, but no passengers were allowed ashore. I remember saying to myself, "I want to come back here some day." (And I did, nearly twenty years later in my Green Beret with teams of Special Forces troops.)

The next morning we weighed anchor and steamed slowly west the length of the Sea of Marmara, and had a good look at the old Fort Gelibolu, which is Turkish for Gallipoli, the site of the British battle years before at the northeast end of the Dardanelles. We then eased southwest through the long narrow straits of the Dardanelles to the Aegean Sea. Again an old song, "Dardanella," came to mind.

It took us another day to thread our way through the beautiful Greek and Turkish islands as we steamed south through the Aegean Sea. Once a British sailor who had often made the trip pointed to the west—starboard—side and said, "Over the horizon there is Athens." Then, pointing east over our port side he added, "Opposite, in Turkey, lies Izmir, which is called Smyrna in the Bible. Next to it is Ephesus, where the Apostle John took Jesus' mother Mary after her son's crucifixion and where she is buried."

Again, much as I wanted to hurry onward, I also hoped I'd come back someday to see those places—and

I did. We passed between the islands of Rhodes and Crete in the Mediterranean; I was fortunate enough to spend some time on Crete years later. We proceeded southwest, leaving Cyprus to our port side. On Monday morning, March 12, we docked and debarked at Port Said, Egypt, at the north end of the Suez Canal.

We were met by American Red Cross ladies, all of whom seemed like angels. Old or young, fat or thin, they were great to see and just as good to talk with. They gave each of us a small bag of new toilet articles: toothbrush, razor and blades, toothpaste, shaving cream, soap, clean towels. We lined up for showers and more DDT, then lined up again at a finance office pay table for a partial pay of one hundred dollars.

After two years without any pay, having money seemed very strange. As soon as we were released from processing in mid-afternoon, Charlie Kouns and I took off for the Souk, the marketplace of Port Said. I bought presents for everyone in the family, mainly items made of camel leather, which seemed appropriate for a gift from Egypt and were most abundant. I bought hand-tooled purses for the ladies, and shaving kits and billfolds for the men, plus assorted toys for the youngsters. As it grew dark, a group of us congregated at a bistro in the off-limits Casbah area, bought a few bottles of wine and cognac, and had a celebration dinner of garlic chicken, lamb shish kebab, salad, and rice.

At our corner table, the food, wine, and conversation flowed rapidly and freely, along with the remainder of our partial pay. I recall that Charlie Kouns and Jack Dobson were there, and Pat Teal and a big engineer officer, a late arrival at Oflag 64. I had been well trained to sit with my back to the corner in a hostile or strange place—and this was a strange place. I glanced up occasionally to see who was coming and going.

After several hours of festivity and nostalgia, I noticed two men in slouch hats and raincoats enter the café and glance around the room; then they split up, one on each side of the room, stopping for a few words, apparently a question, at each table. Those seated would shake their heads, and the questioners moved on.

By the time one reached our table I had a hunch the OSS had arrived. I wasn't the least bit surprised when the stranger leaned toward our table and queried, "Major Sage?"

I grinned at him and said, "Right!"

He said, "There's a car waiting for you outside."

I put the last of my pay on the table, bade my colleagues so long, and went out with the OSS men.

A door opened from the back seat of a long black limousine and out stepped Commodore Hinks. I'd met him before. He was a special liaison officer of President Roosevelt's with the OSS. With him was another senior staff member from the Cairo office of the OSS. They started asking questions as soon as we got rolling, and I gave the first of many debriefings. As we drove south to Ismailia, I could see moonlight glint on the Suez Canal. Then we turned eastward and south again across strips of desert and the fields of the Nile delta toward Cairo. I don't remember when I stopped talking. I just suddenly went to sleep.

They woke me in Cairo, put me into a hotel room at two or three a.m. and let me sleep almost until noon. Then there was a day and a half of briefings for Colonel Aldridge, the station CO and many of the OSS personnel there. Interspersed with this work was quite a range of R&R: visits to the local pyramids and the Sphinx, which fascinated me, and an intramural U.S. basketball game in the evening. Wild Bill Donovan, now a major general, had been cabled that I had arrived and was asked what to do with me. He replied that they were to send me wherever I wanted to go. I said I'd like to go to our advanced headquarters nearest the German border to see if and how I could help the POWs who had been moved south to Bavaria.

The next day I was flown in an OSS plane back across the Mediterranean to Athens, Greece, where we refueled, then on to Naples, Italy. We landed at the same airport where I had landed twenty-five months before as a prisoner in a JU-52. From Naples we drove about fifteen or twenty miles north to the OSS headquarters at Caserta. There I went through the usual debriefings, renewed old acquaintances with a few old-timers— particularly Marian Cooley, a fine lady who had been part of the backbone of OSS administration from the very first back in Washington. She filled me in on the doings and whereabouts of some of my old colleagues.

I asked again if there was anything I could do to help my POW friends in Bavaria. I was told they would study the prospects. In the meantime, I was being sent to a villa on the Isle of Capri for two weeks' rest and recuperation. On Saturday, March 17, I was taken by boat across the Bay of Naples, past the lovely hills of Sorrento. Again I burst forth with song: "Come back to Sorrento, come back my love." Then we went on to the beautiful Isle of Capri and out came another song:

" 'Twas on the Isle of Capri that I found her,
Beneath the shade of an old pasta tree." (I was freewheeling and chuckling here!)

Then I remembered:

"She softly whispered, 'It's best not to linger,'
And then on her pale hand I could see

She had a small golden ring on her finger—
'Twas good-bye on the Isle of Capri."

I didn't really find anybody like that on Capri, but I did have lovely accommodations at the villa of Mrs. Harrison Williams, who lent her house to the OSS for this purpose. There was fine food, drinks, and—best of all—the rest I had come for.

The following morning, Sunday, I went to church in Capri. Though I didn't know that particular service very well, I enjoyed the beauty, the music, and the opportunity to thank the Lord properly in His house for bringing me safely out of the "valley of the shadow of death"—the lethal gray monotony and hardship of the prison camps and the trip across Russia. Then I visited the shining jewel of the Blue Grotto, the aquamarine underwater cave at Capri.

I was too restless, however, to really enjoy anything. I sent a radio message to the OSS in Caserta to meet me at the Naples dock the next morning, Monday, when I caught the first boat to the mainland. I told the chief of the OSS mission at Caserta either to put me to work or to send me home. He told me that General Donovan would not let me go back into Germany, so he would cut me orders for the States.

The next day I took off from Naples and flew to Tunisia, backtracking the route I had taken in the German plane a couple of years before. Then I flew to Oran where I had first landed with my OSS detachment and the place where I'd met my first scorpion on a sleeping bag. Then I flew on west to Casablanca where I slept a bit and then switched to a bigger plane for the Atlantic crossing. Never did I leave the airport to mingle with the Arabs at any North African port. I had been betrayed by them so many times in the winter of 1942–43 that I didn't quite trust myself around them. Since that time, however, I've worked in many Arab countries, and with the best of relations.

As we took off from Casablanca for the Azores Islands and on home on the evening of March 21, I breathed a sigh of relief. After reading a bit on the plane, I dozed off. Some time later when I awoke, a WAC stewardess, the first I had seen, offered me a glass of orange juice before we landed. I said, "Oh, the Azores already?"

She said, "Oh no, Casablanca. We met a storm seven hundred miles out and had to turn back."

I felt as restless and rough as a cob while we waited back in Casablanca for refueling and a weather change. Soon the weather did change, and after brief stops in the Azores and Newfoundland, we made it to New York. As I stepped off the plane, I did not quite kiss American soil, but I sure knelt and patted it lovingly.

General Donovan's people had kept close tabs on my movements, and when my overseas flight landed, our plane was met by the crew of General Donovan's airplane, which had been sent to New York to take me back to Washington, D.C. An OSS car picked me up at the capital's airport and dropped me at the Wardman-Park Hotel. General Donovan himself telephoned me as I was cleaning up, welcomed me back, and told me a car would be at the hotel at ten o'clock the next morning to bring me in to headquarters.

The OSS had given me a month's pay at Cairo, and being hungry as usual, I asked the hotel people where the nearest good restaurant was for a welcome-home dinner. They suggested a place nearby on Connecticut Avenue called the Continental or Napoleon's or something European like that. I then phoned my old friend from Washington State college days, Ernie Krom, stationed in Washington with the Navy.

He shouted, "Where are you?"

I told him that I'd be at that restaurant in about ten minutes and to join me for dinner.

By the time he arrived, I had consumed one steak and salad with all the trimmings, washed down with a bottle of fine wine. Then we ordered two more of the same, one for Ernie and a second for me. It was a great, relaxing evening, and in a few hours we caught up on the doings of lots of old friends. It was then that I learned that our other great friend who played football with me at Washington State and was with me in the OSS, Chris Rumburg, had died while trying to save other people when his ship sank taking them from England to France.

Ernie also told me that Chris had gotten the news of my capture through the OSS. He and Ernie had been out at a bar drowning their sorrows. Ernie told me that Chris, with tears in his eyes, said, "He'll never get back because they'll shoot him. He'll break out. Either way, old Jerry will never stay in that prison camp." That was his biggest worry. Ernie and I then raised a glass to Chris Rumburg, a great friend and a fine soldier.

When I met General Donovan the next morning, Saturday, he welcomed me with a great beaming grin, his penetrating blue eyes sparkling. "I knew you'd get home early, Jerry!" Donovan's daughter-in-law Mary was also there with a warm welcome. While her husband David Donovan was away with the Navy, Mary shared many hostess duties with the general's wife, Ruth. Both were warm, friendly people whom I'd enjoyed knowing in 1942.

Other old friends who were there in the Q Building

to greet me included my silent-killing mentor Delicate Dan Fairbairn of England, and Ainsworth Blogg of Seattle, now both lieutenant colonels. I believe Dick Oliver, who as adjutant had ushered me in to my first meeting with Donovan three years before, was also there. I told Dan Fairbairn that his training really worked, including the sentry kill and everything else he had taught. I then told him about my own classes in silent death for the POW colleagues in Stalag Luft III when Colonel Goodrich directed me to prepare a team to take over the camp in case the Germans started liquidation proceedings.

During the afternoon I gave more briefings, and at one point between briefings, General Donovan told me he was sending me back home for thirty days' rest and recuperation. He then asked me what I wanted to do next. I said that I hadn't fought the Japanese yet and I'd like to take an outfit out against them.

He said, "If you're sure you want to, I'll send you out to the West Coast Training Center and give you a command of a new group to harass the Japanese from North China. You can start calling together the men you want in your outfit."

I was delighted with the idea and said so. Orders were cut that afternoon assigning me to the OSS West Coast Training Center on Catalina Island, about thirty miles off the coast of California across from Long Beach, with a thirty-day delay en route for rest and recuperation. In Donovan's words, "Load up on steaks, sleep, and have fun." And that's what I planned to do.

I was also invited that afternoon to a welcoming dinner in the evening hosted by the Donovans. I said I regretted that my only uniform was the field jacket and trousers that I had been issued in Cairo, plus a new overseas cap and my old parachute boots.

Replied Donovan, "That's great," and he was right: It was a fine evening.

Dinner was served in the dining room at the Q Building, followed by a movie in the conference room. I'm not sure now which division heads of the OSS were there, but there were several. I talked mainly with the general, Ruth Donovan, Mary Donovan, and Ambassador Robert Murphy and his wife. They were all particularly interested in my reports on what I'd seen and heard in Poland and Russia. They knew the Nazis were nearly finished, and the OSS was already shifting gears to deal with the emerging power of the Soviet Union.

I felt quite awkward at this first truly genteel social affair after so many months as a POW, escapee, and displaced person. The dinner was beautifully set and served, and I took my time to refresh my memory of which piece of silver went with which course. For so long the choice of both food and fork had been extremely limited.

Then, after dinner, as we walked toward the conference room theater, I headed for a drinking fountain in the hall. Ambassador Murphy's wife also turned that way and in a bantering tone I said, "Let me buy you a drink!" Mrs. Murphy smiled her thanks and bent over the fountain just as I pushed the button for the water.

That button was trigger-happy. A veritable stream of water spurted up into her face. Fortunately, I was able to offer her a fresh handkerchief as I said, "Oh no, I told Mrs. Donovan how hard I had tried to be civilized during dinner."

Mrs. Murphy, bless her heart, laughing the whole time, patted my arm and said, "You are truly a refreshing man, Jerry Sage!" We chuckled the rest of the way into the movie room. I don't recall what the movie was, but it was definitely part of a fine evening.

The next day I cleaned up some more bits of business, saw a few more friends, assembled my orders and the plane tickets and was soon on my way out to the state of Washington. From March 26 till about April 20, 1945, I visited relatives and friends in Spokane, Tacoma, and Seattle. On a lovely Easter Sunday in Spokane, April 1, I gave credit where credit was due, to the Savior who brought me back safely and kept all my loved ones safe and well during my absence.

Chapter 33

Two days later, April 3, was a surprise highlight. I had spent the day downtown giving a luncheon talk (one of many) to a civic club and visiting friends. I returned about six o'clock to the home Mom and Dad had built in Opportunity in the lush valley of great cantaloupes and vegetables just east of Spokane.

My sister Nita met me at the door with, "It's about time!" and a chiding smile.

I said, "Sorry I'm so late, but where are all the folks?" The house seemed deserted.

Nita smiled and said, "We're dining in the recreation room," and led me down the basement stairs. As I stepped down, I was greeted by a chorus of "Hark, the Herald Angels Sing." There in one end of the room was a full-spreading Christmas tree—complete with our traditional angel at the top of the tree, gaily colored lights, ornaments galore, and shiny silver icicles glittering over all. Everyone in that room shouted, "Merry Christmas!"

All the family gave me teary-eyed hugs. There were presents for me for Christmases 1943 and 1944, the lean ones spent in prison camps. I spent a bit of time blowing my nose and getting things out of my eyes with a handkerchief. Then I looked at the festive table. It was all there: a huge brown turkey, dressing, cranberry sauce, loads of fresh salad, steamed vegetables, my favorite pumpkin pie, and Mother's special Christmas plum pudding, steamed, with the delicious vanilla sauce.

It was a great double Christmas that third of April 1945, crazy and wonderful, like the family's approach to war work. Nita told me that when they heard I was in a POW camp they immediately held a family powwow, posing the question, "How can we get Jerry out of there the fastest?"

Spokane had only one really big war industry. Kaiser had built a huge aluminum plant there. The folks figured that the faster American fighting airplanes could be made from that aluminum, the faster the war would end. So they all quit what they were doing and reported to the Kaiser plant. Dad left his business, wholesale jobbing of candy and tobacco, and signed on to the Kaiser security force as a guard. Nita quit her job at the bank and Mother stopped building houses; both got jobs in the business office. My little brother Gene even tried to join the Marines, but they told him they weren't accepting fourteen-year-olds. (Later Gene was a Marine for four years and then a lawyer in Seattle.)

All this happened on receiving the news of my capture in early 1943. When they heard from General Donovan that I was loose and coming home, Mom and Nita both left Kaiser and returned to their former lives. The personal part of the war was over, and by March of 1945 they figured we had all the airplanes we could use. Dad stayed on at the plant for the rest of the war, just to make sure.

One of the talks I especially enjoyed giving in Spokane was at my old alma mater, North Central High

School. The faculty held a combined meeting and reception for me. There was a brief debriefing (if there is such a thing), then a question period and general bull session over cookies, coffee and lemonade. I realized what truly good friends these teachers had been to me. But there was also bad news.

One of the first teachers I asked about was my football coach, Archie Buckley. It was a sad shock to learn he had been killed as a Navy officer fighting the Japanese in the Pacific.

Archie's fighting spirit and enthusiasm had been contagious. He was a great quarterback for Coach Babe Hollingbery at Washington State, sometimes pulling the team out to victory over a bigger and better opponent by sheer competitive fire.

Babe Hollingbery was a great guy too, a fine, clean-cut coach who was always a good example to us and always full of enthusiasm. His motto was, "A team that won't be beat can't be beat." To get myself through college with only a fifty dollar scholarship for all A's and a thirty-five dollar monthly National Youth Administration football scholarship, I lived with three other football players for a year in the Hollingberys' basement.

But the afternoon that was the big step into confident manhood for me was under Archie Buckley at North Central High. I was a tall, skinny sixteen-year-old playing second string end on defense while the first team ran all out against us in scrimmage. I guess I was doing pretty well stopping the plays around my end, but on one play a couple of us tackled our big fullback, Louis Contos. His pile-driving legs kept churning and one set of cleats slammed square into my face.

Nose guards hadn't been invented then. I saw red in all directions, much inside my head, a lot running down my shirt. I guess there was adrenalin mixed with the pain; I raged into the backfield on nearly every play from then on and even made crossfield tackles toward the other end. Archie looked at me a couple of times and asked if I hadn't better sit out for a while. I yelled, "I'm not leaving," and dug in for the next play.

Later, in the shower room while a trainer taped my broken nose into place and made various repairs to my mouth, cheeks, and the corners of my eyes, Coach Buckley said, "Jerry, I don't know if you knew what you were doing, but you sure were doing it right."

From that afternoon on my confidence seemed to soar. I learned that pain could not dominate me. I started on the first string the next day in the city-league opener at long side end and played every minute of the rest of the season. We won the regional championship.

I still get a thrill in watching high-school football games, with their enthusiasm, color, cheerleaders, top-flight bands, and spirit of clean fun. At Spring Valley High and Airport High in Columbia, South Carolina, and now at Enterprise High School in Alabama, every opening kickoff recalls the kickoffs of our championship team at North Central in 1933.

Coach Buckley usually chose to kick off rather than receive the ball because we all got down so fast underneath the ball that we always pinned the opponents back near their goal line. Bob Carey, the opposite end, was a particular friend, and we had a kickoff ritual. As the outside men of our lineup, we had the job of seeing that the receiver did not get around us—that we penned him inside. Just before the kick, Bob and I looked at each other and waved in a combination of encouragement and a dare to see who could get there first. At any rate, it seemed to bring luck; no kick return got around us all that year.

I remember best the people in my life who helped me, or made me, stretch and grow. I learned from my coaches a lot about winning, losing, trying a bit harder, giving everything you've got, then a bit more, and overcoming pain to reach a goal.

Other teachers stretched and challenged me too. Mr. Nygaard, the shy dedicated math teacher at North Central High, one day in 1932 or '33, handed me a little pamphlet and said, "You might be interested in this, Jerry."

It was a tract by Einstein on his theory of relativity. There was a great deal I didn't understand, but I struggled with it until I had glimmers of what Einstein was proposing. I was able to probe it further with Mr. Nygaard's help. His confidence in me made me react by stretching my brain to follow new paths. That may be what education is all about.

Other high-school teachers were stimulating in their own fields. Miss Mary McKenna extended my taste for poetry and good books in her English literature class. I was already hooked on Sir Walter Scott, Alexander Dumas, and Rudyard Kipling by Mother. Dad added Robert W. Service: As I've said, he loved "The Shooting of Dan McGrew" and "The Cremation of Sam McGee." Our speech and drama teacher, Mrs. Grace Leonard, drove and cajoled us into speaking on a variety of subjects, building our confidence in public speaking. Miss Marjorie Freakes got me interested in journalism and I wound up as editor of the high-school paper.

It was great to see them again eleven years and a long war after my graduation, and to have the chance to thank them all for their wisdom, friendship, teaching, and patience.

* * *

Another talk I enjoyed giving in the Spokane area was at Central Valley High School, where my younger brother Gene was playing football and preparing to go on to Washington State. The youngsters were very much alive, bright-eyed, and curious, and they asked great questions.

There was of course no television to speak of in those days, but I was invited to talk on several radio shows. One of the biggest was The Breakfast Club of America. The Army's public information office lined it up—and there my first prior censorship occurred. They asked me to say nothing of my views on the Russians and what they did in Poland, but to stick to the evildoings of the Nazis, the prison camp experiences, and the escapes. The rationale seemed to be not to upset the Russians now.

At that very time, the spring of 1945, in San Francisco, President and Mrs. Roosevelt and the State Department were trying to build the United Nations to "make the world safe for democracy." The same thing had been attempted after World War I. The effort now was to build a better international organization than the League of Nations, which Woodrow Wilson had tried and failed to sell to the U.S. Congress after World War I. Our government knew the United Nations could not get off the ground unless the second most powerful nation in the world joined.

I could see the problem but always regretted that we couldn't do more to help the nations turned into communist puppets, whose fates, in a sense, we aided and abetted. I have the feeling that at the international meetings—the Big Three meetings, as they were called—of Roosevelt, Churchill, and Stalin at Teheran and Yalta, the two great men of the United States and Great Britain were past their prime and allowed themselves to be outfoxed by the younger, stronger, more ambitious Joseph Stalin.

Another vivid memory during that holiday was my visit to an Army dentist at Madigan General Hospital in Fort Lewis, Washington. This occurred—according to my little red book—on April 12, 1945. The dentist was merrily drilling away to the Andrews Sisters singing on the radio when an announcer interrupted with the news that President Roosevelt had just died. The dentist almost put the drill through my cheek. It was a sobering moment for all of us. But our nation safely changed horses in midstream, and Harry Truman, with due humility, considerable experience in Washington, and a lot of courage, took up the reins of war.

Among the many warm welcome-home messages that came in during that R&R in Washington state were two particularly memorable telegrams. An official one from the OSS announcing my promotion in April to lieutenant colonel was occasion for several celebration parties. The other one, from Steve Byzek, had a special meaning to both Dad and me.

Dad had been an enlisted man in the Navy in World War I and had a few unpleasant experiences with "the brass." When I first showed up in uniform wearing lieutenant's bars, Dad said only half jokingly, "Yuk, you look like a cock-eyed ensign." Then more seriously, he added, "I'm sure you know this, son, but never forget that every man wants to be treated like a man, and whether officer or enlisted, each guy puts his pants on the same way—one leg at a time."

Steve Byzek's message to me read to this effect: "Congratulations. Heard you made a home run. Knew you would. Know you'll be taking another outfit out. Want to go with you. Send for me. Best regards, Steve Byzek."

Dad asked, "Who's Byzek?" I told him he was one of the fine enlisted men, a sergeant, with me in North Africa.

Dad said, "Enlisted, eh? That's mighty nice, son." He was far more impressed by this request from an enlisted man to serve again with me than by the news of my promotion.

Not long thereafter I reported to the OSS West Coast Training Center on Catalina Island. One of the first things I did was to start an official request for Steve Byzek to join me there. It turned out that by that time he was an officer.

Phil Allen, a fine officer and former headmaster at Andover, as I recall, was running the West Coast Training Center. Donovan evidently had passed the word there to let me teach any classes I wanted and take any refresher training that would be useful while they worked out details with the Far East commander's staff. I refreshed myself on the use of all hand-held weapons and soon was shooting as well as ever. The hunting was good on Catalina Island. There were wild goats on the hilltops and wild razorback boars, fine-flavored from roaming under the old oak trees and eating lots of acorns. We had several delicious barbecues of both goat and pig.

I helped teach silent killing, demolitions, and sabotage, and exchanged ideas on survival, escape, and evasion with other old colleagues. We passed on our experiences to the new men. Two other OSS officers who had been involuntary guests of the Germans showed up at the training center that summer.

Peter Ortiz, as I recall, was the son of a U.S. Foreign Service officer and had lived in France much of his youth. He joined the French Foreign Legion and was captured by the Germans in 1940. He escaped from a POW camp in Austria and made his way to the United States. He was commissioned in the Marines and joined the OSS. In 1944 he became a leader of the French Maquis Resistance Forces and was so successful in destroying German troop trains and their supplies that the Germans put a price on his head. His underground band was finally surrounded in a village in the southern Alps of France and Ortiz had to surrender to save the village from extinction by the Germans. He was hauled off to a prisoner-of-war camp in northern Germany.

Another was a Navy man named Taylor, Jack or Dick. I believe he had been a dentist in southern California. He'd been one of my students at an earlier OSS camp. Then he later was parachuted in to Eastern Europe to foment resistance. He was captured and thrown into the notorious concentration camp at Mauthausen. One arm was badly torn up when the Germans were interrogating him. His upper arm had been held fast while his lower arm was rotated like a crank. The Lord must have played a major role in bringing all three—Ortiz, Taylor, and Sage—back to this meeting on Catalina Island.

I celebrated the German surrender on VE Day in May 1945 with my old Procter & Gamble buddy, Gail Stewart, in Long Beach, California. Gail was in the Navy and had been out in New Guinea and other far reaches of the Pacific fighting the Japanese. Now he was stationed at a naval supply depot in the San Pedro area, near Long Beach. On VE Day I also shaved off the moustache I had had ever since North Camp in Stalag Luft III.

Monday to Friday I was on Catalina Island, but I returned to the mainland on the weekends and had some great reunions with former kriegie friends as they showed up in southern California. It was here that Don Stine came to see me, bringing his oil painting of me. "Silent Death" had been done on cardboard in Stalag Luft III in 1943 and carried across Europe and America to reach me at last.

I also ran into Wings Kimball that summer and we cooked up a fun event. Kimball was one of the pilots who escaped out of the boxcar with me near Sfax, Tunisia, in February 1943, and we were together at Stalag Luft III until I was purged in June 1944. On Catalina I met the OSS parachuting specialist and instructor Sergeant "Hoppy" Hopkins: I mentioned to him that I wanted to do a water jump some day. He replied that he had 2,399 jumps and would enjoy jumping out over the water with me for his 2,400th jump. OSS people weren't necessarily crazy, they just sometimes did unusual things.

Hopkins had been a stunt pilot, wing walker, and stunt parachutist for some time before the war and he had jumped more than anyone I knew. Later on he jumped out of a plane and landed on Devil's Peak in the southwest part of the United States, which caused a heck of a fuss because park rangers and mountaineers had to go to a lot of trouble to rescue him. The winds were so bad up there they couldn't land the chopper to pick him up and it was a long way to climb.

One weekend, Kimball and Hopkins and I got together and worked out our jump scenario. Wings arranged to borrow a small plane, a C-45, from an Army Air Corps field at Santa Ana, not far away. There was one other principal in this little skit. Sunday night I called the OSS headquarters on Catalina and talked with Chief Roberts—that's chief boatswain's mate—a fine Navy man with whom I'd served at the Indian Head, Maryland, camp on the Potomac back in 1942. I asked him to be ready with the OSS crash boat to pick us up out of the bay after we jumped out of the airplane Monday morning. I said we'd buzz the camp first to alert them.

On Monday morning Kimball drove us out to the Santa Ana airport. The C-45 is a little plane with room for a pilot and copilot and four seats in the back. We had static-line harnesses and were prepared to hook up the static line to the braces where the seats were bolted into the floor of the airplane. Our only problem was that the C-45 had twin vertical stabilizers on the tail and was a short plane, so if we jumped out with the plane straight and level, we were apt to cut off our heads on the tail. Hoppy and Kimball figured we'd have to be in a 45-degree dive when we jumped from the cabin to keep from hitting the tail. Hoppy said he'd be the jumpmaster and I said, "That's fine." He said he'd be right behind.

We took off on a beautiful sunny day. We were wearing light khaki shirts and pants uniforms; Hopkins and I wore light tennis shoes for our dip in the water. As we flew along, Hopkins and I reviewed procedures for rapidly getting out of the chute harness as we neared or entered the water. As we got to Catalina Island, I pointed out the OSS camp and boat dock to Kimball. He buzzed the area a couple of times while I waved out the door until some blue-shirted lads in sailor hats waved back at us and started up the crash boat.

Then on Hoppy's signal we climbed to a bit above our jump altitude. I squatted in the door. We'd already hooked up the static lines and now Kimball nosed the plane into a 45-degree dive. Hoppy tapped me on the shoulder and I jumped. The chute opened properly and I had a lovely quiet view of the island as I drifted down to the water. I could see the crash boat turning to head toward my splashdown point.

I started unfastening my chute as I neared the water. When I splashed down I was completely free of it, with one elbow hooked through the harness so I wouldn't lose the chute. The only problem was that at water level a strong breeze was blowing off the island. It kept my chute inflated, towing me back toward the mainland at a good clip. I could see the crash boat leap forward as it sped up to catch me. Then the boat started to run me down. I had to release the chute and use both arms and legs to fend off the side of the bow. It darned near sank me.

From the boat was coming an awful string of invectives. Chief Roberts was a great seaman, but he detested parachutes. He was perfectly at home on the sea, but he got nervous around parachutes and was cussing them and me out in no uncertain terms. Then he swung a long pole over the side to me, rapping me smartly on the head as he did. I grabbed the pole, he pulled me alongside, jerked me by the belt as I was climbing aboard, and dumped me unceremoniously on the deck.

I kept grinning at him until he ran out of cuss words, then he grinned too and we shook hands, ran down the parachute and pulled it aboard. About that time Hoppy made his jump. We picked him up with no problems and made for shore. Chief Roberts returned to his usual proper military vocabulary and we added this experience to a long list of memories of OSS training, the arenas of war, and the camaraderie of high-spirited men.

Another good day that summer was spent with Navy captain and movie director John Ford, who was back in Hollywood directing the movie *They Were Expendable*. This became the great Navy story starring John Wayne, Robert Montgomery, and Donna Reed. As I've mentioned, John Ford had directed me in parts of an OSS training film in 1942 and invited me to visit him on the set. His invitation through the West Coast Training Center was to see a bit of Hollywood in action. It was great fun. I had long admired John Wayne, usually called Duke there. He had played football for the University of Southern California just a few years before I played at Washington State. I had also admired Robert Montgomery, a very smooth actor. These were the stars playing Navy officers.

I liked the fresh open smile of Donna Reed from our first greeting. She was playing a Navy nurse. This was the heroic story of the PT boats, the torpedo boats in World War II. I thoroughly enjoyed the actors' work. They were real pros under Ford's first-class directing and I enjoyed talking with them when they gathered around at coffee breaks and at lunch. John Ford had evidently told them a bit about me and they asked quite a few questions about my experiences with the Germans. Everyone seemed genuinely interested in each other and we just had a good old-fashioned bull session.

In the afternoon John Ford asked one of his assistants to show me around some of the adjacent Hollywood sets. Most were unoccupied but I could see mockups of Wild West streets, of a Roman gladiator arena, and of various indoor stages. One set was busy as a beehive. It seemed to be a huge ballroom in a grand hotel or on an ocean liner, with a raised platform at one end. On this platform was a great organ and just seating herself on the bench before the banks of keys was a tiny lady.

I asked, "Who is that?"

The guide answered, "Ethel Smith."

Just then her fingers and toes seemed to start dancing on the keys and the foot pedals. It was the first time I could remember hearing Ethel Smith at the organ, but

I became a solid fan right there. She was playing a catchy Latin American tune I later learned was called "Tico, Tico." It was beautiful as it resounded throughout the great hall.

My guide said they were shooting a musical called *Early to Wed*, starring Van Johnson and Esther Williams. I recognized Van Johnson striding across the far end of the room about the time the director said, "Take five!" and everybody took a break.

During the break a marimba band, obviously part of the picture, started playing, and a few people started dancing. One of the numbers had the same kind of a catchy beat as the tune Ethel Smith had played. I guess I started tapping a foot and moving a bit with the rhythm. A tall, pretty, dark-haired girl with a great shape and broad shoulders walked up to me and said, "You look as though you like to dance. Would you?"

I said, "I do like to dance—I used to rhumba before the war, but this beat is different. What is it?"

She said, "This is a samba and its movements are more back and forth than sideways as in the rhumba. Come, I'll show you."

She was a fine dancer and a good teacher. It didn't take long to get the patterns and we began just enjoying the dance.

I said, "By the way, I'm Jerry Sage. What's your name?"

She said with a friendly grin, "I'm Esther Williams."

I said, "Boy, that explains your beautiful shoulders. I remember you used to win a lot of swimming medals in Seattle."

She laughed and said, "Yes, and I'm still swimming a lot in my pictures." She was a beautiful lady and I was proud to learn the samba from her.

On the Fourth of July, 1945, I gave heartfelt thanks for independence and celebrated more quietly and more reverently than the last two Fourths of July in prison camps. I thought of the contrast: the rowdy obstreperous Yanks among the British RAF fliers at Stalag Luft III in 1943 and then the milder and a bit more lonely day of a solitary American among the British Army officers at Eichstadt in 1944.

Chapter 34

The OSS groups on Catalina Island were in good shape, ready for deployment overseas, and marking time for orders that never came. By mid-July we could almost smell the end of the war. Radio newscasters had been describing a series of fire raids by B-29s that laid Tokyo to waste. Admiral Halsey's Third Fleet was ranging at will along the main islands, the heartland of Japan, shelling, bombing and strafing airfields, harbors, planes, railroads, and ships. Japanese transportation had nearly ground to a halt.

Then a British fleet moved north to aid Halsey in the destruction and more war-seasoned American troops released from Europe started landing in the Philippines. On July 26 the Allied heads of state, meeting in Potsdam, Germany, gave a formal warning to Japan to surrender or be annihilated. Japan replied that she was ignoring the Potsdam Declaration. In less than two weeks, the United States delivered the coup de grace.

On the sixth of August a single B-20, the *Enola Gay*, flew over Hiroshima, a city of over a third of a million people, and dropped a small atomic bomb. When the great rolling mushroom of smoke and debris cleared, well over half the city was gone. President Truman gave the Japanese an ultimatum for surrender, which also was ignored. On the eighth of August a second atomic bomb completely destroyed the city of Nagasaki.

A few days later, under the American threat of more atomic bombs, the Japanese agreed to accept the Potsdam terms of surrender. Hirohito sent his messengers out to the far-flung forces of Japan, telling them to stand down and cease fighting, and the Allies moved into position for the final surrender. These events culminated in the historic signing of the surrender papers on the battleship *Missouri* on September 2, 1945. The war was finally over.

But a dark cloud lingered on the horizon. The Soviet Union, which had done nothing to help in the struggle against Japan, declared war on that crippled nation only on August 8, the day of our atomic bombing of Nagasaki. Red Army forces charged into Manchuria to ensure their share of the spoils in eastern Asia. Like a hyena the Soviet Union leaped on the mortally wounded nation and chewed off parts for itself on the Pacific shores These it could add to the ten communist puppet states fast being established by Red Army forces in Eastern Europe.

When the atomic bombs were dropped, I was as surprised as millions of others, and just as stunned by the implications of the new weapons. It took me a few days to digest the news of the A-bombs, the belated moves of the Russian bandits to the Pacific, and the surrender arrangements, and to realize the war was finally drawing to a close. What next?

I had a lot of thinking to do, so I hiked off by myself and climbed to the top of the highest hill near our Catalina OSS camp and sat down and thought.

Back in solitary confinement in 1943 and 1944, I came to the conclusion that after the war I could best serve my fellowman and community as a teacher. But now, in August 1945, when Germany and Japan were defeated, I was still uneasy. I could not feel truly at peace. After what I'd seen in Poland, I just did not trust the Russian communists. I remembered the youth, vigor, and size of the Red Army—and the absolute control exerted over millions of people by the small, fanatical elite of the Communist party.

Communist puppets were now in position to control all of Eastern Europe from the Baltic to the Mediterranean, and the Soviet Union had secure footholds on islands and peninsulas of the Pacific shores, very close to Alaska.

The most powerful weapons in history were here—a quantum leap in destructive power, at the time fortunately in American hands. But in peacetime we never have been good at keeping secrets. What we developed others could develop, learn about, or steal.

International efforts at keeping the peace were under way. How much promise did they show?

The charter of the new United Nations was signed on June 26, 1945, by all countries in the San Francisco Conference of April 25, while I was on leave on the West Coast. This was the culmination of Roosevelt's continuing efforts to correct the weaknesses in the old League of Nations and to build a framework for a permanent system as far back as the Atlantic Charter in 1941 and at each of their successive meetings during the war. I read a great deal about the new organization, wondering if it offered some role I might take in keeping the peace after the war.

Of special interest to me was the Security Council of the United Nations, which had been given the prime responsibility for maintaining peace and international order. The U.N. was definitely not a supra-national or world government with enforceable laws. It could only recommend concerted action against an aggressor, and the two major powers—the United States and the Soviet Union—both insisted on wielding veto power in the Security Council. The charter provided a military staff committee for the Security Council. This looked especially interesting to me. I thought it might be a good place to keep an eye on the Russians. I didn't trust them as far as I could throw the whole Red Army.

These were just some of my thoughts on the hill that quiet day in Catalina Island. When I walked down the hill, I had come to these decisions for my future: First, my civilian teaching career had to wait until the world's future looked much more peaceful. Second, I would investigate the possibilities of serving on the military staff committee of the United Nations. Third, if there was no place for me there, I'd stay with Donovan's OSS, since the United States would have to maintain the best intelligence possible to meet future contingencies. I was also convinced that the OSS style of special operations, such as guerrilla fighting and sabotage, had already proved its worth in World War II.

I asked for orders to go from the West Coast back to OSS headquarters. These came through with no hitches and I was in Washington by the first of September. My OSS friends in Washington knew no more about the military staff committee of the Security Council than I did, and they put me in touch with the State Department agency dealing with U.N. affairs. There I was routed through many offices, but no one knew of anything definite being done about setting up the committee in question nor in general about any type of enforcement agencies of the United Nations. When I asked further if there was any place at all they knew of in the United Nations where I might be able to use my training and experience in either a military or civilian capacity, the responses were so negative that I finally gave up and returned to OSS headquarters.

Most of us had hoped that the OSS would continue as the central agency for intelligence and special and clandestine operations, but there were all kinds of rumors that the President might have different ideas. In a few days the rumors proved to be true. On September 20, 1945, the President issued an executive order releasing General Donovan from his OSS leadership and ordering the entire OSS closed down within two weeks. Some OSS activities, such as research and analysis, were given to the State Department. The remains of secret intelligence and special operations were transferred to the War Department under Brigadier General John Magruder in what was called the Strategic Services Unit. The good ship OSS had been scuttled and I still had not found a meaningful job where I could be of service.

At this point I think the good Lord stepped in. Lieutenant Colonel Dick Oliver, the last military executive officer of OSS headquarters and an old friend from 1942, handed me an Army circular he had just noted and said, "Jerry, you might be interested in this."

I was. It announced that senior field-grade officers interested in rebuilding Europe were invited to apply for fourteen weeks of intensive study at Columbia University in New York beginning late in October. The program was called The European Senior Staff Officers Studies Course, taught by top experts in such areas as economics, international trade, European governments, and geopolitical problems. The graduates were to serve on the highest staff of the Army Command in Europe and in military governments over Germany and Austria.

This sounded fine to me. I'd be stationed in the

heart of the action in Europe, in Germany, which had already been divided into four zones of occupation, each controlled by one of the Allies: the United States, Great Britain, France, and the Soviet Union. I was quite familiar with the geography of much of Europe and spoke bits of several of its languages. I hoped I could help rebuild a sensible, democratic Europe and perhaps be of some service to my friends in Poland and other victims of totalitarian powers, both Nazi and Russian.

I applied for the course, was accepted, broadened my European background at Columbia, joined the staff at Headquarters European Command in Frankfurt, received a regular Army commission, stayed in the Army and was happy about the decision from the very start.

During those years after the war I had the opportunity to see Donovan on several occasions. When I was at Columbia University, I occasionally had some time off, and Donovan would invite me to some of the breakfasts he held for his friends.

He still had a Scandinavian cook and a chauffeur from OSS days. The Swedish hotcakes and omelets were excellent. Over coffee we'd have wide-ranging conversations about geopolitics and current affairs around the world. We talked about the status of the Cold War, what Stalin was doing, and what might happen next.

It was always a great pleasure for me to be with Donovan. We would dive right into meaningful talks, picking up where we had left off before.

Many years later, when I was teaching at the Command and General Staff College in Fort Leavenworth, Kansas, I saw Donovan for the last time. Having recently suffered a stroke, William Donovan was in Walter Reed Hospital, and I knew his condition was serious. Leaving my teaching, I traveled to Washington, D.C., to see him. It was a kind of pilgrimage, a final chance to meet my old boss before he met the big boss upstairs.

The nurse attending the hospital suite obviously had the duty of guarding her patient from too many visitors.

"Who are you?" she asked as I came in, quickly adding, "General Donovan isn't seeing anyone."

"Well, I've come all the way from Kansas," I replied. "Would you just tell him that Jerry Sage is out here?"

The nurse went into the bedroom and soon returned. "The general will see you," she said, "but please be brief."

I went in. There, lying in the bed, was Wild Bill, just waking up from a nap. He brought his eyes into focus and there it was again—that familiar, piercing look in his Delft-blue eyes.

He smiled as I took his hand.

"Gee," I said, "it's grand to see you. You're looking great!"

He gave me a big grin and held my hand in a tight grip for a moment. Then he looked up and said, "Jerry, we sure gave 'em hell, didn't we?"

And that was about it. I was glad I had come to see him. I said a quiet prayer over him and left, and he passed away within a week.

Epilogue

My initial three and a half years of World War II service stretched to well over thirty years of active duty for Uncle Sam—other assignments, other conflict, more great memories.

In March 1946 I was back in Frankfurt, a few miles from the former German Luftwaffe POW screening center Dulag Luft, where I had spent many days in the hospital or the cooler with its heat treatment. This time my address was Headquarters European Command, in the Civil Affairs Division, as Chief of the Field Contact Branch. I was working with displaced persons: Estonian, Latvian, Lithuanian, Polish, Czech, Yugoslav, Romanian, Bulgarian and Jewish peoples away from their home countries, and many released from concentration camps. I was chosen for this work because I understood some of the problems of ex-prisoners and slave laborers under the Germans and spoke a little of their languages. I also understood the reasons why so many from Eastern Europe were still in displaced persons (DP) camps in Germany. Most of them had refused repatriation because of their fear of the Russians and their distaste for the communist governments recently imposed by the

Red Army. The Jews wanted to go to a free country, usually to the United States or to Palestine.

As the U.S. Army had the overall responsibility for the camps, officers and non-commissioned officers from local units were responsible for immediate supervision, while most of the day-to-day administration was carried out by the United Nations Relief and Rehabilitation Agency (UNRRA), ably assisted by a staff of displaced persons themselves. My duties were mainly routine inspections and visits to ensure that the crowded camps were kept sanitary and the people adequately fed and clothed, provided with education and training as needed, all in a fair and equitable manner.

Occasionally I was called upon to calm down displaced persons when they were frightened or upset by rumors. They seemed to trust and confide in me a bit more freely than others, probably because of my POW experiences and my ability to communicate with them using bits of their own tongue to establish rapport, then continuing in German, which all of the DPs perforce understood.

One day I received a message that some elderly Ukrainian ladies were lying down on the railroad tracks in front of a locomotive outside a camp in southern Bavaria. The local authorities were merely trying to consolidate two camps that were only partly filled and were taking them by train, but the people were deathly afraid that the train meant deportation to the Soviet Union. A EUCOM headquarters pilot flew me down in a light Army plane and landed near the camp. It took all of my persuasive powers to get the Ukrainians aboard the train, and I felt I had to stay with them to keep them calm until they reached the new camp.

Men from General Anders' Polish troops who fought so heroically alongside American and British troops against the Germans in Italy were now serving in guard companies at U.S. installations. Some were repatriated following promises of the new communist government that they would not be harassed, but these assurances proved to be false. We learned that as a repatriation train stopped at the checkpoint between the Soviet zone of occupation and the U.S. zone, each returning Pole was interrogated by men of the Polish secret police, the UB, aided by the Russian KGB.

Polish-speaking American officers who accompanied the train overheard these agents threatening some of the returnees with death or imprisonment if they did not become informers for the UB. After several such reports reached the European Command, I was sent back into Poland to learn more about what was happening to Polish DPs.

In Poland it was easy to verify that returning soldiers from General Anders' forces were, at a minimum, kept under constant surveillance, that many had been arrested, and some had disappeared. One of the young ladies whose family had helped Charlie Kouns and me was now working as an interpreter for UNRRA and helping in the Warsaw office. Like most Poles working for U.S. or U.N. agencies, she was terribly frightened of the UB. She had been picked up by them, taken to headquarters, and interrogated for three or four hours with a pistol to her head. The UB threatened her, saying she and her family would be killed if she would not agree to spy on UNRRA and to reveal its communications with the U.S. embassy.

When the American ambassador, Arthur Bliss Lane, verified this, we made plans to get her out to the U.S. zone. The American aircraft that picked me up was too closely watched to allow me to take her with me on my return, but other arrangements made earlier did work, and she arrived in the U.S. zone with a small group of refugees who had walked under very difficult conditions all the way across the Soviet zone of Germany from Poland. We took care of her until she was admitted to the United States on a scholarship; she later became a stewardess for Pan American Airlines.

Also on this trip I was able to witness the first "election" in Poland under the communists. It was merely a referendum on three general propositions, but the communists built it up to make it look like a vote of confidence for their regime. The government permitted no publicity against these three measures. They controlled all the media and they sent truckloads of armed men to help ensure that the government would get a favorable vote on all three issues. Then, to guarantee a landslide, most of the ballot boxes were pulled out to the Communist party headquarters to be counted. The communists could then announce that over ninety per cent of the people had agreed with the government's stand. On the other hand, a secret poll conducted by the U.S. embassy at selected polling places showed that the vote was really going almost the opposite way on one measure—that over eighty per cent of the people had voted against it—but that view was never publicized.

Many Jewish DPs wanted to go to Palestine; the younger ones who survived concentration camps were very ready to fight for a home there. Occasionally at night on my field trips I'd find groups of young Jews training vigorously for military action with broomsticks and other makeshift weapons for arms. I talked with a few men who had come recruiting from the underground groups in Palestine, Haganah and Irgun.

In the early summer of 1947 I was called back to Washington to work out of the office of General Marshall, then Secretary of State, giving testimony to the Senate and House committees on immigration as to the worthiness of admitting more DPs into the United States by special legislation. In the spring of 1948 I was called back again to speak about the DP problem on nationwide television on the *New York Herald Tribune Forum on European Affairs*. I enjoyed meeting experts in many fields and gave my presentation between the addresses of two people I respected highly. I spoke just after Trigve Lie, the Norwegian secretary-general of the United Nations, and just before Eleanor Roosevelt, a real leader in humanitarian causes. I gave my address over television before I had ever seen a television receiver.

The problems of the persons displaced and abused in World War II by the Nazis and then afraid to go home to the new communist masters were very complex ones. It was one job where I had no doubts that I was truly helping people who needed my help.

I visited friends at West Point after the *Herald Tribune* forum and at a reception there I met a grand man, Colonel Herman Beukema, senior professor of the department of social services at the U.S. Military Academy. We promptly got into a long bull session on the problems of the world, especially Europe. At one point he asked, "How would you like to teach here?"

I said, "I've never thought about it, but I have no objection."

Colonel Beukema evidently had plenty of clout in the Pentagon, because orders arrived bringing me back to the States before Christmas of 1948 to attend Columbia University for more graduate work in the spring term, then to report to the U.S. Military Academy in June.

For the next three years I taught upperclassmen history, geography, and government, along with seminars in international relations. At night I completed a master's degree in public law and administration and all requirements for a doctorate in international relations—except for writing the dissertation—at Columbia.

In the summer of 1952 I took an advanced infantry course at Fort Benning, Georgia, then flew to Korea. Though that war was winding down, I enjoyed my infantry duties with the Fifth Regimental Combat Team, a counterattack force, both as the second in command of the RCT, and as a battalion commander. After about a year of troop duty I was called up for a few months to General Maxwell Taylor's Headquarters Eighth Army to be in charge of Special Services.

In the summer of 1954 I was ordered to Headquarters Sixth Army at the Presidio of San Francisco, where I had started my active duty in 1941, for a year of personnel work (G-1). From there I was sent to Fort Leavenworth, Kansas, to attend the Command and General Staff College Course, during which my promotion to colonel came through. On graduation I was chosen to remain on the staff and faculty for the next three years, 1956–1959, serving first as an instructor, then class supervisor (like a dean of students). I was then sent to the Army War College at Carlisle Barracks, Pennsylvania, for concentrated studies of international relations, power factors and strategy, graduating in 1960.

Assigned thereafter to the general staff of the Department of the Army (DA) in the Pentagon, working on special operations, plans, and programs, I dealt with further development of Special Forces Groups (Green Berets) and psychological warfare. I heartily believed in the value of such irregular operations from early OSS days and had written papers and lectured to that effect at every service school I attended.

At the end of the year I was chosen to join the Joint Staff, working directly for the Joint Chiefs of Staff in the same general field—the office for counter-insurgency operations. A highlight: In the fall of 1961 my boss, Major General Billy Craig, took a colonel or equivalent from each of the services on a fact-finding trip to Southeast Asia for President Kennedy. I was the Army representative working with Special Forces problems and investigating the use of third-country troops such as Filipinos to aid in the struggle against the communists of North Vietnam.

We spent some time with General Vang Pao and his Meo tribesmen, just south of the Plaines de Jarres in Laos. His men were real fighters, many trained by our Green Berets; the Viet Cong from the north and their Russian advisors soon learned to respect—and hate—them. I traded my pistol to Vang Pao for his crossbow. He was not only a gutsy fighter, but also a lover. I gathered that he had seven wives and about five dozen children. He may well have been growing his own recruits.

My heart bleeds now, as it did earlier for the Poles and other nations of Europe, for the Meo tribesmen and other groups, some Cambodians, whom we armed and trained to fight the communists. Since the Americans left, they have been subjected to nothing short of an extermination program by the new communist rulers.

It was on this trip that I first landed an airplane on my own at the Vientiane airport in Laos. The pilot, a CIA man who had more guts than brains, let me do it.

After two years with the Joint Staff, 1961–1963, I got a grand assignment to be commander of the Tenth Special Forces Group (Airborne) with headquarters at Bad Tolz in the Bavarian Alps. This was another outfit the Russian communists hated. They knew that if they ever attacked Western Europe, teams of Green Berets were ready to parachute into their backyards, take advantage of the wealth of dissident feelings brewing under communist rule, and organize guerrilla units behind enemy lines.

As the situation stabilized into the uncertain peace of the Cold War, we not only trained hard in the Alps of Germany and exercised airborne operations from various airfields in Europe, we also trained with NATO allies and answered requests from many nations to assist them in tougher training for their forces in counter-insurgency operations. Two years of experience (1963–65) as the commander of Tenth Special Forces—years liberally sprinkled with high adventure, high spirits, good humor, purposeful operations, relieved by a touch of comedy—are probably worthy of another book some day.

We particularly enjoyed training a special force for King Hussein of Jordan in 1964, with side trips through the Holy Land from Christ's birthplace in Bethlehem to the baptismal spot in the Jordan River. From there we proceeded to Jerusalem and the Via Dolorosa, the route of the Crucifixion. We also visited the Roman city of Jarrash, where innumerable chariot wheels made deep ruts in the ancient marble road. Later we were led to the hidden city of Petra, hand-carved out of rose-red stone, a narrow slit in the cliffs its only entry. The next day we enjoyed tea and water-skiing with King Hussein and his family at Aqaba on the Red Sea.

In Pakistan we developed well-qualified jumpmasters among the Pakistani paratroopers near historic Peshawar and Rawalpindi. I walked across the border into Afghanistan from this Kipling territory and overlooked Kabul, now invaded by the Soviet Army.

We also trained a special force for the Shah of Iran and helped train other units of the Iranian First Army. Much later the leader of the special force, Lieutenant Colonel Khosrodad, a fine officer, was executed as a general on Ayatollah Khomeini's orders. On another mission we trained parachutists in Saudi Arabia, a country dry in everything but oil.

We conducted realistic guerrilla exercises with special troops of both Greece and Turkey out of an advance base on Crete. At night we Green Berets tried Greek dances (Zorba style) with the toughest anti-communist fighters in Greece, the Hellenic Raiding Force. One evening their commander, General Constantine Kollias, and I slit our wrists and became blood brothers. (Kollias was my third blood brother; the first was the chief of the Nez Perce Indians, a football teammate of mine in college. The second was Jan Staubo of Norway, when he heard about the Indian blood brother.) From the Turkish mountain men I learned how to skin a sheep easily by pricking through the outer skin and blowing air between the outer skin and the inner diaphragm-like layer. It took great lung power, but the sheepskin then peeled off readily.

In exchange training with Norwegians we traded some of our special techniques for Norse tips on cross-country skiing across the great Hardanger Vita.

In England we maneuvered with the British SAS, my old colleagues of OSS days, and with a parachute brigade, across the Yorkshire moors. The visit included a private showing of the Crown Jewels by the colonel of the Tower of London, and a great reunion with Wings Day and other RAF friends.

Other Green Beret teams cross-trained with the para-military carabinieri of Italy and military units in France, Spain, Belgium, and Denmark. For infiltration by sea and frogman jobs we worked with submarines and scuba gear in the waters of the Mediterranean (warm) and the North Sea (cold).

We in turn hosted and trained individuals or groups from nearly every European country in our Bad Tolz Alpine backyard. During the two years I parachuted about a hundred times on a variety of drop zones, at our home base and abroad, with soldiers from many lands.

As you can see, we were never bored, and it wasn't all hell for leather. Some of our best achievements were by our medics, highly trained non-commissioned officers who did fine triage and repair work on the wounded and who served as midwives in the boondocks of less developed countries. Our Green Beret medics won many friends, especially among the women and children—and their appreciative men—of the poorer lands. But all good things must end—a colonel could have a tactical command for only eighteen to twenty-four months by headquarters regulations. I had a wonderful twenty-four-month tour of duty.

I still chuckle over clippings of stories printed in the official newspapers from Moscow and from the communist puppet states. We were certainly a target for Soviet spies; their information was not always complete, and if they needed some propaganda item, they'd bend the facts to fit.

During the uprising of the people of Czechoslovakia in the late 1960s (cruelly and ruthlessly put down by the Red Army), Moscow media blamed the Tenth Special Forces Group for the uprising. Friends in intelligence sent me clippings of this item in Russian, German, and English. For instance, the Moscow *Literary Gazette* in August 1968 printed a long propaganda article to justify the need for Soviety military intervention in Czechoslovakia. It read:

> "The center of operations for counterrevolutionary [anti-Communist] forces was the Tenth Special Forces Group near Bad Tolz. Their object is to carry out a silent war behind the front in east European countries. The group is commanded by Colonel Jerry Sage, a specialist in subversive war. Sage has commanded American intelligence operations in Southeast Asia and North Africa, but now he is occupied with sabotage against Czechoslovakia."

I would have been proud and happy to help the Czech people but that story isn't true.

I was glad to see that Soviet intelligence had a bit of a time lag. They were off by three years. Their August 1968 story still had me as commander of the Tenth Special Forces, but I finished my tour there in July of 1965 and had been back in the United States for over a year in August 1968. In East German papers and Moscow's *Pravda* I was also accused of helping refugees escape over the Berlin Wall from communist East Germany to freedom in the West. The stories had a small kernel of truth but were fabrications as to the particulars.

Following my Special Forces tour, I didn't want to go back to staff work and was happily given an administrative command over the North Bavaria district with headquarters just outside Nuremberg—where I had been in the B-17 air raid, after which the German guards had dumped me off at Eichstadt. There, from 1965 to 1967, I had housekeeping responsibilities for over seventy thousand Americans with schools, hospitals, sports facilities, post exchanges and commissaries.

Back in the United States I served at Headquarters Continental Army Command (CONARC) at Fort Monroe, Virginia, in the Unit Training Division, and became reacquainted with U.S. installations by inspecting unit training from Fort Drum, New York, to Fort Irwin, California, and from Fort Lewis, Washington, to an airborne maneuver in Florida. In the spring of 1968 I asked for and received a fine assignment for the last two or three years of my allotted thirty.

I became the deputy chief of staff for ROTC affairs at Headquarters Third Army at Fort McPherson (Atlanta) Georgia. The job included supervision of ROTC at colleges and high schools throughout about ten southeastern states, Puerto Rico, and the Virgin Islands. We considerably increased our ROTC units at both the college and high-school levels and I had a good look at educational institutions in the South, giving commissioning and graduation addresses at several of them. I was keeping my eyes open for a good place to teach all this time. I retired on March 1, 1972, with over thirty years of active military service.

By this time, the heavy traffic in Atlanta had dulled my enthusiasm for that growing city, and I moved to Columbia, South Carolina. There I started teaching at Airport High School. The principal, Hayward Moore, had offered me a job there during an ROTC visit a year or two before. When we again met over lunch, Hayward asked, "What do you like to teach?"

I replied, "God and country!"

He grinned and said, "Good, but let's call it civics."

In December of my second school year at Airport High, Dr. Tom Jones, then president of the University of South Carolina, asked me to develop a policies-and-procedures manual for the entire university and its many branches—working on a part-time basis. In connection with this assignment, I enrolled in the university's doctoral program—my second—this time in education. With two jobs, graduate work, and scattered speaking engagements each month, I was left little time for work and even less for sleep, and finally I had to stop teaching at Airport High after two pleasant years there.

I finished the university manual just as my boss was replaced as president and just as I was laid up in the hospital for many months by a ruptured disk or two in June of 1975. That old back had taken a beating by Nazi rifle butts, night parachute jumps onto farm machinery, and a jeep rolling over me. Now, after a girl driving a minibus hit my car in the rear at high speed, I could hardly use my left leg. After an operation and much therapy, it improved enough so that I was mobile by the summer of 1976.

In August, Mrs. Mary Corley, head of the social studies department of Spring Valley High School on the eastern side of Columbia, South Carolina, told me about an opening in her department. I went back into high-school teaching, which I actually find more challenging and satisfying than college.

I thoroughly enjoyed the work at Spring Valley and the kids were great, as I find they are everywhere. I developed my own courses in world geography with lots of emphasis on curiosity, love of people, and God and country. Before my third year was over, I was voted Teacher of the Year at Spring Valley. I'm proud to say that the students had voted me this award first, followed by the faculty. I was then elected Teacher of the Year for the whole state of South Carolina. This seemed a greater honor to me than many military awards.

My teaching in South Carolina ended in 1980 after a decision to move to Enterprise, Alabama, near Fort Rucker, the huge Army helicopter school. I left behind many great friends at Spring Valley High, the university, the Retired Officers Association, and the Military Order of World Wars, as well as many fine neighbors.

I now keep busy in Enterprise, Alabama, a delightful town of under twenty thousand, with a great high-school football team, a splendid band, and lots of school spirit. I give enrichment lectures in the school systems nearby and talks to the many civic, educational, sports, youth, and church groups. No matter what the subject matter, I always try to bring out the value of developing a strong faith and cherishing the value of the individual.

In talking with young people, I urge them to find and develop the talents the good Lord has given them and to shun the shoddy, the cheap, and the easy. I've noted that too many teenagers are lured into drugs and alcohol by pushers and peer pressure, so I do what I can to fight this "sheep complex," the going along with the worst aspects of the gang. I tell them if they want to be sheep, be the bell sheep that leads the others to safety.

Youngsters admire courage and they understand straight talk. I try to stress the importance of having the courage to choose the harder right over the easier wrong and to lift others up rather than tear them down.

To keep in shape, fight off the arthritis, and keep the old scar tissue elastic, I swim half a mile every day except Sunday.

One of my latest projects is helping to develop a Civitan Club in Enterprise to help the needy and handicapped and thereby pay my civic dues. We raise money by selling Claxton fruitcake for Thanksgiving and Christmas, installing candy boxes near cash registers of restaurants and other businesses where people can pick up nicely wrapped mint candy and leave donations for retarded children. We also have suppers, rummage sales, and other projects.

We spend the proceeds on schools and training centers for retarded and physically handicapped people. We donate our personal services to the Special Olympics competitions, whose motto is "to make each handicapped participant feel like a winner." Our Enterprise Civitan Club is composed of men and women of all orders, creeds, and occupations. Our criteria for membership are the highest and simplest: a friendly, compassionate spirit and a willingness to help others less fortunate.

I'm a very happy man and a very grateful one. I plan to spend the rest of my days thanking God for His care and help and my country for the rich opportunities I've been given. Helping my fellowman in this great country seems to be the best possible way of showing my gratitude.